IN THE SHADE OF THE QUR'ĀN

with an introduction by:
Professor Muhammad Qutb

Fi-Zhilal al-Qur'ān

بسم الله الرحمن الرحيم

IN THE SHADE OF THE QUR'ĀN

Vol. 30

SAYYID QUTB

Translated by
M. Adil Salahi
Ashur A. Shamis

 mwH London Publishers

All rights reserved. No part of this publication may be reproduced, stored in a retrieval system, or transmitted in any form or by any means, electronic, mechanical, photocopying, recording or otherwise, without written permission from the publishers.

© 1979 by MWH London Publishers

Reprinted 1981

ISBN for complete set of 30 volumes (paperback):
 0 906194 16 4

ISBN for this volume (paperback):
 0 906194 07 5

ISBN for complete set of 30 volumes (casebound):
 0 906194 15 6

ISBN for this volume (casebound):
 0 906194 06 7

cover: A late 14th century Qur'an at
 the mosque of Sultan Barqouq, Cairo.

233 Seven Sisters Road
LONDON
N4 2DA
England

Printed and bound in Great Britain by
Redwood Burn Limited
Trowbridge & Esher

CONTENTS

Surah No.	Title	Page
	Preface	vii
	Acknowledgements	x
	Introduction	xi
78	The Tiding (*an-Naba'*)	1
79	The Pluckers (*an-Nazi'aat*)	19
80	The Frowning (*Abas*)	37
81	The Darkening (*at-Takweer*)	61
82	Cleaving Asunder (*al-Infitar*)	73
83	The Stinters (*al-Mutaffifoon*)	85
84	The Rending (*al-Inshiqaq*)	101
85	The Constellations (*al-Burooj*)	111
86	The Night Visitor (*at-Tariq*)	121
87	The Most High (*al-'Aala*)	129
88	The Enveloper (*al-Ghashiyah*)	149
89	The Dawn (*al-Fajr*)	159
90	The City (*al-Balad*)	171
91	The Sun (*ash-Shams*)	183
92	The Night (*al-Lail*)	191
93	The Forenoon (*ad-Dhuha*)	199
94	Solace (*ash-Sharh*)	205
95	The Fig (*at-Teen*)	211
96	The Blood Clots (*al-Alaq*)	217
97	Power (*al-Qadr*)	233
98	The Clear Proof (*al-Bayyinah*)	239
99	The Earthquake (*az-Zalzalah*)	253
100	The Coursers (*al-'Adiyat*)	259
101	The Striker (*al-Qari'ah*)	265

In the Shade of the Qur'an

Surah No.	Title	Page
102	Rivalry for Worldly Gain (*at-Takathur*)	269
103	The Declining Day (*al-'asr*)	273
104	The Slanderer (*al-Humazah*)	289
105	The Elephant (*al-Feel*)	293
106	Quraish	309
107	Small Kindness (*al-Ma'oun*)	315
108	Abundance (*al-Kawthar*)	321
109	The Disbelievers (*al-Kafiroon*)	327
110	Victory (*an-Nasr*)	335
111	Fire Flames (*al-Masad*)	343
112	Purity of Faith (*al-Ikhlas*)	349
113	The Daybreak (*al-Falaq*)	357
114	Men (*an-Nas*)	363

PREFACE TO THE ENGLISH EDITION

It is more by coincidence than by design that volume 30 of Sayyid Qutb's most important work "*In the Shade of the Qur'an*" should be the first to appear in English. Indeed Professor Muhammad Qutb, the author's brother, only reluctantly approved its publication in book form now. The reason for starting with Volume 30 was simply that the greater part of it had already been translated and serialised in "*The Muslim*", the organ of the Federation of the Students Islamic Societies in UK and Eire. The plan is, however, that volume 1 will follow shortly and the translation of the rest of this work will, Allah willing, proceed in the normal order.

The reasons for selecting *In the Shade of the Qur'an* for translation are self-evident. Ever since its first appearance this work has been welcomed throughout the Arab world as a major contribution to a clearer understanding of the Qur'an by contemporary Arab readers. The book has been translated into several languages. Its appearance in English will provide the students of Islamic thought with a reference book of great value and high esteem. It will give researchers and scholars an insight into modern Islamic thinking in the Arab World. Its paramount value, however, is that it will provide a medium for a comprehensive understanding of the Islamic principles as outlined in the Qur'an, for the many millions of Muslims throughout the world to whom English is the medium of instruction.

The translators wish to point out that in rendering in English the meaning of the *surahs* included in the present volume they did not adopt any of the many translations of the Qur'an. Each of these has its merits and its shortcomings. The translators produced their own version which, they hope, will be found to convey the Qur'anic meanings more fully while avoiding many of the shortcomings of the other translations. They acknowledge, however, that producing an

In the Shade of the Qur'an

English text of the meanings of the Qur'an which achieves the same degree of excellence as the Arabic text is a task far beyond human endeavour. The Qur'an is Allah's book and no man can aspire to express Allah's message as He Himself has done.

In addition to the usual problems of translation this work has presented us with the difficulty of trying to render in English passages which deal with purely literary or linguistic aspects of the Qur'anic text. The reader will better appreciate this problem when he takes into consideration the fact that in translation the Qur'anic text might not retain these aspects. Rather than omit such passages or reduce them to footnotes, we have modified the text slightly so as to incorporate such passages, indicating at the same time the variance between the two editions. All such passages are easily identifiable by the reader. At one point, however, it was necessary to omit a passage dealing with a linguistic problem which is relevant only to the Arabic text.

Readers of Islamic books in English often find Arabic terms used as if they are part of the English language. Such usage is usually employed because the author or the translator feels that the connotations of the Arabic term cannot be conveyed by any English equivalent. This may be so. But if the usage of Arabic terms is found to be an easy way out it has its disadvantages. It narrows the readership of such books to only those who have prior knowledge of Islamic terminology. It is felt, however, that *"In the Shade of the Qur'an"* can be of great benefit to the reader who wishes to learn about Islam and the Qur'an and who is totally unfamiliar with Islamic terminology. Hence we have refrained from using Arabic terms despite the inadequacy of some English equivalents. With wider usage such English terms may in time acquire new connotations when used in an Islamic context so as to convey the required meaning.

A Turkish friend who has had some experience in translation once remarked that he feels uneasy about using the English term "prayers" for the Turkish *"namaz"* or the Arabic *"salah"*. The English term, he said, is much too general to convey the precise meaning of *"salah"* or its Turkish equivalent. This is certainly true, but before the advent of Islam the Arabic term did not convey much more than what an Englishman understands by "prayers". What did the term *"namaz"* connote, we wonder, before the Turkish people adopted the religion of Islam?

Preface

One exception is the retention of the term "*surah*", which indicates a separate and independent part of the Qur'an. An obvious English term which may be suggested for it is "chapter". But "chapter" is inadequate as a substitute for "*surah*" because a chapter is supposed to deal with a single topic. None of the longer *surahs* of the Qur'an is confined to the discussion of one single idea. Furthermore, the Arabic term is used to refer to parts of the Qur'an only. No other book is divided into *surahs*, not even the books of the Prophet's traditions. Since it is a special word in Arabic, its retention in the English edition is unavoidable.

The verses of *surahs* have been indicated by starting a new line for each verse. Verses, however, do not start with a capital letter except where a verse begins a new sentence. If a verse runs in more than one line the continuity is indicated by giving the second line a wider margin. This arrangement has been followed so as to avoid giving any impression of similarity between the Qur'an and poetry.

Despite the hard work that has been put into this translation of Sayyid Qutb's work, this English edition is nowhere near the Arabic original for excellence of style and perfection of expression. Whatever shortcomings this edition suffers from, the translators acknowledge as their own. The author is in no way responsible for them. But those who have had some experience in translation, and in the translation of Islamic texts in particular, recognise the difficulty of the task we have undertaken and will acknowledge that, humble as it may be, the result, in some measure, serves the purpose.

As this is the first English volume of "*In the Shade of the Qur'an*", comments on the translation are invited so as to incorporate any useful suggestions in the following volumes.

Finally, the translators wish to record their deep gratitude to Dr. Abdullah Jibril Oyekan who, as editor of *The Muslim*, gave them immense help and encouragement in the early stages of their work. His successors also deserve our thanks. Dr. Carol Miles of King Alfred's College, Winchester edited the English text with meticulous care and made numerous improvements for which we express our thanks.

M.A.Salahi
A.A.Shamis

ACKNOWLEDGEMENTS

MWH London Publishers wish to record their gratitude to

THE KING ABDUL AZIZ UNIVERSITY, MAKKA

and

THE KARA ESTABLISHMENT, MAKKA

for their financial assistance in the translation and publication of this volume

INTRODUCTION
By
Professor Muhammad Qutb*

It gives me great pleasure to write this introduction to *In the Shade of the Qur'an* in its English version. The book is the fruit of the most productive years of its author's intellectual life and, at the same time, a vivid expression of the sacred battle which he fought and which culminated in his martyrdom in 1966.

The larger part of this work was written when the author was in jail in the period 1954–64. This was a period of complete solitude, when writing was the main preoccupation of the author and during which he lived totally "in the shade of the Qur'an".

The author's vigorous struggle, for which he was imprisoned, then killed, was, at the practical level, an attempt to achieve the implementation of Islam in the shape of a community which practises Islam in its life and preaches the need for its realisation until it becomes the actual code of practice for the society as a whole. At the intellectual level, however, the author's life struggle is embodied in a collection of books devoted to explaining the true nature of Islam, its fundamentals, values and laws. The largest and most important of these works is undoubtedly *In the Shade of the Qur'an*.

The book is a "campaign of struggle" because it is, indeed, much more than a "commentary" on the Qur'an.

The Qur'an is the book of Islam. Hardly a generation has passed since the dawn of Islam without the appearance of one or more commentaries which explain the meaning of the Qur'an. Having spent a considerable part of his life "in the shade of the Qur'an" and, having joined the struggle for the sake of Islam, the author of this

---

* Professor Muhammad Qutb is the author's brother. He himself has written several books on Islam, some of which have been translated into English and other languages. He is considered one of the most distinguished contemporary writers on Islam.

work did not intend to write just another commentary. He had a different objective which he felt could be attained through writing his commentary.

Our present age has its own features which, perhaps, have never existed in any period of history. They are the ones which give this commentary its own colouring and determine its points of emphasis.

The Muslims, for their part, are now far removed in their practical life from the true nature of Islam. The image of Islam they present by their way of life is nothing more than the indistinguishable negative of the true image of Islam as it was practised by the early Islamic generations, who perfectly fulfilled Allah's own description of them: *"You are indeed the best nation that has ever been raised up for mankind: you enjoin the doing of what is right and forbid the doing of what is wrong and you believe in Allah."*[1] Hence they were able to write that incomparable page in human history. They established truth and justice on earth and raised for mankind an inimitable civilisation which builds up its structure in the material and spiritual worlds at the same time. It is a civilisation which unites the two worlds and achieves harmony between body and soul, religion and politics, faith and science, the present life and the hereafter, the practical and the ideal.

The non-Muslims, on the other hand, confront humanity with a host of philosophical, social, political and economic doctrines which banish religion from practical life and at best restrict it to a tiny corner of man's conscience so that it may become purely a relationship between the individual and his Lord that has no bearing whatsoever on society and its active life, or, at worst, fight it tooth and nail and bar its very existence. As a result, human life is full of many sorts of political, social and economic injustice which know no limits. It witnesses various types of intellectual and moral perversion unknown in history. The advocates of such perversion and deviation try nevertheless to dress their erring ways in a scientific garment and they hold to them as if they were truth itself or the ideal sought after. This they do despite all that they suffer in consequence of nervous and psychological diseases – worry and restlessness, madness and suicide, alcoholism, drug addiction and crime.

What is worse is that these deviant philosophical, social, political

---

[1] The Qur'an 3; 110

and economic doctrines now dominate the lives of contemporary Muslims, wearing the false disguise of a "modern human civilisation". Thus they poison the lives of the Muslim peoples to a larger degree than they do the life of the West because the Muslims of today have deserted Islam and are unaware of its true nature and fundamental value.

Hence the vigorous intellectual and practical "campaign of struggle" to which the author devoted himself was an attempt to explain to contemporary Muslims the true nature of Islam. His driving objective was that the Muslims of today should be able to live and practise true Islam in the same way as the early Islamic generations. They would then rescue themselves and would be able to show all mankind the road to salvation.

The Qur'an is the constitution revealed by Allah to regulate and govern human life. It is the book which educated the Islamic nation until it attained the standard which earned it the title "the best nation ever raised up for mankind". Light should, therefore, be thrown on it from two angles. The first is the angle of education: this shows how the Qur'an, at the levels of the individual, the family, the community and the nation, leads man to achieve the highest degree of moral and spiritual nobility possible in this life. The other angle is that of the practical code which regulates human life in its noblest form and in all its spheres political, economic, social, intellectual and moral; that is, a life which is befitting to man whom Allah has ennobled and raised above all species of His creation and entrusted with the task the heavens, the earth and the mountains have all dreaded to shoulder.

This is the method the author has followed in explaining the meanings of the Qur'an. He does not dwell long on individual words or expressions, unless there is a special need for that. Rather, he takes the whole verse or a number of verses and explains their relevance to the education of man according to the Divine method, or to the practical code which regulates the life of Islamic society in all spheres.

Faith is the central point of Islamic education and the Islamic practical code. It takes up the larger part of the Qur'an and its *surahs*. Consequently, it takes up the larger part of *In the Shade of the Qur'an*. As presented by the Qur'an, faith is not merely a word to be uttered and then forgotten as man goes about his diverse practical affairs, heedless of the significance of faith and its controls. Faith is indeed the pivot around which all life turns: the conscience, the intellect and the practical sense all alike.

The belief in the unity of Allah goes deep into the very structure of the universe as well as into the human self. It provides a complete conception of life and human existence which differs greatly, in fundamentals and in details, from any concept which is not based on the same essential fact.

The believer, in whose heart this fundamental fact is firmly established, finds that his feelings, ideas and concepts as well as his private and social actions, are totally different from those of a man who conducts his life affairs on a different basis or who views faith as an abstract, philosophical idea which has little or no influence on his life. The same applies to the community whose life is governed by faith. Its aims, ambitions, behaviour and practical achievements are different from those of any other community which does not share its Islamic concepts of God, the universe, life and man.

The Qur'an projects this image in full detail: the image of the believer as his soul is moulded by the acceptance of the reality of the unity of Allah, in contrast with the erring soul who does not submit to this cardinal truth; and the image of the faithful community which conducts its life on the basis that there is no deity but Allah, in contrast with the erring communities which adopt different doctrines and ignoble values. Through this projection the Qur'an educates the individual believer and the community of believers so that they may attain their highest standards. It then provides them with the practical code which regulates the various aspects of life and establishes "the best nation ever raised up for mankind."

The author actually lives with the Qur'an as it projects these images. He then tries to show his reader the image of a believer content with his faith, delineating the feelings, ideas, values, concepts as well as the practical conduct of the believer as described in the Qur'an. He also tries to explain the practical code Allah has laid down for human life. This is indeed the basic theme of this work: *In the Shade of the Qur'an.*

It dwells at length on faith and how it penetrates the human self, as well as on its influence on the various aspects of life especially in the area of the implementation of Divine legislation. There are two reasons for this: the first is that the Qur'an itself dwells for long on all these aspects. It describes how faith leaves its mark on *all* human actions, in all situations and conditions: in security or fear, in ease or hardship, in wealth or poverty, in society or solitude, in peace or war, in strength or weakness, in resisting personal desires or struggling against the enemies. The Qur'an also repeatedly declares in clear terms that accepting the faith means submission to the Divine law and the rejection of all other laws. Failing that submission the declaration of faith by any person becomes a hollow statement, with no real substance and unacceptable to Allah. The other reason is that these very implications are the ones that have been forgotten by, or are completely unknown to, the Muslims of today. This applies more particularly in the case of submission to the Divine law as an essential part of faith, without which one's faith is incomplete and faulty. For unless the Divine law is upheld the true image of Islam remains non-existent at both the individual and the social levels.

The author also speaks at length on the numerous signs in the universe which indicate the Divine existence, making occasional but cautious use of some of the conclusions arrived at by modern science. This he does because the Qur'an often dwells on these signs since they are sure to stimulate the human heart to conscious recognition of the unity of the Creator and his infinite majesty and greatness and, consequently to worship and submit to Him alone. He also describes scenes of the hereafter, because the Qur'an paints these in great detail as they are important means to awaken the religious conscience of man and to establish a dual relationship between Allah and man based on the two strongest and parallel feelings in man, namely, fear and hope.

He also dwells a great deal on the various Islamic systems, in their basic, unchangeable principles, as opposed to the multitude of deviant and *Ignorant* systems which rule the earth today. His aim here is to show how wide the gulf is between the rule of Allah and that of *Ignorance*, and to explain the serious consequences of man's refusal to comply with the Divine instructions, his obstinate disregard of His wisdom and his spurning of Divine revelations, claiming at the same time that he knows his needs and can judge what is most suitable for him better than Allah.

The author also speaks comprehensively on the Islamic method of educating the individual and the community, with the dual purpose of shedding light on the Qur'anic instructions on the one hand and on the other enriching the contemporary Islamic revivalist movement in this field. This enrichment is badly needed at this particular stage as the Islamic movement strives to establish an Islamic presence in the midst of *Ignorant* surroundings which are hostile to Islam trying to suppress it or, at least, to move away from it. In this area the author lays strong emphasis on "education through events" to delineate the Qur'anic method of making use of great events in disciplining the human soul, so that it may be moulded in the required shape while it is still vividly impressed by the event. Thus, it takes the right mould permanently and becomes immune to deviation.

These are the main themes of this work. As the reader undoubtedly realises, they are not merely a "commentary" on the Qur'an. Should we, however, wish to use the term we need to qualify it by saying it is a commentary with a definite aim. Its aim is to disseminate the Islamic call and to delineate its system of education and discipline which is essential for its continuity and progress today as it was essential for its prosperity throughout its unique history.

Special mention should be made of a unique characteristic in this "commentary", of which the author was aware and to which he draws the attention of his reader. It is indeed the net result of his own active involvement in the call to Islam and the trials he had to endure for such involvement. It is the fact the Qur'an cannot be truly and correctly understood and it does not produce all its dynamic effect except through the practical and active participation in the campaign of "no deity but Allah." For "no deity but Allah" represents a massive campaign within the human conscience and in the social set-up of human communities. It is not something static which may be put in a special corner where it settles down. It is a dynamic, ever-active force which never weakens or subsides. Internally, within the individual, it is a self-sustaining force which tries to elevate man above worldly desires and enable him to lead a life which is pure, elevated, noble and consistent, through his continuous attempt to draw nearer to Allah, seeking His pleasure and avoiding His anger. In society, it is a permanent movement which aims to make all mankind submit to the Divine constitution: *"until there is no more oppression and all submit to Allah alone."*[1]

---

[1] The Qur'an: 8; 39

Introduction   In the Shade of the Qur'an

If one reads the Qur'an in a sort of a passive, detached state one is sure to miss a lot of its indications and purposes. But when one reads it while actually involved in the cause trying to establish that "there is no deity but Allah", one's heart will open to receive its meanings which one would otherwise have missed, and will draw inferences of which one was totally unaware. The present work is itself a proof of this fact. The author wrote the earlier edition of a number of volumes before he engaged in the real battle, when he had not yet devoted himself fully to the campaign of "no deity but Allah". Then he rewrote the early volumes from within. The difference between the two editions cannot be exaggerated. It is a difference produced by the new light shed by actually practising the meanings of the Qur'an.

Another arresting feature of this "commentary", in its Arabic original at least, is its literary style. The author started his life as a man of letters, preoccupied with the artistic side of life. His attitude to life and to the universe was that of a keen artist who has a lively and genuine response to whatever is beautiful and who goes through the practical life with an idealistic outlook. This, however, did not prevent him from becoming involved in the political issues of the day. The latter part of his life, on the other hand, was devoted to his vigorous struggle for the cause that had become his sole preoccupation. To the cause of Islam he devoted his thoughts and his feelings, his nights and his days, and indeed his whole life. But did he ever lose his artistic feeling which was so prominent in his earlier career? Indeed not. The Qur'an itself, in whose shade the author has lived, is characterised by a fine style of surpassing excellence, even as it portrays the on-going battle of "no deity but Allah."

I extend my greetings to the readers of this English translation hoping that they will live with the author "In the Shade of the Qur'an."

MUHAMMAD QUTB
Professor of Islamic Studies
King Abdul Aziz University
Makka-Saudi Arabia

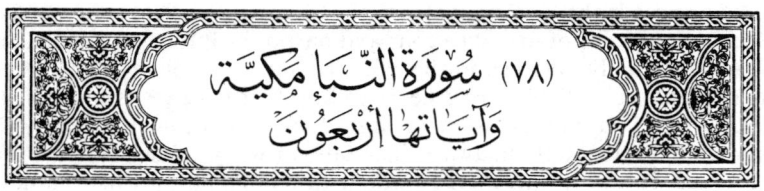

بِسْمِ اللهِ الرَّحْمٰنِ الرَّحِيمِ

عَمَّ يَتَسَاءَلُونَ ۝ عَنِ النَّبَإِ الْعَظِيمِ ۝ الَّذِي هُمْ فِيهِ مُخْتَلِفُونَ ۝ كَلَّا سَيَعْلَمُونَ ۝ ثُمَّ كَلَّا سَيَعْلَمُونَ ۝ أَلَمْ نَجْعَلِ الْأَرْضَ مِهَادًا ۝ وَالْجِبَالَ أَوْتَادًا ۝ وَخَلَقْنَاكُمْ أَزْوَاجًا ۝ وَجَعَلْنَا نَوْمَكُمْ سُبَاتًا ۝ وَجَعَلْنَا اللَّيْلَ لِبَاسًا ۝ وَجَعَلْنَا النَّهَارَ مَعَاشًا ۝ وَبَنَيْنَا فَوْقَكُمْ سَبْعًا شِدَادًا ۝ وَجَعَلْنَا سِرَاجًا وَهَّاجًا ۝ وَأَنْزَلْنَا مِنَ الْمُعْصِرَاتِ مَاءً ثَجَّاجًا ۝ لِنُخْرِجَ بِهِ حَبًّا وَنَبَاتًا ۝ وَجَنَّاتٍ أَلْفَافًا ۝ إِنَّ يَوْمَ الْفَصْلِ كَانَ مِيقَاتًا ۝ يَوْمَ يُنْفَخُ فِي الصُّورِ فَتَأْتُونَ أَفْوَاجًا ۝ وَفُتِحَتِ السَّمَاءُ فَكَانَتْ أَبْوَابًا ۝ وَسُيِّرَتِ الْجِبَالُ فَكَانَتْ سَرَابًا ۝ إِنَّ جَهَنَّمَ كَانَتْ مِرْصَادًا ۝ لِلطَّاغِينَ مَآبًا ۝ لَابِثِينَ فِيهَا أَحْقَابًا ۝ لَا يَذُوقُونَ فِيهَا بَرْدًا وَلَا شَرَابًا ۝ إِلَّا حَمِيمًا وَغَسَّاقًا ۝ جَزَاءً وِفَاقًا ۝ إِنَّهُمْ كَانُوا لَا يَرْجُونَ حِسَابًا ۝ وَكَذَّبُوا بِآيَاتِنَا كِذَّابًا ۝ وَكُلَّ شَيْءٍ أَحْصَيْنَاهُ كِتَابًا ۝ فَذُوقُوا فَلَنْ نَزِيدَكُمْ إِلَّا عَذَابًا ۝ إِنَّ لِلْمُتَّقِينَ مَفَازًا ۝ حَدَائِقَ وَأَعْنَابًا ۝ وَكَوَاعِبَ أَتْرَابًا ۝ وَكَأْسًا دِهَاقًا ۝ لَا يَسْمَعُونَ فِيهَا لَغْوًا وَلَا كِذَّابًا ۝ جَزَاءً مِنْ رَبِّكَ عَطَاءً حِسَابًا ۝ رَبِّ السَّمَاوَاتِ وَالْأَرْضِ وَمَا بَيْنَهُمَا الرَّحْمٰنِ لَا يَمْلِكُونَ مِنْهُ خِطَابًا ۝ يَوْمَ يَقُومُ الرُّوحُ وَالْمَلَائِكَةُ صَفًّا لَا يَتَكَلَّمُونَ إِلَّا مَنْ أَذِنَ لَهُ الرَّحْمٰنُ وَقَالَ صَوَابًا ۝ ذَلِكَ الْيَوْمُ الْحَقُّ فَمَنْ شَاءَ اتَّخَذَ إِلَى رَبِّهِ مَآبًا ۝ إِنَّا أَنْذَرْنَاكُمْ عَذَابًا قَرِيبًا يَوْمَ يَنْظُرُ الْمَرْءُ مَا قَدَّمَتْ يَدَاهُ وَيَقُولُ الْكَافِرُ يَا لَيْتَنِي كُنْتُ تُرَابًا ۝

SURAH 78

THE TIDING
AN-NABA'

In the name of Allah, the Beneficent, the Merciful.

About what are they asking?
About the fateful tiding
on which they are at variance.
No indeed; they shall certainly know!
Again, no indeed; they shall certainly know.
Have We not spread and levelled the earth,
and made the mountains as pegs?
We created you in pairs,
and made your sleep a cessation of activity.
We made the night a mantle,
and appointed the day for gaining a livelihood.
We built above you seven mighty ones,
and placed therein a blazing lamp.
We send down out of the rain-clouds water in abundance,
by which We bring forth grain and varied plants,
and gardens thick with trees.
Fixed is the Day of Decision.
On that day the Trumpet is blown and you shall come in crowds,
and heaven is opened, and becomes gates,

and the mountains are set in motion, and seem to have been a mirage.
Hell stands as a vigilant watchguard,
a home for the tyrants and the transgressors.
Therein they shall abide for ages,
tasting neither coolness nor any drink,
save boiling fluid and decaying filth:
a fitting recompense.
They did not expect to be faced with a reckoning,
and roundly denied Our revelations.
But We noted and recorded all,
(and We shall say:) "Taste this, then;
the only increase you shall have is increase of torment."
The godfearing shall have a place of security,
gardens and vineyards
and high-bosomed maidens, of equal age, for companions,
and a cup overflowing.
There they shall hear no idle talk, nor any falsehood.
Such is the recompense of your Lord: a truly sufficient gift:
Lord of the heavens and earth and all that lies between them, the All-Merciful, with Whom they have no power to speak.
On the day when the Spirit and the angels stand in ranks, they shall not speak, save him to whom the All-Merciful has given leave, and who shall say what is right.
That day is a certainty. Let him who will seek a way back to his Lord.
We have forewarned you of an imminent scourge, on the day when a man will look on what his hands have forwarded and the disbeliever will cry: "Would that I were dust"!

Surah 78 — The Tiding (*An-Naba'*)

This thirtieth part of the Qur'an has a special, distinctive colour. All the *surahs* it includes are Makkan, except two, namely, "The Clear Proof" and "Victory". Although they vary in length, they are all short. More significant, however, is the fact that they form a single group with more or less the same theme. They have the same characteristics of rhythm, images, connotations and overall style. They are, indeed, like a persistent and strong knocking on a door, or loud shouts seeking to awaken some people who are fast asleep, or some drunken men who have lost consciousness, or are in a night club, completely absorbed with their dancing or entertainment. The knocks and the shouts come one after the other: Wake up! Look around you! Think! Reflect! There is a God! There is planning, trial, liability, reckoning, reward, severe punishment and lasting bliss. The same warning is repeated time after time. A strong hand shakes them violently. They seem to open their eyes, look around for a second and return to unconsciousness. The strong hand shakes them again, the shouts and knocks are repeated even more loudly. They may wake up once or twice to say obstinately, "No!" They may stone the person warning them or insult him and then resume their position of inattention. He shakes them anew.

This is how I feel when I read this part of the Qur'an. It puts strong emphasis on a small number of highly important facts and strikes certain notes which touch men's hearts. It concentrates on certain scenes in the universe and in the world of the human soul, as well as certain events which take place on the Day of Decision. I note how they are repeated in different ways, which suggests that the repetition is intended.

This is how one feels when one reads: *"Let man reflect on the food he eats..."*[1] Or *"Let man then consider of what he was created..."*[2] Or *"Let them reflect on the camels, and how they were created; the heaven, how it was raised on high; the mountains, how they were set down; the earth, how it was levelled flat."*[3] Or *"Which is stronger in constitution: you or the heaven He has built? He raised it high and gave it its perfect shape, and gave darkness to its night, and brought out its daylight. After that He spread the earth. He brought out water from it, and brought forth its pastures; and the mountains He set firm, for you and your cattle to delight in."*[4] Or *"Have We not spread and levelled the*

---

[1] The Qur'an. 80; 24.
[2] Ibid. 86; 5.
[3] Ibid. 88; 17—20.
[4] Ibid. 79; 27–33.

earth, and made the mountains as pegs? We created you in pairs, and gave you sleep a cessation of activity. We made the night a mantle and appointed the day for gaining a livelihood. We built above you the seven mighty ones and placed therein a blazing lamp. We send down out of the rain-clouds water in abundance, by means of which we bring forth grain and varied plants, and gardens thick with trees."[1]

Or "Let man reflect on the food he eats: how We pour down the rain in torrents, and cleave the earth in fissures; how We bring forth the corn, the grapes and the fresh vegetation, the olive and the palm, the dense-treed gardens, the fruit-trees and the green pastures, for you and your cattle to delight in."[2] Or "O man, what has lured you away from your gracious Lord, Who created and moulded you and gave you an upright shape. He can give you whatever form He wills."[3] Or "Praise the name of your Lord, the Most High, Who creates and proportions well, Who determines and guides, Who brings forth the pasturage, then turns it into withered grass."[4] Or "We indeed have created man in the fairest shape and form: then We brought him down to the lowest of the low, except for those who believe and do righteous deeds, for theirs shall be an unfailing recompense. Who, then, can give you the lie as to the Last Judgement? Is not Allah the most Just of judges?"[5] Or "When the sun is darkened, when the stars fall and disperse, when the mountains are made to move away, when the camels, ten months pregnant, are left untended, when the wild beasts are brought together, when the seas are set alight, when men's souls are paired (like with like), when the infant girl, buried alive, is asked for what crime she was slain, when the records are laid open, when the sky is stripped bare, when Hell is made to burn fiercely, when Paradise is brought near, every soul shall know what it has put forward."[6]

Or "When the heaven is cleft asunder, when the stars are scattered, when the oceans are made to explode, when the graves are hurled about, each soul shall know its earlier actions and its later ones."[7] Or, "When the sky is rent asunder, obeying her Lord in true submission, when the earth is stretched out and casts forth all that is within her and becomes empty, obeying her Lord in true submission."[8] Or "When the earth is rocked with her (final) earthquake, when the earth shakes off her bur-

---

[1] The Qur'an. *78; 6–16.*
[2] Ibid. *80; 24–32.*
[3] Ibid. *82; 6–8.*
[4] Ibid. *87; 1–5.*
[5] Ibid. *95; 4–8.*
[6] Ibid. *81; 1–14.*
[7] Ibid. *82; 1–5.*
[8] Ibid. *84; 1–5.*

dens, and man cries: 'what is the matter with her?' On that day she will tell her news, that your Lord has inspired her."[1]

We experience the same feeling as we meditate over the scenes of the universe portrayed at the beginning or in the middle of some of the *surahs* in this part of the Qur'an: *"I swear by the turning stars, which move swiftly and hide themselves away, and by the night as it comes darkening on, and the first breath of dawn."*[2] Or *"I swear by the twilight, and by the night and what it envelops, and by the moon in her full perfection."*[3] Or, *"By the dawn, by the ten nights by that which is even and that which is odd, by the night as it journeys on."*[4] Or *"By the sun and his morning brightness, by the moon as she follows him, by the day which reveals its splendour, by the night when it enshrouds him, by the heaven and its construction, by the earth and its spreading, by the soul and its moulding, and inspiration with knowledge of wickedness and piety."*[5] Or *"By the night when she lets fall her darkness, by the day in full splendour by Him who created the male and the female."*[6] Or *"By the white forenoon and the brooding night."*[7]

Strong emphasis is laid, throughout this thirtieth part of the Qur'an, on the origin of man as well as the origin of life, in both its vegetable and animal forms. Emphasis is also given to various scenes in the universe, such as scenes of the Day of Resurrection, which is described in different places as "the Greatest Catastrophe", "the Stunning Blast", "the Enveloper", etc. Scenes of the reckoning, fine reward and severe retribution are also given prominence. They are drawn with images which leave a stunning effect. All these are given as a proof of the reality of creation and elaborate planning of the universe by Allah, as well as evidence confirming the reality of the life to come, and its decisive reckoning. These scenes are, at times, combined with scenes of the fate of some of the nations who rejected the Divine messages. The whole of this part exemplifies all this. We will make, however, a brief reference in this introduction to some examples.

The present *surah*, "The Tiding" is an example of the emphasis laid on the realities of creation and resurrection, and the prominence given to the scenes of the universe and the hereafter. The same

---

[1] The Qur'an 99; 1–5.
[2] Ibid. 81; 15–18.
[3] Ibid. 84; 16–18.
[4] Ibid. 89; 1–4.
[5] Ibid. 91; 1–8.
[6] Ibid. 92; 1–3.
[7] Ibid 93; 1–2.

applies to the next *surah*, entitled "The Pluckers". The third *surah* in this part, "The Frowning" starts with a reference to a certain event of the early days of Islam. The rest of the *surah* is devoted to a discussion of the origins of man and plants before it tackles the "Stunning Blast":

"On that day each man will forsake his brother, his mother and his father, his wife and his children: for each one of them will on that day have enough preoccupations of his own. Some faces on that day shall be beaming, smiling and joyful. Some other faces on that day shall be covered with dust, veiled with darkness." [1]

Surah "The Darkening" portrays scenes of the great upheaval which envelops the whole universe on the Day of Resurrection. It also draws some fine and inspiring scenes of the universe in the context of affirming the reality of revelation and the honesty of the Prophet.

Surah "Cleaving Asunder" includes scenes of the universal upheaval, coupled with scenes of perfect happiness and eternal suffering in the hereafter. As it portrays these scenes it attempts to shake and awaken men's hearts: *"O man! What has lured you away from your gracious Lord ..."* [2] Scenes of both types are also portrayed in the *surah* entitled, "The Rending" *Surah* "The Constellations" touches very briefly on some scenes of the universe and the hereafter by way of introduction to the main theme. The *surah* tackles the history of a group of believers who were subjected by the disbelievers to severe torture with fire. It also states how Allah will inflict greater and more severe torture with fire on those disbelievers.

Surah "The Night Visitor" gives some scenes of the universe and speaks of the origins of man and plants prior to an oath, by all these, affirming *"Surely it is a decisive word; it is no frivolity."* [3] The *surah* entitled "The Most High" speaks of creation, planning, Divine guidance and the various stages of the growth of pastures. All this is given by way of introduction to the theme of the hereafter, reckoning, reward and retribution. *Surah* "The Enveloper" gives some images of the happiness of the believers in the hereafter, and the misery of the disbelievers. It also draws attention to the creation of camels, heaven, earth and mountains. The same applies right through to the end of this thirtieth part, with the exception of a few *surahs* which are

---

[1] The Qur'an. *80; 34–41.*   [3] Ibid. *86; 13–14.*
[2] Ibid. *82; 6.*

Surah 78   The Tiding (*An-Naba'*)

devoted to the exposition of the fundamental principles of faith, such as the *surahs* entitled "Purity of Faith", "The Disbelievers", "Small Kindness", "The Declining Day", "Power", and "Victory", and with the exception of a few more *surahs* which give encouragement and solace to the Prophet and direct him to seek the refuge of his Lord against all evil, such as those entitled, "The Forenoon", "Solace", "Abundance", "The Daybreak" and "Men".

Another aspect of the style of this part is its artistic use of fine expressions, images, rhythm, meter and rhyme to touch upon areas of exceptional beauty in the human soul and in the universe at large. It does this in order to achieve better results as it addresses those who have lost sight of the truth, trying to attract their attention and awaken their feelings. This is clearly evident, for example, in its portrait of the stars as they turn in their orbits, rise and set, in the image of deer disappearing in their dens then appearing again, its image of the night as a living being walking quietly in the dark, and the dawn breathing with the first rays of light: *"I swear by the turning stars, which move swiftly and hide themselves away, and by the night as it comes darkening on, and the first breath of dawn."* [1]

It is also clear in the description of sunset, the night and the moon: *"I swear by the twilight, and by the night and what it envelops, and by the moon, in her full perfection –"*,[2] and in the scenes of dawn and the travelling night: *"By the dawn, by the ten nights, by that which is even and that which is odd, by the night as it journeys on,"*[3] or *"By the white forenoon and the brooding night."*[4]

Again it is markedly evident in the inspiring address to the human heart; *"O man, what has lured you away from your gracious Lord, Who created and moulded you and gave you an upright shape? He can give you whatever form He wills";*[5] in the description of Heaven: *"Other faces on that day are jocund, well-pleased with their striving, in a sublime garden, where they hear no babble,"*[6] and of Hell: *"But he whose scales are light, shall have the abyss for his home. Would that you knew what that is like! It is a raging fire."*[7]

Allegory is often employed and an unusual derivation is sometimes preferred in order to obtain the intended musical effect. All this

---

[1] The Qur'an. *81; 15–18.*
[2] *Ibid. 84; 16–18.*
[3] *Ibid. 89; 1–4.*
[4] *Ibid. 93; 1–2.*
[5] *Ibid. 82; 6–8.*
[6] *Ibid. 88; 8–11.*
[7] *Ibid. 101; 8–11.*

shows the artistry which so entirely pervades this part of the Qur'an.

The present *surah* is a good example of the general bent of this part, its themes, the fundamental principles it seeks to establish, the scenes and images it portrays, its inferences, its music and its fine touches, as well as its artistic selection and manipulation of terms and expressions to enhance its effect. It opens with a form of question which imparts a sense of gravity to the matter in dispute; yet it is something that admits of no dispute. This is followed by an immediate warning of what will happen on the day when they will realise its nature: *"About what are they asking? About the fateful tiding on which they are at variance. No indeed; they shall certainly know! Again, no indeed; they shall certainly know."* Discussion of this fateful tiding is then temporarily dropped. The *surah* draws attention to what we see around us in the universe and what we feel in our souls which give an unmistakable indication of what will follow: *"Have We not spread and levelled the earth, and made the mountains as pegs? We created you in pairs, and made your sleep a cessation of activity. We made the night a mantle and appointed the day for gaining a livelihood. We built above you seven mighty ones, and placed therein a blazing lamp. We send down out of the rain-clouds water in abundance, by which We bring forth grain and varied plants, and gardens thick with trees."*

After this multitude of images taken from actual life the *surah* takes up the issue of the event of which they have been warned. It explains to them its nature and how it takes place: *"Fixed is the Day of Decision. On that day the Trumpet is blown and you shall come in crowds, and heaven is opened, and becomes gates, and the mountains are set in motion, and seem to have been a mirage."*

Then follows the scene of misery, violent, infinitely powerful: *"Hell stands as a vigilant watchguard, a home for the tyrants and the transgressors. Therein they shall abide for ages, tasting neither coolness nor any drink, save boiling fluid and decaying filth: a fitting recompense. They did not expect to be faced with a reckoning and roundly denied Our revelations. But We noted and recorded all, (and We shall say): 'Taste this, then; the only increase you shall have is increase of torment.' "* The scene of happiness, on the other hand, overflows with beauty: *"The godfearing shall have a place of security, gardens and vineyards and high-bosomed maidens, of equal age, for companions, and a cup overflowing. There they shall hear no idle talk, nor any falsehood. Such is the recompense of your Lord: a truly sufficient gift."*

The *surah* closes with a distinctive note which accompanies a ma-

Surah 78 — The Tiding (*An-Naba'*)

jestic scene of the day when all this takes place: *"Lord of the heavens and earth and all that lies between them, the All-Merciful, with Whom they have no power to speak. On the day when the spirit and the angels stand in rank, they shall not speak, save him to whom the All-Merciful has given leave, and Who shall say what is right. That day is a certainty. Let him who will seek a way back to his Lord. We have forewarned you of an imminent scourge, on the day when a man will look on what his hands have forwarded and the disbeliever will cry: 'Would that I were dust!'"*

This is the fateful tiding about which they ask, and this is what will happen on the day when they will realise the true nature of this great event.

"About what are they asking? About the fateful tiding on which they are at variance. No indeed; they shall certainly know. Again, no indeed; they shall certainly know."

The *surah* opens by shunning the enquirers and the enquiry. It wonders that anyone should raise any doubts about resurrection and judgement, which were the centre points of bitter controversy. For the disbelievers could hardly imagine that resurrection is at all possible, despite the fact that it is most logical. The *surah* asks what they are talking about: *"About what are they asking?"* We are then given the answer. The question is not meant to solicit information but to draw attention to the singularity of their questioning by putting forward the subject of their questions and stating its nature: *"About the fateful tiding on which they are at variance."* The answer does not name the event but describes it to enhance the feeling of wonder and amazement at such people. The variance was between those who believed in resurrection and those who denied it, but the questions were raised by the latter only.

The *surah* does not provide any more details about the event in question. It simply describes it as great before adding an implicit threat which is much more frightening than a direct answer. *"No indeed, they shall certainly know. Again, no indeed, they shall certainly know."* The phrase "no indeed" is used here as the nearest possible rendering of the Arabic term *"kalla"*, which denotes strong shunning. The whole sentence is repeated to add force to the threat implied.

The *surah* then puts aside, apparently, that great event which is at the centre of controversy, only to pick it up later on. The *surah* takes us on a quick round of the universe in which we see a multitude of scenes, creatures and phenomena. Contemplation of these would strongly shake any human heart: *"Have We not spread and levelled the earth, and made the mountains as pegs? We created you in pairs, and made your sleep a cessation of activity. We made the night a mantle and appointed the day for gaining a livelihood. We built above you seven mighty ones, and placed therein a blazing lamp. We send down out of the rain-clouds water in abundance, by which We bring forth grain and varied plants, and gardens thick with trees."*

In this round we go across the vast universe, observing a great multitude of scenes and phenomena, which are sketched out with great economy of words and phrases. This helps make the rhythm sharp and penetrating, like incessant hammering. The form of question implying a statement is used here on purpose. It may be likened to a strong hand shaking those unaware, it draws their attention to all these creatures and phenomena which give strong evidence of the deliberate planning and designing which go into their creation, the ability to create and recreate, and the wisdom behind creation, which dictates that no creature will be left out of the great reckoning. Hence we come back to the fateful tiding, the subject of argument.

The first leg in our round takes in the earth and the mountains: *"Have We not spread and levelled the earth, and made the mountains as pegs?"* Both facts mentioned here can be easily recognised and appreciated by everyone. Indeed, even primitive man can be affected by them once his attention is drawn to them.

As human knowledge advances and man acquires better insight into the nature of the universe and its varied phenomena, his appreciation of these two aspects is enhanced. He recognises more fully Allah's elaborate planning of the universe, the accurate balance maintained between the individual kinds of creation and their respective needs, the preparation of the earth for human existence and man's adaptability to his environment. That the earth has been specially prepared as a comfortable home for human life in particular is irrefutable evidence of the careful designing of this existence. It is sufficient to break one relation in the conditions available on earth or in the conditions and proportions required for life and the earth would no longer be that comfortable home for men to tread on.

Man recognises easily, by eyesight, that the mountains are very much like the pegs of a tent. From the Qur'an we learn that they steady the earth and keep its balance. This may be because the mountains' height offsets the depth of the seas and oceans. An alternative explanation is that mountains balance out the inner with the outer movements of our planet. Or probably they merely increase the weight of the earth at certain spots to prevent its violent shaking with earthquakes, volcanoes or internal tremors. There may be another explanation not yet known to man. In the Qur'an we find numerous references to natural laws the essence of which was completely unknown to man at the time of revelation, but knowledge of them has been acquired a few centuries later.

In its second leg our round touches upon various aspects of human existence: *"We created you in pairs."* Again, this is a well established phenomenon, easily recognised by every human being. Allah has made the survival and continuity of mankind conditional on each of the two different sexes, male and female, playing its role in life fully. Not much knowledge is required for appreciating what this involves of comfort, pleasure and recreation. Hence the Qur'anic statement stands to be appreciated by every society in every age according to that society's abilities and knowledge.

Beyond the primitive feeling of the importance of this fact there is a wider scope of contemplation as man's knowledge increases and his feelings become more refined. We may contemplate how one sperm produces a male child while another, absolutely similar to the first, produces a female child. Our contemplation, however penetrating, is bound to lead us to the inescapable conclusion that it is the perfect planning of Allah which gives each sperm its distinctive characteristics so that we may have a male and a female, for life to continue.

"And made your sleep a cessation of activity. We made the night a mantle and appointed the day for gaining a livelihood." Allah has willed that sleep should overpower man and make him lose consciousness and activity. When asleep, man is in a state which is unlike life and unlike death. It ensures rest for his body and mind and compensates both for whatever effort they have exerted during wakefulness. All this happens in a way the true nature of which man cannot conceive. His will plays no part in it and it is impossible for him to discover how it happens to him. When awake, man does not know his condition while he is asleep. He is also unable, when asleep, to observe his condition and how sleep affects him. It is one of the secrets of the constitution of man and all living creatures, unknown except to the Creator Who has made sleep essential for life. For there is no living creature who can stay without sleep except for a limited period. If he were forced, by external means, to stay awake he would certainly die.

In the Shade of the Qur'an

Sleep does not merely satisfy some of man's physical and mental needs. It is, indeed, a truce for the human soul from the fierce struggle of life. It is a respite which allows man to lay down his armour, willingly or unwillingly, and enjoy a period of perfect peace which he needs no less than he needs food and drink. Sometimes, when one is low-spirited, mentally exhausted, possessed by fear and alarm, sleep may overpower one, for a few minutes perhaps, and bring about a total change in one's condition. Sleep does not merely renew one's strength, but it may revive one as if one wakes up a new person altogether. This is miraculous but still very true. It happened on a large scale to the early Muslims who fought in the battles of Badr and Uhud. Allah mentions both occasions in the Qur'an, reminding the Muslims of His favours. *"He made slumber overcome you as a reassurance from Him."* [1] *"Then, after grief, He let peace and security fall upon you – a sleep which overtook some of you . . ."* [2] Many other people had the same experience in similar conditions.

Cessation of activity and consciousness through sleep is a prerequisite for the continuity of life. Yet it can be given only by Allah. It is mentioned here by way of inviting man to contemplate his own creation and constitution.

Allah's perfection of creation has provided a correspondence between the movement of the universe and that of living creatures. As man requires sleep after his day's work, so Allah has provided the night as a covering mantle for man to enjoy his slumber. Day is also provided as a period of activity for man to pursue his livelihood. Thus perfect harmony is established. The world is perfectly suitable for the creatures who live in it, and Allah's creation is endowed with the characteristics which fit in easily and gently with the characteristics of the universe. What perfect planning by a scrupulous Designer!

The final leg of our round touches on the creation of heaven; *"We built above you seven mighty ones, and placed therein a blazing lamp. We send down out of the rain-clouds water in abundance, by which We bring forth grain and varied plants, and gardens thick with trees."* The seven mighty ones Allah has built above the earth are the seven heavens or skies, the precise nature of which is known only to Allah. They may be seven galaxies (a galaxy is a group of stars the number

---

[1] The Qur'an. *8; 11 (This verse relates to the battle of Badr).*
[2] Ibid. *3; 154 (This verse relates to the battle of Uhud).*

of which may exceed one hundred million) which have a bearing on our planet or on our solar system. The phrase may also refer to something else which we do not know. What we know for certain, however, is that these seven have strong constitution and do not easily disintegrate. This much we know about the stars and we observe in what we call "the sky". The *surah* also points out that the construction of the seven mighty ones is in perfect harmony with the creation of the earth and the world of man. This is implied in the following verses: *"And placed therein a blazing lamp."* This is a reference to the sun which shines and gives the heat necessary for the earth and its living creatures. It also plays an important part in forming the clouds by evaporating sea water: *"We send down out of the rainclouds water in abundance."* The Arabic text refers to these clouds as something squeezable. But who squeezes them to extract their juice? The winds, maybe, or perhaps some kind of electric charge in the atmosphere. Beyond both types, however, there is the hand of the Designer, who has assigned to everything in the universe its respective qualities.

The use of the word "lamp" to refer to the sun is very apt, for a lamp gives heat and light and it shines as if it is ablaze. The heat and the light provided by the sun combine with the water flowing in abundance time after time from the "squeezable" clouds to help the seeds send out their shoots. This is how grains, vegetables, bushes and wide-branching trees grow. This consonance in the design of the universe could not have been achieved without the careful Designer and the wise Planner. Any man would appreciate this if his attention were drawn to it. If he acquired advanced knowledge he would find much more consonance and congruity in the universe, which would leave him wondering in complete amazement. He would then find completely insupportable the argument that all this had been the result of coincidence. He would consider those who evade admitting the fact of elaborate and conscious planning pig-headed, unworthy of respect.

The Qur'an refers to this multitude of scenes and phenomena in the universe in a very significant succession: making the earth level, the mountains its pegs, mankind pairs, sleep a cessation of activity, the night a covering mantle, the day a period of bustling activity, building the seven mighty ones, providing the blazing lamp and the abundant flow of water so that vegetation, grains and trees can shoot forth and grow. This succession confirms the perfect consonance and produces a very strong feeling of the great Wisdom that has planned all this. It inspires the heart with the realisation of the purpose of this life . . . Hence, we pick up again the theme of the fateful tiding, the subject of controversy.

All this has been for work and pleasure, but there are reckoning and reward to follow, on the appointed Day of Decision: *"Fixed is the Day of Decision. On that day the Trumpet is blown and you shall come in crowds, and heaven is opened and becomes gates, and the mountains are set in motion, and seem to have been a mirage."* Creation is not without purpose. The Creator Who has accurately measured human life and carefully provided perfect harmony between it and the universe cannot let people just live and die in vain. Reason cannot accept that those who do good and the evil-doers should both end in dust. The rightly guided and the straying folk, the just and the tyrants cannot have the same fate. There must be a day when everything is judged and evaluated. The day is appointed by Allah: *"Fixed is the Day of Decision."*

It is a day when upheaval overtakes the universe and destroys its systems. *"On that day the Trumpet is blown and you shall come in crowds, and heaven is opened and becomes gates, and the mountains are set in motion, and seem to have been a mirage."* The "Trumpet" is a kind of horn of which we know nothing except its name and that it will be blown. We need not waste our time trying to discover how, for such discovery will not strengthen our faith.

Allah has revealed to us what we need to know of the secrets of the universe so that we may not waste our energy in futile pursuit of useless knowledge. We can imagine, however, a blow on the Trumpet which men answer by coming in crowds. We can visualise such a scene when all generations of mankind, which succeeded one another on this earth, rise up, walking in multitudes, from all directions to attend the great reckoning. We can imagine the fearful sight of people rising up from graves and the great crowd, huge, endless. We can feel the horror of the day with such an unprecedented crowd, helpless, horror-stricken. We do not know where will this happen, for the universe is full of great events: *"and heaven is opened and becomes gates, and the mountains are set in motion, and seem to have been a mirage."*

Heaven, the mighty heaven, is opened up so that it becomes gates. It is, as described elsewhere in the Qur'an, rent asunder. So, it will

Surah 78   The Tiding (*An-Naba'*)

look very unfamiliar to us. The firmly dug-in pegs, namely, the mountains are set in motion. They are hammered, scattered, turned into dust, blown by the wind, as other Qur'anic verses describe. Hence, they become non-existent, like a mirage which has no reality. Or, probably, different rays are reflected against them after they have been turned into dust and they look like a mirage.

All in all, it is horror apparent in the upheaval which envelops the universe as well as in men's resurrection after blowing the Trumpet. Such is the Day of Decision carefully and wisely fixed.

The *surah* takes another step, beyond resurrection, to describe the fate of the tyrant disbelievers and that of the righteous. It begins with the former group who raise doubts about the fateful tiding: *"Hell stands as a vigilant watchguard, a home for the tyrants and the transgressors. Therein they shall abide for ages, tasting neither coolness nor any drink, save boiling fluid and decaying filth: a fitting recompense. They did not expect to be faced with a reckoning and roundly denied Our revelations. But We noted and recorded all, (and We shall say:) 'Taste this, then; the only increase you shall have is increase of torment.'"* Hell has been created so that it may watch the tyrants and transgressors and await their arrival. They come to find it well prepared to receive them, as if they return to their natural home after having gone on a journey to the earth. It is a home in which they stay endlessly. But they taste *"neither coolness nor any drink."* The next verse gives an exception to that, but the exception is even worse: *"save boiling fluid and decaying filth."* Their throats and stomachs burn as they drink their boiling fluid, which is the "coolness" they have, while their other drink is the filth of the burning bodies, decaying by the enormous heat. The Qur'an comments that this is *"a fitting recompense."* It is in keeping with what they have done in their lives. For they thought they would never return to Allah: *"They did not expect to be faced with a reckoning and roundly denied Our revelations."* Their denial, as the Arabic verse suggests, is strongly emphatic and stubbornly upheld. But Allah keeps a meticulous record which does not leave out anything they do or say: *"But We noted and recorded all."* Then follows a reproach coupled with the tiding that they can hope for no change in their condition and no abatement of its intensity: *"Taste this, then; the only increase you shall have is increase of torment."*

We then have the corresponding scene of the righteous in complete bliss. *"The godfearing shall have a place of security, gardens and vineyards, and high-bosomed maidens, of equal age, for companions, and a cup overflowing. There they shall hear no idle talk, nor any falsehood. Such is the recompense of your Lord: a truly sufficient gift."* If Hell is a vigilant watchguard which the tyrants cannot escape, the righteous, the godfearing, will end in a place of security. What a place it is: *"gardens and vineyards."* The vine tree is specifically mentioned because it is well known to the addressees. The godfearing will also have companions who are described here as high-bosomed and of equal age. They also drink of a cup overflowing with drink.

These luxuries are given a physical description so that they may be appreciated by human beings. The precise nature of these luxuries and how they may be enjoyed remain unknown to us as our understanding is restricted by our limited world. But the enjoyment provided to the righteous is not purely physical. *"There they shall hear no idle talk, nor any falsehood."* So it is a pure life there, free of the idle chatting and falsehood which give rise to controversy. The reality is known to everyone, which means that there is no room for futile argument. It is a sublime state of affairs suitable for the eternal life. Then follows the Qur'anic comment: *"Such is the recompense of your Lord: a truly sufficient gift."*

The *surah* closes with the final scene of the day when all this happens. It is a scene in which we see Jibril, the Holy Spirit, and all the angels standing in ranks before Allah, their All-Merciful Lord. They stand in awe of Him; no-one dares utter a word without prior permission from the Merciful. *"Lord of the heavens and earth and all that lies between them, the All-Merciful, with Whom they have no power to speak. On the day when the Spirit and the angels stand in ranks, they shall not speak, save him to whom the All-Merciful has given leave, and who shall say what is right."*

The recompense given to the righteous and to the tyrant transgressors, which was detailed in the previous section is from *"your Lord ... Lord of the heavens and earth and all that lies between them, the All-Merciful."* What a befitting context to reaffirm the eternal truth of godhead. Allah is the Supreme Lord of man, heavens and earth, this life and the next, Who metes out reward for righteousness and punishment for tyranny. But above all He is the All-Merciful. The reward He assigns to each group is a manifestation of His mercy. Even the torment endured by the transgressors originates from Allah's mercy. For it is indeed part of mercy that evil should be punished and that it should not have the same end as good.

The other Divine attribute implied here is majesty: *"with Whom they have no power to speak."* In this highly awesome situation no man or angel can speak without permission from the All-Merciful. Whatever is said will be right because He does not permit anyone to speak whom He knows will not be saying what is right.

When we think that the angels, who are favoured by Allah, and absolutely pure from sin, stand silent in front of Allah and dare not speak without His permission, we are bound to feel how awesome the atmosphere is. Having motivated such a feeling the *surah* gives a cry of warning to those who have chosen not to hear or see: *"That day is a certainty. Let him who will, seek a way back to his Lord. We have warned you of an imminent scourge, on the day when a man will look on what his hands have forwarded and the disbeliever will cry: 'Would that I were dust!'"*

Those who raise doubts and question the reality of the Day of Decision are given a violent shake: *"That day is a certainty."* There is no room left for doubts and controversy. Yet there *is* time for mending one's erring ways before the fearful watchguard, i.e. Hell, becomes a permanent home: *"Let him who will, seek a way back to his Lord."* The warning is stern enough to make the drunken awake: *"We have forewarned you of an imminent scourge."* It will not be long coming, for man's life is but a short period. The scourge is so fearful that the disbelievers, when faced with it, will send up that great cry expressing the wish that they had never lived: *"on the day when a man will look on what his hands have forwarded and the disbeliever will cry: 'Would that I were dust!'"*

It is a cry of one who is in great distress, who feels ashamedly for what has been and what one has done. He feels that it is better not to be, or to be something as worthless as dust, than to witness such a fearful occasion. This horrifying position of the disbelievers is the subject of the questions and doubts they raise concerning that fateful tiding.

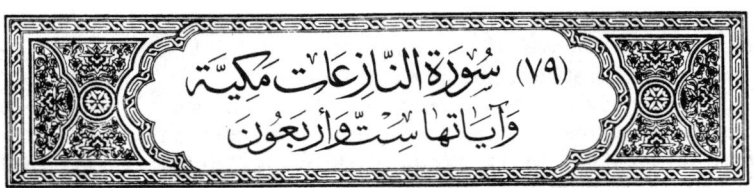

بِسْمِ اللهِ الرَّحْمَنِ الرَّحِيمِ

وَالنَّازِعَاتِ غَرْقًا ۝ وَالنَّاشِطَاتِ نَشْطًا ۝ وَالسَّابِحَاتِ سَبْحًا ۝ فَالسَّابِقَاتِ سَبْقًا ۝ فَالْمُدَبِّرَاتِ أَمْرًا ۝ يَوْمَ تَرْجُفُ الرَّاجِفَةُ ۝ تَتْبَعُهَا الرَّادِفَةُ ۝ قُلُوبٌ يَوْمَئِذٍ وَاجِفَةٌ ۝ أَبْصَارُهَا خَاشِعَةٌ ۝ يَقُولُونَ أَإِنَّا لَمَرْدُودُونَ فِي الْحَافِرَةِ ۝ أَإِذَا كُنَّا عِظَامًا نَخِرَةً ۝ قَالُوا تِلْكَ إِذًا كَرَّةٌ خَاسِرَةٌ ۝ فَإِنَّمَا هِيَ زَجْرَةٌ وَاحِدَةٌ ۝ فَإِذَا هُمْ بِالسَّاهِرَةِ ۝

هَلْ أَتَاكَ حَدِيثُ مُوسَى ۝ إِذْ نَادَاهُ رَبُّهُ بِالْوَادِ الْمُقَدَّسِ طُوًى ۝ اذْهَبْ إِلَى فِرْعَوْنَ إِنَّهُ طَغَى ۝ فَقُلْ هَلْ لَكَ إِلَى أَنْ تَزَكَّى ۝ وَأَهْدِيَكَ إِلَى رَبِّكَ فَتَخْشَى ۝ فَأَرَاهُ الْآيَةَ الْكُبْرَى ۝ فَكَذَّبَ وَعَصَى ۝ ثُمَّ أَدْبَرَ يَسْعَى ۝ فَحَشَرَ فَنَادَى ۝ فَقَالَ أَنَا رَبُّكُمُ الْأَعْلَى ۝ فَأَخَذَهُ اللَّهُ نَكَالَ الْآخِرَةِ وَالْأُولَى ۝ إِنَّ فِي ذَلِكَ لَعِبْرَةً لِمَنْ يَخْشَى ۝ أَأَنْتُمْ أَشَدُّ خَلْقًا أَمِ السَّمَاءُ بَنَاهَا ۝ رَفَعَ سَمْكَهَا فَسَوَّاهَا ۝ وَأَغْطَشَ لَيْلَهَا وَأَخْرَجَ ضُحَاهَا ۝ وَالْأَرْضَ بَعْدَ ذَلِكَ دَحَاهَا ۝ أَخْرَجَ مِنْهَا مَاءَهَا وَمَرْعَاهَا ۝ وَالْجِبَالَ أَرْسَاهَا ۝ مَتَاعًا لَكُمْ وَلِأَنْعَامِكُمْ ۝

فَإِذَا جَاءَتِ الطَّامَّةُ الْكُبْرَى ۝ يَوْمَ يَتَذَكَّرُ الْإِنْسَانُ مَا سَعَى ۝ وَبُرِّزَتِ الْجَحِيمُ لِمَنْ يَرَى ۝ فَأَمَّا مَنْ طَغَى ۝ وَآثَرَ الْحَيَاةَ الدُّنْيَا ۝ فَإِنَّ الْجَحِيمَ هِيَ الْمَأْوَى ۝ وَأَمَّا مَنْ خَافَ مَقَامَ رَبِّهِ وَنَهَى النَّفْسَ عَنِ الْهَوَى ۝ فَإِنَّ الْجَنَّةَ هِيَ الْمَأْوَى ۝ يَسْأَلُونَكَ عَنِ السَّاعَةِ أَيَّانَ مُرْسَاهَا ۝ فِيمَ أَنْتَ مِنْ ذِكْرَاهَا ۝ إِلَى رَبِّكَ مُنْتَهَاهَا ۝ إِنَّمَا أَنْتَ مُنْذِرُ مَنْ يَخْشَاهَا ۝ كَأَنَّهُمْ يَوْمَ يَرَوْنَهَا لَمْ يَلْبَثُوا إِلَّا عَشِيَّةً أَوْ ضُحَاهَا ۝

SURAH 79

THE PLUCKERS
AN-NAZI'AAT

In the name of Allah, the Beneficent, the Merciful.

By those that pluck out vehemently
and those that move forward rapidly;
by those that swim vigorously
and those that outstrip swiftly
and those that conduct a certain affair.
On the day when the earth shall quake,
followed soon afterwards by the sky,
all hearts shall be filled with terror,
and all eyes shall be downcast.
They say, "What, are we being restored as we were before?
What, when we have been turned to old, hollow bones?
They say, "That will be a losing return."
But with just one blast
they shall be alive on earth.
Have you heard the history of Moses?
His Lord called out to him in the holy valley of Towa,
saying: "Go to Pharoah: he has tyrannised and transgressed all bounds,
and say to him: 'Would you like to reform yourself?

I will guide you to your Lord, so that you may be in awe of Him.' "
He showed Pharaoh the mightiest miracle,
but Pharaoh cried lies and rebelled.
He then turned away hastily.
He summoned all his men and made a proclamation to them:
"I am your supreme Lord", he said.
Allah smote him with the scourge of the life to come
and that of this life as well.
Surely in this there is a lesson for the godfearing.
Which is stronger in constitution: you or the heaven He has built?
He raised it high and gave it its perfect shape,
and gave darkness to its night, and brought out its daylight.
After that He spread out the earth.
He brought out water from it, and brought forth its pastures;
and the mountains He set firm,
for you and your cattle to delight in.
Then, when the Greatest Catastrophe comes
on the day when man shall call to mind what he has done,
When Hell is brought in sight of all who are looking on;
then, he who tyrannised and transgressed
and chose this present life
will have Hell for his dwelling place.
But he who feared to stand before his Lord
and forbade his soul its caprice
will dwell in Paradise.
They question you about the Hour of Doom, when will it come?
But why should you be concerned with its exact timing?
The final word concerning it belongs to your Lord.
Your mission is merely to warn those who fear it.
On the day when they see that hour, it will seem to them that their life
on earth had spanned only one evening, or one morning.

Surah 79   The Pluckers (*An-Nazi'aat*)

This *surah* is just one example of many in this thirtieth part of the Qur'an which have one common objective, namely, to drive home to man the reality of the hereafter, its inevitability, and its awesome and serious nature, and to stress its importance to the Divine planning of man's life in this world. Such planning culminates in man's death and subsequent resurrection for the life to come. As it sets out to drive this idea home to man, the *surah* touches the emotions in different ways which are directly relevant to its central idea.

First we have an ambiguous opening which creates an air of fear and worried expectation. The rhythm here is quick and throbbing; it helps evoke feelings of fear, surprise and wonder: *"By those that pluck out vehemently, and those that move out rapidly, by those that swim vigorously, and those that outstrip swiftly, and those that conduct a certain affair."*

This equivocal, shaking opening is followed by the first of the scenes of the hereafter. The scene shares style and tempo with the opening which thus serves as a framework for the scene: *"On the day when the earth shall quake, followed soon afterwards by the sky, all hearts shall be filled with terror, and all eyes shall be downcast. They say, 'What, are we being restored as we were before? What, when we have been turned to old, hollow bones?' They say, 'That will be a losing return.' But with just one blast they shall be alive on earth."*

Having spread an air of awe, the *surah* gives an account of the end met by some of the disbelievers in the story of Moses and Pharaoh. Here the rhythm is quieter and more relaxed to suit the narrative style: *"Have you heard the history of Moses? His Lord called out to him in the holy valley of Towa, saying: 'Go to Pharaoh: He has transgressed all bounds, and say to him; "Would you like to reform yourself? I will guide you to your Lord, so that you may be in awe of Him." ' He showed Pharaoh the mightiest miracle, but Pharaoh cried lies and rebelled. He then turned away hastily. He summoned all his men and made a proclamation to them: 'I am your supreme Lord,' he said. Allah smote him with the scourge of the life to come and that of this life as well. Surely in this there is a lesson for the godfearing."* This account serves as an introduction to the great principle the *surah* aims to establish.

Leaving history aside, the *surah* takes up the open book of the universe. It paints some of the great scenes of the universe which testify to the limitless power and careful planning of Allah, the Creator of the universe Who controls its destiny both in this life and in the life to come. These scenes are drawn here with powerful style and strong rhythm in harmony with the opening of the *surah* and its general cadence. *"Which is stronger in constitution: you or the heaven He has built? He raised it high and gave it its perfect shape, and gave darkness to its night, and brought out its daylight. After that He spread out the earth. He brought out water from it and brought forth its pastures; And the mountains He set firm, for you and your cattle to delight in."*

After all these introductory scenes and inspiring touches comes the statement concerning the "Greatest Catastrophe" accompanied by the distribution of rewards for actions alone in this life. The rewards are portrayed in scenes which fit in harmoniously with the Greatest Catastrophe: *"Then, when the Greatest Catastrophe comes, on the day when man will call to mind what he has done, when Hell is brought in sight of all who are looking on; then, he who has transgressed and chosen this present life will have Hell for his dwelling place. But he who feared to stand before His Lord and forbade his soul its caprice will dwell in Paradise."*

At this point, when we are overwhelmed with the effects of the scenes of the Greatest Catastrophe, Hell brought near, the end of the transgressors who prefer this life to the next, and that of the god-fearing who restrain themselves and do not give in to their own caprice – at this point, the *surah* turns to those who deny resurrection and ask the Prophet to fix its time. The rhythm here is superb: it adds to the feeling of awe produced by the account of the Hour of Doom. *"They question you about the Hour of Doom, when will it come? But why should you be concerned with its exact timing. The final word concerning it belongs to your Lord. Your duty is merely to warn those who fear it. On the day when they see that hour, it will seem to them that their life on earth had spanned only one evening, or one morning."* Perhaps we should note that these verses end with the sound *"aaha"* which adds length to the meter, intensifying the effect of majesty and awe.

"By those that pluck vehemently and those that move forward rapidly; by those that swim vigorously and those that outstrip swiftly and those that conduct a certain affair." Some commentators say of these verses that they refer to the angels who pluck out the souls vehemently, move along actively with ease and speed, swim along as they move in the outer world, outstrip other creatures to embrace the faith and carry out Allah's commands and conduct whatever affairs they are charged with. Other commentators maintain that they refer

Surah 79   The Pluckers (*An-Nazi'aat*)

to the stars who pluck out as they run in their orbits, move rapidly in phases, swim in space, outstrip others as they run fast and bring about certain phenomena and results which are entrusted to them by Allah and which affect life on earth. A third group of commentators are of the view that the pluckers, runners, swimmers and outstrippers refer to the stars while the conductors of affairs are the angels. Another group believe that the pluckers, runners and swimmers are the stars while the outstrippers and conductors of affairs are the angels.

Whatever the referents of these terms are, we feel from the general Qur'anic sense that mentioning them in this particular manner produces a shock and a feeling of expectation of something fearful. Thus, they contribute, right at the outset, to preparing our minds for the fearful account of the first and second quakes and of the Greatest Catastrophe later on in the *surah*.

Perhaps it is better not to go into great detail in trying to explain and discuss these verses. It is perhaps more fruitful to let these verses produce their effect naturally. The Qur'an seeks to achieve its objective of awakening men's hearts in different ways. If we do this we simply follow the example of Umar ibn Al-Khattab. He once read the *surah* entitled "The Frowning". When he reached the verse which reads *"wa fakihatan wa abba"*[1] he wondered, "We know the fruit trees *'fakihatan'*, but what is *'abba'*?" But then he reproached himself saying: "You Ibn Al-Khattab, are being really fussy today! What harm is there in your not knowing the meaning of a word used in Allah's book?" He then said to the people around: "Follow what you understand of this book; what you do not understand you may leave alone." His statement, aimed at discouraging people from trying to explain what may be equivocal to them without the backing of perfectly sound authority, represents an attitude of veneration towards Allah's words, some of which may have been deliberately left equivocal so that they may fulfil a certain objective.

The opening of the *surah* takes the form of an oath, to confirm the event related in the following few verses: *"On the day when the earth shall quake, followed soon afterwards by the sky, all hearts shall be filled with terror, and all eyes shall be downcast. They say, 'What, are*

---

[1] This verse may be rendered in English as "and the fruit trees and the green pastures." The term *"abba"* i.e. "green pastures" was not commonly used, which explains Umar's question. – Translator's note.

In the Shade of the Qur'an

we being restored as we were before? What, when we have been turned to old, hollow bones?' They say, 'That will be a losing return.' But with just one blast they shall be alive on earth.'" [1] It has been suggested that the "quaker" is the earth. This is based on what the Qur'an says in another *surah*: *"On the day when the earth and the mountains will quake"* [2] It has also been suggested that the "follower" is the sky, as it follows the earth and witnesses its own upheaval which causes it to split and causes the stars to scatter. An alternative suggestion claims that the "quaker" refers to the first blast on the Trumpet which causes the earth, the mountains and all creation to quake and tremble and makes all who are in heaven and on earth fall down fainting, except those who shall be spared by Allah. "The follower" it is claimed, refers to the second blow on the Trumpet which brings all creation back to life (as stated in *surah* 39, verse 68).

Whichever suggestion is the correct one, the very verses make men's hearts feel the quake and shake with fear and worry. They prepare them to realise what sort of terror will fill the hearts on the day of judgement: *"All hearts shall be filled with terror and all eyes shall be downcast."* Thus, it is a combination of worry, fear, humiliation and breakdown. This is what happens on that day, and it is the fact which the oath at the opening of the *surah* seeks to establish. In both sense and rhythm, the scene portrayed by these verses fits in perfectly with the opening.

The *surah* goes on to speak of their surprise and wonder when they are resurrected: *"They say, 'What, are we being restored as we were before? What, when we have been turned to old, hollow bones?'"* They wonder whether they are being returned to life again. Amazed, they ask how this can be done after they have been dead for so long that their bones have become hollow. Then they realise that their awakening does not take them back to their life on earth, but to their second life. At this point they feel their great loss and cry: *"They say, 'That will be a losing return.'"* They have not banked on such a return, and have not prepared for it, so they have everything to lose by it. The Qur'anic comment is to state what will actually happen. *"But with*

---

[1] The Arabic text does not specify the earth as the thing which will quake, or the sky as following. The first two verses in this section may be rendered in a more strictly literal translation as: "On the day when the quaker shall quake, followed by the follower." Hence the author attempts to explain the meaning of these verses in his own familiar way. – Translator's note.
[2] The Qur'an. *73; 14.*

Surah 79   The Pluckers (*An-Nazi'aat*)

just one blast they shall be alive on earth."

The "blast" is a shout, but it is described here as a blast to emphasise its force, and to strike a note of perfect harmony between this scene and the other scenes of the *surah*. The term used for "the earth" here refers to a bright white earth which is the land of resurrection. We do not know its exact location. All we know of it is that which the Qur'an or the authentic traditions of the Prophet relate. We have no intention of adding anything unauthoritative to their account. Other Qur'anic statements lead us to the conclusion that this one blast is most probably the second blow on the Trumpet, i.e. the blow of resurrection. The expression used here gives a sense of speed. The blast itself is associated with speed, and the general rhythm of the *surah* is a rapid one. The terrified hearts also beat fast. Hence the perfect harmony between the sense, the rhythm, the scenes and the *surah* as a whole.

The rhythm then slows down a bit in order to suit the style of narration. For next we have an account of what had taken place between Moses and Pharaoh, and the end which Pharaoh met after he had tyrannised and transgressed all bounds: *"Have you heard the history of Moses? His Lord called out to him in the holy valley of Towa, saying: 'Go to Pharaoh: he has transgressed all bounds, and say to him: "Would you like to reform yourself? I will guide you to your Lord, so that you may have fear of Him."' He showed Pharaoh the mightiest miracle, but he cried lies and rebelled. He then turned away hastily. He summoned all his men and made to them a proclamation: 'I am your supreme Lord,' he said. Allah smote him with the scourge of the life to come and that of this life as well. Surely in this there is a lesson for the godfearing."*

The story of Moses is the most frequent and most detailed of the Qur'anic stories. It is mentioned in many other *surahs*, in different styles and with varying emphasis. At times, certain episodes are given greater prominence. This variation of style and emphasis aims at striking harmony between the historical account and the *surah* in which it occurs. Thus, the story helps to make the message of the *surah* clearer. This method is characteristic of the Qur'an.[1] Here the

---

[1] For a full discussion of this method see the chapter entitled "The Use of Narrative in the Qur'an" in the author's book *"The Qur'anic Art of Picture Drawing."*

In the Shade of the Qur'an

historical account is given in quick successive scenes which open with the call Moses receives in the holy valley and end with the destruction of Pharaoh in this life and the life to come. Thus, it fits very well with the main theme of the *surah*, namely the hereafter. The part given here of Moses's history spans a long period, but it is covered by a few short verses, so that it may fit in well with the rhythm and message of the *surah*. These short verses include several stages and scenes of the story.

They start with an introductory question addressed to the Prophet, *"Have you heard the history of Moses?"* The question serves to prepare us to listen to the history and contemplate its lessons. Moses's story is described here as history to emphasise that it has actually happened. It starts with the scene of Moses being called by Allah: *"His Lord called out to him in the holy valley of Towa."* Towa is probably the name of the valley which lies to the right of the Mount Toor, as one comes up from Madian in North Hijaz.

The moment when this call was made was awesome. The call from Allah Himself to one of His servants, great beyond description, embodies a secret of Divinity, and a secret of how Allah has made man susceptible to receiving His call. No one can comprehend what is involved here without inspiration from Allah Himself.

The communication between Allah and Moses is discussed in more detail elsewhere in the Qur'an. In this *surah*, however, it is touched upon briefly, before Allah's command to Moses is stated: *"Go to Pharaoh: He has tyrannised and transgressed all bounds, and say to him 'Would you like to reform yourself? I will guide you to your Lord, so that you may be in awe of Him.'"*

"Go to Pharaoh: he has tyrannised and transgressed all bounds." Tyranny and transgression should not have taken place and must not go on. They lead to corruption and to what displeases Allah. So, Allah (praised be He) selects one of His noble servants and charges him with the task of trying to put an end to them. They are indeed so hateful that Allah Himself commands one of His servants to go to the tyrant in an attempt to turn him away from his erring ways, so that he may have no excuse should Allah decide to exact His retribution.

"Go to Pharaoh: he has tyrannised and transgressed all bounds." Allah then teaches Moses how to address the tyrant in the most persuasive manner, so that he may desist and try not to incur upon himself the displeasure of Allah: *"and say to him: 'Would you like to*

Surah 79   The Pluckers (*An-Nazi'aat*)

reform yourself?'" The first question to be put to the tyrant is whether he would like to purify himself of the stains of tyranny and the filth of disobedience to Allah. Would he like to know the path of the pious, the blessed: *"I will guide you to your Lord, so that you may be in awe of Him."* The offer made here to Pharaoh is to be shown the way acceptable to Allah. Once he knows it, he will feel the fear of Allah in his heart. Man does not transgress and tyrannise unless he loses his way and finds himself taking a road which does not lead to Allah. His heart hardens as a result, and he rebels and tyrannises.

Moses has been told this in the scene of Allah's call to him. He of course puts these questions to Pharaoh when he encounters him. The *surah*, however, does not repeat them when it describes the encounter. It skips over what happens after Allah's call to Moses and deletes what Moses says when he conveys his message. It is as if the curtain falls after the scene of the call. When it is lifted again, we are presented with the end of the encounter scene: *"He showed Pharaoh the mightiest miracle, but Pharaoh cried lies and rebelled."*

Thus, Moses conveys the message with which he has been entrusted in the manner Allah has taught him. This warm, friendly attitude, however, cannot win over a heart that has been hardened by tyranny and ignorance of the Lord of the universe. So Moses shows him the great miracles of the stick turning into a snake and Moses's hand becoming brilliant white in colour, (as they are explained in other *surahs*), *"but he cried lies and rebelled."* The scene of Moses's encounter with Pharaoh and his conveying the message to him ends with Pharaoh's rejection and rebellion. It is then followed by a scene in which Pharaoh turns away to mobilise his forces and bring forward his magicians for an encounter between magic and the truth. Pharaoh adopted this course of action because he was determined not to accept the truth or submit to right. *"He then turned away hastily. He summoned all his men and made a proclamation to them: 'I am your supreme Lord,' he said."*

The *surah* does not give any details of Pharaoh's efforts to muster his magicians and sorcerers and summon all his men. It simply says that he went away to do that, and then boasted with his impertinent proclamation which betrays his infinite ignorance and conceit: *"'I am your supreme Lord', he said."*

Pharaoh's declaration betrays the fact that he was deceived by his people's ignorance and their submission to his authority. Nothing deceives tyrants more than the ignorance and the abject submission of the masses. A tyrant is in fact an individual who has no real power or authority. The ignorant, submissive masses simply bend their backs for him to ride, stretch out their necks for him to fit them with reins, hang down their heads to give him a chance to show his conceit, and forego their rights to be respected and honoured, thus giving him a chance to tyrannise. The masses do all this because they are deceived and afraid at the same time. Their fear has no real basis except in their imagination. The tyrant, an individual, can never be stronger than thousands or millions, should they attach the proper value to their humanity, dignity, self-respect and freedom. Every individual in the nation is a match for the tyrant in terms of power. No one could tyrannise in a nation which is sane, or which knows its true Lord, believes in Him and refuses to submit to any creature who has no power over its destiny.

Pharaoh, however, found his people so ignorant, submissive and devoid of faith that he was able to make his insolent, blasphemous declaration, *"I am your supreme Lord!"* He would have never dared to make it had he found that his nation had the qualities of general awareness, self-respect and faith in Allah.

With such an intolerable insolence on Pharaoh's part coming on top of his grim tyranny, the Supreme Power moved in: *"Allah smote him with the scourge of the life to come and that of this life as well."* The scourge of the life to come is mentioned first because it is much harsher and perpetual. It is indeed the real punishment for the tyrants and the transgressors because of its severity and endlessness. It is also more appropriate to give it prominence since the life to come is the main theme of the *surah*. Besides, it fits perfectly with the general rhythm of the *surah*.

The scourge of this life is fearful and severe, but that of the life to come is much more so. Pharaoh had power, authority and glory, yet none of that was of any use to him. One can only imagine what will be the fate of the disbelievers who do not have similar power, authority or glory but still resist the call of Islam and try to suppress it.

"Surely in this there is a lesson for the godfearing." Only those who know their true Lord and fear Him will benefit from the lessons of Pharaoh's history. Those who do not fear Allah will continue in their erring ways until they reach their appointed end, when they shall suffer the scourge of both this life and the life to come.

Surah 79   The Pluckers (*An-Nazi'aat*)

Having mentioned the end met by the tyrants who thought themselves very powerful, the *surah* turns to the present disbelievers who also depend on their own power. It directs their attention to some manifestations of the work of the Supreme Power in the universe. Their power does not stand any comparison with that of Allah: *"Which is stronger in constitution: you or the heaven He has built? He raised it high and gave it its perfect shape, and gave darkness to its night, and brought out its daylight. After that He spread out the earth. He brought out water from its depth, and brought forth its pastures; And the mountains He set firm, for you and your cattle to delight in."*

The question these verses start with: *"Which is stronger in constitution: you or the heaven He has built?"* admits of one answer only: Heaven. So the question seems to infer another: "Why should you think so highly of your own power when heaven is much stronger in constitution than you and the Lord Who created it is much stronger than it?" The question may also be carried forward in a different direction: "Why do you think resurrection impossible? He has created heaven, the creation of which requires more power than your own creation? Resurrection is merely a repetition of creation. It follows that He who has built heaven will find your resurrection an easier proposition."

"He has built" heaven. The term "build" suggests strength and firm constitution. Heaven is so indeed. Its planets are held together in a perfect system. They neither scatter, nor fall away from their orbits.

"He raised it high and gave it its perfect shape." A glance is enough to recognise the perfect coherence and harmony in the building of heaven. Knowledge of the laws which govern the existence of the creatures in the sky above us and provide a perfect balance between their movements and between their mutual effects enhances awareness of the significance of this verse. It intensifies the feeling of the limitlessness of their very real world, of which human knowledge has uncovered only a small part. This part, however, is enough to make man overwhelmed with wonder and astonishment. He stands speechless at the infinite beauty of the universe. He can give no explanation for it except that a superhuman power has planned it and governs it. This explanation is now accepted even by those who profess not to believe in any religion.

"And gave darkness to its night, and brought out its daylight." The Arabic words used in this verse add to the strength of the general

tone. They also have stronger connotations than the translation suggests. They are used here because they are more fitting with the general context. The succession of darkness at night and light in the morning is a phenomenon recognised by all, but it may be overlooked because of its being so familiar. Here, the Qur'an reminds us of its permanent novelty. For it is repeated anew every day, producing the same effects and reactions. The natural laws governing this phenomenon are so precise and miraculous that they continue to impress and astonish man as his knowledge increases.

"After that He spread out the earth. He brought out water from it, and brought forth its pastures; and the mountains He set firm." Spreading out the earth is a reference to the levelling of its surface so that it becomes easy to walk on, and to the formation of a layer of soil suitable for cultivation. Setting the mountains firm is a result of the final shaping of the surface of the earth and its cooling down to a level suitable for the emergence of living organisms. Allah also brought out water from the earth. This applies to the springs that allow the deep waters to flow out on the surface of the earth. It applies also to the rain water, since it comes originally from the earth. He also brought forth the pastures, which is, in this context, a reference to all plants upon which man and animals feed, and which directly and indirectly sustain life.

All this happened after the heaven was built, the night darkened and the earth spread. The recent theories of astrology support this Qur'anic statement, for they assume that the earth was moving in its orbit, with day and night succeeding each other for hundreds of millions of years before it was levelled and spread out, became suitable for the growth of vegetation, and before its surface took its final, present shape of plains, valleys and mountains.

The Qur'an declares that all this is *"for you and your cattle to delight in."* This is a reminder for man of what Allah has made for him, and of His perfect and elaborate planning. It is not by chance that the heaven was built in this fashion and that the earth was spread out to take its present shape. Man's existence, as Allah's vicegerent, was taken into account. Man's existence and development depend on so many factors which operate in the universe generally, and in the solar system in particular, and more particularly in the earth itself. All these factors must be made to function in absolute harmony.

Following the Qur'anic approach of giving a short statement which embodies the basic fact, yet is rich with hints and inferences,

Surah 79   The Pluckers *(An-Nazi'aat)*

the *surah* names just a few of these harmonised factors – the building of heaven, darkening of the night, bringing out the daylight, spreading out the earth, bringing out its waters and pastures and setting the mountains firm – for man and his cattle to delight in. This statement makes the idea of elaborate planning of the universe understood by everybody. It makes use of some of its manifestations which require no particular standard of education to appreciate. This enables the Qur'an to be a universal address, to all men, in all ages and societies, whether primitive or advanced. The reality of meticulous and elaborate planning of the whole universe, however, goes far beyond the level mentioned here. The very nature of this universe rules out any possibility of its formation by chance, for no chance could result in such perfect and absolute harmony on such an immeasurable scale. The harmony starts with the fact that our solar system is unique among millions and millions of planetary systems, and our earth is also a unique planet with regard to its location in the solar system. It is this uniqueness which makes life on earth possible. We have not yet discovered among the many thousands of similar planets anyone which enjoys similar harmonisation of the essential factors which help the emergence and sustenance of life.

Life may appear on a certain planet if certain conditions are met: the planet must be of suitable size, at a medium distance from the sun, and it has to be of a composition which mixes the elements in the right proportion to permit the emergence of life. The suitable size is necessary because the atmosphere of the planet is conditioned by the force of its gravity. The medium distance is also a necessary condition because the planets which are near to the sun are so hot that nothing can solidify on them, and those that are far from the sun are so cold that nothing on them can have any measure of elasticity. The right composition of elements is necessary because such a composition in the right proportion is a must for the growth of vegetation which is, in turn, essential for the sustenance of life. The Earth has the ideal location to satisfy all these conditions which help the emergence of life in the only form which we now know.[1]

The establishment of the fact of elaborate planning of the grand universe, and giving man a special place in it prepares man's heart

---

[1] A. M. Al-Akkad, *Beliefs of Twentieth Century Thinkers*, p. 36.

In the Shade of the Qur'an

and mind to receive and accept the statement of the reality of the hereafter and its final judgement and rewards with a feeling of reassurance. If the origins of the universe and of man are so, then the cycle must be completed, and everyone must have his reward. It is inconceivable that the final end comes with the end of man's short life in this world, or that evil and tyranny can get away without retribution, or that good, justice and right can be left to suffer whatever hardship is visited on them in this life, without there being a chance to put matters right. Such an assumption is, in its very essence, contrary to the fact of elaborate planning, so apparent everywhere in the universe. Hence the reality touched upon in this part of the *surah* serves as an introduction to the reality of the hereafter which is the main theme of the *surah*.

"Then, when the Greatest Catastrophe comes, on the day when man will call to mind what he has done, when Hell is brought in sight of all who are looking on; then, he who transgressed and chose this present life will have Hell for his dwelling place. But he who feared to stand before his Lord and forbade his soul its caprice will dwell in Paradise." This present life is a period of comfort and enjoyment which are given in precise and accurate measure. Its duration is determined according to the overall planning relating to the universe and human life. Its comfort and enjoyment will end at the time appointed for their expiry. When the Greatest Catastrophe comes it ravages all and overwhelms all. The fleeting comfort of this life is extinguished, the whole universe, its built heaven, spread out earth, firm mountains are overturned and all living creatures are overwhelmed. At that moment *"man will call to mind what he has done."* He might have been distracted by the events and comforts of this life and he might have overlooked what he had done. But he will recall it all then, when remembrance brings to him nothing but sadness and grief as he realises what miserable end he is facing. *"When Hell is brought in sight of all who are looking on."* The term used here for "bringing in sight" is particularly powerful. It is rich in its connotations and makes the rhythm even stronger. The result is that the image is so vivid that we almost see the whole scene in front of us now.

Then, people will have different destinies and the aim of the earlier planning of the first life will be revealed: *"Then, he who tyrannised and transgressed and chose this present life will have Hell for his dwelling place."* The two verbs "tyrannise" and "transgress" are used

Surah 79   The Pluckers *(An-Nazi'aat)*

here to render the meaning of one Arabic term, namely, "tyrannise" which is used here, as elsewhere in the Qur'an, in a much wider sense than strict despotism of rulers and dictators. "Tyranny" is used here as synonymous with exceeding the limits of right and truth. Hence these three verses refer to all those who transgress the boundaries of right, prefer this life to the future life, taking no heed of the latter. Since consciousness of the hereafter defines the values and standards to be applied, he who prefers this present life will suffer a breakdown of values and standards which results in his adoption of faulty standards of behaviour. This puts him in the category of despots and transgressors. Thus, Hell which is brought in sight of everybody on the day of the Catastrophe will be *"his dwelling place"*.

"But he who feared to stand before his Lord and forbade his soul its caprice will dwell in Paradise." The one who fears to stand in front of Allah does not indulge in sin. If he slips and commits a sin, in a moment of human weakness, his fear of facing Allah will lead him to repent and pray for forgiveness. Thus he remains within the area of obedience, the central point of which is the control of one's caprice and desires. Indulgence of desire and caprice is essentially the cause of all forms of tyranny and transgression. It is the spring of evil. Man hardly ever falls for any reason other than succumbing to caprice and desire. Ignorance is easy to cure. Desire, after ignorance has been cured, is the plague which requires a long and hard struggle to overcome. The fear of Allah is the solid defence against the violent attacks of desire. Indeed, there is hardly any other defence which can withstand such attacks. Hence, the *surah* mentions the fear of Allah and the control of caprice together in one verse. This fact is here asserted by Allah, the Creator of man and the only one Who knows the human soul, its weaknesses and their effective cure.

Allah does not ask man to suppress his desires, because He knows that it is not possible for him to do so. He simply asks man to control his desires and not to let them control him. He tells him that fear of standing before his Lord, the Almighty, should be of great help to him. He has fixed his reward for this hard struggle: Paradise as a dwelling place. For Allah knows perfectly well the hardships involved in this struggle and the high standards to which man is elevated by it. This struggle, self-control and elevation help man fulfil his humanity. Such fulfilment cannot be achieved by giving way to all desires, and following caprice wherever it leads, on the pretext that desire and caprice are part of human nature. Allah, who made man sensitive to certain urges, also gave him the ability to control such urges by self discipline. He also gives him Paradise as a reward when he wins and elevates himself to the high standard of humanity.

There are two types of freedom. The first is the one achieved through scoring a victory over one's desires and releasing oneself from the chains of caprice. When man achieves such a victory he finds himself able to fulfil these desires and caprices in a controlled and balanced way which emphasises man's freedom of choice. This type of freedom is the human type, the one which suits the honour Allah has bestowed on man. The other type is the animal freedom, represented in man's defeat, his enslavement by his desires, and his loss of control over himself. This type of freedom is advocated only by those who have lost their humanity, so they try to cover their slavery with a dress of deceptive freedom.

The first type is enjoyed by those who elevate and prepare themselves for the sublime and free life in their future dwelling place of Paradise. The second is indulged in by those who sink into the cesspool of desire, thus preparing themselves for Hell where they are deprived of their humanity. The end is the natural one, in both cases, according to Islam which gives everything its true and proper value.

The last part of the *surah* is expressed in a rhythm which evokes awe. *"They question you about the Hour of Doom, when will it come? But why should you be concerned with its exact timing? The final word concerning it belongs to your Lord. Your mission is merely to warn those who fear it. On the day when they see that hour, it will seem to them that their life on earth had spanned only one evening, or one morning."* Every time the diehards of the polytheists heard a description of the fearful events of the Day of Judgement, and the reckoning which takes place then, they used to ask the Prophet (peace be on him) to specify its time: *"When will it come?"* The answer given here to such questions is a rhetorical question, *"But why should you be concerned with its exact timing?"* It is an answer which suggests that the Hour of Doom, or the Day of Judgement, is so great and majestic that the questions put by the disbelievers concerning it sound stupid and pitiful. Moreover, such questions can be put forward only by the impudent. The great Prophet himself is asked, *"Why should you be concerned with its exact timing?"* It is so great that neither you nor anyone else should ask to be informed of its exact time. This knowledge belongs to Allah alone, not to anybody else. *"The final word concerning it belongs to your Lord."* He himself is the master of everything which relates to it. The Prophet's own duties, and the limits he should not, and need not exceed are well defined: *"Your mission is merely to warn those who fear it."* He is to warn those who will benefit by such warnings. Such people will feel that it is true and fear the outcome, so they conduct their lives according to their firm belief that it will arrive at the time appointed by Allah.

The majesty and awe of the Hour of Doom is explained through the description of its effects on men's feelings and the comparison they draw between its duration and the length of this present life. *"On the day when they see that hour, it will seem to them that their life on earth had spanned only one evening, or one morning."* It so grips the soul that our present life with all its epics, events and luxuries will seem to those who lived them shorter than a single day; just one evening or one morning. So, the whole world, its centuries and ages will shrink to nothing longer than one morning or one evening in the sight of the very people who quarrel and fight for it, preferring it to their share in the life to come, and who commit all sorts of sin, tyranny and transgression to achieve their ends in it, yielding to their desire and caprice. Yet for such a passing enjoyment they abandon the hereafter and forego the certain prospect of dwelling in Paradise. That is definitely the greatest stupidity of all, which no man who has ears and eyes to hear and see can ever perpetrate.

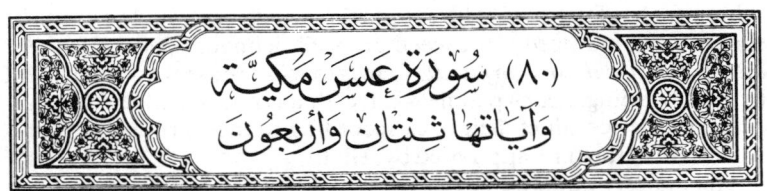

بِسْمِ اللهِ الرَّحْمٰنِ الرَّحِيمِ

عَبَسَ وَتَوَلَّىٰ ۝ أَن جَاءَهُ الْأَعْمَىٰ ۝ وَمَا يُدْرِيكَ لَعَلَّهُ يَزَّكَّىٰ ۝ أَوْ يَذَّكَّرُ فَتَنفَعَهُ الذِّكْرَىٰ ۝ أَمَّا مَنِ اسْتَغْنَىٰ ۝ فَأَنتَ لَهُ تَصَدَّىٰ ۝ وَمَا عَلَيْكَ أَلَّا يَزَّكَّىٰ ۝ وَأَمَّا مَن جَاءَكَ يَسْعَىٰ ۝ وَهُوَ يَخْشَىٰ ۝ فَأَنتَ عَنْهُ تَلَهَّىٰ ۝ كَلَّا إِنَّهَا تَذْكِرَةٌ ۝ فَمَن شَاءَ ذَكَرَهُ ۝ فِي صُحُفٍ مُّكَرَّمَةٍ ۝ مَّرْفُوعَةٍ مُّطَهَّرَةٍ ۝ بِأَيْدِي سَفَرَةٍ ۝ كِرَامٍ بَرَرَةٍ ۝

قُتِلَ الْإِنسَانُ مَا أَكْفَرَهُ ۝ مِنْ أَيِّ شَيْءٍ خَلَقَهُ ۝ مِن نُّطْفَةٍ خَلَقَهُ فَقَدَّرَهُ ۝ ثُمَّ السَّبِيلَ يَسَّرَهُ ۝ ثُمَّ أَمَاتَهُ فَأَقْبَرَهُ ۝ ثُمَّ إِذَا شَاءَ أَنشَرَهُ ۝ كَلَّا لَمَّا يَقْضِ مَا أَمَرَهُ ۝ فَلْيَنظُرِ الْإِنسَانُ إِلَىٰ طَعَامِهِ ۝ أَنَّا صَبَبْنَا الْمَاءَ صَبًّا ۝ ثُمَّ شَقَقْنَا الْأَرْضَ شَقًّا ۝ فَأَنبَتْنَا فِيهَا حَبًّا ۝ وَعِنَبًا وَقَضْبًا ۝ وَزَيْتُونًا وَنَخْلًا ۝ وَحَدَائِقَ غُلْبًا ۝ وَفَاكِهَةً وَأَبًّا ۝ مَّتَاعًا لَّكُمْ وَلِأَنْعَامِكُمْ ۝

فَإِذَا جَاءَتِ الصَّاخَّةُ ۝ يَوْمَ يَفِرُّ الْمَرْءُ مِنْ أَخِيهِ ۝ وَأُمِّهِ وَأَبِيهِ ۝ وَصَاحِبَتِهِ وَبَنِيهِ ۝ لِكُلِّ امْرِئٍ مِّنْهُمْ يَوْمَئِذٍ شَأْنٌ يُغْنِيهِ ۝ وُجُوهٌ يَوْمَئِذٍ مُّسْفِرَةٌ ۝ ضَاحِكَةٌ مُّسْتَبْشِرَةٌ ۝ وَوُجُوهٌ يَوْمَئِذٍ عَلَيْهَا غَبَرَةٌ ۝ تَرْهَقُهَا قَتَرَةٌ ۝ أُولَٰئِكَ هُمُ الْكَفَرَةُ الْفَجَرَةُ ۝

SURAH 80

THE FROWNING
ABAS

In the name of Allah, the Beneficent, the Merciful.

He frowned and turned his back
when the blind man came to him.
How could you tell? He might have sought to purify himself.
He might have been forewarned and the reminder might have
    profited him.
But to the one who considered himself self-sufficient
you were all attention.
Yet the fault would not be yours if he remained uncleansed.
As to him who comes to you with zeal
and with a feeling of fear in his heart –
him you ignore and busy yourself with trifles.
    No indeed! This is an admonition;
let him who will, bear it in mind.
It is written on honoured pages,
exalted, purified,
by the hands of noble and devout scribes.
Perish man! How ungrateful he is!
Of what did Allah create him?
Of a little germ. He created him and proportioned him.

In the Shade of the Qur'an

He makes his path smooth for him.
He then causes him to die and puts him in his grave.
He will surely bring him back to life when He pleases.
But by no means has man fulfilled His bidding.
Let man reflect on the food he eats:
how We pour down the rain in torrents,
and cleave the earth in fissures;
how We bring forth the corn,
the grapes, and the fresh vegetation,
the olive and the palm,
the dense-tree'd gardens.
the fruit-trees and the green pastures,
for you and your cattle to delight in.
But when the stunning blast is sounded,
on that day each man will forsake his brother,
his mother and his father,
his wife and his children:
for each one of them will on that day have enough preoccupations
 of his own.
Some faces on that day shall be beaming,
smiling and joyful.
Some other faces on that day shall be covered with dust,
veiled with darkness.
These shall be the faces of the disbelievers, the hardened in sin.

Surah 80   The Frowning *(Abas)*

This *surah* discusses certain principles of grave importance. It is unique in its images and the impressions it leaves, combining its marked spiritual effect with superb musical rhythm.

Its first part treats a certain incident which took place in the early days of Islam. The Prophet (peace be on him) was busy with a few dignatories of the tribe of Quraish, explaining to them the message of Islam, when Ibn Umm Maktoom, a poor blind man, interrupted him. Unaware that the Prophet was busy with those people, the blind man asked him repeatedly to teach him some verses of the Qur'an. The Prophet (peace be on him) was not very pleased at this interruption. He frowned and turned away from Ibn Umm Maktoom. This *surah* opens by criticizing the Prophet's behaviour in this incident. It lays down clearly the values and principles upon which Islamic society is founded and states the true nature of the message of Islam. *"He frowned and turned his back when the blind man came to him. How could you tell? He might have sought to purify himself. He might have been forewarned and the reminder might have profited him. But to the one who considered himself self-sufficient you were all attention. Yet the fault would not be yours if he remained uncleansed. As to him who comes to you with zeal and with a feeling of fear in his heart – him you ignore and busy yourself with trifles. No indeed! This is an admonition; let him who will, bear it in mind. It is written on honoured pages, exalted, purified, by the hands of noble and devout scribes."*

Man's ungrateful attitude to Allah and his denial of Him come up for discussion in the second part. Here man is reminded of his origin of how his life is made easy; of how Allah determines his death and resurrection; and of how, after all, he fails to carry out His orders: *"Perish man! how ungrateful he is! Of what did Allah create him? Of a little germ. He created him and proportioned him. He makes his path smooth for him. He then causes him to die and puts him in his grave. He will surely bring him to life when He pleases. But by no means has man fulfilled His bidding."*

The third part directs man to reflect upon things of immediate concern to him, namely, his food. Absolute perfection of creation is obvious in the provision of food for man as it is obvious in the creation, proportioning and development of man himself. *"Let man reflect on the food he eats: how We pour down the rain in torrents, and cleave the earth in fissures; how We bring forth the corn, the grapes, and the fresh vegetation, the olive and the palm, the dense-tree'd gardens, the fruit-trees and the green pastures, for you and your cattle to delight in."*

The final part touches upon "the stunning blast" and its fearful effects. The very sound of the words gives an impression of horror. It makes people unaware of anything around them. Their faces, however, give a lucid account of what is happening to them. *"But when the stunning blast is sounded, on that day each will forsake his brother, his mother and his father, his wife and his children: for each one of them will on that day have enough preoccupations of his own. Some faces on that day shall be beaming, smiling and joyful. Some other faces on that day shall be covered with dust, veiled with darkness. These shall be the faces of the disbelievers, the wicked."*

This quick preview of the *surah* leaves a profound effect on the reader. Its message and its implications are so powerful that no human heart can avoid being deeply touched, even by a quick perusal of it.

In the following pages we will attempt to illustrate some of the very far-reaching effects of certain parts of the *surah* which may not be immediately apparent.

"He frowned and turned his back when the blind man came to him. How could you tell? He might have sought to purify himself. He might have been forewarned and the reminder might have profited him. But to the one who considered himself self-sufficient you were all attention. Yet the fault would not be yours if he remained uncleansed. As to him who comes to you with zeal and with a feeling of fear in his heart – him you ignore and busy yourself with trifles. No indeed! This is an admonition; let him who will, bear it in mind. It is written on honoured pages, exalted, purified, by the hands of noble and devout scribes."

The Divine instructions which followed this incident are much more far-reaching than appears at first sight. They are indeed a miracle. These instructions, the principles they seek to establish and the change they aim to accomplish in human society are, perhaps, the first and greatest miracle of Islam. But the instructions are made here as a direct comment on a single incident. It is part of the Qur'anic method to make use of isolated incidents in order to lay down fundamental and permanent principles. The principles established here and their practical effects, as seen in the early Islamic society, are indeed Islam itself. They constitute the truth which Islam and the earlier Divine religions seek to plant in human life.

The point at issue here is not merely how an individual or a class of people should be treated. This is indeed the significance of the

Surah 80 The Frowning (*Abas*)

Qur'anic comment on the incident itself, taken in isolation. The heart of the matter is, however, something far more important. It is: how should people evaluate everything in their lives? From where should they derive their values and their standards for such an evaluation.

What the Divine instructions contained in the opening part of the *surah* seek to establish is that men must base their values and standards on Divine considerations, laid down by Allah.

No social circumstances, traditions or practices, nor any concept of life derived from them should be allowed either to encumber or determine these values and standards. There is no denying the difficulties involved in conducting human life on the basis of values and standards laid down by the Divine Being, free from the pressure of all worldly considerations.

If we consider the heavy pressure of society on the individual's feelings and attitudes – traditional values, family and social ties, and environmental values, for example – we can appreciate the difficulty of carrying out these Divine instructions. We can appreciate such difficulty even better when we remember that in order to convey it to people, Muhammad himself (peace be on him) needed this special directive, or rather this censure. Reference to this is sufficient to convey the gravity of the matter. For Muhammad (peace be on him) has reached greater heights of sublimity and greatness than any man can aspire to. Yet the fact that special instructions were required for him to convey a certain principle makes that principle greater than greatness, unique in sublimity.

This is indeed, a true description of the principle established here, namely, that mankind should derive their values and standards from the Divine Being, after they have freed themselves from the pressure of their social set-up with all its values and standards.

The basic standard Allah has, through His prophets, commanded mankind to adopt is: *"The noblest of you in Allah's sight is he who fears Him most."*[1] This is the standard by which all values, traditions and practices should be evaluated. It establishes a purely Divine criterion which has nothing to do with any worldly considerations. But people live on earth and establish a multitude of ties, each having its own weight and gravity. They have considerations of family relations, power and wealth. The distribution or concentration of these creates certain practical and economic results which determine the

---

[1] The Qur'an. *49; 13.*

position of every man or every class of people in relation to others. Thus some acquire a position superior to that of others, in worldly standards.

When Islam declares: *"The noblest of you in Allah's sight is he who fears Him most"*, it simply indicates that all these values and considerations are void, however important they seem to men. It substitutes for them a single value derived directly from Allah, the only value accepted by Him. The incident itself serves to establish this value in an actual situation. Thus the essential principle is established: the scales recognised are those of Allah; the supreme value which should govern man's life is the Divine one. Hence, all human values, standards, traditions and concepts must be abandoned by the Islamic nation.

Let us now consider the incident itself. Ibn Umm Maktoom, a poor blind man, comes to the Prophet (peace be on him) at a time when he is busy with a group of the most powerful and influential personalities in Makka, including Utbah and Shaibah, the two sons of Rabi'ah, Abu Jahl Amr ibn Hisham, Umayyah ibn Khalaf, Al-Waleed ibn Al-Mogheerah. Also present is Al-Abbas ibn Abdel-Muttalib, the Prophet's uncle. It is a crucial meeting. The Prophet explains the message of Islam to them and hopes for a favourable response. He feels that the cause of Islam will gain a lot by such a response. The time is very hard for Islam in Makka. Those very people have been using all their wealth, power and influence to check its advancement, and to stop people from accepting it. They have managed to freeze Islam in Makka and hinder its progress elsewhere. Outside Makka, the other tribes have adopted an attitude of wait and see. For they feel that that is their best stand in a tribal society such as theirs which gives to the tribe's attitude paramount importance. They are aware that against Muhammad, the Prophet of Islam, stand his own kinsmen, who, theoretically speaking, should be his most ardent supporters.

It must be emphasised that when we say that the Prophet is busy with those people, he has no personal interest with them. He is simply working for the interest of Islam. Acceptance of Islam by these influential and powerful people means the removal of all impediments from the path of Islam in Makka. It also ensures for Islam the freedom to progress outside Makka.

While this crucial meeting is in progress, a poor man comes and interrupts the Prophet (peace be on him) saying: "Messenger of Allah!

Surah 80   The Frowning (*Abas*)

teach me some verses of what Allah has taught you." Despite his awareness that the Prophet (peace be on him) is busy, he repeats his request several times. The Prophet dislikes this interruption. His face, which remains unseen by the blind man, expresses his aversion. He frowns and looks away from the poor man, who has interrupted the crucial meeting of which the Prophet has great hopes for his message. Indeed, the Prophet's motive has been his great enthusiasm to win badly-needed support for Islam.

Here, heaven intervenes to say the final word in this matter and to put the landmarks along the whole length of the road. Thus we are given the scales by which to weigh our values regardless of all considerations, including the consideration of what serves the interests of Islam, as seen by men, and even by the greatest man, Muhammad (peace be on him). This is why the Prophet who has been described elsewhere in the Qur'an as having *"great and sublime nature"*, [1] is strongly censured by Allah, the Most High. It is the only point in the Qur'an that the Prophet, who is very dear to Allah, is told *"kalla"* (inadequately translated as "no indeed"). *Kalla* is a term of censure and an order to desist. That is because the contravened principle is central to this religion.

The reproof is made in unique style, which defies translation into ordinary language. Written language has to apply certain rules and observe some well defined norms. These would dampen the effects of the very vivid style of the Qur'an, which is characterised in this instance by its rapid touches and short phrases which are more like feeling reactions and instant pictures.

"He frowned and turned his back when the blind man came to him." The use of the third person form here is significant. It suggests that the subject-matter is so distasteful to Allah that He does not like to confront His beloved messenger with it. This in itself is a gesture of mercy and kindness to the Prophet. Thus, the action which necessitated the reproof has been disguised with great subtlety. The reproof then takes the form of direct address, starting somewhat mildly: *"How could you tell? He might have sought to purify himself. He might have been forewarned and the reminder might have profited him."* How could you tell but that a great gain might have been made? That is to say that the poor, blind man who came to you seeking light might have profited by Allah's reminder and set about purifying himself.

---

[1] The Qur'an. *68; 4.*

In the Shade of the Qur'an

His heart might have brightened by Allah's light and he might become like a lighthouse, guiding people to safety. This is exactly what happens every time a human being genuinely accepts the faith. It is, indeed, what carries real weight in Allah's scales.

The reproof then takes a stronger tone. It wonders at the action in question: *"But to the one who considered himself self-sufficient you were all attention. Yet the fault would not be yours if he remained uncleansed. As to him who comes to you with zeal and with a feeling of fear in his heart – him you ignore and busy yourself with trifles!"* The one who pretends that he can do without you and your religion, light, goodness and purity is the one who receives your attention! You go to him yourself when he turns away, and you are at pains to try to persuade him to accept the faith. *"Yet the fault would not be yours if he remained uncleansed."* What is it to you if he chooses to remain in filth? You are not answerable for his sinful actions. He will not secure your victory. *"As to him who comes to you with zeal"*, out of his own free will, *"and with a feeling of fear in his heart,"* groping his way with outstretched hands, fearful of pitfalls, *"him you ignore and busy yourself with trifles!"* What a strong description of the act of not paying due attention to the man who came to seek the right guidance.

The tone gets even stronger and the reproof becomes outright censure: *"kalla"* or *"No indeed"*, this must never be the case.

There follows a statement affirming that Islam is an honourable and noble call. It has no need for anybody's support. It cares only for the one who accepts it on its merits, regardless of his position in human society! *"This is an admonition; let him who will, bear it in mind. It is written on honoured pages, exalted, purified, by the hands of noble and devout scribes."* It is a noble and honoured message in every respect. Its pages are purified and exalted, entrusted to "noble and devout" angel ambassadors who convey it to those human beings selected for the task of conveying it to their people. It is also dignified. No one who pretends that he is self-sufficient need be approached about accepting this message of Islam. It is only for those who know its value and seek to be purified by it.

So this is the Divine standard by which all values and considerations should be evaluated, and all men should be judged. This is also Allah's word, which is the final judgement in all situations.

But where and when was this laid down? The answer is in Makka, when the Muslims were few in number, and Islam was the weaker side in an unequal battle. The attempt to win a group of powerful and

Surah 80   The Frowning (*Abas*)

influential men was not motivated by any personal interest. Ignoring the poor blind man was not occasioned by any personal consideration. All was for the sake of the new message. But the message itself calls for the adoption and application of this very standard and these very values. For Islam can never acquire any real power or achieve any true victory except through the establishment of these values and standards.

As stated earlier, the essential principle involved is far greater and wider in scope than this single incident. It is that man should derive his values and standards from Allah, not from any worldly source. *"The noblest of you in Allah's sight is he who fears Him most."* Indeed, the one whom Allah considers noble is the one who deserves to be attended to and looked after, even if he is completely lacking in family relations, power and wealth, the assets highly valued according to worldly standards. These and all other worldly values become worthless when they part ways with faith and the fear of Allah. This is the great issue which the Divine instructions in this *surah* seek to settle.

The Prophet was deeply and powerfully touched by these Divine instructions and by Allah's reproof. Throughout his life, he worked tirelessly for the establishment of this great principle in Islamic society.

The first action taken by him was to announce these instructions and the reproof in public. This in itself is something very great. Taken from any point of view, no person other than a Messenger of Allah could have announced in public that he had been censured so strongly, in such a singular manner, for a slip he had made. It would have been enough for any other great man to recognise his mistake and to avoid a repetition in future. With the Messenger of Allah, however, things acquire different proportions. No person other than Allah's messenger could have had the courage, in such circumstances as Islam was facing, to make this declaration, challenging with it the masters of Qur'aish, who were very proud of their lineage, power and wealth.

These were at the time the only considerations of any importance in Makkan society, where people wondered: *"Why was this Qur'an not revealed to some great man from the two towns?"*[1]* They were, of

---

[1] The Qur'an. *43; 31.*
* The two towns are Makka and Taif. – Translator's note.

course, aware of Muhammad's lineage, and that he was the descendant of the noblest family in Arabia. His ancestors were masters of Makka. Nevertheless they asked such a question simply because Muhammad himself did not occupy a position of power in Makka before prophethood.

In such a society, at that particular time, such a great principle could have never been the product of any earthly factor, or host of factors. It could have had only one source: Allah. No power could have pushed it through other than the Divine will. The Islamic society received it directly from the Prophet. It was soon well established and it acquired depth and momentum, which helped it to continue its operation in the Islamic nation over the centuries.

The establishment of this principle was, indeed, a rebirth of humanity. It was greater in importance than the first birth of man. Man was able to free himself from all worldly bonds and standards, and substitute for them a set of heavenly values which are independent of all earthly considerations. The new values were soon understood and accepted by everybody. Soon the grave matter which necessitated that Muhammad himself be issued with a special directive in order to convey it became the operative principle of the Islamic conscience and the basic code of the Islamic society. It remained so for a very long period.

Perhaps we cannot appreciate fully the true nature of the rebirth of humanity. The reason for our inability is that we cannot conceive the practical significance of our release from the pressures of society, its values, standards, traditions and practices. In order to appreciate the magnitude of these pressures we have only to remember that the advocates of the materialistic view of history consider that the economic condition of a certain society determines the beliefs, arts, literature, laws, customs of that society, as well as its view of life and its destiny. What a narrow and mistaken view of the true nature of man!

With this basic principle, Islam accomplished the miracle of the rebirth of man.

Since then the values attached to this great principle have become supreme. Their ascendancy, however, was by no means easy, neither in the Arabian society, nor in the minds of the Muslims themselves. Through his actions and directives, coloured by the profound effect the Divine instructions in this *surah* left on him, the Prophet was able to implant this basic principle of Islam in the consciences of his companions and in the life of the Islamic society he had established. He looked after his new plant with unfailing care until it had established deep roots and spread its branches wide. This was why this principle remained for centuries the guiding principle of the Muslim community, in spite of a multitude of opposing factors.

After this incident the Prophet always gave Ibn Umm Maktoom a warm welcome. Whenever he met him, he said: "Welcome to the man for whose sake my Lord reproved me." He appointed him twice as his deputy governor of Medina when he had to be away.

The Prophet married his own cousin Zainab bint Jahsh of the Assad clan to his former slave Zaid ibn Harithah. Marriage has always been a very delicate issue, and it was particularly so in the Arabian Peninsula at that time. The Prophet's motive was to deal a deadly blow to all the social values and standards based on worldly considerations.

Soon after the Makkan Muslims settled in Medina the Prophet established a bond of brotherhood between every two Muslims. He made his own uncle, Hamza, a brother to his former slave, Zaid; and Khalid ibn Rowaiha of the Khath'am tribe and Bilal, the former slave, were made brothers.

He appointed Zaid as Commander-in-Chief of the Muslim army which fought the battle of Mu'tah. Zaid's first deputy was the Prophet's own cousin Ja'afar ibn Abu Talib. The second deputy was Abdullah ibn Rawaha of Al-Ansar. A number of well-known personalities from Makka and Medina were in that army of three thousand men, including the most famous Muslim commander of all time, Khalid ibn Al-Waleed. The Prophet himself went out to bid them farewell. It is also worth mentioning that Zaid and his two deputies were killed in that battle.

The last action of the Prophet was to appoint Ussaamah ibn Zaid, a young man in his teens, as commander of an army he raised to fight the Romans. In the army was a large number of the early Muslims, of both *Al-Muhajireen* (the Makkans) and Al-Ansar (the Medinans), including his two most distinguished companions and immediate successors, Abu Bakr and Umar, as well as his own relative Sa'ad ibn Abi Waqqas, one of the very earliest people to embrace Islam. Some people grumbled about the fact that Ussaamah was made commander, because he was so young. Abdullah ibn Umar takes up the story: "When some people complained about giving the army command to Ussaamah, the Prophet said: 'You are deprecating his appointment as commander in the same way as you previously deprecated his father's appointment. By Allah, his father was a worthy commander, and one of the dearest people to me. Ussaamah is also one of the dearest people to me.'"[1]

Some people spoke in derogatory terms about the Prophet's companion, Salman, the Persian. They took a narrow nationalistic view and spoke of the inferiority of Persians in relation to Arabs. The Prophet took a decisive step to put down all such narrow tendencies. He declared: "Salman belongs to the Prophet's family."[2] The Prophet's statement transcends all lineage, tribal and national considerations, which were of immense weight in Arabia.

Some disagreement occurred between two of the highly esteemed companions of the Prophet, Abu Tharr and Bilal. Out of temper, Abu Tharr called Bilal "you, son of a black woman". The Prophet was extremely upset by what Abu Tharr said. He rebuked him saying: "That is too much, Abu Tharr. He who has a white mother has no advantage which makes him better than the son of a black mother."[3] Thus the Prophet put the dispute in its proper perspective. What distinguishes people is their faith, not their colour. This is the Islamic criterion, which is so unlike the worldly criteria of *Ignorant*[4] societies. The Prophet's rebuke had a profound effect on Abu Tharr, who was a very sensitive person. He wanted to atone for his mistake, so he put his head on the ground swearing that he would not raise it until Bilal had put his foot over it.

---

[1] Transmitted by Al-Bukhari, Muslim and At-Termithi.
[2] Transmitted by At-Tabarani and Al-Hakim.
[3] Transmitted in two different versions by Ibn Al-Mubarak in his two books *Al-Birr* and *As-Salah*.
[4] *"Ignorant"*, i.e. un-Islamic. Islam divides all societies, beliefs and practices into two groups: Islamic and Ignorant (*Jahili*). Whatever is in conflict with Islam can only be derived from ignorance. For knowledge of the Supreme Creator, His message, the method He commands mankind to follow and the social order He wants them to set up will lead mankind in one direction, namely, the Islamic direction. So, when people adopt un-Islamic beliefs, values and practices their action can only stem from their lack of such knowledge, or from their deliberate disregard to such knowledge. Hence, Islam describes such attitude as one of *Ignorance (Jahiliyyah)*, and whatever social set up it produces as *Ignorant*.

Surah 80   The Frowning (*Abas*)

Bilal achieved a position of great distinction in the Islamic society. What made his achievement possible was the application of Heaven's values. Abu Huraira related that the Prophet once said to Bilal: "Tell me what action of yours you hope to be most rewarding to you, for last night I heard your footsteps as you drew near to me in heaven." Bilal answered: "I don't think that since becoming a Muslim I have ever done anything which I hope to be more rewarding than that every time I have ablution at any time of day or night I pray whatever I can."[1]

Once Ammar ibn Yassir asked permission to see the Prophet. The Prophet said: "Let him come in; welcome to the cleansed good man."[2] He also said of Ammar: "Ammar is full of faith to the top of his head."[3] Huthaifa related that the Prophet said: "I do not know how long I shall be with you, so accept the leadership of the two who will follow me (and he pointed to Abu Bakr and Umar), and follow the guidance of Ammar. Believe whatever Ibn Massoud tells you."[4]

Ibn Massoud was so close to the Prophet that any stranger in Medina would have thought him a member of the Prophet's household. Abu Mussa said: "I came to Medina from the Yemen with my brother. We were for quite sometime under the impression that Ibn Massoud and his mother belonged to the Prophet's household, an impression we had formed because of the frequency of their coming in and out of the Prophet's homes, and their long companionship with him."[5]

The Prophet himself sought the hand of an Ansari woman in marriage for Julaibeeb, a former slave. Her parents were reluctant to sanction such a marriage. She, however, said to them: "Do you mean to reject the Prophet's suit? If the Prophet thinks that this man is suitable for us, then let this marriage go through." So they gave their consent.[6] Soon after his marriage, Julaibeen took part in an armed expedition. After the battle, which resulted in a victory for the Muslims, the Prophet asked his companions: "Is anybody missing?" They named a few people. He repeated the question and they named

---

[1] Transmitted by Al-Bukhari and Muslim.
[2] Transmitted by At-Termithi.
[3] Transmitted by An-Nissai.
[4] Transmitted by At-Termithi.
[5] Transmitted by Al-Bukhari, Muslim and At.Termithi.
[6] Transmitted by Imam Ahmad.

In the Shade of the Qur'an

a few others. He asked the same question for the third time and they answered in the negative. He said: "I think Julaibeeb is missing." They looked for him and found his body next to seven enemy soldiers whom he had killed. The Prophet came over, stood near him, and said: "He killed seven people before he was killed. This man belongs to me and I belong to him." He lifted him on his arms until a grave was dug for him. He then put him in his grave. The tradition does not say whether Julaibeeb was given a death wash.[1]

With this Divine instruction and the guidance of the Prophet, the rebirth of humanity was accomplished in a unique manner. Thus a new society came into existence, which imported its values and standards from heaven, and lives on earth, unhampered by earthly restrictions. This is the greatest miracle of Islam, a miracle which could not have happened except by the will of Allah, and through the actions of the Prophet. This miracle is in itself a proof that Islam is a religion revealed by Allah, and that the man who conveyed it to us is His messenger.

It was the Divine will that the leadership of the Islamic society, after the death of the Prophet, should be assigned successively to Abu Bakr and Umar, the two persons who were most keenly aware of the true nature of Islam and most vividly impressed by the guidance of the Prophet. Indeed, Abu Bakr and Umar surpassed everybody else with their love of the Prophet and determination to follow very closely in his footsteps.

Abu Bakr was well aware of the Prophet's object in assigning the army command to Ussaamah. His first action after he became Caliph was to send the army raised by the Prophet and commanded by Ussaamah on its original mission. Abu Bakr, the Caliph, went along with the army to the outskirts of Medina to bid it farewell. It was a strange scene: Abu Bakr the old Caliph walking, and Ussaamah the young commander on his horse. Ussaamah felt ashamed and begged Abu Bakr to ride or else he would walk alongside him. Abu Bakr refused saying: "You shall not walk and I shall not ride. It will do me no harm to walk for an hour if my walking is for the cause of Allah."

Abu Bakr felt that he needed Umar to help him shoulder the responsibilities of government. Umar, however, was a soldier in Ussaamah's army, so he had to ask Ussaamah's permission to

---

[1] Transmitted by Muslim.

Surah 80   The Frowning *(Abas)*

discharge him. Hence, the Caliph, the Head of the State, said to his army commander: "If you think you could spare me Umar to help me, then please do so"! What a request! It is the height of magnanimity, attainable only with Allah's will, by individuals well taught by Allah's Messenger.

A few years go by and we see Umar assuming the leadership of the Islamic society, as its second Caliph. One of his actions was to appoint Ammar ibn Yassir, who formerly belonged to the lower classes of Makka, as governor of the Kufa region in Iraq.

One day a number of dignatories from Qur'aish, including Suhail ibn Amr and Abu Sufian, sought to see Umar. He let them wait and admitted first Suhaib and Bilal, two former slaves, on grounds of their early acceptance of Islam and their taking part in the battle of Badr. Abu Sufian felt very angry and said: "I have never seen a day like this. These slaves are admitted and we are kept waiting!" Suhail, who was more keenly aware of the true nature of Islam, said: "Gentlemen! I see in your faces an expression of what you feel, but I say to you that if you are angry you should be angry with yourselves. Both they and you were called upon to accept Islam at the same time. They were quick to respond but you were slow. What will you do if on the Day of Judgement you find that they are included among the chosen people and you are left behind?"

Umar allotted Ussaamah ibn Zaid a larger share of the spoils of war than he allotted his own son Abdullah. When Abdullah queried his father's decision Umar said: "Son, the Prophet used to love Zaid more than he loved your father, and he loved Ussaamah more than he loved you. What I did was simply to attach to the Prophet's love higher value than I attached to my own love."[1] As he said this Umar was, of course, fully aware that the Prophet measured his love by the Divine standards.

Umar sent Ammar to question Khalid ibn Al-Waleed, the victorious commander of the Muslim army and the descendant of a noble family, about certain charges. Ammar tied Khalid's robes round his neck. Some reports add that he tied Khalid's hands throughout the interrogation with the cloth of his own turban. When the investigation proved Khalid's innocence Ammar untied him and put Khalid's turban back on his head with his own hand. Khalid did not object to this treatment. He knew that Ammar was one of the early

---

[1] Transmitted by At-Tirmithi.

companions of the Prophet. Khalid also knew what the Prophet used to say about Ammar.

It was Umar himself who used to say about Abu Bakr and Bilal: "Abu Bakr is our master and he freed our master." This refers to the days when Bilal was a slave of Umayyah ibn Khalaf, who used to torture him mercilessly, in order to turn him away from Islam. Abu Bakr bought Bilal from Umayyah and set him free. This former slave, Bilal, is described by Umar, the Caliph, as "our master".

Umar was the one who said, "Had Saalim, the former slave of Abu Huthaifa, been alive I would have nominated him to succeed me." This statement must be taken against the background that Umar did not nominate anyone to succeed him, not even Othman, Ali, Talha or Zubair. He only appointed a consultative committee of six, so that the next Caliph should be chosen from among them.

Ali ibn Abu Talib sent Ammar and Al-Hassan, his own son, to Kufa to seek their support against Aisha (may Allah be pleased with her). His message said, "I know that she is your Prophet's wife in this life and in the hereafter. You are, however, faced with a test which will prove whether *you follow your Prophet or his wife*."[1] The people of Kufa accepted his case against Aisha, mother of the believers and Abu Bakr's daughter, (may Allah be pleased with them all).

Bilal was asked by his brother in Islam, Abu Ruwaiha of Khath'am, to speak for him to the family of a Yemeni woman he wished to marry. Bilal went to them and said: "I am Bilal ibn Rabah and this is my brother, Abu Ruwaiha. He lacks good manners and firm belief. You may please yourselves whether you give him your daughter in marriage or not." He did not deceive them by hiding the truth, nor did he behave as a mediator, unmindful of his answerability to Allah. The family concerned were pleased with such honesty. They married their daughter to Abu Ruwaiha, the noble Arab whose advocate was Bilal, the former slave from Abyssinia.

This fundamental principle remained for centuries firmly established in the Islamic society, despite the various factors working for the bringing about of a setback to that society. "Abdullah ibn Abbas was always remembered with his slave Ikrimah, while Abdullah ibn Umar was remembered with his slave Nafi'. Anas ibn Malik was always associated with his slave Ibn Sirin, as was Abu Huraira with his slave Abdurrahman ibn Hormuz. The most distinguished men of

---

[1] Transmitted by Al-Bukhari.

Surah 80   The Frowning (*Abas*)

learning were Al-Hassan in Basra, Mujahid ibn Jabr, Attaa ibn Rabah and Tawoos ibn Kaissan[1]. In Egypt, Yazeed ibn Abi Habeeb, a black slave from Dengla, was the grand Mufti (holder of the highest position of religious authority) during the reign of Umar ibn Abdulaziz."[2]

This Divine standard continued to win high respect for the pious and godfearing, even when they were deprived of all things to which worldly considerations attached great value. It was only recently that this Divine standard ceased to operate after the whole world had been overwhelmed by the tide of *Ignorance*. In the United States, the leading country of the West, a man is valued according to the size of his bank balance. In the Soviet Union, the leading country of the East, where materialism reigns supreme, a man is worth less than a machine. The land of Islam, on the other hand, has sunk back into *Ignorance,* from which Islam had saved it a long time ago. *Ignorant* creeds which Islam had rooted out have been revived. The Divine standard has been abandoned in favour of *Ignorant* values which are completely alien to Islam.

The only hope that remains is that the new Islamic movement will be able to rescue mankind once again from the clutches of *Ignorance* and bring about a second rebirth of humanity, similar to the one announced by the decisive verses at the opening of this *surah.*

The second part of the *surah* wonders at man's conceited attitude as he turns his back to the true faith, despite his being called upon to adopt it. It wonders how man forgets his humble origin and is totally oblivious of the care Allah has taken of him and of His complete power over every stage of his existence, both in this life and in the hereafter. In his attitude of utter ungratefulness man fulfils nothing of his duties towards his Lord, Who has created and sustained him and Who will hold him to account for his actions: *"Perish man! How ungrateful he is! Of what did Allah create him? Of a little germ. He created him and proportioned him. He makes his path smooth for him. He then causes him to die and puts him in his grave. He will surely bring him back to life when He pleases. But by no means has man fulfilled His bidding!"*

"Perish man!" He deserves to be killed for his abominable attitude.

---

[1] All these men would have belonged to a low class, had they lived – Translator's note.

[2] A. Al-Guindi, *Abu Haneefa.*

The mode of expression adds to the sense of horror excited by this attitude. *"How ungrateful he is!"* He strongly denies the claims of his creation. Had he been mindful of these claims he would have shown humble gratitude to His Lord who created him; he would have shown no conceit and would have remembered the end he will have to meet. Indeed, how can man be so arrogant and conceited? What are his origins: *"Of what did Allah create him?"* It is a very humble origin, worthless indeed except for the grace of Allah. *"Of a little germ. He created him and proportioned him."* A little germ of no significance; that is man's beginning. Allah, the Creator, has then proportioned him. The Arabic verb used here denotes precise and meticulous proportioning. It also denotes bestowing weight and value. This is how man has been created, honoured and raised from his humble origin to a high position in which the whole world has been put at his disposal.

"He makes his path smooth for him": The path of life has been smoothed for him. He has also been given the ability to recognise and follow the right path.

When the journey of life is over, when every living being meets the inevitable end, *"He then causes him to die and puts him in his grave".* So in the end the case is just the same as in the beginning: man submits to his Lord Who brings him to life when He wills and ends his life when He wills. He honours him by making the earth his last abode, rather than leaving him as food to wild animals. He has made it part of human nature to bury the dead. When the time He has appointed arrives, He brings him back to life for the reckoning: *"He will surely bring him back to life when He pleases."* So man will not be left without reward or retribution.

But has man prepared himself for this reckoning? *"But by no means has man fulfilled His bidding."* Mankind as a whole, and all human generations, from the very first man created up to the last breath of the last human being, will not have fulfilled Allah's bidding. This is the inference of the Arabic expression used here. Man will always remain negligent of his duties. He will never remember his origin and creation as he should, nor will he thank and praise his Creator Who has guided him and looked after him as He should be thanked and praised. He does not prepare himself in this life for the day of reward and retribution. This applies to humanity as a whole. In addition, the great majority of men turn their backs arrogantly on the Divine guidance.

Surah 80   The Frowning (*Abas*)

Next the *surah* invites man to reflect upon his food and the food of his cattle, which is one of the great many things Allah has provided for him: *"Let man reflect on the food he eats: how We pour down the rain in torrents, and cleave the earth in fissures; how We bring forth the corn, the grapes, and the fresh vegetation, the olive and the palm, the dense-tree'd gardens, the fruit-trees and the green pastures, for you and your cattle to delight in."*
This is the full story of man's food, related here stage by stage. Let man reflect: does he play any significant role in it? Can he determine or change its course? Indeed, the same hand which has brought him to life has brought forth the food to sustain him.
"Let man reflect on the food he eats." Food, the first necessity of human life, deserves a few thoughts. It is made readily available, day after day. But it has a simple and wonderful story. Yet its simplicity makes man forget its wonder. Nevertheless, it is as miraculous as man's own creation. Every step is determined by the Supreme Will which has created man.
"How we pour down the rain in torrents". Pouring down the rain is a fact known to every human being, wherever he lives, regardless of his level of experience or knowledge. It is, therefore, taken up in this address to all human beings. As man's knowledge has increased, he is now able to appreciate the meaning of this verse more fully. He knows that something happened a long time before the daily phenomenon of rain came to be established. Perhaps the theory closest to the truth concerning the formation of the oceans, whose water evaporates and then falls down as rain, claims that they were formed somewhere above the earth and then were poured down in torrents. A contemporary scientist says on this subject:

> If it is true that the temperature of the earth at the time of its separation from the sun was about 12,000 degrees, or that of the surface of the sun, then all the elements were free and, therefore, no chemical combination of importance could exist. Gradually, as the earth, or the earth-forming fragments, cooled, combinations would take place and a nucleus of the world as we know it is formed. Oxygen and hydrogen could not combine until the temperature was reduced to 4,000 degrees Fahrenheit. At this point these elements would rush together and form water. What we know as the atmosphere must have been enormous at that time. All the oceans were in the sky and all those elements not combined

were in the air as gases. Water, having formed in the outer atmosphere, fell towards the earth but could not reach it, as the temperature near the earth was higher than it was thousands of miles out. Of course, the time came when the deluge would reach the earth only to fly up again as steam. With whole oceans in the air, floods that would result as cooling progressed are beyond calculation. . . .[1]

Although we do not claim any definite link between this theory and this particular Qur'anic statement, we acknowledge that the theory gives us a better understanding of what it means and the period of history it refers to, i.e., the period of pouring water down in torrents. The theory may be proved right. On the other hand, other theories may be put forward to explain the origins of water. The Qur'anic statement, however, remains valid for all ages and societies.

This is how the production of food starts: *"We pour down the rain in torrents"*. No one can claim either to have produced water, at any stage of its formation, or to have poured it down, so that the process of food production may be set in motion.

"And cleave the earth in fissures". All human societies may be asked to reflect on this second stage, which follows the pouring down of rain. The primitive man sees the rain falling and realises that he has no power over it. He sees the water splitting the earth and penetrating the soil. He also sees the plant cleaving the earth with the Creator's will and growing over its surface. He notices that the plant is thin and the earth heavy; yet the Creator's hand enables the plant to split the earth and move through it. Anyone who contemplates how plants grow can recognise the miracle involved here. He can feel the operation of the latent power inside the gentle, little plant.

As human knowledge expands, a new understanding of this statement may be developed. The cleaving of the earth so that it becomes suitable for the growth of vegetation may have taken place long time ago. The Qur'anic statement may refer to the multiple break up of the rocks of the surface of the earth caused by the great floods and by the various climatic factors which, according to modern scientists, contributed to the formation of a soil layer where vegetation can grow. This interpretation fits more closely with the sequence of events as it is reported here.

---

[1] A. Cressy Morrison, *Man Does Not Stand Alone*, London, 1962, pp. 25–6.

Surah 80　　　　　　　　　　　　　　　The Frowning *(Abas)*

In either case, the third stage is that of the growth of all kinds of vegetation. The kind mentioned here is the best known to the people immediately addressed by the Qur'an, and the kind most common in the food of man and animal. *"How we bring forth the corn"*. "The corn" refers to all cereals and grains used for human or animal food. *"The grapes, and the fresh vegetation"*. The reference here is to the well-known vine fruits and to all vegetables which can be eaten raw and can be picked time after time. *"The olive and the palm, the dense-tree'd gardens, the fruit trees and the green pastures."* The olive and the palm fruits are well-known to all Arabs. "The gardens" refer to the fenced fields of fruit trees. They are described here as being dense with trees. The Arabic term *"abb"* translated here as "green pastures" refers in all probability to the herbage used for cattle. As mentioned in the commentary on the preceeding *surah*, Umar asked what the *"abb"* meant and then blamed himself for asking. So we follow Umar's suit and add nothing to what has already been mentioned.

This is the story of food, the provision of which is carefully planned by the hand which created man. Man plays no role in any of its stages. Even the seeds and grains he may throw in the earth are not of his making. The miraculous aspect here lies in the original production of these seeds and grains, which is beyond man's comprehension. Various seeds may be planted in the same piece of land, irrigated by one kind of water; yet each one produces its own fruit. It is the hand of the Creator which makes this infinite collection of plants and their fruits, and preserves in the little seed the characteristics of its mother plant so that they may reappear in the plant which issues from it. Man remains ignorant of the secrets of this process. He has no power over it. It is Allah's own production: *"For you and your cattle to delight in"*. This delight is, however, for a limited period. There follows something totally different which needs to be carefully considered by man before it actually arrives.

"But when the stunning blast is sounded, on that day each man will forsake his brother, his mother and his father, his wife and his children: for each one of them will on that day have enough preoccupations of his own. Some faces on that day shall be beaming, smiling and joyful. Some other faces on that day shall be covered with dust, veiled with darkness. These shall be the faces of the disbelievers, the wicked."

This is the end of all delight and enjoyment. It fits perfectly with the long planning and comprehensive designing which include every

In the Shade of the Qur'an

stage in the development of man. The end portrayed in this scene comes into perfect harmony with the scene portrayed at the beginning of the *surah* which shows someone coming forward with zeal and with a feeling of fear in his heart, and another considering himself self-sufficient and turning away from the Divine guidance. Here we have an exposition of their standing in Allah's view.

"The stunning blast" is the nearest translation of an Arabic term which carries a very sharp tone; it almost pierces through the ears. This effect simply prepares us for the following scene in which we see *"each man will forsake his brother, his mother and his father, his wife and his children."* These ties between the man and his nearest relations cannot be severed in the normal course of events. Yet the stunning blast destroys these very links and ties and throws them into the air.

The fearfulness depicted in this scene is purely psychological. It strikes the soul, isolates it and holds it in its grip. The result is that each one will think only of himself. He shall have no time or power to think of others: *"for each one of them will on that day have enough preoccupations of his own".* The description is vivid; yet there could not be a shorter and more comprehensive statement to describe the general condition of worried minds and souls: *"for each one of them will on that day have enough preoccupations of his own."*[1]

This condition is universal when the stunning blast takes place. Then follows a description of the condition of the believers and that of the disbelievers after the two groups have been assigned their values by the Divine standards: *"some faces on that day shall be beaming, smiling and joyful."* These faces are beaming with happiness, overflowing with delight, lit up with a broad smile. They are hopeful and reassured because they feel that the Lord is pleased with them. The people of this class are spared the terror of the stunning blast, so they can afford to smile and show their happiness. Or probably the smiles and manifestations of happiness are seen after these people have realised the good end awaiting them.

"Some other faces on that day shall be covered with dust, veiled with darkness. These shall be the faces of the disbelievers, the hardened in sin." These faces are covered with the dust of sadness and misery,

---

[1] Quoted from *"The Qur'anic Scenes of the Day of Judgement"* by the author.

Surah 80   The Frowning (*Abas*)

darkened with humiliation and depression. They know what they have done in this life and they await their inevitable punishment. *"These shall be the faces of the disbelievers, the hardened in sin."* The people of this class are devoid of faith. They do not believe in Allah or in the Divine message. Moreover, they are hardened in their erring and sinful ways. They persistently violate the Divine commandments.

The destiny of each group is portrayed in their faces. It is a vivid portrait drawn with words and expressions – a fact which testifies to the immense power characteristic of the Qur'anic style.

The opening and the close of the *surah* are in perfect harmony. The opening lays down a fundamental principle and a general standard, and the close shows us the results of applying this standard. The *surah* is a short one; yet it states a number of major facts and principles, portraying a large number of scenes, utilising different rhythms. The style brings out all the images in full relief.

بِسْمِ اللهِ الرَّحْمَنِ الرَّحِيمِ

إِذَا الشَّمْسُ كُوِّرَتْ ۝ وَإِذَا النُّجُومُ انكَدَرَتْ ۝ وَإِذَا الْجِبَالُ سُيِّرَتْ ۝ وَإِذَا الْعِشَارُ عُطِّلَتْ ۝ وَإِذَا الْوُحُوشُ حُشِرَتْ ۝ وَإِذَا الْبِحَارُ سُجِّرَتْ ۝ وَإِذَا النُّفُوسُ زُوِّجَتْ ۝ وَإِذَا الْمَوْءُودَةُ سُئِلَتْ ۝ بِأَيِّ ذَنبٍ قُتِلَتْ ۝ وَإِذَا الصُّحُفُ نُشِرَتْ ۝ وَإِذَا السَّمَاءُ كُشِطَتْ ۝ وَإِذَا الْجَحِيمُ سُعِّرَتْ ۝ وَإِذَا الْجَنَّةُ أُزْلِفَتْ ۝ عَلِمَتْ نَفْسٌ مَّا أَحْضَرَتْ ۝

فَلَا أُقْسِمُ بِالْخُنَّسِ ۝ الْجَوَارِ الْكُنَّسِ ۝ وَاللَّيْلِ إِذَا عَسْعَسَ ۝ وَالصُّبْحِ إِذَا تَنَفَّسَ ۝ إِنَّهُ لَقَوْلُ رَسُولٍ كَرِيمٍ ۝ ذِي قُوَّةٍ عِندَ ذِي الْعَرْشِ مَكِينٍ ۝ مُطَاعٍ ثَمَّ أَمِينٍ ۝ وَمَا صَاحِبُكُم بِمَجْنُونٍ ۝ وَلَقَدْ رَآهُ بِالْأُفُقِ الْمُبِينِ ۝ وَمَا هُوَ عَلَى الْغَيْبِ بِضَنِينٍ ۝ وَمَا هُوَ بِقَوْلِ شَيْطَانٍ رَجِيمٍ ۝ فَأَيْنَ تَذْهَبُونَ ۝ إِنْ هُوَ إِلَّا ذِكْرٌ لِّلْعَالَمِينَ ۝ لِمَن شَاءَ مِنكُمْ أَن يَسْتَقِيمَ ۝ وَمَا تَشَاءُونَ إِلَّا أَن يَشَاءَ اللَّهُ رَبُّ الْعَالَمِينَ ۝

SURAH 81

THE DARKENING
AT-TAKWEER

In the Name of Allah, the Beneficent, the Merciful.

When the sun is darkened,
when the stars fall and disperse,
when the mountains are made to move away,
when the camels, ten months pregnant, are left untended,
when the wild beasts are brought together,
when the seas are set alight,
when men's souls are paired (like with like),
when the infant girl, buried alive, is asked for what crime she was slain,
when the records are laid open,
when the sky is stripped bare,
when Hell is made to burn fiercely,
when Paradise is brought near,
Every soul shall know what it has put forward.
I swear by the turning stars,
which move swiftly and hide themselves away,
and by the night as it comes darkening on,
and by the dawn as it starts to breathe,
this is truly the word of a noble and mighty messenger,
who enjoys a secure position with the Lord of the Throne.
He is obeyed in heaven, faithful to his trust.
Your old friend is not mad.
He saw him on the clear horizon.
He does not grudge the secrets of the unseen.
It is not the word of an accursed devil.
Whither then are you going?
This is only a reminder to all men,
to those of you whose will is to be upright.
Yet, you cannot will except by the will of Allah, Lord of all the Worlds.

In the Shade of the Qur'an

This *surah* may be divided into two parts, each of them treating one major principle of faith. The first is the principle of Resurrection accompanied by a great upheaval in the universe, which affects the sun and the stars, the mountains and the seas, heaven and earth, wild and domestic animals, as well as man. The second principle, discussed in the second half of the *surah*, is the principle of revelation. The *surah* has something to say about the angel carrying the Divine revelation, the Prophet receiving it, the people addressed by it, and the Supreme Will which has shaped their nature and sent down to them this revelation.

The rhythm of the *surah* is one of violent movement which leaves nothing in its place. Everything is thrown, smashed or scattered away. The movement is so violent that it excites and frightens. It alters every familiar situation and shakes men's hearts violently for a long period so that they feel deprived of both shelter and reassurance. In such a violent destructive storm the human heart is no more than a little feather, blown in every direction. No protection and, indeed, no safety can then be found except what is granted by Allah, the Eternal Being. Thus, the rhythm of the *surah* has on its own, the effect of pulling man's heart and soul away from everything associated with safety and security, in order to seek peace, safety and protection in Allah.

The *surah* is also a gem of striking images drawn from the universe in both its present beautiful condition which is familiar to us and its condition on the Day of Resurrection when every familiar thing is changed beyond recognition. The *surah* is, moreover, rich in fine expressions which add colour to the images portrayed. As the *surah* is so short, the rhythm, images and fine expressions combine together to produce a very strong and lasting effect.

Had it not been for the fact that the *surah* contains some words which are no longer familiar to us today, I would have preferred not to comment on it. Its rhythm and images leave a far stronger effect than any human interpretation can aspire to achieve.

"When the sun is darkened, when the stars fall and disperse, when the mountains are made to move away, when camels, ten months pregnant, are left untended, when the wild beasts are brought together, when the seas are set alight, when men's souls are paired (like with like), when the infant girl, buried alive, is asked for what crime she was slain, when the

Surah 81   The Darkening (*At-Takweer*)

records are laid open, when the sky is stripped bare, when Hell is made to burn fiercely, when Paradise is brought near, every soul shall know what it has put forward.''

These verses sketch a scene of a great upheaval which envelops the whole universe. It is an event which reveals every guarded secret and leaves nothing hidden away. Every human being faces what he has put forward for the day of reckoning and judgement.

The great events mentioned indicate that the present familiar state of the universe, with its perfect harmony, measured movement, controlled relations, perfected by a meticulous and able Maker will suffer a breakdown of its system. It will have completed its role. Along with all creation, it will move into a new predetermined phase of life, unlike anything known to us in this world.

The *surah* aims to get this idea of the inevitable upheaval well established in men's hearts and minds so that they may attach little or no importance to the values and riches of this world, though these may seem to be of lasting consequence. The hearts and minds of people should establish a firm bond with the everlasting truth, i.e. the truth of Allah the Eternal, Who never changes when everything else changes and disappears. They should break the chains of what is familiar in this life in order to recognise the absolute truth which admits no restrictions of time, place, finite faculties or temporal standards.

As one goes through the events of this universal upheaval, one cannot fail to observe an inner feeling for this affirmation.

As to what exactly happens to all these types of creation during the Resurrection we can only say that it is known to Allah alone. We can only comprehend what we have experienced. When we think of a great upheaval in the world our imagination cannot stretch beyond a violent earthquake or volcano, or, perhaps, the fall of a bomb. Floods are perhaps the most destructive manifestation of the power of water known to us. The most powerful events in the universe we have monitored were some limited explosions in the sun, which is millions of miles away from us. All these events, great as they may be, seem so small when they are compared to that universal upheaval which will take place on the Day of Resurrection that they may be considered akin to children's play. If we really want to know what will happen then, we can do no more than attempt to draw some sort of comparison with what we have experienced in this life.

The darkening of the sun probably means that it will cool down and its flames which stretch out for thousands of miles in space will dwindle and die down. As the sun is now in gas form because of its intense heat, which reaches a maximum of 12,000 degrees, its darkening probably means its transformation by freezing to a form similar to that of the surface of the earth. It may adopt a circular shape without becoming stretched out.

This is probably the meaning of the opening verse, but it could also mean something different. As to how it will happen, or what will cause it to happen, we can only say that this is known only to Allah.

The falling of the stars probably means that they will break away from the system which holds them together and lose their light and brightness. Only Allah knows which stars will be affected by this event: will it affect only a small group of stars, say, our own solar system, or our galaxy, which comprises hundreds of millions of stars, or will it affect all the stars in their millions of millions? It is a well-known fact that the universe comprises an almost infinite number of galaxies, each with its own space.

The forcing away of the mountains probably means that they will be crushed and blown away as indicated in other *surahs*: *"They ask you about the mountains. Say: 'My Lord will crush them to fine dust and leave them a desolate waste.'*[1] *"When the mountains crumble away and scatter into fine dust"*[2] *"And the mountains shall pass away as if they were mirage"*.[3] All these verses refer to a certain event which will affect the mountains and do away with their firm foundation and stability. This may be the beginning of the quake which will shake the earth violently, and which is mentioned in *surah* 99 "The Earthquake". *"When the Earth is rocked in her last convulsion, when the earth shakes off her burdens"*.[4] All these events will take place on that very long day.

"When the camels, ten months pregnant, are left untended". The Arabic description of the camel here specifies that she is in her tenth month of pregnancy. When in this state, she is to the Arab his most valuable possession because she is about to add to his wealth by a highly valued young camel, and to give him a lot of milk which he and his family will share with the new born animal. However, on that day, which will witness such overwhelming events, such priceless

---

[1] The Qur'an. *20; 105.*
[2] *Ibid. 56;5.*
[3] *Ibid. 78;20.*
[4] *Ibid. 99; 1–2.*

Surah 81   The Darkening (*At-Takweer*)

camels will be left without care, completely untended. The Arabs who were the first to be addressed by this verse never left such camels untended, except for the gravest of dangers.

"*When the wild beasts are brought together*". The great terror which overwhelms the wild beasts in their jungles is the cause of their coming together. They forget their mutual enmities, and move together, unaware of their direction. They neither seek their homes nor chase their prey as they usually do. The overwhelming terror changes the character of even the wildest of beasts. What would it do to man?

"*When the seas are set alight*". The Arabic term used here may mean that the seas will be over-filled with water, from floods similar to those which characterised the early stages of life on earth. On the other hand, earthquakes and volcanoes may remove the barriers now separating the seas so that the water of one will flow into the other. The Arabic expression may also mean that the seas will experience explosions which set them ablaze, as mentioned elsewhere in the Qur'an: "*When the oceans are made to explode*".[1] The explosions may result from separating the oxygen and the hydrogen which make the sea water. They could also be atomic explosions of some sort. If the explosion of a limited number of atoms in a hydrogen or atom bomb produces such dreadful consequences as we have seen, then the atomic explosion of the waters of the oceans, in whatever manner it may occur, will produce something much too fearful for our minds to visualise. Similarly, we cannot conceive the reality of Hell, which stands beyond these vast oceans.

"*When men's souls are paired (like with like)*". The pairing of souls may mean the reunion of body and soul at the time of resurrection. It may also mean their grouping, like with like, as mentioned elsewhere in the Qur'an: "*You will be divided into three groups*"[2] – the chosen elite, the people of the right, and the people of the left. It may also mean some other way of grouping.

"*When the infant girl, buried alive, is asked for what crime she was slain*". The value of human life must have sunk very low in pre-Islamic Arabian society. There existed a convention of burying young girls alive, for fear of shame or poverty. The Qur'an describes this practice in order to portray its horror and record its *Ignorance*, i.e. *Jahiliyyah*. Its condemnation fits in perfectly with the declared

---

[1] The Qur'an. *81; 3.*   [2] *Ibid. 56; 7.*

aim of Islam, to destroy *Ignorance* and save mankind from sinking to its depth. In *surah* 16 "The Bee" we read in translation: *"When the birth of a girl is announced to one of them, his face grows dark and he is filled with rage and inward gloom. Because of the bad news he hides himself from everybody; should he keep her with disgrace or bury her under the dust? How will they judge"*.[1] And in *surah* 17 "The Night Journey" we read *"You shall not kill your children for fear of want. We will provide for them and for you"*.[2]

Girls were killed in an extremely cruel way. They were buried alive! Those Arabs who did not kill their young daughters or send them to mind cattle, had different methods of ill-treating women. If a man died, the head of the clan would throw his gown over the widow. This was a gesture of acquisition which meant that the widow could not re-marry anyone except the owner of the gown. If he fancied her, he would marry her, paying no regard whatsoever to her feelings in the matter. If he did not marry her, he would keep her until she died so as to inherit her wealth.

Such was the attitude of the *Ignorant* society in Arabia to women. Islam condemns this attitude and spurns all these practices. It forbids the murder of young girls and expresses its horrifying nature. It makes it one of the subjects of reckoning on the Day of Judgement. Here, the *surah* mentions it as one of the great events which overwhelm the universe in a total upheaval. We are told that the murdered girl will be questioned about her murder. The *surah* leaves us to imagine how the murderer will be brought to account.

The *Ignorant* social order of the pre-Islamic period would never have helped women to gain a respectable, dignified position. That had to be decreed by Allah. The way of life Allah has chosen for mankind secures a dignified position for both men and women who share the honour of having a measure of the Divine spirit breathed into them. Women owe their respectable position to Islam, not to any factor of environment or social set-up.

When the new man with heavenly values came into being, women became respected and honoured. The woman's weakness of being a financial burden to her family was no longer of any consequence in determining her position and the respect she enjoyed. These considerations have no weight in the scales of heaven. Real weight

---

[1] The Qur'an. *16; 58–9.*   [2] *Ibid. 17; 31.*

Surah 81   The Darkening (*At-Takweer*)

belongs to the noble human soul when it maintains its relationship with Allah. In this man and woman are equal.

When one puts forward the arguments in support of the fact that Islam is a Divine religion, and that it has been conveyed to us by Allah's Messenger who has received His revelations, one should state the change made by Islam in the social status of women as one of the irrefutable arguments. Nothing in the social set-up of Arabia at the time pointed to such an elevation of the woman's position. No social or economic consideration made it necessary or desirable. It was a deliberate move made by Islam for reasons which are totally different from those of this world and from those of the *Ignorant* society in particular.

"When the records are laid open". This is a reference to the records of people's deeds. They are laid open in order that they may be known to everybody. This, in itself, is hard to bear. Many a breast has closely hidden a secret, the remembrance of which brings a feeling of shame and a shudder to its owner. Yet all secrets are made public on that eventful day. This publicity, representative of the great upheaval which envelops the whole universe, is part of the fearful events which fill men's hearts with horror on the day.

"When the sky is stripped bare". This image corresponds closely to throwing open people's secrets. When the word "sky" is used, our first thoughts reach to the blue cover hoisted over our heads. Its stripping means the removal of that cover. How this would happen remains to us a matter of conjecture. It is enough to say that when we look up we will no longer see our familiar blue dome. This may be brought about by any change affecting the *status quo* in the universe which causes this phenomenon to exist. The last scene of that fearful day is portrayed by the next two verses: *"When Hell is made to burn fiercely, when Paradise is brought near"*. Where is Hell? How does it burn? What fuel is used in lighting and feeding its fire? The only thing we know of that is that it *"has fuel of men and stones"*.[1] This is, of course, after they have been thrown in it. Its true nature and its fuel prior to that is part of Allah's knowledge.

"Every soul shall know what it has put forward". In the midst of all these overwhelming events, every soul shall know for certain what sort of deeds it has brought with itself. Every soul shall also know that it cannot change, omit from or add to what it has done.

---

[1] The Qur'an. 66; 6.

In the Shade of the Qur'an

People will find themselves completely separated from all that has been familiar to them, and from their world as a whole. Everything will have undergone a total change except Allah. If man turns to Allah he will find that His support is forthcoming when the whole universe is overwhelmed by change.

Thus ends the first part of this *surah* which fills both mind and heart with a vivid impression of the universal upheaval on the Day of Resurrection.

The second part of the *surah* opens with a certain form of oath by some very beautiful scenes in the universe. The oath, in fine expressions, is made to assert the nature of revelation, the angel carrying it, and the messenger receiving and conveying it as well as people's attitudes to it, all in accordance with Allah's will: *"I swear by the turning stars, which move swiftly and hide themselves away, and by the night as it comes darkening on, and by dawn as it starts to breathe, this is truly the word of a noble and mighty messenger, who enjoys a secure position with the Lord of the Throne. He is obeyed in heaven, faithful to his trust. Your old friend is not mad. He saw him on the clear horizon. He does not grudge the secrets of the unseen. It is not the word of an accursed devil. Whither then are you going? This is only a reminder to all men, to those of you whose will is to be upright. Yet, you cannot will except by the will of Allah, Lord of all the worlds."*

The stars referred to here are those which turn in their orbit, and are characterized by their swift movement and temporary disappearance. In translating the text we have to forego the sustained metaphor used in Arabic which draws an analogy between these stars and the deer as they run at great speed towards their homes, disappear for a while and then reappear at a different point. The Arabic metaphor adds considerable liveliness and beauty to the description of the movement of the stars, which corresponds to the rhythmic beauty of the expression.

Again, the rhythm of the Arabic verse translated as *"and by the night as it comes darkening on"* gives a feeling of life, depicting the night as a living being. The beauty of the Arabic expression is of surpassing excellence.*

The same applies to the next verse: *"and by dawn as it starts to*

---

* It is indeed impossible to achieve the same degree of excellence when translating Qur'anic verses into another language – Translator's note.

Surah 81   The Darkening (*At-Takweer*)

breathe''. This verse is indeed more effective in portraying dawn as alive, breathing. Its breath is the spreading light and the life that begins to stir in everything. I doubt whether the Arabic language, with its inexhaustible wealth of fine imagery and vivid expressions, can produce an image portraying dawn which can be considered equal to this Qur'anic image in aesthetic effect. After a fine night, one can almost feel that dawn is breathing.

Any aesthete will readily perceive that the Divine words of the first four verses of this second part of the *surah* constitute a gem of fine expression and vivid description: *"I swear by the turning stars, which move swiftly and hid themselves away, and by the night as it comes darkening on, and by dawn as it starts to breathe."* This descriptive wealth adds power to man's feelings as he responds to the natural phenomena to which the verses refer.

As the Qur'an makes this brief, full-of-life description of these phenomena it establishes a spiritual link between them and man, with the result that, as we read, we feel the power which created these phenomena, and the truth which we are called upon to believe. This truth is then stated in a manner which fits in superbly with the general theme of the *surah*: *"This is truly the word of a noble and mighty messenger, who enjoys a secure position with the Lord of the Throne. He is obeyed in heaven, faithful to his trust."* This Qur'an with its description of the Day of Judgement is the word of a noble messenger, i.e. Jibril, the angel who carried and conveyed it to Muhammad (peace be on him).

The *surah* then gives a description of this chosen messenger. He is *"noble"*, honoured by Allah who says that he is *"mighty"*, which suggests that considerable strength is required to carry and convey the Qur'an. *"Who enjoys a secure position with the Lord of the Throne."* What a great honour for Jibril to enjoy such a position with the Lord of the universe. *"He is obeyed in heaven"*, i.e. by the other angels. He is also *"faithful to his trust"*, carrying and discharging the message.

These qualities add up to a definite conclusion: that the Qur'an is a noble, mighty and exalted message and that Allah takes special care of man. It is a manifestation of this care that He has chosen an angel of the calibre of Jibril to convey His revelation to the man He has chosen as His Messenger. As man reflects on this Divine care he should feel humble. For he himself is worth very little in the kingdom of Allah, were it not for the care Allah takes of him and the honour He bestows on him.

In the Shade of the Qur'an

There follows a description of the Prophet who conveys this revelation to the people. The *surah* seems to say to them: You have known Muhammad very well over a considerable length of time. He is your old honest, trusted friend. Why, then, are you fabricating tales about him, when he has been telling you the simple truth which he has been entrusted to convey to you: *"Your old friend is not mad. He saw him on the clear horizon. He does not grudge the secrets of the unseen. It is not the word of an accursed devil. Whither then are you going? This is only a reminder to all men."*

They knew the Prophet perfectly well. They knew that he was a man of steady character, great sagacity and complete honesty. But in spite of all this they claimed that he was mad, and that he received his revelations from the devil. Some of them adopted this attitude as a basis for their sustained attack on the Prophet and his Islamic message. Others did so out of amazement and wonder at his revelation, which is unlike anything said or written by man. Their claim confirmed their traditional belief that each poet had a devil who wrote his poems, and each monk had a devil who uncovered for him the secrets of the unknown world. They also believed that the devil may come in contact with some people causing them to say some very strange things. They ignored the only valid explanation, that the Qur'an is revealed by Allah, the Lord of all the Worlds.

The *surah* counters this attitude by a reference to the surpassing beauty of Allah's creation, noticeable everywhere in the universe, and by portraying some universal scenes, as they appear, full of life. This method of reply suggests that the Qur'an comes from the same creative power which endowed the universe with matchless beauty. It also tells them about the two messengers entrusted with the Qur'an, the one who brought it down and the one who conveyed it to them, i.e. their own friend whom they know to be sane, not mad. The *surah* tells them that he has indeed seen the other noble messenger, Jibril, with his own eyes, on the clear horizon where no confusion is possible. He is faithful to his trust and cannot be suspected of telling anything but the truth. After all, they have never associated him with anything dishonest. *"It is not the word of an accursed devil"*. Devils, by nature, cannot provide such a straightforward and consistent code of conduct. Hence the *surah* asks disapprovingly: 'Whither then are you going?' How far can you err in your judgement. And where can you go away from the truth which stares you in the face wherever you go?

Surah 81   The Darkening (*At-Takweer*)

"This is only a reminder to all men." It reminds them of the nature of their existence, their origin and the nature of the universe around them. The reminder is *"to all men"*. Islam here declares the universal nature of its call right from the start, in Makka, where it was subjected to an unabating campaign of persecution.

The *surah* then reminds us that it is up to every individual to choose whether to follow the right path or not. Since Allah has granted everyone his or her free will, then every human being is responsible for himself: *"To those of you whose will is to be upright"*, that is to say, to follow Allah's guidance. All doubts have been dispelled, all excuses answered by this clear statement of all the relevant facts. The right path has been indicated for everyone who wishes to be upright. Anyone who follows a different path shall, therefore, bear the responsibility for his action.

There are, in the human soul and in the universe at large, numerous signs which beckon every man and woman to follow the path of faith. These are so clearly visible and so powerful in their effect that one needs to make a determined effort to turn one's back on them, especially when one's attention is drawn to them in the stirring, persuasive manner of the Qur'an. It is, therefore, man's own will which leads him away from Allah's guidance. He has no other excuse or justification.

The *surah* concludes by stating that the operative will behind everything is the will of Allah: *"You cannot will except by the will of Allah, Lord of all the Worlds."* We notice that the Qur'an makes a statement of this type whenever the will of human beings or creatures generally is mentioned. The reason for this is that the Qur'an wants to keep the fundamental concepts of faith absolutely clear. These include the fact that everything in the universe is subject to the will of Allah. No one has a will which is independent from that of Allah. That He grants man a free will is part of His own Divine Will, like everything else. The same applies to His granting the angels the ability to show complete and absolute obedience to Him and to carry out all His commandments.

This fundamental fact must be clearly understood by the believers, so that they may have a clear concept of the absolute truth. When they acquire such a concept they will turn to the Divine Will for guidance and support, and regulate their affairs according to this Will.

بِسْمِ اللهِ الرَّحْمٰنِ الرَّحِيْمِ

إِذَا السَّمَاءُ انْفَطَرَتْ ۝ وَإِذَا الْكَوَاكِبُ انْتَثَرَتْ ۝ وَإِذَا الْبِحَارُ فُجِّرَتْ ۝ وَإِذَا الْقُبُورُ بُعْثِرَتْ ۝ عَلِمَتْ نَفْسٌ مَا قَدَّمَتْ وَأَخَّرَتْ ۝ يَا أَيُّهَا الْإِنْسَانُ مَا غَرَّكَ بِرَبِّكَ الْكَرِيمِ ۝ الَّذِي خَلَقَكَ فَسَوَّاكَ فَعَدَلَكَ ۝ فِي أَيِّ صُورَةٍ مَا شَاءَ رَكَّبَكَ ۝ كَلَّا بَلْ تُكَذِّبُونَ بِالدِّينِ ۝ وَإِنَّ عَلَيْكُمْ لَحَافِظِينَ ۝ كِرَامًا كَاتِبِينَ ۝ يَعْلَمُونَ مَا تَفْعَلُونَ ۝ إِنَّ الْأَبْرَارَ لَفِي نَعِيمٍ ۝ وَإِنَّ الْفُجَّارَ لَفِي جَحِيمٍ ۝ يَصْلَوْنَهَا يَوْمَ الدِّينِ ۝ وَمَا هُمْ عَنْهَا بِغَائِبِينَ ۝ وَمَا أَدْرَاكَ مَا يَوْمُ الدِّينِ ۝ ثُمَّ مَا أَدْرَاكَ مَا يَوْمُ الدِّينِ ۝ يَوْمَ لَا تَمْلِكُ نَفْسٌ لِنَفْسٍ شَيْئًا وَالْأَمْرُ يَوْمَئِذٍ لِلَّهِ ۝

SURAH 82

CLEAVING ASUNDER
AL-INFITAR

In the Name of Allah, the Beneficent, the Merciful.

When the heaven is cleft asunder,
when the stars are scattered,
when the oceans are made to explode,
when the graves are hurled about,
each soul shall know its earlier actions and its later ones.
O man, what has lured you away from your gracious Lord,
Who created and moulded you and gave you an upright shape?
He can give you whatever form He wills.
Shun it! but you deny the Last Judgement.
Yet there are guardians watching over you,
noble recorders,
who know all your actions.
Surely the righteous shall be in bliss,
while the wicked shall be in Hell,
where they shall be thrown on the Day of Judgement;
nor shall they ever be absent from it.
Would that you knew what the Day of Judgement is!
Oh, would that you knew what the Day of Judgement is!
It is the day when no soul can be of any help to any other soul and when
    Allah reigns supreme.

In the Shade of the Qur'an

This short *surah* refers to the great upheaval discussed in the previous *surah* "The Darkening", but gives it a special colour. It has a different rhythm, deep and calm. It adds a touch of expostulation coupled with an implicit threat. Hence, it does not detail the scenes of the great upheaval as in the previous *surah*, where these scenes are dominant. The scenes here are shorter, in order to suit its quieter atmosphere and slower rhythm.

At the opening the *surah* mentions the cleaving of the sky, the scattering of the stars, the bursting of the oceans and the hurling of the graves as simultaneous with every soul's knowledge of its earlier and later actions, on that solemn day.

The second part starts with the remonstrance combined with an implicit threat to man who is the recipient of abundant grace; yet he does not show any gratitude for Allah's grace. *"O man what has lured you away from your gracious Lord, Who created and moulded you and gave you an upright shape. He can give you whatever form He wills."*

The third part provides the reason for such an ungrateful attitude. The denial of reckoning and judgement, the *surah* tells us, is the source of every evil. The reality of the meting out of reward and punishment at the Last Judgement is re-emphasised; *"Shun it! but you deny the Last Judgement. Yet there are guardians watching over you, noble recorders, who know all your actions. Surely the righteous shall be in bliss, while the wicked shall be in Hell, where they shall be thrown on the Day of Judgement; nor shall they ever be absent from it."*

The final part gives an idea of how fearful the Day of Judgement is, how everyone is absolutely helpless and all power belongs to Allah: *"Would that you knew what the Day of Judgement is! Oh, would that you knew what the Day of Judgement is! It is the day when no soul can be of any help to any other soul and Allah reigns supreme."*

So the *surah* represents yet another way of portraying the same basic principles stressed in this thirtieth part of the Qur'an in various methods and styles. *"When the heaven is cleft asunder, when the stars are scattered when the oceans are made to explode, when the graves are hurled about, each soul shall know its earlier actions and its later ones."*

In the commentary on the previous *surah* we described the feelings generated in people when they visualise the universe undergoing a change so violent that it leaves nothing in its familiar shape and condition. We also said that such feelings tend to pull man away from anything which gives him a sense of security, with the exception of Allah, the Creator of the universe, the One Who lives on after every-

Surah 82   Cleaving Asunder (*Al-Infitar*)

thing has died and withered away. Man's heart is thus made to turn to the only true being Who neither changes nor dies, to seek His support and security in the face of the general upheaval which destroys everything that seemed once to be permanent. For nothing lives for ever except the Creator Who is the only one worthy of being worshipped.

The first aspect mentioned here of the universal upheaval is the cleaving or rending of the sky, which is mentioned in other *surahs:* "*When the sky is split asunder and becomes rose red, like stained leather.*"[1] "*The sky will be rent asunder, for on that day it is frail and tottering.*"[2] "*When the sky is rent asunder.*"[3] That the sky will be split or rent asunder on that hectic day is certain. What is meant exactly by such rending, and how the sky will look after it has been rent are difficult to say. All that we are left with is a feeling of violent change which overwhelms the universe, as we see it, and a realisation that its perfect system will no longer be in operation.

The violent upheaval in the universe causes the stars to scatter after they have been held together by a system which makes every star keep to its orbit, along which it may move fearfully fast, without swerving out of it. If the system is broken at any time, as will happen when the life of the stars comes to its end, they will just disappear in the wide space, as does a particle of dust running loose.

The explosion of the oceans may refer to their being overfull to the extent that they drown the dry land and swallow the rivers. It may, alternatively, mean an explosion which separates oxygen from hydrogen, the two gases which form water. Thus water returns to its original gas condition. The verse may also be taken to refer to a nuclear explosion of the atoms of the two gases. If this is the case, then the explosion would be so fearful that our nuclear devices of today would seem, in comparison, like children's toys. The explosion may also take a different form, totally unknown to us. One thing, however, we know for certain is that there will be horror far greater than any man could have ever experienced.

The hurling about of the graves may be a result of one of the events mentioned above. It may also be a separate event which occurs on that eventful day. As the graves are hurled about people are resurrected and stand up again, back in life, to face the reckoning and

---

[1] The Qur'an. *55:37.*   [3] *Ibid. 84:1.*
[2] *Ibid. 69:16.*

In the Shade of the Qur'an

receive their reward or punishment. This is complemented by the verse which follows the description of these events: *"Each soul shall know its earlier actions and its later ones."* That is, each soul shall come face to face with what it has done and what it left behind of the consequences of its actions; or, what it has enjoyed in this present life and what it has saved for the hereafter. The knowledge, however, will accompany these horrific events. It will indeed be one of them, for it terrifies the soul no less than any of the other events mentioned earlier.

The Arabic expression used here may be translated literally as "a soul shall know . . .". It is, however, in Arabic a neater and more effective denotation of "each soul shall know . . .". Furthermore, the knowledge by every soul is not the end of the matter. It has consequences which are as violent as the scenes portrayed here of the great upheaval. The consequences are merely implied, not stated here, which is again more effective. After this opening which alerts men's senses and consciences, the *surah*, by means of gentle remonstrance coupled with an implicit threat, touches the hearts of men who busy themselves with trivialities. It reminds man of Allah's very first act of grace towards him, namely, his moulding in such an upright perfectly proportioned shape. Allah could have easily given him any form He wished. Yet man is ungrateful: *"O man, what has lured you away from your gracious Lord, Who created and moulded you and gave you an upright shape? He can give you whatever form He wills."* The address appeals to man's most noble quality, his humanity, which distinguishes him from all creatures and assigns to him the highest position among them. This quality represents Allah's gracious blessing to man and His abundant generosity to him.

This appeal is immediately followed by a gentle remonstrance: *"What has lured you away from your gracious Lord?"* What makes you neglect your duties to your Lord and behave impudently towards Him when He has given you your humanity which raises you above all His creation and provides you with the ability to distinguish between right and wrong. A few details of Allah's generosity are then added: *"O man, what has lured you away from your gracious Lord, Who created and moulded you and gave you an upright shape."* It is an address which appeals straight to man's heart. He listens to the remonstrance of Allah when He reminds him of His grace while he continues with his erring ways and impudent behaviour towards Him.

Surah 82   Cleaving Asunder (*Al-Infitar*)

    Indeed, man should reflect deeply over his creation, his physically and physiologically perfect constitution. Reflection should prompt him to show his genuine gratitude, deep respect and real love to Allah, his gracious Lord, Who has blessed him with such constitution; perfect, upright and handsome. The miraculous aspects in man's constitution are far greater than what he sees all around him and what he can imagine. Perfection and the right balance are easily evident in man's physical, mental and spiritual constitution. Full volumes have been written on the perfection of creation as evidenced by man. It is perhaps useful to include here one or two quotations from such works.

    The human body is composed of a number of specialised systems: the skeleton, the muscular system, the skin, the digestive system, the blood circulation system, the respiratory system, the procreative system, the lymphatic system, the nervous system, the urinal system and the senses of tasting, smelling, hearing and seeing. Everyone of these systems is miraculous and far more wonderful than any scientific achievement which makes man possessed with wonder. Yet man tends to overlook the wonders of his own constitution!

    A contributor to the British Scientific Journal* writes:

    Man's hand is one of the most remarkable wonders of nature. It is extremely difficult, indeed impossible, to invent a device which can match the human hand for simplicity, efficiency, ability and instant adaptability. When you read a book you take it in your hand, then you hold it in the position most suitable for your reading. The same hand will automatically correct the position of your book whenever a correction of position is necessary. When you turn a page you place your finger underneath the paper and apply the amount of pressure needed for turning the page. When the page is turned no more pressure is applied. You also use your hand to hold a pen and to write. With your hand you use all the tools you need such as a spoon, a knife or a pen. You use it to open or

---

* The original passages of this 'Journal' could not be traced by the translators, so a re-translation is given to put back into English the two passages quoted here. The author quotes them from Mr. Abdurrazaq Nawfal, *Allah and Modern Science*. Mr. Nawfal does not, however, specify the name and number of the 'Journal' he quotes from – Translators' note.

close the window and to carry anything you wish to carry. . . . Man's hand has 27 pieces of bone in addition to 19 groups of muscles.[1]

A part of the human ear is a series of some four thousand minute but complex arches graduated with exquisite regularity in size and shape. These may be said to resemble a musical instrument, and they seem adjusted to catch, and transmit in some manner to the brain, every cadence of sound or noise, from the thunderclap to the whisper of the pines and the exquisite blending of the tones and harmonies of every instrument in the orchestra. If in forming the ear the cells were impelled to evolve strict efficiency only that man might survive, why did they not extend the range and develop a superacutness? Perhaps the power behind these cells' activities anticipated man's coming need of intellectual enjoyment, or did they by accident build better than they knew?[1]

The visual functions are carried out mainly by the eye with its 130 million retinal light receptors. The eyelids with the eyelashes at their tips protect the eyes day and night. Their movement, which is involuntary, keeps out dust particles and other alien bodies. The eyelashes throw their shades over the eye to lessen the intensity of light. Furthermore, by their movement the eyelids prevent the eyes from becoming dry. The fluid around the eye, which we call tears, is a highly effective, most powerful disinfectant . . .

In human beings, the taste function is carried out by the tongue, through groups of the taste cells which are located in the taste buds of the mucosal surface of the tongue. These buds are of different shapes: some are filamentary, some mushroom-shaped and others are lenticular. They are supplied by fine branches of the glosso-pharangeal nerve as well as the nerve which carries the taste sense. When we eat, these fine branches of the taste nerve are stimulated and convey the impulses of the taste sensation to the brain. This system is located at the front of the tongue, so that we may reject what we sense to be harmful. It is this system which helps us sense whether what we eat is bitter or sweet, hot or cold, sour or salty, etc. The tongue contains nine thousand of these

---

[1] A. Nawfal, *Allah and Modern Science*, Cairo, 1957 (Arabic).
[2] A. C. Morrison, *Man Does Not Stand Alone*, London, 1962, pp. 63–64.

Surah 82   Cleaving Asunder *(Al-Infitar)*

fine taste buds, each of which is linked with the brain by more than one nerve. Hence we may wonder: 'How many nerves have we? What are their sizes? How do they function individually and how do they combine to give the brain their various types of sensation? ...
The nervous system, which effectively controls the body, is composed of fine neurons which cover every part of the body. The neurons are linked to larger nerves which are, in turn, linked to the central nervous system. Whenever any part of the body feels any sensation, even the slightest change of temperature, the neurons convey this sensation to the peripheral nerves which, in turn, convey it to the brain so that it may order the necessary action. The signals are carried through the nerves at the speed of 100 metres per second ...'[1]

If we think of digestion as a process in a chemical laboratory and of the food that we eat as raw materials, we immediately discover that it is a wonderful process which will digest anything edible except the stomach itself.

First into this laboratory we put a variety of food as a raw material without the slightest regard for the laboratory or how the chemistry of digestion will handle it. We eat steak, cabbage, corn and fried fish, wash it down with any quantity of water, and top it off with alcohol, bread, and beans. We may add sulphur and molasses as spring medicine. Out of this mixture the stomach selects those things which are useful by breaking down into its chemical molecules every item of food, discarding the waste, and reconstructs the residue into new proteins, which become the food of the various cells. The digestive tract selects calcium, sulphur, iodine, iron and any other substances which are necessary, takes care that the essential molecules are not lost, that the hormones can be produced and that all of the valid necessities of life are on hand in regulated quantities, ready to meet every necessity. It stores fat and other reserves to meet such an emergency as starvation, and does all this in spite of human thought or reason. We pour this infinite variety of substances into this chemical laboratory with almost total disregard of what we take in, depending on what we consider the automatic process to keep us alive. When

---

[1] A. Nawfal, *Allah and Modern Science*, Cairo, 1957 (Arabic).

these foods have been broken down and are again prepared, they are delivered constantly to each of our billions of cells, a greater number than all the human beings on earth. The delivery to each individual cell must be constant, and only those substances which the particular cell needs to transform them into bones, nails, flesh, hair, eyes, and teeth are taken up by the proper cell. Here is a chemical laboratory producing more substances than any laboratory which human ingenuity has devised. Here is a delivery system greater than any method of transportation or distribution the world has ever known, all being conducted in perfect order.[1]

A lot may be said about every other system of the human body. But wonderful as these systems are, man may have them in common with animals. He, however, is privileged to possess his unique mental and spiritual qualities which are regarded in this *surah* as a special favour from Allah. After the *surah* has dealt with the humanity of man, it mentions the perfection of his creation and the right proportioning of his mould: *"O man, what has lured you away from your gracious Lord Who created and moulded you and gave you an upright shape."*

Let us reflect on our powers of comprehension, the nature of which is unknown to us. The mind is the medium of comprehension but the working of our minds and how they function remain to us incomprehensible. If we suppose that what we grasp is transmitted to the brain through the nerves, where and how does the brain store its information? If we compare the brain to a magnetic recording tape, every man needs in his average lifetime of sixty years a great many billion metres on which to record such a huge multitude of pictures, words, meanings, feelings and responses so that he may, as he actually does, remember them several decades later. Furthermore, how does man sort out individual words, meanings, events and pictures to mould them together in a sort of coherent education? How does he transform information and experiences into knowledge?

Yet this is by no means the most significant of man's distinctive qualities. There is that wonderful ray of Allah's spirit which provides a link between man and the beauty of the universe and its Creator. As this link is established, man can experience at clear, bright moments a sense of communion with the infinite, the absolute, which prepares

---

[1] A. C. Morrison, *op. cit.* pp. 88–89.

him for a blissful eternal life in Allah's paradise. Yet man has no power to comprehend the nature of his spirit, which is Allah's greatest favour to him and which makes him a man. Hence Allah addresses him by this quality of his *"O man!"* then remonstrates with him directly: *"What lures you away from your gracious Lord?"* Thus man is reminded of Allah's greatest favour, but he stands impudent, negligent of his duties to Allah, unashamed and ungrateful. But man does not need more than to realise the source of this remonstrance and what attitude he adopts when he stands before his Lord to be absolutely overwhelmed by shame: *"O man! what lures you away from your gracious Lord, Who created and moulded you and gave you an upright shape. He can give you whatever form He wills."*

The *surah* moves on to explain the reason for man's impudence and negligence, namely, the denial of the Last Judgement. It emphatically confirms the reality of reckoning, reward and punishment: *"Shun it! but you deny the Last Judgement. Yet there are guardians watching over you, noble recorders, who know all your actions. Surely the righteous shall be in bliss, while the wicked shall be in Hell, where they shall be thrown on the Day of Judgement: nor they shall ever be absent from it."* The English expression "shun it" is used here to render the meaning of the Arabic word *"kalla"* which is a command to desist and an indication of a change of subject and style. Hence, the following verses are in the form of a statement.

"Shun it! but you deny the Last Judgement." You think that reckoning and accountability are falsehoods, and this is precisely the cause of your impudence and negligence of your duties. How can any person disbelieve in the Judgement and still lead a life based on goodness and right guidance? Some people may achieve a higher degree of faith: they worship Allah because they love Him, not out of fear of punishment nor in hope of reward. But these people continue to believe in the Last Judgement. They fear it and look forward to it at the same time, because they hope to be with their beloved Lord. When man, however, flatly rejects the Day of Judgement he will be devoid of politeness and light; his heart and conscience are dead.

You deny the Day of Judgement when you will certainly face it. Everything you do in this life will be counted for or against you. Nothing is lost, nothing forgotten: *"Yet there are guardians watching over you, noble recorders, who know all your actions."* These recorders are the angels charged with accompanying men, watching them and recording all what they do and say. We do not know, and are not required to know how this takes place. Allah knows that we are neither given the ability to understand it nor are we going to benefit by understanding it because it does not affect the purpose of our existence. Hence it is useless to attempt to explain by our means what Allah has chosen not to reveal to us of the world of the imperceptible. Sufficient it is to us to feel that we do not live in vain and that there are noble recorders who note what we do, in order to be alert and prudent.

Since the atmosphere of the *surah* is one of benevolence and nobility, the description of those recorders given here is that they are "noble", so that we may feel shy and try to be polite in the presence of these noble angels. It is natural for people to exercise extra care not to say or do anything impolite or disgraceful when they are in the presence of noble people. How careful would they be if they realised that they were all the time in the presence of angels. The *surah* indeed arouses the most noble feelings of our upright nature by portraying this fact in such a familiar way.

We are then told of the destinies of the righteous and the wicked, which are determined by the reckoning based on the recordings by the noble angels: *"Surely the righteous shall be in bliss, while the wicked shall be in Hell, where they shall be thrown on the Day of Judgement, nor shall they ever be absent from it."* The end is certain. That the righteous shall dwell in blissful happiness and the wicked shall end up in Hell is already determined. A "righteous" person is the one who consistently does "right" actions, i.e. good deeds of all kinds, until doing them becomes an intrinsic quality of his. The adjective "righteous" has connotations which fit in well with nobility and humanity. The contrasting quality, "wickedness", carries connotations of insolence and impudence as the wicked indulge in their sinful actions. Hell is a proper recompense for wickedness. The *surah* emphasises the certainty of this punishment: *"where they shall be thrown on the Day of Judgement."* Then it re-emphasises it: *"nor they shall ever be absent from it."* They cannot escape it in the first place, nor will they be allowed to leave it, not even for a short while.

Having stated what happens on the Day of Judgement, the *surah* emphasises again the certainty of that day, since it is denied by some. The emphasis is provided here in the form of a rhetorical question which enhances the mystery surrounding the object of the question. The *surah* then states the complete helplessness of everyone, the absolute impossibility of giving or receiving support and that Allah is the absolute sovereign on that awesome day: *"Would that you knew what the Day of Judgement is! Oh, would that you knew what the Day of Judgement is! It is the day when no soul can be of any help to any other soul and Allah reigns supreme."* The form "would that you knew . . ." is in Arabic a form of rhetorical question often used in the Qur'an. It suggests that the matter under discussion is far beyond our imagining and understanding. This is stressed here by repetition of the question before details about conditions on the day concerned are given: *"It is the day when no soul can be of any help to any other soul."* It is total helplessness when everyone stands alone, busy with his own problems, unable to think of anyone else, relative or friend. *"And Allah reigns supreme."* He indeed reigns supreme in this life and the next. This fact, however, becomes so clear on that day that no one can overlook it, as the ignorant and the conceited do in this life.

The *surah* closes with an air of fear and speechless expectation, which contrasts with the air of violent horrors of the opening. In between the two man is addressed with that remonstrance which overwhelms him with a feeling of shame.

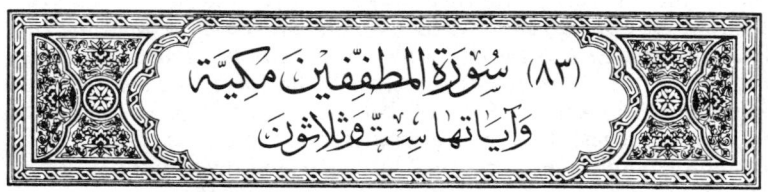

بِسْمِ اللَّهِ الرَّحْمَنِ الرَّحِيمِ

وَيْلٌ لِلْمُطَفِّفِينَ ۝ الَّذِينَ إِذَا اكْتَالُوا عَلَى النَّاسِ يَسْتَوْفُونَ ۝ وَإِذَا كَالُوهُمْ أَو وَزَنُوهُمْ يُخْسِرُونَ ۝ أَلَا يَظُنُّ أُولَٰئِكَ أَنَّهُم مَّبْعُوثُونَ ۝ لِيَوْمٍ عَظِيمٍ ۝ يَوْمَ يَقُومُ النَّاسُ لِرَبِّ الْعَالَمِينَ ۝ كَلَّا إِنَّ كِتَابَ الْفُجَّارِ لَفِي سِجِّينٍ ۝ وَمَا أَدْرَاكَ مَا سِجِّينٌ ۝ كِتَابٌ مَّرْقُومٌ ۝ وَيْلٌ يَوْمَئِذٍ لِلْمُكَذِّبِينَ ۝ الَّذِينَ يُكَذِّبُونَ بِيَوْمِ الدِّينِ ۝ وَمَا يُكَذِّبُ بِهِ إِلَّا كُلُّ مُعْتَدٍ أَثِيمٍ ۝ إِذَا تُتْلَىٰ عَلَيْهِ آيَاتُنَا قَالَ أَسَاطِيرُ الْأَوَّلِينَ ۝ كَلَّا بَلْ رَانَ عَلَىٰ قُلُوبِهِم مَّا كَانُوا يَكْسِبُونَ ۝ كَلَّا إِنَّهُمْ عَن رَّبِّهِمْ يَوْمَئِذٍ لَمَحْجُوبُونَ ۝ ثُمَّ إِنَّهُمْ لَصَالُو الْجَحِيمِ ۝ ثُمَّ يُقَالُ هَٰذَا الَّذِي كُنتُم بِهِ تُكَذِّبُونَ ۝ كَلَّا إِنَّ كِتَابَ الْأَبْرَارِ لَفِي عِلِّيِّينَ ۝ وَمَا أَدْرَاكَ مَا عِلِّيُّونَ ۝ كِتَابٌ مَّرْقُومٌ ۝ يَشْهَدُهُ الْمُقَرَّبُونَ ۝ إِنَّ الْأَبْرَارَ لَفِي نَعِيمٍ ۝ عَلَى الْأَرَائِكِ يَنظُرُونَ ۝ تَعْرِفُ فِي وُجُوهِهِمْ نَضْرَةَ النَّعِيمِ ۝ يُسْقَوْنَ مِن رَّحِيقٍ مَّخْتُومٍ ۝ خِتَامُهُ مِسْكٌ وَفِي ذَٰلِكَ فَلْيَتَنَافَسِ الْمُتَنَافِسُونَ ۝ وَمِزَاجُهُ مِن تَسْنِيمٍ ۝ عَيْنًا يَشْرَبُ بِهَا الْمُقَرَّبُونَ ۝ إِنَّ الَّذِينَ أَجْرَمُوا كَانُوا مِنَ الَّذِينَ آمَنُوا يَضْحَكُونَ ۝ وَإِذَا مَرُّوا بِهِمْ يَتَغَامَزُونَ ۝ وَإِذَا انقَلَبُوا إِلَىٰ أَهْلِهِمُ انقَلَبُوا فَكِهِينَ ۝ وَإِذَا رَأَوْهُمْ قَالُوا إِنَّ هَٰؤُلَاءِ لَضَالُّونَ ۝ وَمَا أُرْسِلُوا عَلَيْهِمْ حَافِظِينَ ۝ فَالْيَوْمَ الَّذِينَ آمَنُوا مِنَ الْكُفَّارِ يَضْحَكُونَ ۝ عَلَى الْأَرَائِكِ يَنظُرُونَ ۝ هَلْ ثُوِّبَ الْكُفَّارُ مَا كَانُوا يَفْعَلُونَ ۝

SURAH 83

THE STINTERS
AL-MUTAFFIFOON

In the name of Allah, the Beneficent, the Merciful.

Woe to the stinters
who, when others measure for them, exact in full,
but who, when they measure or weigh for others, defraud them.
Do such men not think that they will be raised to life
on a great day,
the day when all mankind shall stand before the Lord of all creation?
No indeed; the record of the transgressors is in Sijjeen.
Would that you knew what Sijjeen is!
It is a sealed book.
Woe on that day to the disbelievers
who deny the Day of Judgement.
None denies it but the guilty aggressors, the evil-doers,
who, when Our revelations are recited to them, cry: "Fables of the ancients!"
No indeed; their own deeds have cast a layer of rust over their hearts.
No indeed; on that day they shall be shut out from their Lord.
They shall roast in Hell,
and a voice will say to them: "This is (the reality) which you denied!"
But the record of the righteous is in Illiyun.

In the Shade of the Qur'an

Would that you knew what Illiyun is!
It is a sealed book,
witnessed only by those who are closest to Allah.
The righteous shall surely dwell in bliss.
Reclining upon soft couches they will look around them
In their faces you shall mark the glow of joy.
They shall be given to drink of a pure-drink, securely sealed,
with a seal of musk –
for this let the strivers emulously strive.
It is a drink mixed with the waters of Tassneem
a fountain at which the favoured will drink.
The evil-doers scoff at the faithful
and wink at one another as they pass by them.
When they go back to their folk they speak of them with jests,
and when they see them they say: "These are erring men!"
Yet they have not been assigned the mission of being their guardians.
So on that day the faithful will mock the disbelievers,
as they recline upon their couches and look around them.
Shall not the disbelievers be rewarded according to their deeds.

Surah 83   The Stinters (*Al-Mutaffifoon*)

The *surah* describes the conditions the Islamic call was facing in Makka. Its other objective is to awaken the hearts of men and draw their attention to the new event which would cause the life of the Arabs, and mankind in general, to take a new turn. The event in question is the arrival of Heaven's message to earth.

The general state of affairs in Arabian society is portrayed at the outset, as the *surah* threatens the stinters with a woe which will befall them on the great day, *"the day when all mankind shall stand before the Lord of all creation"*. The reason for such a threat is revealed at the end, when the *surah* gives a sketch of the manners of the evildoers, their attitude towards the believers, their scoffing at them, winking to one another as they pass by and their assertion that the believers *"are erring men"*.

The *surah* may be divided into four parts. The first opens with a declaration of war against the stinters: *"Woe to the stinters who, when others measure for them, exact in full, but who, when they measure or weigh for others, defraud them. Do such men not think that they will be raised to life on a great day, the day when all mankind shall stand before the Lord of all creation?"*

The second part warns the transgressors and denounces them in strong terms. It threatens them with woe and ruin and establishes their guilt and aggression. It explains the reasons for their blindness and describes the punishment on the Day of Judgement: *"No indeed; the record of the transgressors is in Sijjeen. Would that you knew what Sijjeen is! It is a sealed book. Woe on that day to the disbelievers who deny the Day of Judgement. None denies it but the guilty aggressors, the evil-doers, who, when Our revelations are recited to them, cry: 'Fables of the ancients!' No indeed; their own deeds have cast a layer of rust over their hearts. No indeed; on that day they shall be shut out from their hearts. No indeed; on that day they shall be shut out from their Lord. They shall roast in Hell, and a voice will say to them: 'this is (the reality) which you denied'."*

The third part gives an account of the righteous. It describes their high rank, the bliss they will enjoy, the delight showing in their faces, and the pure drink they will have while they recline on their soft couches, and look all around them. It is a delightful image of happiness: *"But the record of the righteous is in Illiyun. Would that you knew what Illiyun is! It is a sealed book, witnessed only by those who are closest to Allah. The righteous shall surely dwell in bliss. Reclining upon soft couches they will look around them. In their faces you shall mark the glow of joy. They shall be given to drink of a pure drink, securely sealed, with a seal of musk – for this let the strivers emulously strive. It is a drink mixed with the waters of Tassneem, a fountain at which the favoured will drink".*

The last part of the *surah* describes what the transgressors mete out to the righteous in this world of conceit and hollow vanity: harsh treatment, ridicule and bad manners. Juxtaposed are descriptions of the ultimate situation of each group, the transgressors and the righteous, in the world of truth and immortality: *"The evil-doers scoff at the faithful, and wink at one another as they pass by them. When they go back to their folk they speak of them with jests, and when they see them they say: 'These are erring men!' Yet they have not been assigned the mission of being their guardians. So on that day the faithful will mock the disbelievers, as they recline upon their couches and look around them. Shall not the disbelievers be rewarded according to their deeds?"*

The *surah* depicts a social environment, and is also an account of the Islamic way of dealing with the world as it exists and with the human mind. This is what we shall attempt to explain as we consider the *surah* in detail.

"Woe to the stinters who, when others measure for them, exact in full, but who, when they measure or weigh for others, defraud them. Do such men not think that they will be raised to life on a great day, the day when all mankind shall stand before the Lord of all creation?"

The *surah* opens with Allah's declaration of war against the stinters *"Woe to the stinters"*. The Arabic term used for "woe" implies destruction and ruin. The implication is the same whether we consider this verse as a statement of a future eventuality or a curse – for a curse made by Allah has the same effect as that of a statement of what is going to happen. The next two verses explain the meaning of the *"stinters"* or defrauders as intended in the *surah*. They are those *"who when others measure for them, exact in full, but who, when they measure or weigh for others, defraud them."* They are those who want their merchandise complete and intact when they buy, but they do not give the right amount when they sell. The following three verses wonder at the defrauders, who behave as if they will not have to account for what they gain in this life. *"Do such men not think that they will be raised to life on a great day, the day when all mankind shall*

Surah 83   The Stinters *(Al-Mutaffifoon)*

stand before the Lord of all creation?"

The fact that the behaviour of the defrauders is tackled in this manner in a Makkan revelation is very interesting. Makkan *surahs* generally concentrate on the fundamentals, such as the assertion of the unity of Allah, the supremacy of His will and His dominion over the universe and over mankind, and the assertion of the truth of revelation and prophethood, the truth of the Day of Judgement, the reckoning and the reward. The Makkan revelations also endeavour to form and develop the moral sense and relate it to the fundamentals of faith. The tackling of a specific issue of morality, such as the stinting of weights and measures, or business dealings in general, is a later concern; it is characteristic of Medinan revelations, which regulate the life of the community in an Islamic state. The fact that this Makkan *surah* makes the issue of stinting its focal point therefore deserves to be considered carefully.

The first point to note is that in Makka the nobility were very rich, were unscrupulous and exercised complete monopoly of trade in their business concerns. They organised the export and import trade using caravans which travelled to Yemen in winter and to Syria in summer. They had their seasonal trade fairs such as the Okaz Fair which was held in the pilgrimage season. The fairs were for business dealings as well as literary activities.

The text suggests that the defrauders against whom war was declared belonged to the nobility and wielded much power and influence which enabled them to force others to succumb to their wishes. The Arabic expression connotes that for some unspecified reason they were able to impose their will and exact in full. The meaning implied is not that they exacted their full due; for this would not justify the declaration of war against them. What is meant is that they obtained by sheer force what they had no right to demand. But when it was their turn to weigh or measure for others, they exercised their power by giving them less than their due.

Indeed this warning, coming so early in the Makkan period, gives an idea of the nature of the religion of Islam. It points out that Islam embraces all sides of life and aims to establish a firm moral code which accords with the basic principles of the Divine teachings. At the time when this *surah* was revealed the Muslim community was still weak. The followers of Islam had not yet won power in order to organise society and the life of the community according to Islamic principles. Yet Islam demonstrated its opposition to those acts of flagrant injustice and unethical dealings. It declared war against the stinters and threatened them with woe and destruction at the time when they were the powerful rulers of Makka. It declared its uncompromising stand against the injustice suffered by the masses whom it has never sought to lull into a state of lethargy and apathy.

This gives us an insight into the real motives behind the stubborn opposition to Islam by the masters of Makka. They were undoubtedly keenly aware that what Muhammad (peace be on him) was calling for was not merely a matter of personal conviction which demanded no more than a verbal assertion of the unity of Allah and the prophethood of Muhammad, and a form of prayers addressed to Allah and not to idols. They realised that the new faith would establish a way of life which would cause the very basis of their positions and interests to crumble. They were fully aware that the new religion, by its very nature, did not admit any partnership or compromise with any worldly concepts, alien to its Divine basis, and that it posed a mighty threat to all the base earthly values of *Ignorance*. This is why they launched their offensive, which continued in full force both before and after the Muslim emigration. It was an offensive launched to defend their way of life in its entirety, not only a set of concepts which have no effect beyond individual acceptance and personal conviction.

Those who attempt in any age or land to prevent it from organising and ruling human life also realise these essential facts. They know very well that the pure and straightforward Islamic way of life endangers their unjust order, interests, hollow structure and deviant practices. Indeed the tyrannical stinters (whatever form their stinting takes and wherever it is, in money and finance, or in the area of rights and duties) are those who fear most the ascendancy of Islam and the implementation of its just methods.

The representatives of the two Medinan tribes, Aws and Khazraj, who pledged their support and loyalty to the Prophet were also aware of all this. Ibn Ishaaq, the Prophet's biographer, wrote: "Assim ibn Umar ibn Qataadah told me that when the Medinan Muslims came to give their pledge to the Prophet, Al-Abbas ibn Ubaadah Al-Ansari, who belonged to the clan of Salim ibn Awf, addressed them and said: "You Khazraj! Do you know what your pledge to this man really means?" They answered 'Yes, we do'. His rejoinder was, 'You are pledging to fight the rest of mankind, white and black alike! So it would be better to leave him alone now if you

Surah 83   The Stinters *(Al-Mutaffifoon)*

think you would give him up to his enemies in the event of your sustaining material losses or losing your leaders. If you do such a thing you will bring upon yourselves great humiliation both in this life and in the life hereafter. But if you feel that you will honour your pledges despite any sacrifice in money or men, then go ahead, because this will be best for you here and in the hereafter!' They said, 'We offer our loyality and support and declare our readiness to sustain any sacrifice, material or personal!' Turning to the Prophet, they asked him, 'What will be our reward if we honour our pledges?' He said, 'Heaven'. They said, 'Give us your hand'. He did and they gave him their pledges of support".

These supporters, like the Makkan tyrants, were keenly aware of the nature of Islam. They realised that it stands for absolute justice and fairness in the social order it seeks to create. It accepts no tyranny, oppression, conceit, injustice or exploitation. Hence it faces the combined forces of all forms of despotism, arrogance and exploitation. *"Do such men not think that they will be raised to life on a great day, the day when all mankind shall stand before the Lord of all creation?"*

Their attitude is singularly strange. The mere idea of being raised to life again on that great day, when all mankind shall stand as ordinary individuals in front of the Lord of the Universe, awaiting His just judgement, without support from any quarter, should be enough to make them change course. But they persist, as if the thought of being raised to life after death has never crossed their minds.

They are called "stinters" in the first part of the *surah*; in the second they are described as "transgressors". The *surah* proceeds to describe the standing of this group with Allah, their situation in this life, and what awaits them on the great day. *"No indeed; the record of the transgressors is in Sijjeen. Would that you knew what Sijjeen is! It is a sealed book. Woe on that day to the disbelievers who deny the Day of Judgement. None denies it but the guilty aggressors, the evil-doers, who, when Our revelations are recited to them, cry: 'Fables of the ancients!' No indeed! their own deeds have cast a layer of rust over their hearts. No indeed; on that day they shall be shut out from their Lord. They shall roast in Hell, and a voice will say to them: 'This is (the reality) which you denied!' "* They think they will not be raised to life after death, so the Qur'an rebukes them and affirms that a record of their actions is kept. The location of that record is specified as an additional confirmation of the fact, albeit a location unknown to man. They are threatened with woe and ruin on that day when their sealed book shall be reviewed: *"No indeed; the record of the transgressors is in Sijjeen. Would that you knew what Sijjeen is! It is a sealed book. Woe on that day to the disbelievers."*

The transgressors, as the Arabic term here connotes, are those who indulge excessively in sin. Their book is the record of their deeds. We do not know the nature of this book and we are not required to know. The whole matter belongs, in point of fact, to the realm of which we know nothing except what we are told by Allah, the Lord of that realm. This statement, that there is a record in *Sijjeen* of the transgressors' deeds, is followed by the familiar Qur'anic form of expression associated with connotation of greatness, *"Would that you knew what Sijjeen is!"* Thus, the addressee is made to feel that the whole matter is too great for his complete understanding.

The *surah* then gives further description of the transgressors' record: *"It is a sealed book".* There is no possibility of addition or omission until it is thrown open on that great day. When this takes place, *"woe on that day to the disbelievers."* Then we are given information about the subject of disbelief, and the true character of the disbelievers *"who deny the Day of Judgement. None denies it but the guilty aggressors, the evil-doers, who, when Our revelations are recited to them, cry: 'Fables of the ancients!'"* So, aggression and bad deeds lead the perpetrator to deny the Day of Judgement and to take a rude and ill-mannered attitude towards the Qur'an, describing it as *"Fables of the ancients!"* This description by the disbelievers is, of course, based on the fact that the Qur'an contains some historical accounts of former nations. These accounts are related as a lesson for later generations as they demonstrate with much clarity the working of the Divine rules to which all nations and generations are subject.

They are strongly rebuked and reprobated for their rudeness and disbelief. These connotations, carried by the Arabic term *"Kalla"* (translated here as "No indeed"), are coupled with an assertion that their allegations are unfounded. We are then given an insight into the motives of their insolence and disbelief and the reasons for their inability to see the obvious truth or respond to it: *"their own deeds have cast a layer of rust over their hearts".* Indeed the hearts of those who indulge in sin become dull, as if they are veiled with a thick curtain which keeps them in total darkness, unable to see the light. Thus they gradually lose their sensitivity and become lifeless. It has been transmitted by Ibn Jareer, At-Tirmithi, An-Nissaie and Ibn Majah that the Prophet said: "When a man commits a sin, it throws a black spot over his heart. If he repents, his heart is polished; but if he persists in his practice, the stains increase". At-Tirmithi described this tradition of the Prophet as authentic. An-Nissaie's version differs in wording but not in import. His version may be translated as follows: "When a man commits a sin, a black spot is formed on his heart. If he desists, prays for forgiveness and repents, his heart will be polished; but if he persists, the spot grows bigger until it has covered his whole heart." This is what Allah refers to when he says: *"No indeed, their own deeds have cast a layer of rust over their hearts."* Explaining this verse, Imam Al-Hassan Al-Basri said: "It is a case of one sin on top of another until the heart is blinded and dies."

Thus we have learnt the situation of the transgressing disbelievers, as well as their motives for transgression and disbelief. Then we are told what will happen to them on that great day, a destiny which befits their evil deeds and denial of the truth: *"No indeed! on that day they shall be shut out from their Lord. They shall roast in Hell, and a voice will say to them: 'This is (the reality) which you denied!'"* Because their sins have cast a thick veil over their hearts, they are unable in this life to feel the presence of Allah, and it is only appropriate that they will not be allowed to see His glorious face. They will be deprived of this great happiness, which is bestowed only on those whose hearts and souls are so clean and transparent that they deserve to be with their Lord, without any form of separation or isolation. Such people are described in *surah* 75 'The Resurrection': *"On that day there shall be joyous faces, looking towards their Lord."*[1]

This separation from their Lord is the greatest and most agonising punishment and deprivation. It is a miserable end of a man whose very humanity is derived from only one source, namely his contact with Allah, his benevolent Lord. When man is torn away from this source of nobleness he loses all his qualities as a human being and sinks to a level which makes him deserve to be thrown in Hell. *"They shall roast in Hell."* On top of that, there is something much worse and much more agonising, namely, rebuke. *"And a voice will say to them, 'This is (the reality) which you denied!'"*

Then follows an account of the other group, the righteous. This is

---

[1] The Qur'an. 75; 22–3.

given in the customary Qur'anic manner of providing two elaborately contrasting images, so that a detailed comparison may be drawn: *"But the record of the righteous is in Illiyun. Would that you knew what Illiyun is! It is a sealed book, witnessed only by those who are closest to Allah. The righteous shall surely dwell in bliss. Reclining upon soft couches they will look around them. In their faces you shall mark the glow of joy. They shall be given to drink of a pure drink, securely sealed, with a seal of musk – for this let the strivers emulously strive. It is a drink mixed with the waters of Tassneem, a fountain at which the favoured will drink."*

This section of the *surah* starts with the Arabic term *"kalla"* which connotes strong reproach and a firm command to the transgressors to desist from their denial of the truth. It then proceeds to speak about the righteous. Since the record of the transgressors is in *Sijjeen*, that of the righteous is in *Illiyun*. The term "righteous" refers to the obedient who do good. They are the exact opposite of the transgressors, who indulge in every excess. The name *"Illiyun"* connotes elevation and sublimity, which suggests that *"Sijjeen"* is associated with baseness and ignominy. The name is followed by the form of exclamation often used in the Qur'an to cast shades of mystery and grandeur: *"Would that you knew what Illiyun is!"*

The *surah* then states that the record of the righteous is *"a sealed book, witnessed only by those who are closest to Allah."* We have already stated what is meant by *"a sealed book"*. We are told here that the angels closest to Allah do see this book and witness it. This statement gives the feeling that the record of the righteous is associated with nobility, purity and sublimity. The angels closest to Allah look at it and enjoy its description of noble deeds and glorious characteristics. The whole image is provided as an evidence of the honour the righteous receive.

There follows an account of the situation in which the righteous find themselves. We are told of the bliss they enjoy on that great day: *"The righteous shall surely dwell in bliss"*. This contrasts with Hell, in which the transgressors dwell. *"Reclining upon soft couches they will look around them"*. This means that they are given a place of honour. They look wherever they wish. They do not have to look down, out of humility; and they suffer nothing which distracts their attention.

In their bliss, the righteous live in mental and physical comfort. Their faces are radiant with unmistakable joy; *"In their faces you shall mark the glow of joy. They shall be given to drink of a pure drink,*

Surah 83   The Stinters (*Al-Mutaffifoon*)

securely sealed, with a seal of musk". Their drink is absolutely pure without any unwanted additions or particles of dust. Describing it as *"securely sealed"* with musk indicates, perhaps, that it is ready made in secured containers to be opened when a drink is needed. All this adds to the impression of the meticulous care being taken. The fact that the seal is of musk adds an element of elegance and luxury. The whole picture, however, is understood only within the limits of human experience in this world. In the Hereafter people will have different concepts, tastes and standards which will be free from all the bonds of this limited world. The description is carried further in the following two verses: *"It is a drink mixed with the waters of Tassneem, a fountain at which the favoured will drink."* So, this pure, securely sealed drink is opened and mixed with a measure of the water of a fountain called Tassneem and described as the one from which the favoured drink. Before this last part of the description is given we have a highly significant instruction: *"For this let the strivers emulously strive"*.

Those stinters who defraud their fellow men pay no regard to the Day of Judgement, and, worse still, deny that such a Day of Reckoning will come. Hardened by their sins and excesses, they strive endlessly for the petty riches of this world. Each of them tries to outdo the others and gain as much as possible. Hence, he indulges in all types of injustice and vice for the sake of ephemeral luxuries which should never be an object of competition. It is the other type of luxury and honour which deserves emulous striving: *"For this let the strivers emulously strive"*.

Those who strive for an object of this world, no matter how superb, grand or honourable it is, are in reality striving for something hollow, cheap and temporary. This world, in its totality, is not worth, in Allah's view, one mosquito's wing. It is the hereafter which carries real weight with Him. So, it should be the goal for strenuous competition and zealous striving.

It is remarkable that striving for the hereafter elevates the souls of all the strivers, while competition for worldly objects sinks their souls to low depths. As man works continuously to achieve the happiness of the hereafter, his work makes this world a happy and pure one for everybody. On the other hand, efforts made for the achievement of worldly ends turn this world into a filthy marsh, where animals devour one another and insects bite the flesh of the righteous.

Striving for the hereafter does not turn the earth into a barren desert, as some transgressors imagine. Islam considers this world a farm, and the hereafter its fruits. It defines the role of the true believer as the building of this world while following the path of piety and righteousness. Islam stipulates that man must look on his task as an act of worship which fulfils the purpose of his existence as defined by Allah: *"I created mankind and the jinn so that they worship me."*[1] The statement, *"For this let the strivers emulously strive"*, inspires man to look far beyond this finite, little world, as he sets out to fulfil his mission as Allah's vicegerent on earth. Thus as they work on purifying the filthy marsh of this world their souls are elevated to new heights.

Man's life on earth is limited while his future life is of limitless duration. The luxuries of this world are also limited while the happiness of Paradise is much too great for us to conceive. The elements of happiness in this life are well known to everyone, but in the next world they are on a level befitting a life which is everlasting.

What comparison can then hold between the two spheres of competition or the two goals, even when we apply the human method of balancing losses against profits? It is, indeed, one race and a single competition: *"For this let the strivers emulously strive"*.

The beatitude enjoyed by the righteous is discussed at length in order to give a detailed account of the hardships, humiliation and insolence they are made to suffer by the transgressors. The final comment of the *surah* taunts the disbelievers as they behold the righteous enjoying their heavenly bliss: *"The evil-doers used to deride the faithful, and wink at one another as they pass by them. When they go back to their own folk they would speak of them with jests, and when they see them they would say: 'These are certainly erring men!' Yet they have not been assigned the mission of being their guardians. So on that day the faithful will mock the disbelievers as they recline upon their couches and look around them. Shall not the disbelievers be rewarded according to their deeds"*.

The images portrayed by the Qur'an of the evil-doers' derision of the faithful, their rudeness and insolence, and their description of the faithful, as "erring men" are taken directly from the real life of Makka at the time. But the same actions happen over and over again

---

[1] A fuller treatment of this idea of the purpose of creation is given by the author in his commentary on the quoted verse: (*surah 51*; verse 56).

Surah 83   The Stinters (*Al-Mutaffifoon*)

in all ages and places. Many people in our own age have witnessed similar actions, as though this *surah* was revealed to describe what these contemporary people have seen with their own eyes.[1] This proves that the attitude of the transgressors and the evil-doers to the believers hardly ever changes from one country to another or from one period of time to another.

"The evil-doers used to deride the faithful." Notice here the use of the term *"used to"*! The *surah* takes us away from this world to the hereafter to see the righteous in their bliss while we hear what used to happen to them in this world. The believers were made to suffer ridicule and derision by the transgressors, either because they were poor or weak or because their self-respect would not allow them to return the abuse of the base evil-doers. What a contrast of attitudes: the evil-doers persecute the believers and laugh at them shamelessly while the believers stick to their attitude of dignified perserverance and self-respect.

"And wink at one another as they pass by them". They wink at one another or make certain actions intended as mockery and derision. Such behaviour betrays their baseness and bad manners. They try to make the believers feel embarrassed and helpless. *"When they go back to their folk they would speak of them with jests".* When they have nourished their little, evil minds with such mockery and injurious actions aimed at the believers they would go back to their folk to *"speak of them with jests".* They feel satisfied with what they have done. Although they have sunk to the lowest depths in their behaviour, they cannot imagine how contemptible they are.

"And when they see them they would say: 'These are certainly erring men!'" This is even more singular! Nothing is more absurd than that those transgressors should speak about the right ways and the erring ways, or that they should say that the believers are erring. Transgression knows no limits. The transgressors never feel ashamed of what they do or say. Their description of the believers as *"erring men"* is a clear manifestation of this fact. The Qur'an does not try to defend the believers or refute this evil accusation levelled at them, because it is not worth refuting. It laughs loudly, however, at those who involve

---

[1] This can be taken as a reference to what the author himself and members of the Muslim Brotherhood suffered in Egyptian prisons in the period 1954–73, as well as to the persecution of the advocates of Islam in many Muslim countries. – Translator's note.

themselves impudently in something which does not concern them, *"Yet they have not been assigned the mission of being their guardians!"* No one has asked them to look after the believers, or to watch over them, or to assess their situation. So why do they give their unsolicited opinion?

This sarcasm concludes the narration of what the transgressors do in this life. The *surah* relates it as if it is something of the past, and gives an image of the present, i.e. in the hereafter, when the believers rejoice in their heavenly bliss: *"So, on that day the faithful will mock the disbelievers, as they recline upon their couches and look around them"*. On that day the disbelievers are shut out from their Lord, suffering this isolation combined with the torture of Hell when they are told: *"This is (the reality) which you denied!"* At the other end the believers recline on their couches, in total beatitude, partaking of their pure drink which is secured with a seal of musk and mixed with the waters of Tassneem. As the *surah* gives the two images, it shows how the tables are turned; for then it is the believers who laugh at the disbelievers.

The *surah* concludes with another loud, ironic question: *"Shall not the disbelievers be rewarded according to their deeds?"* Their *"reward"* is not a good one, as the term used here connotes in ordinary usage. We have just been given an image of their doom, which is described here sarcastically, as their *"reward"*.

The scene of the evil-doers' ridicule of the believers merits further discussion. It is portrayed in considerable detail, in the same way as the earlier scene of the righteous in their heavenly bliss. The detailed description is highly artistic. It also has a marked psychological effect which is soothing. The Muslim minority in Makka was facing a sustained, demoralising onslaught by the polytheists, but Allah did not leave the Muslims on their own: He comforted them and urged them to persevere.

They feel comforted by the very fact that their sufferings as a result of the harsh treatment they receive from the polytheists are outlined by Allah in detail. He sees what the believers suffer and does not ignore what He sees, although He may let the disbelievers do as they wish, only for a while. He also sees how the transgressors laugh unrepentantly at the sufferings of the faithful. Since He describes all this in the Qur'an, then He must take it into account. This, in itself, is enough consolation for the believers.

Surah 83   The Stinters (*Al-Mutaffifoon*)

There are also those ironic remarks about the evil-doers. They may go unnoticed by the disbelievers because their indulgence in their sinful practices have made them insensitive. The highly sensitive hearts of the believers, however, are touched and comforted by them.

It must be noted that the only consolation offered by Allah to the believers who were subjected to harsh treatment and painful ridicule was Heaven for the believers and Hell for the disbelievers. This, again, was the only promise the Prophet (peace be on him) made to the believers when they pledged their wealth and their lives for the cause of Islam. Victory in this life was never mentioned in the Makkan chapters of the Qur'an as a consolation or as an incentive to persevere. The Qur'an was cultivating the hearts of the believers, and preparing them to fulfil the task with which they have been entrusted. It was necessary that these hearts should attain a high standard of strength and self-denial so that they would give everything and suffer all hardships without looking for anything in this life. They seek only the Hereafter and to win the pleasure of Allah. They should be prepared to go through the whole journey of life suffering all sorts of hardships and deprivations without the promise of any reward in this life, not even victory for the cause of Islam.

Such a group of people must be first established. When this happens and Allah knows that they are sincere and determined in what they have pledged themselves to do, then He will give them victory in this life. Victory will not be theirs as a personal reward. They will be given power as trustees appointed for the implementation of the Islamic way of life. They will be worthy trustees because they were neither promised nor did they look for any worldly gain. They pledged themselves truly for Allah at a time when they were unaware of any benefit that may befall them except that they would win Allah's pleasure.

All the Qur'anic verses which speak of victory were revealed later in Medina when this was no longer an issue. Victory was given because Allah willed that successive human generations should have an actual, definite and practical example of the Islamic way of life. It was not a reward for sacrifices made or hardships suffered.

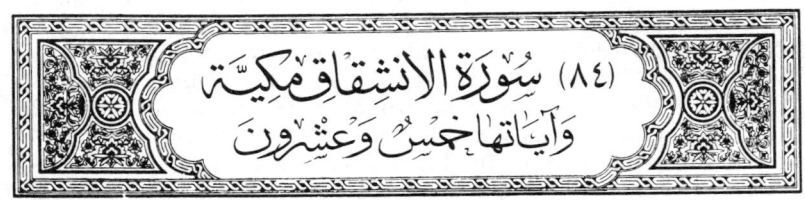

بِسْمِ اللَّهِ الرَّحْمَنِ الرَّحِيمِ

إِذَا السَّمَاءُ انشَقَّتْ ۝ وَأَذِنَتْ لِرَبِّهَا وَحُقَّتْ ۝ وَإِذَا الْأَرْضُ مُدَّتْ ۝ وَأَلْقَتْ مَا فِيهَا وَتَخَلَّتْ ۝ وَأَذِنَتْ لِرَبِّهَا وَحُقَّتْ ۝ يَا أَيُّهَا الْإِنسَانُ إِنَّكَ كَادِحٌ إِلَىٰ رَبِّكَ كَدْحًا فَمُلَاقِيهِ ۝ فَأَمَّا مَنْ أُوتِيَ كِتَابَهُ بِيَمِينِهِ ۝ فَسَوْفَ يُحَاسَبُ حِسَابًا يَسِيرًا ۝ وَيَنقَلِبُ إِلَىٰ أَهْلِهِ مَسْرُورًا ۝ وَأَمَّا مَنْ أُوتِيَ كِتَابَهُ وَرَاءَ ظَهْرِهِ ۝ فَسَوْفَ يَدْعُو ثُبُورًا ۝ وَيَصْلَىٰ سَعِيرًا ۝ إِنَّهُ كَانَ فِي أَهْلِهِ مَسْرُورًا ۝ إِنَّهُ ظَنَّ أَن لَّن يَحُورَ ۝

بَلَىٰ إِنَّ رَبَّهُ كَانَ بِهِ بَصِيرًا ۝ فَلَا أُقْسِمُ بِالشَّفَقِ ۝ وَاللَّيْلِ وَمَا وَسَقَ ۝ وَالْقَمَرِ إِذَا اتَّسَقَ ۝ لَتَرْكَبُنَّ طَبَقًا عَن طَبَقٍ ۝ فَمَا لَهُمْ لَا يُؤْمِنُونَ ۝ وَإِذَا قُرِئَ عَلَيْهِمُ الْقُرْآنُ لَا يَسْجُدُونَ ۩ ۝ بَلِ الَّذِينَ كَفَرُوا يُكَذِّبُونَ ۝ وَاللَّهُ أَعْلَمُ بِمَا يُوعُونَ ۝ فَبَشِّرْهُم بِعَذَابٍ أَلِيمٍ ۝ إِلَّا الَّذِينَ آمَنُوا وَعَمِلُوا الصَّالِحَاتِ لَهُمْ أَجْرٌ غَيْرُ مَمْنُونٍ ۝

SURAH 84

THE RENDING
AL-INSHIQAQ

In the name of Allah, the Beneficent, the Merciful.

When the sky is rent asunder,
obeying her Lord in true submission;
When the earth is stretched out
and casts forth all that is within her and becomes empty,
obeying her Lord in true submission!
O man! You labour hard unto your Lord, and you shall meet Him.
He who is given his book in his right hand
shall have a lenient reckoning
and return rejoicing to his people.
But he who is given his book behind his back
shall call down destruction upon himself
and shall roast in the fire of Hell.
He lived among his family joyfully.
He surely thought he would never return.
Yes, indeed; his Lord was watching over him.
I swear by the twilight,
and by the night and what it envelops,
and by the moon in her full perfection,
that you shall certainly ride,
that you shall certainly ride, stage after stage.
Why then do they not accept the faith,
or kneel in prayer when the Qur'an is read to them?
But the disbelievers are crying lies,
and Allah knows very well what they are hiding.
So give them the tidings of a woeful doom,
save those who embrace the true faith and do good deeds; for theirs
is an unfailing recompense.

In the Shade of the Qur'an

The *surah* opens by sketching some of the scenes of universal upheaval which were dealt with in greater detail in *surahs* 81, 82 and earlier in *surah* 78; "The Darkening", "The Cleaving Asunder" and "The Tiding", respectively. These scenes, however, are now given a special tone arising from emphasis on the complete submission by heaven and earth to Allah: *"When the sky is rent asunder, obeying her Lord in true submission; when the earth is stretched out and casts forth all that is within her and becomes empty, obeying her Lord in true submission."*

This powerful opening with its emphasis on submission to Allah is a foreword to the subsequent address to man, to make him feel his humbleness in front of his Lord. Man is reminded of his position and his ultimate destiny when he returns to Allah: *"O man! You labour hard unto your Lord, and you shall meet Him. He who is given his book in his right hand shall have a lenient reckoning and return rejoicing to his people. But he who is given his book behind his back shall call down destruction upon himself and shall roast in the fire of Hell. He lived among his family joyfully. He surely thought he would never return. Yes, indeed; his Lord was watching over him".*

The third part of the *surah* sketches certain scenes of life on earth which are well known to man. These have their significance as they point to Allah's planning, which is elaborate, and faultless. An oath is made to assert that men must live through deliberately planned stages which they cannot escape journeying through and experiencing: *"I swear by the twilight, and by the night and what it envelops, and by the moon in her full perfection, that you shall certainly ride, stage after stage."*

The last part of the *surah* wonders at those who deny the faith when their position is as described in the previous two parts, and the end of their world is as described in the beginning of the *surah*: *"Why then do they not accept the faith, or kneel in prayer when the Qur'an is read to them?"* Then follows an assertion that Allah knows what they conceal within themselves and an ultimatum is given on their inevitable end: *"But the disbelievers are crying lies, and Allah knows very well what they are hiding, so give them the tiding of woeful doom, save those who embrace the true faith and do good deeds; for theirs is an unfailing recompense."*

Two main qualities are evident in this *surah*: its quiet rhythm and its earnest message. Both are evident even in the images of the universal upheaval the *surah* contains, which are portrayed with

Surah 84   The Rending (*Al-Inshiqaq*)

much more violence elsewhere (*surah* 81, "The Darkening"). Here the attitude of sympathetic and compassionate cautioning is adopted. The cautioning is gradual, easy and presented in a quiet, inspiring statement beginning with the words *"O man"*. This awakens the conscience.

The various parts of the *surah* are ordered according to a special plan. It carries the reader through a variety of scenes, some relating to the universe, others to man himself. The scenes are sketched one after the other in a thoughtful order starting with the scene of universal submission to Allah, which leaves a gentle but real impression on the reader's heart. Then we have the scene of the reckoning, reward and retribution, followed by a contemporary scene of life on earth and its phenomena. Then follows a statement of wonder at those who, after all this, still refuse to accept the faith. The statement is combined with a warning of severe punishment, and a promise of unfailing reward to the believers.

All this is embodied in the few lines which compose this short *surah*. Succinctness of style is just one aspect of the miraculous nature of the Qur'an. The ideas the *surah* sets out to explain could not normally be tackled with such power and to such effect, even if entire books were devoted to the task. But the Qur'an achieves its purpose because it addresses hearts directly. No wonder! It is the word of the Lord Who knows all.

"When the sky is rent asunder, obeying her Lord in true submission; when the earth is stretched out and casts forth all that is within her and becomes empty, obeying her Lord in true submission." The splitting of the sky has been dwelt upon in the commentary on other *surahs*. One new element here is the submission by the sky to her Lord and her complete obedience: *"obeying her Lord in true submission."*[1] Another new element is the stretching of the earth: *"when the earth is stretched out."* This means perhaps an expansion of her size or shape as a result of a disruption of the laws of nature which govern her and preserve

---

[1] This verse of the *surah* is extremely difficult to translate. All translators of the Qur'an, without exception, have found it impossible to render in English because even in Arabic its structure is of a very special type. Literal translation would make it appear self contradictory. The commentary dwells here on the phraseology of the verse, explaining its connotations. Since this relates to a purely linguistic problem, it is not given here – Translator's note.

her in her present shape. The statement, made in the passive, suggests that this will be carried out through the intervention of an outside force, *"and casts forth all that is within her and becomes empty."* This image portrays the earth as a living entity casting out what is within her and getting rid of it.

There are indeed a great many things within her, countless types of creation that have lived, died and were buried over a long period of time, the span of which is known to no one but Allah. It also includes abundant resources of metals, water and other secrets unknown except to the Creator. The earth carries all this load one generation after another until that final day when it casts forth all that is within her and gets rid of it. *"Obeying her Lord in true submission"*. She follows the sky's suit and declares total obedience and complete submission to Allah.

These short verses with their vivid description show both the sky and the earth as living, receiving their orders and instantly complying with them. Their obedience is a manifestation of their conscious and dutiful submission.

Although the scene sketched here is one of universal upheaval which takes place on the Day of Judgement, its shades of humility, solemnity and tranquility are brought out in full relief. The impression it leaves, therefore, is one of humble and obedient submission to Allah.

In such an atmosphere of conscious obedience, man is addressed from high: *"O man! You labour hard unto your Lord, and you shall meet Him."*

"O man!" your Lord has made you in a perfect way. He has given you your humanity which distinguishes you from the rest of creation. Your humanity endows you with certain characteristics which should have made you more conscious of your Lord, and more obedient and submissive to Him than both the sky and the earth. He has given man of His own spirit and endowed him with the ability to communicate with Him, receive His light, ennoble himself with Allah's grace in order to achieve the highest degree of perfection attainable by man. This is no little distinction. *"O man! You labour hard unto your Lord and you shall meet Him."* Man certainly labours hard in this life, shouldering his responsibilities and exerting himself. All this he does in order to return, in the end, like all the rest of creation, to Allah. Man labours even for what he enjoys! Nothing in this life comes easily or without effort: if sometimes no physical labour is

Surah 84   The Rending (*Al-Inshiqaq*)

needed, then surely some mental and emotional effort will be required. In this the rich and poor are alike, although the labour exerted may differ in kind and form. This address reminds man that labouring hard, in a variety of ways, is the lot of all in this life on earth. But when men meet their Lord, they will fall into two groups: one will suffer hardship incomparable to that suffered on earth; another consisting of those who have demonstrated their obedience and true submission, will enjoy the blessings of a rest in which the suffering of this life will be forgotten.

"He who is given his book in his right hand shall have a lenient reckoning and return rejoicing to his people". He who is given his book in his right hand is the happy one who was true to his faith. Allah is pleased with him and rewards him well. He will have a lenient reckoning, that is to say that he will not be called to account for what he did in his life. This is abundantly clear in the traditions of the Prophet. "Aisha (may Allah be pleased with her) related that the Messenger said, 'He who is called to account will suffer affliction'. I pointed out, she said, that Allah says, 'He ... shall have a lenient reckoning'. The Messenger answered, 'That is not what is meant by reckoning and accountability. *Lenient reckoning* signifies no more than showing his record. He who is called to account on the Day of Judgement will suffer affliction.'"[1]

Aisha also related: "I heard Allah's messenger (peace be upon him) saying in his prayers 'My Lord, make my reckoning a lenient one'. When he had finished his prayers I asked him, 'What is the lenient reckoning?' He answered: 'He who receives lenient reckoning will have his record looked into and will be forgiven, but he who is called to account on that day will perish.'"[2]

This is, then the lenient reckoning accorded to him who receives his book in his right hand. He shall win *"and return rejoicing to his people"*, who will also have won and arrived in heaven ahead of him. We deduce from this statement that those who accept the faith in this life and adhere to the right path will gather together in heaven. Everyone ends up with those whom he loves and enjoys their company. We also have an image of the winner's all-important test: he returns with his face overflowing with happiness.

This image is the extreme opposite of what happens to the afflicted

---

[1] Transmitted by Al-Bukhari, Muslim, At-Tirmithi and An-Nissaie.
[2] Transmitted by Imam Ahmad.

who has to account for his evil deeds and receives his book with reluctance. *"But he who is given his book behind his back shall call down destruction upon himself and shall roast in the fire of Hell."*
The Qur'an usually makes a distinction between receiving the book with one's right hand or left hand. Here we have a new image: the book is given from behind the back. There is no reason to prevent the combination of anyone being given the book in his left hand and from behind his back at the same time. It is an image of one who feels great shame and hates to be confronted with what he has done. We have no real knowledge of the nature of this book or how it is given in one's right or left hand or behind one's back. But we comprehend from the first expression the reality of escape, and from the second the reality of doom.

This is indeed what we are meant to appreciate. The various forms of expression are used mainly to drive the point to us and to enhance its effects. The exact knowledge of what will happen and how it will happen belongs to Allah.

So, the unfortunate one who lived his life on earth labouring hard, but disobeying Allah and indulging in what is forbidden will know his destiny. He realises that what lies in front of him is more suffering and hard labour with the only difference that this time the suffering is greater, uninterrupted and endless. So, he shall call destruction upon himself, for he will see his own destruction as his only means of salvation from what will befall him. When man seeks refuge in his own destruction, then he is certainly in a helpless position. His own non-existence becomes his strongest desire. His helplessness is beyond description. This is the meaning implied by the Arab poet, Al-Mutanabbi, in his poem which starts with what may be rendered in English as: "Suffice it a malady that you should think death a cure. It says much that doom should be desired." It is certainly a case of indescribable distress and misery. *"And (he) shall roast in the fire of Hell."* This is the end from which he wishes to escape by means of his own destruction; but there is no way out.

Having portrayed this miserable scene, the *surah* gives us a glimpse of the sufferer's past which led him to this endless misery: *"He lived among his family joyfully. He surely thought he would never return."* The past tense is used here because we feel that we are on the Day of Judgement, after this life has ended. The indulgence and the joy had taken place in this life. *"He lived among his family joyfully."* He cared for nothing beyond the moment he was in, and made no preparation

Surah 84   The Rending (*Al-Inshiqaq*)

for the hereafter. *"He surely thought he would never return"* to his Lord. Had he thought about the return at the end of his journey through life, he would have carried with him some provisions to sustain him. *"Yes, indeed; his Lord was watching over him"*. Indeed Allah has always been aware of man's thoughts, actions and feelings. Allah knows that, contrary to what man had thought, there would be a return to Him to receive the reward merited by actions on earth. This is indeed what happens when all return to Allah to meet their appointed destiny, when what Allah has ordained would take place.

The image of the miserable one when he was joyful among his family in his short life on earth, characterised by its hard labour, in one form or another, has a counterpart in the image of the happy one who returns rejoicing to his people to live with them an eternal happy life, free from all hardship.

The *surah* then refers briefly to some scenes of the world which man inhabits. Men, however, continue to overlook the evidence such scenes provide of the deliberate planning that has gone into the making of this world. Indeed, this planning includes the creation of man himself, and his phases and transitions through life: *"I swear by the twilight, and by the night and what it envelops, and by the moon in her full perfection, that you shall certainly journey on, stage after stage."* The oath, which is indirect in the Arabic text, serves to draw man's attention to these scenes of the universe. The connotations here are in perfect harmony with those of the opening of the *surah* and the scenes portrayed there. The twilight refers to that period of stillness after sunset when the soul is overwhelmed by a deep feeling of awe. The heart feels, at such a time, the significance of parting with a beloved companion, and the feelings of quiet sadness and deep melancholy this involves. It also experiences a feeling of fear of the approaching darkness.

"And by the night and what it envelops." What the night envelops is left unspecified to enhance the effect. Imagination can travel far and wide as one thinks of what the night may conceal of events and feelings. But the travels of the imagination cannot capture all the images generated by the short Qur'anic verse: *"And by the night and what it envelops."* Man is left with an overwhelming feeling and reverence which is in perfect harmony with the stillness and awe associated with the twilight.

"And by the moon in her full perfection". This is another quiet and

splendid scene, describing the full moon as her light descends over the earth. The full moon is always associated with tranquility. The general impression implied here is closely associated with the twilight, and the dark night as it conceals everything. There is here a complementary feeling of stillness and reverence.

"That you shall certainly ride, stage after stage," that is to say, you will pass from one stage of suffering to another to what has been predestined for you. The Qur'an uses the term "ride" to denote the undergoing of various stages of suffering. *"Ride"* is frequently used in Arabic to signify the passage through risk and difficulty. This usage suggests that difficulties and risks are like horses or mules to be ridden. Each one will take the riders the stage predestined for it and for them. Thus each one will deliver them to a new stage which is again predetermined, in the same way as the universal stages, i.e. the twilight, the night and the perfect moon, are predetermined. They eventually end with their meeting with Allah, which has been mentioned in the preceding part. This coherent ordering of the parts of the *surah* and the smooth movement from one point to another is a characteristic of the superb Qur'anic style.

Following on from these sketches portrayed in the *surah* there comes an expression of wonder at those who persist in their denial of the faith when they have all these signs and all this abundant evidence within themselves and in the world at large which indicates the truth: *"Why then do they not accept the faith, or kneel in prayer when the Qur'an is read to them?"* Indeed, why do they not accept the faith? There are numerous indications in the universe and within the soul which point out that the path of faith is the right path. They are at once numerous, deep and powerful, so they besiege the heart if it tries to run away from facing them. But if a man listens to them, then they address him in a manner which is friendly and affectionate.

"Why then do they not accept the faith, or kneel in prayer when the Qur'an is read to them?" The Qur'an addresses them in the language of pure human nature. It opens the heart to the truth and points out its evidence both within themselves and over the horizon. It kindles in the hearts the feelings of God-consciousness, humbleness, obedience and submission to the Creator of the universe. The expression, *"kneel in prayer"* refers to these feelings. The universe is splendid and inspiring: it offers a multitude of signs, mental stimuli and moments of purity which combine to arouse in the human heart a ready response and a willing submission. The Qur'an is also superb and

inspiring; it links the heart with the splendid universe and, consequently, with the Creator who made the universe. It gives the heart a feeling of the truth about the universe which also demonstrates the truth of creation and the Creator. Hence the wonder: *"Why then do they not accept the faith, or kneel in prayer when the Qur'an is read to them?"*

It is indeed amazing, but the Qur'an does not dwell on it for long. It proceeds to describe the behaviour of the disbelievers and the end which awaits them. *"But the disbelievers are crying lies, and Allah knows very well what they are hiding, so give them the tiding of a woeful doom."* The disbelievers cry lies, but the object of their denunciation as lies is unspecified. In Arabic, omission of the object serves to widen the scope of references of the verb. Thus, here we understand that "crying lies" is an entrenched habit and a characteristic of the disbelievers. But Allah is fully aware of the evil they conceal in their hearts and He knows perfectly well their motives for belying the truth.

The *surah* leaves off to address the Messenger (peace be on him): *"So give them the tiding of a woeful doom,"* an unpleasant tiding for anyone who is awaiting any news of his future. At the same time the *surah* describes what awaits the believers who prepare for their future by their good deeds. The description is made in the form of an exception from what awaits the disbelievers: *"save those who embrace the faith and do good deeds; for theirs is an unfailing recompense."* This type of exception is known in Arabic linguistics as "unrelated exception". The believers, not originally among the recipients of the black tidings, are then excepted from it. This form of expression serves to draw attention to what follows. The unfailing recompense is one which is continuous and unceasing, and will be given in the hereafter, where men are immortal.

On this decisive note the *surah* ends. It is a *surah* of short verses and powerful effect.

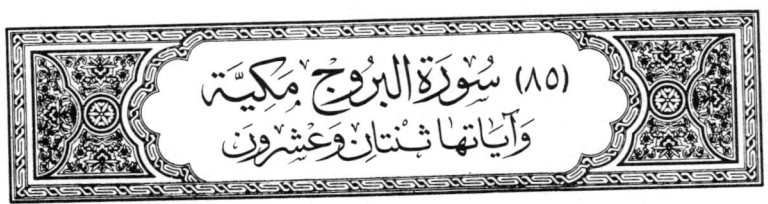

بِسْمِ اللَّهِ الرَّحْمَنِ الرَّحِيمِ

وَالسَّمَاءِ ذَاتِ الْبُرُوجِ ۞ وَالْيَوْمِ الْمَوْعُودِ ۞ وَشَاهِدٍ وَمَشْهُودٍ ۞ قُتِلَ أَصْحَابُ الْأُخْدُودِ ۞ النَّارِ ذَاتِ الْوَقُودِ ۞ إِذْ هُمْ عَلَيْهَا قُعُودٌ ۞ وَهُمْ عَلَىٰ مَا يَفْعَلُونَ بِالْمُؤْمِنِينَ شُهُودٌ ۞ وَمَا نَقَمُوا مِنْهُمْ إِلَّا أَن يُؤْمِنُوا بِاللَّهِ الْعَزِيزِ الْحَمِيدِ ۞ الَّذِي لَهُ مُلْكُ السَّمَاوَاتِ وَالْأَرْضِ ۚ وَاللَّهُ عَلَىٰ كُلِّ شَيْءٍ شَهِيدٌ ۞ إِنَّ الَّذِينَ فَتَنُوا الْمُؤْمِنِينَ وَالْمُؤْمِنَاتِ ثُمَّ لَمْ يَتُوبُوا فَلَهُمْ عَذَابُ جَهَنَّمَ وَلَهُمْ عَذَابُ الْحَرِيقِ ۞ إِنَّ الَّذِينَ آمَنُوا وَعَمِلُوا الصَّالِحَاتِ لَهُمْ جَنَّاتٌ تَجْرِي مِن تَحْتِهَا الْأَنْهَارُ ۚ ذَٰلِكَ الْفَوْزُ الْكَبِيرُ ۞ إِنَّ بَطْشَ رَبِّكَ لَشَدِيدٌ ۞ إِنَّهُ هُوَ يُبْدِئُ وَيُعِيدُ ۞ وَهُوَ الْغَفُورُ الْوَدُودُ ۞ ذُو الْعَرْشِ الْمَجِيدُ ۞ فَعَّالٌ لِمَا يُرِيدُ ۞ هَلْ أَتَاكَ حَدِيثُ الْجُنُودِ ۞ فِرْعَوْنَ وَثَمُودَ ۞ بَلِ الَّذِينَ كَفَرُوا فِي تَكْذِيبٍ ۞ وَاللَّهُ مِن وَرَائِهِم مُّحِيطٌ ۞ بَلْ هُوَ قُرْآنٌ مَجِيدٌ ۞ فِي لَوْحٍ مَحْفُوظٍ ۞

SURAH 85

THE CONSTELLATIONS
AL-BUROOJ

In the name of Allah, the Beneficent, the Merciful

By the heaven with its constellations,
by the Promised Day,
by the witness and that which is witnessed,
slain be the men of the Pit,
the fire abounding in fuel,
when they sat around it,
watching what they did to the believers.
They took vengeance on them for no reason save that they believed in Allah, the Almighty, the Praised One,
the Sovereign of the heavens and the earth, Who witnesses all things.
Those who persecute the believers, men and women, and do not repent shall suffer the chastisement of Hell, the chastisement of burning.
But those who believe and do righteous deeds shall have gardens with flowing rivers; that is the great success.
Stern indeed is your Lord's vengeance.
He is surely the One who originates His creation and re-creates them.
He is All-forgiving, Compassionate,
Lord of the Throne, the Glorious,
Performer of what He wills.
Have you heard the story of the warriors,
of Pharoah and Thamoud?
Yet the disbelievers persist in their denials.
But Allah surrounds them all.
This is indeed a glorious Qur'an,
inscribed on a well-guarded tablet.

In the Shade of the Qur'an

This short *surah* outlines the essentials of faith and the basics of belief as matters of great importance. It sheds a powerful and searching light over these essentials in order to reveal what lies beyond the elementary facts expressed in the text. Every verse, and sometimes every word, in this *surah* virtually opens a window overlooking a limitless world of truth.

The immediate theme of the *surah* is the pit incident, when a community of believers who lived before the advent of Islam (said to be unitarian Christians) were faced by ruthless and tyrannic enemies who sought to force them away from their faith. The believers refused. The tyrants then lit up a great fire in a pit they dug, and threw them into it. The believers were thus burnt to death in front of big crowds which were gathered to witness this ghastly act of extermination. The tyrants sat by, amused by the believers' sufferings: *"They took vengeance on them for no reason save that they believed in Allah, the All-mighty, the Praised One."*

The *surah* starts with an oath: *"By the heaven with its constellations, by the Promised Day, by the witness and that which is witnessed, slain be the men of the Pit . . ."* In this way the *surah* links heaven and its magnificent constellations, the promised day and its great events, the multitudes which witness that day and the events they witness with the pit incident and Allah's anger with the aggressors responsible for it. The *surah* then proceeds to portray the tragic scene in a few, quick glimpses which give a feeling of its horror without dwelling on details.

It includes a reference to the greatness of faith which exalted itself over the atrocious cruelty of men and triumphed over the fire, attaining a level of sublimity which is an honour to all the generations of mankind. It also refers to the heinousness of the crime and the evil and injustice it involves in comparison with the sublimity, innocence and purity of the believers. Then follows a series of short comments stating a number of principles which are highly important to the Islamic call, faith and outlook.

We have firstly a reference to the fact that all heavens and earth are part of Allah's kingdom and to His witnessing of all that takes place in the heavens and on earth. He is *"the Sovereign of the heavens and the earth, Who witnesses all things."*

Secondly, we have a reference to the chastisement of Hell and burning which awaits the wicked tyrants, and a reference to the perfect bliss in heaven awaiting the believers who choose faith in prefer-

Surah 85   The Constellations (*Al-Burooj*)

ence to life itself and exalt themselves despite the persecution by fire. The believers' action is referred to as *the great success:* "*Those who persecute the believers, men and women, and do not repent shall suffer the chastisement of Hell, the chastisement of burning. But those who believe and do righteous deeds, shall have gardens with flowing rivers; that is the great success.*"

A further reference is made to the power with which Allah smites His enemies and to the fact that He creates and re-creates after death: "*Stern indeed is your Lord's vengeance. He is surely the One who originates His creation and re-creates them.*" The fact mentioned here is directly related to the life blotted out in the pit incident.

The *surah* then mentions some of the Divine attributes, each of which has a specific relevance to the subject matter of the *surah*: "*He is All-forgiving, Compassionate.*" He forgives those who repent regardless of the enormity and horror of their sins. He also loves His servants who choose Him. His love is the soothing balsam which heals whatever injuries they may have suffered. "*Lord of the Throne, the All-glorious, Performer of what He wills.*" These attributes portray Allah's absolute will, dominance and power, all of which are relevant to the event discussed in the *surah*. Following that we have a reference to examples of Allah's punishment of the tyrants when they were heavily armed. "*Have you heard the story of the warriors, of Pharoah and Thamoud?*" These were two very different examples of Allah's punishment with widely different effects. Along with the pit event they have numerous implications.

Finally, the *surah* explains the situation of the disbelievers and that Allah surrounds them though they may be unaware of the fact. "*Yet the disbelievers persist in their denials. Allah surrounds them all.*" It concludes with a statement of the truth of the Qur'an and its blessed origin: "*This is indeed a glorious Qur'an inscribed on a well-guarded tablet.*"

This was a brief outline of the theme of the *surah*, the light it sheds and its limitless horizon. A more detailed discussion will now follow.

"*By the heaven with its constellations, by the Promised Day, by the witness and that which is witnessed.*" Before making any reference to the pit incident, the *surah* opens with an oath by the heaven full of constellations. The Arabic term used for 'constellations' may be taken to mean the huge mass of the planets which resemble great towers or palaces built in the sky. In this sense the verse can be related

In the Shade of the Qur'an

to two other verses: *"And heaven – We built it with Our might, and gave it a wide expanse"*,[1] and *"Which is stronger in constitution: you or the heaven He has built?"*[2] The Arabic term may, alternatively, be interpreted as meaning the positions between which these planets move as they go round in orbit. These constitute the spheres within which the planets remain as they move. The reference to the constellations, however, gives an impression of huge creation. This is, indeed, the connotation intended at the outset.

"By the Promised Day." That is the day when judgement is passed on all the events of this life and when the accounts of this world are settled. It is a day Allah has promised will come, and is a great day awaited by all creation.

"By the witness and that which is witnessed." On that day all deeds and creatures are exposed and witnessed. Everybody becomes a witness. Everything becomes known as there is no cover to hide anything from the beholding eyes. References to the heaven and the constellations, the promised day, the witness and what is witnessed all combine together to impart an aura of seriousness, concern, attention and greatness to the manner in which the pit incident is related. They also convey the framework in which the incident is placed, judged and settled on the basis of its true nature. It is a framework stretching far beyond the limits of this short life.

Having thus provided the desired atmosphere and opened up such a horizon, the *surah* then refers to the incident in a few touches. *"Slain be the men of the Pit, the fire abounding in fuel, when they sat around it, watching what they did to the believers. They took vengeance on them for no reason save that they believed in Allah, the All-mighty, the Praised One, the Sovereign of the heavens and the earth, Who witnesses all things."* Reference to the event starts with a declaration of anger with the men of the pit: *"Slain be the men of the Pit"*. It also gives an impression of the enormity of the crime which invokes the displeasure and anger of the All-clement and makes Him threaten the perpetrators. Then we have a description of the pit: *"The fire abounding in fuel"* The literal meaning of "pit" is a hole in the ground, but the *surah* defines it as "the fire" instead of using the term "trench" or "hole" in order to give an impression that the whole pit was turned into a blazing fire.

---

[1] The Qur'an. *51, 47.*   [2] Ibid. *79, 27.*

Surah 85   The Constellations (*Al-Burooj*)

The men of the pit aroused Allah's wrath for the evil crime they committed *"When they sat around it, watching what they did to the believers."* They sat over the fire, very close to this horrifying process, watching the various stages of torture, madly enjoying the burning of human flesh in order to perpetuate in their minds this ghastly scene.

The believers had not committed any crime or evil deed against those people: *"They took vengeance on them for no reason save that they believed in Allah, the All-mighty, the Praised One, the Sovereign of the heavens and the earth, Who witnesses all things."* That was their only crime: that they believed in Allah, the All-mighty Who can do what He wills, the Praised Lord Who deserves praise for every situation and Who is praised even though the *Ignorant* do not praise Him. He is the Lord who deserves to be believed in and worshipped. He is the sole sovereign of the Kingdom of the heavens and the earth. He witnesses all things and He is a witness to what the men of the pit have done to the believers. This verse carries a reassuring touch to the believers and a powerful threat to the conceited tyrants. Allah has been a witness and He suffices for a witness.

The narration of the event is completed in a few short verses which charge the heart with a feeling of repugnance towards the terrible crime and its evil perpetrators. They also invite us to contemplate what lies beyond the event, its importance in the sight of Allah and what it has aroused of Allah's wrath. It is a matter which is not yet completed; its conclusion lies with Allah.

As the narration of the event is concluded we feel our hearts overwhelmed by the magnificence of faith as it exalts the believers and attains its triumph over the hardships and over life itself. We feel the elevation of the believers as they rid themselves of the handicaps of human desires and worldly temptation. The believers could have easily saved their lives by accepting the tyrants' terms. But what a loss humanity as a whole would have incurred! How great the loss would have been had they killed that sublime concept of the worthlessness of life without faith, its ugliness without freedom and its baseness when the tyrants are left free to exercise their tyranny over the souls after they have exercised it over the bodies. But they have won a very noble and sublime concept while they felt the scorch of the fire burning their bodies. Their noble concept has triumphed as it was purified by the fire. They will, later on, have their reward from Allah and their tyrannic enemies will have their retribution. The *surah* goes on to explain both.

"*Those who persecute the believers, men and women, and do not repent shall suffer the chastisement of Hell, the chastisement of burning. But those who believe and do righteous deeds shall have gardens with flowing rivers; that is the great success.*" What has happened on earth in the first life is not the end of the story. There remains a part which will come later. There remains the allocation of awards which will restore the balance of justice and provide the final settlement of what had taken place between the believers and the tyrants. That it will come is certain and confirmed by Allah: "*Those who persecute the believers, men and women*" and persist with their evil ways, careless, unrepentant, "*and do not repent shall suffer the chastisement of Hell, the chastisement of burning.*" Burning is specified although it is also implied by the chastisement of Hell. It earns its specific mention in order to serve as a counterpart to the burning in the pit. Although the same word signifying the action is used, the two types of burning are dissimilar in intensity and duration. The burning here is by fire lit by human beings while the burning in the hereafter is by fire lit by the Creator. The burning here is over in a few minutes while in the hereafter it goes on for ages unknown except to Allah. The burning here is accompanied with Allah's pleasure with the believers, and with the triumph of that noble human concept referred to earlier, while in the hereafter the burning is attended by Allah's anger and man's abject degradation.

Paradise symbolises Allah's pleasure with the righteous believers and His reward to them. "*But those who believe and do righteous deeds shall have gardens with flowing rivers.*" That is the real escape: "*that is the great success.*" The Arabic term used here connotes escape, success and triumph. To escape the punishment of the hereafter is to achieve success. How to describe, then, the reward of gardens where the rivers flow! With this conclusion justice is restored and the whole question is finally resolved. What has taken place on earth is no more than one part; the matter remains unfinished here. This is the fact emphasised by this initial comment on the pit incident, so that it may be fully comprehended by the few believers who have accepted the faith in Makka, and by every group of believers subjected to trail and tyranny in any period of history.

Further comments follow: "*Stern indeed is your Lord's vengeance.*" This is a most suitable comment which contrasts Allah's punishment with the petty and trifling vengeance exacted by the

Surah 85   The Constellations (*Al-Burooj*)

tyrants, and thought by them and by people generally to be very powerful. The really powerful strike is that levelled by the All-mighty, to whom belongs the kingdom of the heavens and the earth, not that levelled by some insignificant people who impose their rule over a limited piece of land for a limited period of time. The statement also emphasises the relationship between the addressee, namely, the Messenger (peace be on him) and the speaker, that is Allah, the All-mighty. He says to him, *"stern indeed is your Lord's vengeance."* He is your Lord, in Whose godhood you believe, and on Whose assistance you rely. This relationship is very significant in a situation where the believers suffer the chastisement inflicted by the tyrants.

"He is surely the One who originates His creation and re-creates them." In their wider connotations origination and re-creation refer to the first and second creations. The two terms, however, signify two events which are constantly taking place. In every moment there is origination as well as re-creation of what has died and decayed. The whole universe is in a state of continuous renovation, and constant decay. Within the context of this ever-repeated cycle of origination and reorigination the whole affair of the pit and its apparent results seem to be, in reality, no more than a beginning of what would be created anew, or a re-creation of what has been already originated. It is a part of a continuous process.

"He is the All-forgiving, the Compassionate." Forgiveness relates to the earlier statement: *"and do not repent":* Forgiveness is part of Allah's mercy and grace which have no limits or restrictions. It is an open door which is never closed in the face of anyone who repents, no matter how grave his sins are. Compassion, however, relates to the stand of the believers who choose their Lord in preference to all things. It is a tender touch of Divine benevolence. Allah elevates His servants who love and choose Him to a grade which the pen would hesitate to describe except for the fact that Allah, out of His blessing, bestows it. It is the grade of friendship between the Lord and the servant. It is a tie of love which exists between Allah and His favoured servants. How insignificant the transitory life they have sacrificed and the momentary afflication they have suffered appear when compared to only a small part of this splendid love or a touch of that loving tenderness. Some slaves of this world, who live in servitude to an individual human being, would take fatal risks in order to win a word of encouragement or receive a sign of pleasure from their

master. They do this although both master and servants are slaves. What, then, should be the attitude of Allah's servants who receive that compassionate love and benevolence from the *"Lord of the Throne, the All-Glorious"*, the All-compeller, the All-sublime. So petty becomes life, so paltry becomes all suffering, and so trifling becomes every treasured object when the pleasure of the loving Lord of the Throne is at stake.

"Performer of what He wills." This is His constantly realised, never-failing attribute. His will is absolute. He may choose, on a certain occasion, that the believers should, by His grace, win victory for a specific purpose He wants to accomplish. He may choose, on other occasions, that faith should triumph over persecution and trial. This may be manifested through the physical elimination of the believers from this transitory life, again to accomplish a specific purpose. He may decide to smite the tyrants in this life, or to delay their punishment to the promised day. Either course of action fulfils a certain purpose behind which Divine wisdom lies. Any action He performs is part of His well-defined scheme and His ability to do what He wills. All this fits very well with the related account of the pit incident and with what comes later of reference to the fates of Pharoah and Thamoud. Beyond all these events and beyond life and the universe there exist the free will and the absolute power of Allah. Examples of this are given: *"Have you heard the story of the warriors of Pharoah and Thamoud?"* This is a reference to two long stories well known to the addressees as they have been mentioned several times in the Qur'an. The two nations concerned are described here by the term "the warriors" in reference to their might and equipment. Have you heard their stories and how Allah did with them as He pleased? Theirs are two different stories in nature and consequences. Pharoah was eliminated with his army when the Children of Israel were saved by Allah. He gave them power to rule for a certain period in order to accomplish a certain scheme of His. As for Thamoud, Allah exterminated them and saved His prophet, Salih, with his few followers. The believers in this instant did not establish a state of their own; they were merely saved from their corrupt enemies. Both stories are manifestation of the Divine will and its performance. They provide two examples of what may befall the advocates of the Islamic call. They are mentioned along with the third possibility which distinguishes the pit incident. The Qur'an explains all three eventualities to the believers in Makka and to all generations of believers.

Surah 85   The Constellations (*Al-Burooj*)

The *surah* concludes with two statements characterised by their sharp and decisive rhythm. Each is a statement of fact and a final verdict. *"Yet the disbelievers persist in their denials. But Allah surrounds them all."* The truth about the disbelievers is that they are in a constant state of disbelief, crying "lies" morning and evening *"But Allah surrounds them all."* They are unaware that Allah's might and His knowledge engulf them, making them even more powerless than mice stranded in a great flood.

"This is indeed a glorious Qur'an inscribed on a well-guarded tablet." The term *"glorious"* signifies nobility and sublimity. Indeed, there is nothing more noble or more sublime or more glorious than the word of Allah, the All-mighty. It is inscribed on a well-guarded tablet, the nature of which we cannot comprehend because it is part of the knowledge Allah has reserved for Himself. We benefit, however, from the connotations of the statement and the impression it leaves that the Qur'an is well preserved and well-guarded. It is the final word in every matter it deals with.

The Qur'an states its judgement in the pit incident and what lies behind it. This judgement is final.

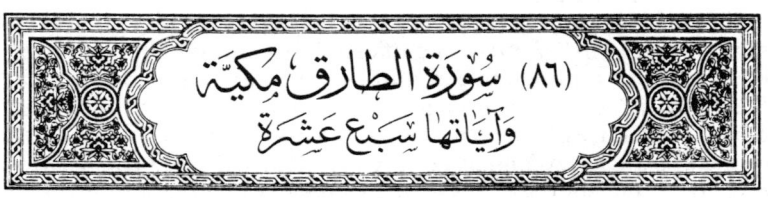

بِسْمِ اللَّهِ الرَّحْمَٰنِ الرَّحِيمِ

وَالسَّمَاءِ وَالطَّارِقِ ۝ وَمَا أَدْرَاكَ مَا الطَّارِقُ ۝ النَّجْمُ الثَّاقِبُ ۝ إِن كُلُّ نَفْسٍ لَّمَّا عَلَيْهَا حَافِظٌ ۝ فَلْيَنظُرِ الْإِنسَانُ مِمَّ خُلِقَ ۝ خُلِقَ مِن مَّاءٍ دَافِقٍ ۝ يَخْرُجُ مِن بَيْنِ الصُّلْبِ وَالتَّرَائِبِ ۝ إِنَّهُ عَلَىٰ رَجْعِهِ لَقَادِرٌ ۝ يَوْمَ تُبْلَى السَّرَائِرُ ۝ فَمَا لَهُ مِن قُوَّةٍ وَلَا نَاصِرٍ ۝ وَالسَّمَاءِ ذَاتِ الرَّجْعِ ۝ وَالْأَرْضِ ذَاتِ الصَّدْعِ ۝ إِنَّهُ لَقَوْلٌ فَصْلٌ ۝ وَمَا هُوَ بِالْهَزْلِ ۝ إِنَّهُمْ يَكِيدُونَ كَيْدًا ۝ وَأَكِيدُ كَيْدًا ۝ فَمَهِّلِ الْكَافِرِينَ أَمْهِلْهُمْ رُوَيْدًا ۝

SURAH 86

THE NIGHT VISITOR
AT-TARIQ

In the name of Allah, the Beneficent, the Merciful.

By heaven and by the night visitor.
Would that you knew what the night visitor is!
It is the star of piercing brightness.
For every soul there is a guardian who watches over it.
Let man then reflect of what he is created:
he is created of gushing water
which issues from between the loins and the chest bones.
Allah is well able to bring him back (to life).
On the day when men's consciences are tried,
he shall be helpless, with no supporter.
By the heaven with its returning rain,
by the earth ever splitting with verdure,
this is surely a decisive word;
it is no frivolity.
They try and scheme against you,
but I too have My schemes.
So give respite to the disbelievers; leave them alone for a while.

In the Shade of the Qur'an

It has been stated in the introduction to this thirtieth part of the Qur'an that its *surahs* are like continuous loud and violent knocks, or like shouts addressed to people who are fast asleep. Both knocks and shouts repeatedly strike their senses with the same message and the same warning: "Wake up! rise! reflect! look around! think! consider! There is a God. There is an organisation and a deliberate system of creation. There is trial and liability, reckoning and reward, severe chastisement and endless happiness." The present *surah* is a typical example of these qualities. Its tone is sharp. The scenes portrayed, the rhythm chosen, the sounds of the individual words and their meanings all contribute to this sharpness of tone. The scenes include the night visitor, the star piercing with brightness, the gushing water, the returning rain and the splitting earth. The meanings include watching over souls: *"For every soul there is a guardian who watches over it"*; the lack of strength and help: *"On the day when men's consciences are tried, he shall be helpless, with no supporter"*; the complete seriousness: *"This is surely a decisive word; it is no frivolity."* The same characteristics apply to the warnings given in this *surah*: *"They try and scheme against you, but I too have My schemes. So give respite to the disbelievers; leave them alone for a while."*

There is complete harmony between the scenes of the universe portrayed in the *surah* and the facts it states. The harmony becomes abundantly clear when the *surah* is carefully considered. *"By heaven and by the night visitor. Would that you knew what the night visitor is! It is the star piercing with brightness. For every soul there is a guardian who watches over it."* This oath includes a scene of the universe and a fact of faith. It opens by mentioning heaven and the night visitor and follows that statement by the form of exclamation made familiar in the Qur'an; *"Would that you knew what the night visitor is!"* This form of exclamation gives the impression that it is mysterious, beyond explanation!

The Qur'an then states its nature and form: *"It is the star of piercing brightness."* It pierces darkness with its penetrating rays. The description applies to all stars. There is no need to attach it to a particular star. Generality is more useful in this kind of context. It makes the meaning read like this: "By heaven and its stars which pierce darkness and penetrate through that veil covering all things." Thus, this reference sheds its own light on the facts outlined in this *surah* and the scenes it portrays, as will be discussed later on.

Allah swears by heaven and its piercing stars that every soul has an

Surah 86   The Night Visitor *(At-Tariq)*

observer appointed by Allah to watch it: *"For every soul there is a guardian who watches over it."* This particular mode of expression implies a strong assertion that there is an agent appointed by Allah to watch every soul and to keep a record of its actions and thoughts. The watch is over the soul because it is there that thoughts and secrets which are responsible for action and its reward lie. Thus, people are not left to roam about over the earth, or to do as they wish without someone to watch what they do. On the contrary, an accurate and immediate record is kept, on the basis of which the reckoning is made.

The awesome inference becomes clear as the soul feels that it is never alone even when without company. There is always the watcher who remains nearby even when one hides from all and is secure against any visitor or intruder. There is the watcher who penetrates all covers and has access to all concealed things, in the same way as the piercing star tears through the night cover. For Allah's method of creation is the same with regard to human souls and the wide horizons. This touch which unites the human soul with the universe is followed by another which emphasises the truth of organised creation and deliberate planning to which Allah has sworn by heaven and the night visitor. The early stages of man's creation constitute a proof of this fact and suggest that man is not forgotten as an insignificant lost item: *"Let man then reflect of what he is created: he is created of gushing water, which issues from between the loins and the chestbones."*

Let man consider his origins and what has become of him. It is a very wide gulf which divides the origins from the final product, the gushing water from man the intelligent, rational being with his highly sophisticated organic, neurological, mental and psychological systems. The reference to this great gulf which the gushing water crosses in order to be made into a communicating being suggests that there is a power beyond the province of man which moves that shapeless and powerless fluid along its remarkable and impressive journey until it is shaped into its magnificent ultimate form. It implies that there is a guardian appointed by Allah to look after that moist germ, and to guide it through its remarkable journey, which is full of wonders much greater than those met by man throughout his life.

This one fertilising cell, of which there are millions in every gush, is hardly visible under the microscope. It is a creature without support, reason or will. But as soon as it settles in the womb it proceeds to search for its food. The guarding hand of Allah equips it with a quality which enables it to convert the lining of the womb around it into a pool of blood, to supply it with fresh nourishment. Once it is sure of the availability of food it starts another process of continuous division to produce new cells. This shapeless and powerless creature which has no reason or will, knows exactly what it is doing and what it wants. The guarding hand watching over it provides it with guidance, knowledge, power and will to enable it to know its way. It is charged with the task of making every group of the newly produced cells specialise in building a part of the magnificent structure of the human body. One group proceeds to produce the skeleton; another group forms the muscles; a third the nervous system; a fourth the lymphatic system. The same applies to every major part of the human structure. But the matter is not as simple as that: it involves a higher degree of specialisation; for every bone, every muscle and every nerve is unique and dissimilar to every other. The structure is accurately planned, and has a wide range of functions. Hence, as every group of cells proceeds to fulfil its appointed task in building this structure, it learns to break up into specialised subdivisions, each having its particular function in the general set up. Every little cell proceeds knowing its way, destination and function. Those cells entrusted with the task of forming the eye know that the eye must be in the face, and that it cannot be situated in the abdomen or the foot or the arm, despite the fact that any of these localities is a suitable place for forming an eye. If the first cell charged with making the eye was taken off course and planted in any of these localities, it would have fulfilled its mission and made an eye there. But when it sets out on its mission it simply goes to the exact spot specified for the eye. Who then has told this cell that this structure needs its eye to be in that particular spot? It is Allah the watching Guardian who guides it, looks after it and shows it its way.

All the cells work individually and collectively within a framework set for them by certain elements functioning inside the cells. These elements are known as the genes which preserve the general characteristics of the species and the distinctive traits of the parents and forefathers. When the eye cell divides and proliferates in order to form the eye, it endeavours at the same time to preserve its shape and particular features so that it turns out to be a human eye and not an eye of any animal. Furthermore, it endeavours to make it an eye of a human being whose forefathers had certain features and charac-

Surah 86   The Night Visitor *(At-Tariq)*

teristics which distinguished their eyes. The slightest error in designing that eye, whether in shape or qualities, forces the forming cell out of its set course. So who has endowed power, ability and knowledge to this insignificant cell which has no reason, will or power of its own? It is Allah Who taught it to design and produce what all mankind can never design or produce. For mankind cannot design an eye or a part of it, if they are charged with this task, while an insignificant cell or group of cells in the human body can accomplish this great mission.

This is merely a quick glance at parts of the remarkable journey which transforms the gushing water into the communicative human being. But there is indeed a great multitude of wonders in the physiological functions of the various organs and systems. It is beyond the scope of this work to trace these wonders but they all constitute evidence of the elaborate planning and organisation and bear the stamp of Allah's guarding, helping and guiding hand. They emphasise the first fact in the *surah* sworn to by heaven and the night visitor, and prepare for the next fact, namely, the resurrection, which was not believed by the polytheists who were among the first to be addressed by the Qur'an.

"Allah is well able to bring him back, on the day when men's consciences are tried, he shall be helpless, with no supporter." Allah, Who has created him and looked after him, is well able to bring him back to life after death. The first creation is evidence of His ability as well as His elaborate planning and organisation. Unless there is a return for a trial of the secrets in order to accord everyone his fair reward, then the highly sophisticated and wise creation would be in vain. *"On the day when men's consciences are tried."* The Arabic terms used by the Qur'an have much wider connotations than *"conscience and trial."* They suggest that that part of the human soul where secrets are safely deposited will be thrown open, searched and exposed in the same way as the night visitor penetrates the covering darkness of the night. As the guarding watcher penetrates through the soul hidden under multiple covers, secrets are tried when man finds himself powerless and without support: *"He shall be helpless, with no supporter."* Standing bare with no cover and being without strength adds to the strains and hardships of the situation. The description has a deep effect on the reader's perception, as it moves from talking of the universe and the human soul to man's creation and his remarkable journey, until he reaches the end when his secrets are exposed

and he stands alone, powerless and without support.

"By the heaven with its returning rain; by the earth ever splitting with verdure; this is surely a decisive word; it is no frivolity." The rain which comes from the sky again and again and the vegetation which splits the earth and springs out are two images describing one of the many manifestations of life, the life of plants and their origins. Water which pours down from heaven and verdure which springs out from the earth, are akin to the water gushing between loins and the breast bones and to the embryo springing out from the darkness of the womb. It is the same life, the same scene, the same movement. It is one system indicating a Maker Who has no competitors.

The rain and verdure scene is not dissimilar to that of the night visitor, the piercing star as it splits covers and curtains. It is also similar to the scene of consciences being searched and all concealments being thrown open. It is again the same style of structure which tells of the Maker. Allah swears by these two creations and their two events, the heaven of the returning rains and the earth splitting with verdure. The impact of the scene portrayed combines with the rhythm to strike a strong note of finality and decisiveness. The oath is that this word, or the Qur'an generally, which states that there is a return and a trial, is the decisive word which admits of no frivolity. It puts an end to all argument and to all doubts and uncertainties. It is a true and final word, to which both the heaven of the returning rain and the earth splitting with verdure are witnesses.

When this final statement of the return and trial is made, there follows an address to Allah's Messenger. At the time of revelation he was with the few believers who supported him in Makka. They were suffering the brunt of the hostility of the polytheists and their plots against the Islamic call. The polytheists were tirelessly trying to smother the call. The address is made to the Messenger to encourage and reassure him, and to disparage what the schemers devise. It states that the scheming is temporary; the battle is in Allah's hand and under His command. So, let the Messenger persevere and be patient, and let him and the believers be reassured: *"They try and scheme against you, but I too have My schemes. So give respite to the disbelievers; leave them alone for a while."*

Those people who are created out of gushing water issuing between the loins and the breast bones, brought forth without any strength, ability or will of their own, guided along their long journey by the Divine power and destined to that return when the secrets are

Surah 86   The Night Visitor (*At-Tariq*)

searched and tried and where they have no strength or support – are devising a scheme against the Prophet and the Muslims! I – the Creator who guides, preserves, directs, brings back to life and puts to trial; the Able; the Victor Who has made the sky, the night visitor, the gushing water and man; the Maker of the heaven with its returning rain and the earth splitting with verdure – I, Allah, am devising a scheme of My own. So, there are the two schemes and a battle. It is, in truth, a one-sided battle but described as one between two sides for the sake of sarcasm.

"So give respite to the disbelievers; leave them alone for a while." Do not be impatient. Do not precipitate the end of the battle when you have seen its true nature. There is a wisdom behind this respite and delay which is short even though it may take up the whole length of this first life; for how short this life appears when compared with a life of limitless duration.

Allah's benevolent and compassionate attitude to His Messenger is noticeable in the final verse: *"So give respite to the disbelievers; leave them alone for a while."* He is addressed here as if he were the final authority, or as if he were the one who decides or approves that they may have a short respite. But the Messenger has no such authority; it is merely an expression of kind and benevolent tenderness which blows an air of compassion over his heart. It is a Divine tenderness which suggests that the Messenger has a say in the whole matter as if he had a share or an interest in it. It lifts all barriers between the Messenger and the Divine domain, where all matters are judged and settled.

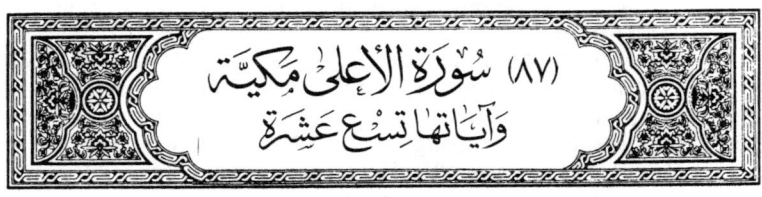

بِسْمِ اللهِ الرَّحْمَنِ الرَّحِيمِ

سَبِّحِ اسْمَ رَبِّكَ الْأَعْلَى ۝ الَّذِي خَلَقَ فَسَوَّى ۝ وَالَّذِي قَدَّرَ فَهَدَى ۝ وَالَّذِي أَخْرَجَ الْمَرْعَى ۝ فَجَعَلَهُ غُثَاءً أَحْوَى ۝ سَنُقْرِئُكَ فَلَا تَنْسَى ۝ إِلَّا مَا شَاءَ اللهُ إِنَّهُ يَعْلَمُ الْجَهْرَ وَمَا يَخْفَى ۝ وَنُيَسِّرُكَ لِلْيُسْرَى ۝ فَذَكِّرْ إِنْ نَفَعَتِ الذِّكْرَى ۝ سَيَذَّكَّرُ مَنْ يَخْشَى ۝ وَيَتَجَنَّبُهَا الْأَشْقَى ۝ الَّذِي يَصْلَى النَّارَ الْكُبْرَى ۝ ثُمَّ لَا يَمُوتُ فِيهَا وَلَا يَحْيَى ۝

قَدْ أَفْلَحَ مَنْ تَزَكَّى ۝ وَذَكَرَ اسْمَ رَبِّهِ فَصَلَّى ۝ بَلْ تُؤْثِرُونَ الْحَيَاةَ الدُّنْيَا ۝ وَالْآخِرَةُ خَيْرٌ وَأَبْقَى ۝ إِنَّ هَذَا لَفِي الصُّحُفِ الْأُولَى ۝ صُحُفِ إِبْرَاهِيمَ وَمُوسَى ۝

SURAH 87

THE MOST HIGH
AL-'AALA

In the Name of Allah, the Beneficent, the Merciful.

Praise the name of your Lord, the Most High,
Who creates and proportions well,
Who determines and guides,
Who brings forth the pasturage,
then turns it into withered grass.
We shall teach you to read and you shall not forget
save what Allah wills. He knows what is manifest and
   what is kept hidden.
And We shall smooth your way to perfect ease.
Give warning, therefore, if warning is of use.
He who fears Allah will heed it,
but the most wretched will turn aside from it,
He shall be cast into the greatest fire,
in which he shall neither die nor live.
Prosperous is he who purifies himself
and glorifies the name of his Lord and prays.
Yet you prefer this present life,
while the life to come is better and longer lasting.
All this is surely written in earlier scriptures;
The scriptures of Abraham and Moses.

In the Shade of the Qur'an

Imam Ahmad Ibn Hanbal has transmitted on the authority of Ali, the Prophet's cousin and companion, that the Prophet used to love this *surah*. The famous traditionalist, Muslim, has also transmitted that the Prophet used to read this *surah* and *surah* 86, "The Enveloper", in the prayers of Islamic festivals and in Friday prayers. If one of the festivals fell on a Friday, the Prophet would be sure to read these two *surahs* in the prayers.

The Prophet is right to love this *surah* as it turns the whole universe into a temple whose four corners echo the praises and glorification of his Lord, the Most High. *"Praise the name of your Lord, the Most High, Who creates and proportions well, Who determines and guides, Who brings forth the pasturage, then turns it into withered grass."* The rhythm of the *surah*, characterised by the long vowels with which each of its verses ends, imparts a feeling of the praises echoed everywhere in the universe.

The Prophet is also right to love this *surah* as it brings him good news. As Allah charges him with the double task of conveying His message and warning people, He promises him: *"We shall teach you to read and you shall not forget, save what Allah wills. He knows what is manifest and what is kept hidden. And We shall smooth your way to perfect ease. Therefore, give warning, if warning is of use."* So Allah takes upon Himself the responsibility of making His Messenger not forget anything of the Qur'an. He also promises that his path will be smoothed in all his affairs, whether they are personal or concern his message. This is certainly a great favour.

Again, the Prophet is right to love this *surah* as it includes the basic ingredients of the Islamic concept of life and existence: the unity of Allah, the Creator; the reality of Divine revelation; and the reality of reward and punishment in the life to come. The *surah* also affirms that these basic principles have well-established roots in the earlier Divine messages. *"All this is surely written in earlier scriptures; the scriptures of Abraham and Moses."* All this is in addition to the impression it imparts of the easy nature of the Islamic ideology, the Messenger who conveys it, and the nation it builds.

"Praise the name of your Lord, the Most High, Who creates and proportions well, Who determines and guides, Who brings forth the pasturage, then turns it into withered grass." The *surah* opens with an order to praise the Lord, which means to glorify Him, recognise His supremacy and infallibility in everything, and remember His Divine attributes. It is much more than verbal repetition of the phrase

Surah 87   The Most High (*Al-'Aala*)

"subhan Allah" or "praise be to Allah". It is a genuine feeling of the sublimity of these attributes.

As the *surah* inspires one with the splendour of a life based on constant appreciation of the Divine attributes, it creates within one a feeling which is very real and very difficult to describe at the same time.

The two immediately presented attributes are Lordship and Highness. The "Lord" or the Arabic equivalent *"Rabb"* is the one Who tends and nurtures. The denotations of this attribute fit in very well with the general atmosphere of the *surah*, its glad tidings and easy rhythm. The "Highness" attribute prompts one to look up to endless horizons. Having a genuinely vivid feeling of this attribute is indeed the essential purpose of praising Allah and glorifying Him.

The *surah* opens with an order addressed by Allah to the Prophet in the first instance: *"Praise the name of your Lord, the Most High."* The order is given with an air of friendliness and compassion almost beyond description.

Whenever the Prophet read this *surah* he used to fulfil this order promptly by stopping after the first verse to say: "All praise be to my Lord, the Most High". Thus, he would receive the order, carry it out promptly and read on. When this *surah* was revealed the Prophet told the Muslims to fulfil the Divine order as they prostrate themselves in their daily prayers. Similarly he told them to carry out the other order of *"Praise the name of your Lord, the Most Great"* as they bow in their prayers. These praises, warm with life, have been included in the prayers as a direct response to a direct order, or more precisely to a direct permission. For Allah's permission to His servants to praise Him is one of the favours He has bestowed on them. It is a permission to them to be in contact with Him in a manner, given their limited abilities, they can appreciate. He, out of His grace, has permitted them to do this so that they may know Him and His attributes as best they can.

"Praise the name of your Lord, the Most High, Who creates and proportions well, Who determines and guides." Everything Allah has created is well proportioned and perfected. Every creature is assigned its own role and given guidance so that it may know its role and play it. It is told the purpose of its creation, given what it needs for sustenance and guided to it. This is clearly visible in everything around us, big or small, important or trivial. (For everything is well perfected and guided to fulfil the purpose of its creation as it can be

fulfilled best.) All things are also collectively perfected so that they may fulfil their collective role.

The single atom is well balanced between its electrons and protons, to the same degree as the solar system, its sun, planets and satellites, are well balanced. Each of the two knows the way it is assigned to travel and fulfils its role. The single living cell is also perfect and well equipped to do everything it is asked to do, in the same measure as the most advanced and complex species. This perfect balance, in the individual and the collective sense, is easily noticeable in every one of numerous kinds of creation that fill the gap between the single atom and the solar system or between the single cell and the most advanced living creature.

This basic fact, evidenced by everything in the universe, is well recognised by the human heart as it contemplates what is in the universe. This sort of inspiration and recognition is within the reach of every man in every age, regardless of his standard of education. All that is required for it is an open mind which contemplates and responds. Increased knowledge then endorses and emphasises with individual examples what inspiration has already proven with the first glance. The results of study and research endorse, within their limited scope, this basic truth which applies to everything in the universe.

The American scientist, A Cressy Morrison, Head of the Science Academy in New York, says in his book *"Man Does Not Stand Alone":*

"Birds have the homing instinct. The robin that nested at your door may go south in the autumn, but will come back to his old nest the next spring. In September, flocks of many of our birds fly south, often over a thousand miles of open sea, but they do not lose their way. The homing pigeon, confused by new sounds on a long journey in a closed box, circles for a moment then heads almost unerringly for home. The bee finds its hive while the wind waving the grasses and trees blots out every visible guide to its whereabouts. This homing sense is slightly developed in man, but he supplements his meagre equipment with instruments of navigation. We need this instinct and our brain provides the answer. The tiny insects must have microscopic eyes, how perfect we do not know, and the hawks, the eagle and the condor must have telescopic vision. Here again man surpasses them with his mechanical instruments. With his telescope he can see a nebula so faint that it requires two million times his vision, and with the electron microscope he can see hitherto invisible bacteria and, so to speak, the little bugs that bite them.

If you let old Dobbin alone he will keep to the road in the blackest night. He can see, dimly perhaps, but he notes the difference in temperature of the road and the sides with eyes that are slightly affected by the infra-red rays of the road. The owl can see the nice warm mouse as he runs in the cooler grass in the blackest night. We turn night into day by creating radiation in that short octave we call light."[1]

"The honey-bee workers make chambers of different sizes in the comb used for breeding. Small chambers are constructed for the workers, larger ones for the drones, and special chambers for the prospective queens. The queen bee lays unfertilized eggs in the cells designed for males, but lays fertilized eggs in the proper chambers for the female workers and the possible queens. The workers, who are the modified females, having long since anticipated the coming of the new generation, are also prepared to furnish food for the young bees by chewing and predigesting honey and pollen. They discontinue the process of chewing, including the predigesting, at a certain stage of the development of the males and females, and feed only honey and pollen. The females so treated become the workers.

For the females in the queen chambers the diet of chewed and predigested food is continued. These specially treated females develop into queen bees, which alone produce fertile eggs. This process of reproduction involves special chambers, special eggs, and the marvellous effect of a change of diet. This means anticipation, discretion, and the application of a discovery of the effect of diet. These changes apply particularly to a community life and seem necessary to its existence. The knowledge and skills required must have been evolved after the beginnings of this community life, and are not necessarily inherent in the structure or the survival of the honey-bee as such. The bee, therefore, seems to have outstripped man in knowledge of the effects of diet under certain conditions.

The dog with an inquiring nose can sense the animal that has

---

[1] A. Cressy Morrison, *op. cit.* pp. 58–59.

In the Shade of the Qur'an

passed. No instrument of human invention has added to our inferior sense of smell, and we hardly know where to begin to investigate its extension. Yet even our sense of smell is so highly developed that it can detect ultra-microscopic particles. How do we know that we all get the same reaction from any single odour? The fact is that we do not. Taste also gives a very different sensation to each of us. How strange that these differences in perception are hereditary.

All animals hear sounds, many of which are outside our range of vibration, with an acuteness that far surpasses our limited sense of hearing. Man by his devices can now hear a fly walking miles away as though it was on his eardrums, and with like instruments record the impact of a cosmic ray."[1]

"One of the water spiders fashions a balloon-shaped nest of cobweb filaments and attaches it to some object under water. Then she ingeniously entangles an air bubble in the hairs of her under-body, carries it into the water, and releases it under the nest. This performance is repeated until the nest is inflated, when she proceeds to bring forth and raise her young safe from attack by air. Here we have a synthesis of the web, engineering, construction, and aeronautics. Chance perhaps, but that still leaves the spider unexplained.

The young salmon spends years at sea, then comes back to his own river, and, what is more, he travels up the side of the river into which flows the tributary in which he was born. The laws of the States on one side of the dividing stream may be strict and the other side not, but these laws affect only the fish which may be said to belong to each side. What brings them back so definitely? If a salmon going up a river is transferred to another tributary he will at once realize he is not in the right tributary and will fight his way down to the main stream and then turn up against the current to finish his destiny. There is, however, a much more difficult reverse problem to solve in the case of the eel. These amazing creatures migrate at maturity from all the ponds and rivers everywhere – those from Europe across thousands of miles of ocean – all go to the abysmal deeps south of Bermuda. There they breed and die. The little ones, with no apparent means of knowing anything

---

[1] A. C. Morrison, *op. cit.* pp. 61–63.

Surah 87   The Most High (*Al-'Aala*)

except that they are in a wilderness of water, start back and find their way to the shore from which their parents came and thence to every river, lake and little pond, so that each body of water is always populated with eels. They have braved the mighty currents, storms and tides, and have conquered the beating waves on every shore. They can now grow and when they are mature, they will, by some mysterious law, go back through it all to complete the cycle. Where does the directing impulse originate? No American eel has ever been caught in European waters and no European eel has ever been caught in American waters. Nature has also delayed the maturity of the European eel by a year or more to make up for its much greater journey. Do atoms and molecules when combined in an eel have a sense of direction and willpower to exercise it?"[1]

"A female moth placed in your attic by the open window will send out some subtle signal. Over an unbelievable area, the male moths of the same species will catch the message and respond in spite of your attempts to produce laboratory odours to disconcert them. Has the little creature a broadcasting station, and has the male moth a mental radio set beside his antennae? Does she shake the ether and does he catch the vibration? The cricket rubs its legs or wings together, and on a still night can be heard half a mile away. It shakes six hundred tons of air and calls its mate. Miss Moth, working in a different realm of physics and, in apparent silence, calls quite as effectively. Before the radio was discovered, scientists decided it was odour that attracted the male moth. It was a miracle either way, because the odour would have to travel in all directions, with or without the wind. The male moth would have to be able to detect a molecule and sense the direction from whence it came. By a vast mechanism, we are developing the same ability to communicate, and the day will come when a young man may call his loved one from a distance and without mechanical medium and she will answer. No lock or bars will stop them. Our telephone and radio are instrumental wonders and give us means of almost instant communication, but we are tied to a wire and a place. The moth is still ahead of us, and we can only envy her until our brain evolves an individual radio Then, in a sense, we will have telepathy.

---

[1] A. C. Morrison, *op. cit.* pp. 64–65.

In the Shade of the Qur'an

"Vegetation makes subtle use of involuntary agents to carry on its existence – insects to carry pollen from flower to flower and the winds and everything that flies or walks to distribute seed. At last, vegetation has trapped masterful man. He has improved nature, and she generously rewards him. But he has multiplied so prodigiously that he is now chained to the plough. He must sow, reap, and store; breed and cross-breed; prune and graft. Should he neglect these tasks starvation would be his lot, civilization would crumble, and earth return to her pristine state."[1]

"Many animals are like a lobster, which, having lost a claw, will by some restimulation of the cells and the reactivation of the genes discover that a part of the body is missing and restore it. When the work is complete, the cells stop work, for in some way they know it is quitting time. A fresh-water polyp divided into halves can reform itself out of one of these halves. Cut off an angle worm's head and he will soon create a new one. We can stimulate healing, but when will our surgeons, if ever, know how to stimulate the cells to produce a new arm, flesh, bones, nails, and activating nerves? An extraordinary fact throws some light on this mystery of re-creation. If cells in the early stages of development are separated, each has the ability to create a complete animal. Therefore, if the original cell divides into two and they are separated, two individuals will be developed. This may account for identical twins, but it means much more – each cell at first is in detail potentially a complete individual. There can be no doubt then, that you are you in every cell and fibre."[2]

"An acorn falls to the ground – its tough brown shell holds it safe. It rolls into some earthy crevice. In the spring the germ awakes, the shell bursts, food is provided by the egglike kernel in which the genes were hidden. They send roots into the earth, and behold a sprout, a sapling, and in years a tree. The germ with its genes has multiplied by trillions and made the trunk, bark and every leaf and acorn identical with that of the oak which gave it birth. For hundreds of years in each of the countless acorns is preserved the exact arrangement of atoms that produced the first oak

---

[1] A. C. Morrison, *op. cit.* pp. 66–67.
[2] A. C. Morrison. *op. cit.* p. 68.

Surah 87   The Most High (*Al-'Aala*)

tree millions of years ago."[1]

The author says in another chapter of his book:

> "Every cell that is produced in any living creature must adapt itself to be part of the flesh, to sacrifice itself as a part of the skin, which will soon be worn off. It must deposit the enamel of teeth, produce the transparent liquid in an eye, or become a nose, or an ear. Each cell must then adapt itself in shape and every other characteristic necessary to fulfil its function. It is hard to think of a cell as right-handed or left-handed, but one becomes part of a right ear, the other becomes part of the left ear. Some crystals that are chemically identical turn the rays of light to the left, others to the right. There seems to be such a tendency in the cells. In the exact place where they belong, they become a part of the right ear or the left ear, and your two ears are opposite each other on your head, and not as in the case of a cricket, on your elbows. Their curves are opposite, and when complete, they are so much alike you cannot tell them apart. Hundreds of thousands of cells seem impelled to do the right thing at the right time in the right place."[2]

Elsewhere in his book Mr Morrison says:

> "In the mêlée of creation many creatures have come to exhibit a high degree of certain forms of instinct, intelligence, or what not. The wasp catches the grasshopper, digs a hole in the earth, stings the grasshopper in exactly the right place so that he becomes unconscious but lives as a form of preserved meat. The wasp lays her eggs exactly in the right place, perhaps not knowing that when they hatch, her children can eat without killing the insect on which they feed, which would be fatal to them. The wasp must have done all this right the first and every time, or there would be no wasps of this species. Science cannot explain this mystery, and yet it cannot be attributed to chance. The wasp covers a hole in the earth, departs cheerfully, and dies. Neither she nor her ancestors have reasoned out the process, nor does she know what happens to her offspring. She doesn't even know that she has worked and lived her life for the preservation of the race."[3]

---

[1] A. C. Morrison, *op. cit.* pp. 86—87.   [2] A. C. Morrison. *op. cit.* pp. 71–72.
[3] A. C. Morrison, *op. cit.* pp. 52–53.

In the same book we also read:

"In some species, the workers bring in little seeds to feed the other ants through the winter. The ants establish what is known as the grinding room, in which those which have developed gigantic jaws especially built for grinding, prepare the food for the colony. This is their sole occupation. When the autumn comes and the seeds are all ground, 'the greatest good for the greatest number' requires that the food supply be conserved and as there will be plenty of grinders in the new generation, the soldier ants kill off the grinders, satisfying their entomological conscience by believing perhaps that the grinders had had reward enough in having had first chance at the food while they ground.

Certain ants, by means of instinct or reasoning (choose which you prefer), cultivate mushrooms for food in what may be called mushroom gardens, and capture certain caterpillars and aphids (plant lice). These creatures are the ants' cows and goats, from which they take certain exudations of a honeylike nature for food. Ants capture and keep slaves. Some ants, when they make their nests, cut the leaves to size, and while certain workers hold the edges in place, use their babies, which in the larval stage are capable of spinning silk, as shuttles to sew them together. The poor baby may be bereft of the opportunity of making a cocoon for himself, but he has served his community.

How do the inanimate atoms and molecules of matter composing an ant set these complicated processes in motion? There must be Intelligence somewhere."[1]

True, there must be a Creator Who guides these and other creatures, big and small. He is the One *"Who creates and proportions well, Who determines and guides"*.

The examples we have quoted above are but few of the large number of remarkable aspects science has recorded in the worlds of plants, insects, birds and animals. But all these aspects reflect only a part of the import of the two verses: *"Who creates and proportions well, Who determines and guides."* For our knowledge covers only a scanty part of what is in the visible universe, beyond which extends a whole world of which we know nothing apart from the few hints

---

[1] A. C. Morrison, *op. cit.* pp. 73–74.

Surah 87   The Most High *(Al-'Aala)*

Allah has chosen to drop to us, as befits our limited abilities.

Having fired such a great volley of praises to Allah to resound in even the remotest corners of the universe, the *surah* complements that with an inspiring touch from the realm of plants: *"Who brings forth the pasturage, then turns it into withered grass."* The "pasturage", as used here, refers to all plants. Every plant is suitable for one sort of species or another. The term then has a much wider sense than the familiar pastures where cattle feed. Allah has created this planet and provided on it enough food to nourish every single living creature which walks, flies or hides itself underground.

The pasturage is green when it first shoots forth, but it withers away and blackens. It may be used for feeding when green, after it blackens and withers, or in between. Thus, it is useful in every condition, and it serves a purpose according to the elaborate planning of the One Who creates, proportions, determines and guides.

The reference here to the life of plants carries also an implicit connotation that all plants are reaped and harvested. Similarly, every living being will come to its appointed end. This connotation fits in well with the reference to the two worlds of man: *"Yet you prefer this present life, while the life to come is better and more lasting."* This life is a pasture which comes to its end when it withers away and blackens, while the life to come is the one which lasts.

As the beginning of the *surah* opens up this limitless horizon, it provides a framework for the fundamental facts tackled in this *surah* to be related to the whole universe. The framework is remarkably suitable, it is perfectly harmonious with the atmosphere of the *surah*, its rhythm and its shades of meaning.[1]

The *surah* then gives the Prophet, and the Muslim nation in general, a very welcome tiding: *"We shall teach you to read and you shall not forget, save what Allah wills. He knows what is manifest and what is kept hidden. And We shall smooth your way to perfect ease. Give warning, therefore, if warning is of use"*. The glad tiding starts with sparing the Prophet the trouble of memorising the Qur'an. All he needs to do is to read as he is taught and Allah will ensure that he will never forget any part of it. *"We shall teach you to read and you shall not forget."* So keen to keep the Qur'an in his memory, the Prophet used to repeat it after Jibril, the angel, had come down with it to him. He felt that it

---

[1] For further discussion of this aspect see the chapter entitled "Artistic Harmony" in the author's book, *"The Quranic Art of Picture Drawing"*.

was part of his responsibility to keep it registered in his memory. But Allah decided that He would look after this task. The tiding is also a happy one for the Islamic nation since it is a reassurance that the faith the Prophet preaches is authentic. It is from Allah and He looks after it. This is part of Allah's grace. It shows how weighty the question of purity of faith is in His scales.

Every time the Qur'an states a definite promise or a constant law, it follows it with a statement implying that the Divine will is free of all limitations and restrictions, even those based on a promise from Allah or a law of His. For His will is absolute beyond any such promise or law. Here, the *surah* emphasises this principle after the promise made to the Prophet that he will never forget anything of the Qur'an: *"Save what Allah wills"*. The two are complementary in the sense that the promise is within the Divine will. So we look forward to Allah's fulfilment of what He has willed to promise.

"He knows what is manifest and what is kept hidden." This is stated here by way of giving a reason for all that has passed: teaching to read, freedom from forgetfulness and the exception made to that. Everything is decided according to the wisdom of the One Who knows the secret and the manifest. He views everything from all angles and makes His decisions on the basis of His unfailing knowledge.

Then follows another tiding, happy and all-embracing: *"And We shall smooth your way to perfect ease."* This is a glad tiding for the Prophet personally and for the Islamic nation at large. It is furthermore a statement of the nature of Islam, its role in human life and in the universe. This verse, which is rendered in Arabic in no more than two words, states one of the most fundamental principles of faith and existence. It provides a link between the nature of the Prophet, the nature of Islam and that of the whole universe. It is a universe created by Allah with ease; it follows its appointed way with ease and draws nearer its final objective with ease. Thus it is an inspiration lighting limitless horizons.

If Allah smooths a certain person's path, he finds ease in everything in his life. For he will move along his way to Allah with the universe which is characterised by its harmony of construction, movement and direction. Hence he does not clash with those who digress – for these are of no importance, compared with the vast universe. Ease will pervade his whole life. It will be evident in his hand, tongue, movement, work, concepts, way of thinking and conducting

Surah 87   The Most High (*Al-'Aala*)

all affairs and tackling all matters; ease with himself and with others as well.

    His wife, Aisha, reports that whenever faced with a choice, the Prophet would always choose the easier of the two alternatives.[1] She also reports: "Whenever the Prophet was alone with his family at home, he was the easiest of men, always smiling and laughing." Al-Bukhari has also transmitted, "A maid servant would take the Prophet by the hand and lead him wherever she wished." His guidance in matters of clothes, food, household furniture and other matters of day to day life points to a preference for what is easy.

    Imam Ibn Qayyim Al-Jawziyyah speaks in his book *"Zaad Al-Ma'ad"* of the Prophet's guidance in matters of dress: "He had a turban which he gave to Ali as a gift, but he used to wear it over a cap. But he also wore either the turban or the cap separately. When he wore the turban, however, he used to leave the end part of it hanging between his shoulders. This has been transmitted by Muslim in his book of authentic traditions, on the authority of Omar ibn Hareeth, who said, 'I saw the Prophet speaking on the platform of the mosque, wearing a black turban with its end hanging between his shoulders'. Muslim has also transmitted on the authority of Jabir ibn Abdullah that the Prophet was wearing a black turban when he entered Makka, but nothing is mentioned here about his leaving its end part hanging. This signifies that the Prophet did not always leave the tail of his turban hanging between his shoulders. It is also said that the Prophet entered Makka wearing his battle dress, with a helmet on his head, which suggests that he used to wear what suited the occasion."

    Ibn Qayyim Al-Jawziyyah says in another chapter of his book: "The best method, it is true, is that followed by the Prophet and which he encouraged his companions to adopt. His guidance regarding dress is, in short, that he used to wear whatever was available, whether woollen or cotton or other types of material. He used Yemeni gowns and had a green gown. He also used different types of dress such as overcoat, long dress, shirts, trousers, top gown, sandals and shoes. He left the end of his turban hanging between his shoulders on occasions, and did not on other occasions."

    On the Prophet's guidance regarding food, the author says: "The Prophet never refused what was available at home, nor did he ever go out of his way to get what was not. He would eat whatever was served

---

[1] Transmitted by Al-Bukhari and Muslim.

of good food and he never slighted any sort of food whatsoever. If he did not like something he would simply not eat it but would not forbid it. An example of his attitude is the case of *dhabb*, which he used not to eat but he did not forbid others eating it. On the contrary, he watched others eating it at his own table. He liked sweets and honey; used to eat dates, fresh and preserved; drank milk, pure and mixed, added water to ice and honey and drank dates drink. He also ate *khazeerah* which is a thick soup made of milk and flour. He ate cucumber with fresh dates, butter, dates with bread, bread with vinegar, dried meat, a dish called *dabba* (which was one of his favourite dishes), boiled meat, rice and meat cooked with fat, cheese, bread with oil, water melon with fresh dates, and he used to like dates cooked with butter. In short, he never refused good food, nor did he go to any trouble to get it. His guidance was to eat what was available. If he did not have anything to eat he would simply go hungry . . . etc."

The author also speaks of the Prophet's guidance concerning sleep and wakefulness: "He used to sleep sometimes on a mattress, sometimes on a simple animal skin. Occasionally he would sleep on a rough mat, or on the cold earth with nothing under him, or on a bed, perhaps a plain bed and perhaps covered with a black bedspread."

The Prophet's traditions urging the adoption of an easy, gentle and tolerant attitude in all matters, especially those which concern religious duties are numerous. From among these we may quote: "This religion is of an easy nature. Anyone who pulls hard against it shall be the loser." (Transmitted by Al-Bukhari). "Do not be hard on yourselves lest it should be made hard for you. A former nation chose to be hard and it was made harder for them." (Transmitted by Abu Dawood). "A rider driving hard neither reaches his destination nor keeps his transport." (Transmitted by Al-Bukhari). "Make it easy, not difficult, for others." (Transmitted by Al-Bukhari and Muslim). Concerning social dealings, the Prophet says: "May Allah have mercy on any person who is tolerant when he buys, sells and asks for his rights." (Transmitted by Al-Bukhari). "A believer is gentle and friendly" (Transmitted by Al-Baihaqi). "A believer gets on well with others and is easy to get on well with." (Transmitted by Al-Daraqutni). "The type of man Allah dislikes most is the quarrelsome one who does not budge." (Transmitted by Al-Bukhari and Muslim).

One of the highly significant features of his character is that he hated hardness even in names and physical features. This shows how

Surah 87 The Most High (*Al-'Aala*)

Allah has moulded his nature and smoothed even his temperament. Saeed ibn Al-Mussayyib reports that the Prophet asked his father what was his name (Al-Mussayyib was his nickname). He answered, "Hazn" (which means rough and difficult). The Prophet said, "No, you are Sahl (plain and easy).[1] The man said, "I will never change a name given to me by my father". Saeed comments, "As a result, we have always had a trace of hardness in our characters." (Transmitted by Al-Bukhari). "Ibn Umar reports that the Prophet changed the name of a woman from 'Aassiyah (disobedient) to Jameelah (pretty)." (Transmitted by Muslim). He also said, "It is part of kindness to receive your brother with a smiling face." (Transmitted by Al-Tirmithi). Thus we realise how refined and gentle the Prophet was to dislike even names and features which smacked of roughness and to try to substitute for them what related to gentility and tolerance.

The life story of the Prophet is composed of pages of gentility, ease, tolerance and understanding in all affairs. Let us quote here an incident which reveals his method of dealing with people of difficult temperament: "Once a bedouin came to the Prophet asking something. The Prophet granted his request then said, 'Have I treated you well?' The bedouin said, 'No, and you have not been kind either!' The Muslims with the Prophet felt very angry and wanted to punish the man. The Prophet, however, motioned them to leave him alone. He then went into his house, sent for the man and gave him something over and above his original request. He then asked him, 'Have I treated you well?' The man said, 'Yes, indeed. May Allah reward you well for you are a good kinsman and a good tribesman'. The Prophet then said to him, 'When you said what you said you made my companions feel angry with you. If you like to tell them what you have just told me so that they would have nothing against you.' The man said, 'I will'. The following day he came and the Prophet said, 'This bedouin said yesterday what you have heard. We gave him more and he claims now that he is satisfied. Is that so?' The bedouin said, 'Yes indeed! May Allah reward you well, for you are a good kinsman and a good tribesman.' The Prophet then said to his companions, 'My affair with this bedouin is similar to that of a man who had a she-camel which ran loose. Other people rushed to try to catch her but they managed only to make her run wild. The owner then appealed to

---

[1] This was how the Prophet changed the names of his companions of which he did not approve – Translator's note.

them to let him alone with his she-camel as he was gentler to her and knew her temperament. The owner then went towards her, having picked something to feed her with. He approached her gently until she responded and sat down. He then saddled her and mounted her back. Had I left you alone when the man said what he said, you would probably have killed him and he would have gone to Hell."

So gentle, simple and compassionate was the Prophet's attitude towards any person of rough nature. Examples of this attitude abound in the records of his life. These examples are practical manifestations of how his path had been smoothed for him to achieve perfect ease in every aspect of life. He had been given a tolerant, understanding nature so that he might carry out his mission as Allah's messenger to mankind. In this way his nature and the nature of Islam, the message he carried and conveyed, are alike. He was able, with Allah's grace, to fulfil the great task with which he had been entrusted. For when his path was smoothed, the heavy burden of his mission became an enjoyable sport.

The Qur'an describes Muhammad, Allah's Messenger, as a source of mercy to humanity, who has come to relieve people of the burdens imposed on them by reason of their being too hard against themselves: *"We have sent you forth only as a mercy to mankind."*[1] *"Those who follow the Messenger, the Prophet who can neither read nor write, whom they shall find described in the Torah and the Gospel. He will enjoin upon them what is right, and forbid them what is evil. He will make all good things lawful to them and prohibit all that is foul. He will relieve them of their burdens and of the shackles that weigh upon them."*[2] The Qur'an also describes the message the Prophet has delivered in statements of like import: *"We have made the Qur'an easy for warning: but will any take heed?"*[3] *"He has laid on you no hardships in the observance of your religion."*[4] *"Allah does not wish to burden you; He seeks only to purify you."*[5] *"Allah does not charge a soul with more than its capacity."*[6] The message of Islam is made easy for people to follow since it takes into consideration the limitations of human abilities. It imposes no burdens which are too heavy. This easy nature of the religion of Islam is readily identifiable in its spirit

---

[1] The Qur'an. *21; 107.*
[2] *Ibid. 7: 157.*
[3] *Ibid. 54: 22.*
[4] *Ibid. 22: 78.*
[5] *Ibid. 5: 6.*
[6] *Ibid. 2: 286.*

Surah 87   The Most High (*Al-'Aala*)

as well as in its commandments: *"Follow the upright nature Allah has endowed mankind with."*[1]

When we look carefully through this religion we find that care has been taken to make it easy for men to follow, without overstraining themselves. It takes into consideration the different situations man finds himself in, and the conditions he faces in different environments. The faith itself is based on concepts which are easy to grasp: a single god; none like Him; He has created everything; He has guided everything to realise the purpose of its existence; He has also sent messengers to remind people of their role in life and to call them back to their Lord Who has created them. All obligations imposed by this faith fit in perfectly together; there are no conflicts, no contradictions. People have to fulfil these obligations according to their abilities: there need be no overstraining, no heavy burdens: "If I give you an order, fulfil it as much as you can; but leave off what I forbid you."[2] Prohibition may be also relaxed *"save under compulsion of necessity."*[3] These basic principles provide the limits within which the Islamic commandments and principles operate.

Hence the Messenger and the message have this basic feature, easy nature, in common. So does the nation of Islam, the easy message, build: it is a middle nation, merciful, the recipient of Divine mercy, easy natured and enjoys a life which is perfectly harmonious with the wider existence in the universe.

The universe itself with its perfect harmony provides a true picture of how Allah's creation moves easily and smoothly, without clash or crash. Millions of millions of stars move in their orbits in the great space Allah has provided, each with its own gravity, yet none moves out of step and none crashes against another. There are millions of millions of living creatures, each moving through life to its appointed aim, near or distant, according to a perfect plan. Each is given the abilities which make its aim easy to achieve. Millions of millions of movements, events and conditions come together then go their separate ways; yet they are much the same as the sounds of the different instruments in an orchestra: so different but combine to give together a beautiful tune.

In short, perfect harmony exists between the nature of the universe, the message, the Messenger and the Islamic nation. They are

---

[1] The Qur'an. *30: 30.*
[2] Transmitted by Al-Bukhari and Muslim.
[3] *op. cit. 6: 119.*

all the creation of Allah, the One, the Most Wise.
"Give warning, therefore, if warning is of use." Allah has taught him to read and not forget, smoothed his way to perfect ease so that he may be able to discharge his great task, namely, to warn. For this he has been the subject of careful preparation. Hence, he is asked to warn whenever he has a chance to address people and to convey to them Allah's message. *"If warning is of use".* Warning is always useful. There will always be, in every land and every generation, those who will listen to the reminders and warnings and will benefit by them, no matter how corrupt their society is and how hardened their people are.

If we ponder a little over the verses in this *surah* and their sequence, we realise the greatness of the message entrusted to the Prophet. To convey it, and to give the warnings he is asked to give he needs special equipment: a smooth way to perfect ease in everything, to be taught to read and Allah's preservation of the message intact.

Once the Prophet has conveyed his message, his task is fulfilled. Everyone is left to choose his way. Their destinies differ according to their choice of the ways they follow: *"He who fears Allah will heed it, but the most wretched will turn aside from it. He shall be cast into the greatest fire, in which he neither dies nor lives. Prosperous is he who purifies himself and glorifies the name of his Lord and prays."* The Prophet is told here that his warnings will benefit him *"who fears Allah"*, and fears His punishment. Any intelligent man will feel a shudder in his soul as soon as he learns that there is a Creator who proportions well, determines and guides. For he realises that such a Creator must hold every man responsible for his actions, good or evil, and will reward him accordingly. Hence he fears and heeds the warnings when he is warned.

"But the most wretched will turn aside from it." If a man does not listen to the warning given, then he is absolutely *"the most wretched"*. He lives in a void, uninspired by the facts surrounding him, turning a deaf ear and a senseless mind to the evidence they give. Such a person lives in constant worry, striving hard to attain the paltry pleasures of this world. Hence he is the most wretched in this life. But he is also the most wretched in the hereafter as he suffers there endless torment: *"He shall be cast into the greatest fire, in which he shall neither die nor live."* The greatest fire is that of Hell. It is indeed the greatest of all fires in intensity, duration and size. He who suffers it finds it endless. He neither dies to rest from its torment, nor

does he live in it a life of rest and security. It is a never-ending agony which makes the sufferer yearn for death as his greatest hope.

At the other end we find prosperity accompanied with self-purification and heeding of the warnings: *"Prosperous is he who purifies himself and glorifies the name of his Lord and prays."* Purification is used here in the widest sense of the word: purification from everything filthy or sinful. The person who seeks to purify himself, glorifies his Lord, feels His power and majesty in his inmost soul and *"prays"*, (whether taken in its general sense or its special Islamic sense) will definitely be *"prosperous"*, as Allah states here. He will be prosperous here in this life as he enjoys his relationship with Allah and the perfect bliss that results from his glorification of Allah. He will also be prosperous in the hereafter as he escapes Hell and is rewarded with perfect happiness in Paradise. How different the two destinies are.

Having sketched the two different ends of the most wretched and the godfearing, the *surah* points out to the addressees the real reason for their great wretchedness, the failure which drives them headlong into the greatest fire: *"Yet you prefer this present life while the life to come is better and longer lasting"*. This short sighted preference for the present life is the real reason for every misery which befalls man. It is indeed the cause of man's taking no heed of the warnings given to him. The Qur'an calls the present life *"dunia"* which connotes both contemptuousness and ease of access. The life to come is better in kind and duration. Only the foolish who are deprived of sound judgement would, in the circumstances, prefer the present life to the next.

In conclusion, the *surah* points out that the message of Islam is not new; its roots go back far deep in time. *"All this is surely written in earlier scriptures, the scriptures of Abraham and Moses."* The basics of the grand faith contained in this *surah* are the same old basic facts outlined in the ancient scriptures of Abraham and Moses.

The truth is one and the faith is one. This results from the fact that their origin is one, Allah, Whose will it was to send messengers to mankind. The messengers deliver basically the same message, the same simple truth. Details of the messages may differ according to local or temporal needs, but the basics are the same. They have one origin: Allah, the Most High, Who creates, proportions well, determines and guides.

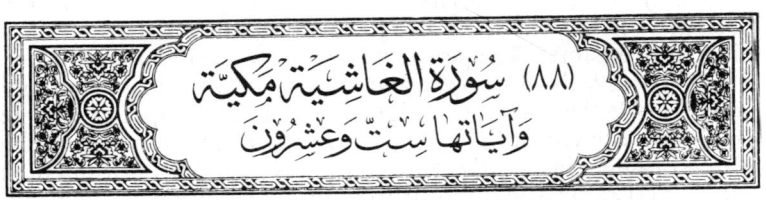

بسم الله الرحمن الرحيم

هَلْ أَتَىٰكَ حَدِيثُ ٱلْغَٰشِيَةِ ۝ وُجُوهٌ يَوْمَئِذٍ خَٰشِعَةٌ ۝ عَامِلَةٌ نَّاصِبَةٌ ۝ تَصْلَىٰ نَارًا حَامِيَةً ۝ تُسْقَىٰ مِنْ عَيْنٍ ءَانِيَةٍ ۝ لَّيْسَ لَهُمْ طَعَامٌ إِلَّا مِن ضَرِيعٍ ۝ لَّا يُسْمِنُ وَلَا يُغْنِى مِن جُوعٍ ۝ وُجُوهٌ يَوْمَئِذٍ نَّاعِمَةٌ ۝ لِّسَعْيِهَا رَاضِيَةٌ ۝ فِى جَنَّةٍ عَالِيَةٍ ۝ لَّا تَسْمَعُ فِيهَا لَٰغِيَةً ۝ فِيهَا عَيْنٌ جَارِيَةٌ ۝ فِيهَا سُرُرٌ مَّرْفُوعَةٌ ۝ وَأَكْوَابٌ مَّوْضُوعَةٌ ۝ وَنَمَارِقُ مَصْفُوفَةٌ ۝ وَزَرَابِىُّ مَبْثُوثَةٌ ۝ أَفَلَا يَنظُرُونَ إِلَى ٱلْإِبِلِ كَيْفَ خُلِقَتْ ۝ وَإِلَى ٱلسَّمَاءِ كَيْفَ رُفِعَتْ ۝ وَإِلَى ٱلْجِبَالِ كَيْفَ نُصِبَتْ ۝ وَإِلَى ٱلْأَرْضِ كَيْفَ سُطِحَتْ ۝ فَذَكِّرْ إِنَّمَا أَنتَ مُذَكِّرٌ ۝ لَّسْتَ عَلَيْهِم بِمُصَيْطِرٍ ۝ إِلَّا مَن تَوَلَّىٰ وَكَفَرَ ۝ فَيُعَذِّبُهُ ٱللَّهُ ٱلْعَذَابَ ٱلْأَكْبَرَ ۝ إِنَّ إِلَيْنَا إِيَابَهُمْ ۝ ثُمَّ إِنَّ عَلَيْنَا حِسَابَهُم ۝

SURAH 88

THE ENVELOPER
AL-GHASHIYAH

In the name of Allah, the Beneficent, the Merciful.

Have you heard the story of the Enveloper?
Some faces on that day are downcast,
labour weary, toilworn,
roasting at a scorching fire,
made to drink from a boiling fountain.
Their only food shall be the fruit of Dhari',
which will neither nourish nor satisfy their hunger.
Other faces on that day are jocund,
well-pleased with their striving,
in a sublime garden,
where they hear no babble.
A running fountain shall be there,
and raised couches,
and goblets set forth,
and cushions laid in order,
and carpets outspread.
Let them reflect how the camel was created;
how heaven was lifted up;
how the mountains were hoisted;
how the earth was outstretched.
Therefore give warning; your mission is only to warn them.
You are not their overseer.
But he who turns his back and disbelieves,
Allah shall inflict on him the greatest chastisement.
To Us they shall surely return,
when We shall bring them to account.

In the Shade of the Qur'an

This *surah* is a deep and calm melody which invites meditation, hope and fear, and warns man to be ready for the day of reckoning. It carries man's heart into two vast spheres: the life hereafter, its limitless world and moving scenes; and the visible sphere of existence, with the signs Allah has spread in all the creatures sharing this existence, held out for everyone to see. After these two great scenarios, the *surah* reminds man of the reckoning on the Day of Judgement, of Allah's power, and of the inevitable return to Him. Throughout, the style is characterised by its depth of tone: it is calm but highly effective, powerful, and awesome.

"Have you heard the story of the Enveloper?" With this introduction, the *surah* wants to make human hearts turn back to Allah, to remind men of His signs in the universe, His reckoning on the Day of Judgement, and His certain reward. It starts with this inquiry, which implies greatness and indicates a positive statement. It points out that the question of the hereafter had already been affirmed and earlier reminders had been given. The Day of Resurrection is here given a new name, "the Enveloper", which suggests that a calamity will befall mankind and envelop them with its horrors. It is one of the evocative names mentioned in the thirtieth part of the Qur'an. Others are: "the Overwhelming", "the Deafening", "the Stunning Event". They are all very suitable to the general tone and nature of this part.

The Prophet (peace be on him) whenever he listened to this *surah* would feel that the address *"Have you heard..."* was directed to him personally, as if he was receiving it from his Lord directly for the first time. He was extremely moved by Allah's address to him. The reality of this Divine address was always present in his mind. A tradition related by Umar ibn Maymoon says that the Prophet once passed by a woman who was reading the *surah*. When she read *"Have you heard the story of the Enveloper....?"* he stopped to listen and said "Yes, I have heard it."

The address is nevertheless a general one, directed to everyone who hears the Qur'an. The story of the Enveloper is the oft-repeated theme in the Qur'an, reminding men of the hereafter, warning them of its punishment, and promising its rewards. It is a story which aims to awaken men's consciences, to arouse their fear and apprehension as well as their hope and expectancy.

After asking *"Have you heard the story of the Enveloper?"*, the *surah* relates a part of this story: *"Some faces on that day are down-*

Surah 88 The Enveloper (*Al-Ghashiyah*)

cast, labour weary, toilworn, roasting at a scorching fire, made to drink from a boiling fountain. Their only food shall be the fruit of Dhari', which will neither nourish nor satisfy their hunger." The scene of suffering and torture is given before the scene of joy, because the former is closer to the connotations and impressions of "the Enveloper".

Thus we are told that there are on that day faces which look humble, downcast and toilworn. They belong to people who have laboured and toiled without any satisfactory results. Indeed the results they get are a total loss, which increases their disappointment, and causes looks of humiliation and exhaustion on their faces. Hence they are described as *"labour weary, toilworn"*. They had laboured and toiled for something different than the cause of Allah. Their work was totally for themselves and their families, for their own ambitions in the worldly life. Then they come to reap the fruits of their toil, not having made any provisions for the future life. Hence they face the end with a mixture of humiliation, exhaustion, misery and hopelessness. In addition to all this they roast *"at a scorching fire."*

They are *"made to drink from a boiling fountain. Their only food shall be the fruit of Dhari', which will neither nourish nor satisfy their hunger." Dhari'* is said to be a tree of fire in Hell. This explanation is based on what has been revealed about the tree of *"zaqqoom"* which grows at the centre of Hell. It is also said to be a kind of cactus thorn, which when green is called *"shabraq"* and is eaten by camels. However, when it is fully grown it cannot be eaten as it becomes poisonous. Whatever it is in reality, it is a kind of food like *"ghisleen"* and *"ghassaaq"* (names given by the Qur'an to refer to the food available in Hell) which neither nourishes nor appeases hunger.

It is obvious that we, in this world, cannot fully comprehend the nature of that suffering and torture in the hereafter. The description is made in order to give our human perceptions the feeling of the greatest possible pain, which is produced by a combination of humiliation, weakness, failure, the scorching fire, drinking and bathing in boiling water, and eating food unacceptable even to the camels. From all these aspects we get a feeling of the ultimate affliction. But the affliction of the hereafter is, nevertheless, greater. Its true nature is incomprehensible except to those who will actually experience it. May Allah never count us among them.

On the other hand we find *"other faces on that day are jocund, well-pleased with their striving, in a sublime garden, where they hear no babble. A running fountain shall be there, and raised couches, and goblets set forth, and cushions laid in order, and carpets outspread."* Here are faces bright with joy, animated with pleasure. They are well-pleased with what they are given. They enjoy that splendid, spiritual feeling of satisfaction with what they have done, as they sense Allah's pleasure with them. There is no better feeling for man than to be reassured of his own actions, and to see the results reflected by Allah's pleasure with him. The Qur'an gives precedence to this kind of happiness over the joys of heaven. Then, it describes heaven and the joys it affords to its happy dwellers: *"in a sublime garden."* It is glorious and sublime, with lofty positions and elevated gardens.

The description of height and elevation gives us a special feeling. *"Where they hear no babble":* this expression creates a sense of calmness, peace, reassurance, affection, satisfaction and pleasant discourse between friends. It also provides a feeling of raising oneself above any vain conversation. This is in itself a kind of joy and happiness, which is better felt when one remembers the first life and its increasing polemics, disputes, contentions, quarrels, din and uproar. When one remembers all this, one relaxes with the feeling of complete calmness, total peace and pleasant happiness generated by the Qur'anic expression *"where they hear no babble".* The very words are endowed with pleasant fragrance. They flow with a gratifying rhythm. It also implies that, as the believers turn away in this life from polemics and vain discourse, their way of life acquires a heavenly element.

As has been said earlier, of all the descriptions of heaven, Allah emphasises first this sublime and brilliant element, before He mentions the joys which satisfy the senses. These are given in a form comprehensible to man, but in heaven they take the form which is suited for the elevated standards of the people of heaven. Thus they remain unknown except to those who actually experience them.

"A running fountain shall be there": the description combines a sense of the appeasement of thirst, with beauty of movement and flow. Running water gives a sense of liveliness and youth. It is pleasant to the eye and the mind, and touches the depths of human feeling.

"And raised couches": the adjective *"raised"* gives an impression of cleanliness and purity. *"And goblets set forth"*, so they are ready for drinking – there is no need to order or prepare them. *"And*

Surah 88   The Enveloper (*Al-Ghashiyah*)

cushions laid in order" are for the dwellers to recline and relax. *"And carpets outspread"* are for the dual purpose of decoration and comfort. All these luxuries are similar to luxuries enjoyed in this life, but these are mentioned merely to make them comprehensible to us. Their true nature, and the nature of their enjoyment, are left for the experience of those successful people whom Allah has rewarded.

It is useless to make comparisons or enquiries concerning the nature of the joys of the hereafter, or the nature of its afflictions. People gain their understanding by means that are limited to this world, and the nature of life in it. When they are in the next life all veils will be lifted and barriers removed. Souls and senses will be free from all restrictions, and the connotations of the very words will alter as a result of the change in feelings they refer to. These Qur'anic descriptions help us to imagine the ultimate of sweetness and joy. This is all that we can do while we live on earth, but when Allah honours us with His grace and pleasure, as we pray He shall, we will know the reality to which the Qur'an refers.

When this account of the hereafter comes to its close, the *surah* refers to the present world, which is in itself a manifestation of the power and perfect planning of Allah, the Almighty: *"Let them reflect how the camel was created, how heaven was lifted up, how the mountains were hoisted, and how the earth was outstretched?"* These four short verses join together the boundaries of the world of the Arabs – the first people to be addressed by the Qur'an. They also group together the prominent ends of creation in the universe as they speak of the sky, earth, mountains and camels. The last of these stands for all animals, although the camel has its own distinctive features and a special value for the Arabs. All these aspects of creation – the sky, earth, mountains and animals – are always in front of man wherever he is. Whatever man's level of civilisation and scientific advancement, they remain within his world and within his sphere of consciousness. When he considers their roles, they suggest to him something of what lies beyond. In each of them there is a miracle of creation. The distinctive, incomparable work of the Creator is clear in them all, and this alone is sufficient to indicate the true faith. Hence the Qur'an directs to them the attention of every human being.

"Let them reflect how the camel was created." The camel was the principal animal for the Arab. It was his means of transport and it carried his belongings. It gave him food and drink. From its hair and

skin he made his clothes and dwellings. Besides, the camel is unique among all animals. Despite its strength, size and firm build, it is tame: a boy can manage it. It gives man a great service and, at the same time, it is inexpensive to keep and its food is easy to find. Moreover, it is the only animal to endure hunger, thirst, hard work and poor conditions. Its shape has also a special characteristic which is in perfect harmony with the portrait drawn here, and this will be discussed later on.

So, the Qur'an asks of its first audience to ponder on how the camel is made. This does not require them to undertake any difficult task or to discover any obscure field of science. *"Let them reflect how the camel was created."* Camels were a part of their world, and they only needed to look and consider how they were made most suitable for their role; how their shape and build fit perfectly with their environment and function. Man did not create camels, nor did camels create themselves. So, they must have been made by the Unique Maker whose work reflects His supreme ability and perfect planning, and proves His existence.

"How heaven was lifted up." The Qur'an repeatedly directs man's reflective faculties to think of the skies. The desert people should be the first to undertake this, because in the desert the sky has a much richer impact and is more inspiring – as if it has a unique existence. The sky – its days brilliant and beaming, its late afternoons captivating and fascinating, its sunsets charming and inspiring, its infinite nights, sparkling stars and friendly whispers, its sunrises live and animating – all this is certainly worth a good deal of reflection and contemplation. They should consider how it was lifted up. Who raised it so high without pillars to support it? Who scattered those innumerable stars? Who endowed it with its beauty and inspiration? They certainly did not lift it up, and it could not have been lifted by itself. A power is responsible for its creation and erection, and intelligent thought is enough to indicate Him.

"How the mountains were hoisted.' For the Arab in particular, a mountain is a refuge and a friend. In general, it always looks majestic and awesome. Next to a mountain, a man appears small and humble. It is natural for a man on a mountain to think of Allah, and feel himself nearer to Him. He feels a distinct detachment from the petty concerns of his worldly life. It was neither a vain whim nor a coincidence that Muhammad (peace be on him) should go to the cave in Mount Hira'a for periods of worship and contemplation (before he was

Surah 88   The Enveloper (*Al-Ghashiyah*)

given the message). It is also not surprising that those who want to spend a period in self-purification should seek to do so in a mountain. The reference here to the mountains speaks of them being *"hoisted"*, because this fits in perfectly with the image portrayed, which will be dealt with later on.

"How the earth was outstretched." The earth is obviously outstretched and made suitable for human life and its full and varied range of activities. Man could not have outstretched it, as it was completed long before his existence. So should not man reflect on and consider who outstretched the earth and made life feasible on it? Intelligent reflection on all these aspects will always inspire the minds and excite the souls into recognition of Allah, the Creator.

Perhaps we should pause a little to consider the perfection with which this image of the universe is portrayed. The Qur'an addresses man's religious conscience in a language of artistic beauty, and both coalesce in the believer's perception to bring the whole image in full relief. The scene portrayed includes the elevated heaven and the outstretched earth. Across such a boundless horizon stand the mountains. They are not described as firmly-rooted, but *"hoisted"*. The camels also stand with their upright humps. It is a majestic scene, vast and infinite, with merely two horizontal lines and two vertical ones. This manipulation of graphic description for the expression of ideas is a distinct characteristic of the Qur'anic style.

Having dealt first with the Hereafter, and pointed out some apparent aspects of the universe, the *surah* now addresses the Prophet, (peace be upon him), laying down the nature of his mission and limits of his role. It then concludes with a final reminder to mankind: *"Therefore give warning; your mission is only to warn them. You are not their overseer. But he who turns his back and disbelieves, Allah shall inflict on him the greatest chastisement. To Us they shall surely return, when We shall bring them to account."* Remind them then of the hereafter and the universe, and all there is in each of them. *"You are not their overseer."* You have no control over their hearts and you cannot compel them to adopt the faith. Men's hearts are in the hands of Allah, the Merciful. *Jihad* (struggle in the cause of Allah), which was later made a duty of the Prophet and all Muslims, did not aim at converting people to Islam by force. Its only aim was to remove all hindrances in the way of the Islamic call, so that it could be conveyed freely, and so that people were not prevented from listening to it or persecuted for doing so. That is the role the Prophet can fulfil: to

In the Shade of the Qur'an

remove the obstacles which prevent him conveying his message.

The notion that the Prophet's mission is confined to reminding and conveying the message is often repeated and stressed in the Qur'an. There are several reasons for this emphasis, the first of which is to relieve the Prophet of the heavy burden of directing the course of the Islamic call once he has conveyed it. He must leave it to Allah to decide its course. The urgency of the human yearning to win victory for the Truth and to get people to benefit from its absolute goodness is so keen that such repetition is required to make the advocates of this call distinguish their own desires and ambitions from their mission. When this distinction is clear, they proceed with the fulfilment of their duty regardless of the response and consequences. Thus the advocates of the call do not worry themselves over who has accepted the faith and who has rejected it. They are not charged with this burden, which becomes particularly heavy at times of adversity, when favourable response becomes a rarity and enemies abound.

But conveyance of the Message, which is the limit of the Prophet's task, is not the end of the matter. The disbelievers are not to be left alone. They cannot deny Allah and be safe. *"But he who turns his back and disbelieves, Allah shall inflict on him the greatest chastisement."* They will no doubt return to Allah, and He will inevitably administer their retribution. The *surah* ends on a decisive and final note: *"To Us they shall surely return, when We shall bring them to account."* The definition of the Prophet's role and the role of every subsequent advocate of Islam is thus completed. They have only to remind and the reckoning will be made by Allah.

It must be stressed, however, that the process of reminding includes the removal of hindrances so that people may be free to listen to the call. This is the aim of *Jihad* as it is understood from the Qur'an and the history of the Prophet. It is a process which neither admits negligence nor permits aggression.

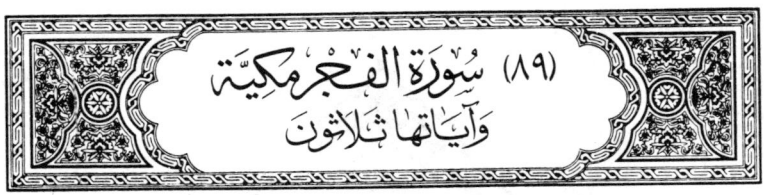

بِسْمِ ٱللَّهِ ٱلرَّحْمَٰنِ ٱلرَّحِيمِ

وَٱلْفَجْرِ ۝ وَلَيَالٍ عَشْرٍ ۝ وَٱلشَّفْعِ وَٱلْوَتْرِ ۝ وَٱلَّيْلِ إِذَا يَسْرِ ۝ هَلْ فِى ذَٰلِكَ قَسَمٌ لِّذِى حِجْرٍ ۝ أَلَمْ تَرَ كَيْفَ فَعَلَ رَبُّكَ بِعَادٍ ۝ إِرَمَ ذَاتِ ٱلْعِمَادِ ۝ ٱلَّتِى لَمْ يُخْلَقْ مِثْلُهَا فِى ٱلْبِلَٰدِ ۝ وَثَمُودَ ٱلَّذِينَ جَابُوا۟ ٱلصَّخْرَ بِٱلْوَادِ ۝ وَفِرْعَوْنَ ذِى ٱلْأَوْتَادِ ۝ ٱلَّذِينَ طَغَوْا۟ فِى ٱلْبِلَٰدِ ۝ فَأَكْثَرُوا۟ فِيهَا ٱلْفَسَادَ ۝ فَصَبَّ عَلَيْهِمْ رَبُّكَ سَوْطَ عَذَابٍ ۝ إِنَّ رَبَّكَ لَبِٱلْمِرْصَادِ ۝

فَأَمَّا ٱلْإِنسَٰنُ إِذَا مَا ٱبْتَلَىٰهُ رَبُّهُۥ فَأَكْرَمَهُۥ وَنَعَّمَهُۥ فَيَقُولُ رَبِّى أَكْرَمَنِ ۝ وَأَمَّا إِذَا مَا ٱبْتَلَىٰهُ فَقَدَرَ عَلَيْهِ رِزْقَهُۥ فَيَقُولُ رَبِّى أَهَٰنَنِ ۝ كَلَّا ۖ بَل لَّا تُكْرِمُونَ ٱلْيَتِيمَ ۝ وَلَا تَحَٰضُّونَ عَلَىٰ طَعَامِ ٱلْمِسْكِينِ ۝ وَتَأْكُلُونَ ٱلتُّرَاثَ أَكْلًا لَّمًّا ۝ وَتُحِبُّونَ ٱلْمَالَ حُبًّا جَمًّا ۝ كَلَّا إِذَا دُكَّتِ ٱلْأَرْضُ دَكًّا دَكًّا ۝ وَجَآءَ رَبُّكَ وَٱلْمَلَكُ صَفًّا صَفًّا ۝ وَجِا۟ىٓءَ يَوْمَئِذٍۭ بِجَهَنَّمَ ۚ يَوْمَئِذٍ يَتَذَكَّرُ ٱلْإِنسَٰنُ وَأَنَّىٰ لَهُ ٱلذِّكْرَىٰ ۝ يَقُولُ يَٰلَيْتَنِى قَدَّمْتُ لِحَيَاتِى ۝ فَيَوْمَئِذٍ لَّا يُعَذِّبُ عَذَابَهُۥٓ أَحَدٌ ۝ وَلَا يُوثِقُ وَثَاقَهُۥٓ أَحَدٌ ۝ يَٰٓأَيَّتُهَا ٱلنَّفْسُ ٱلْمُطْمَئِنَّةُ ۝ ٱرْجِعِىٓ إِلَىٰ رَبِّكِ رَاضِيَةً مَّرْضِيَّةً ۝ فَٱدْخُلِى فِى عِبَٰدِى ۝ وَٱدْخُلِى جَنَّتِى ۝

SURAH 89

THE DAWN
AL-FAJR

In the name of Allah, the Beneficent, the Merciful

By the dawn,
by the ten nights,
by that which is even and that which is odd,
by the night as it journeys on!
Is there not in that an oath for a man of sense?
Have you not heard how your Lord dealt with Aad
Who belonged to Iram and were tall as pillars,
the like of whom had not been created in the whole land?
And with Thamoud, who used to cut the rocks of the valley?
And with Pharoah, of the tent-pegs?
They were all tyrannical and transgressors,
and infested the land with much corruption.
Your Lord let loose on them, therefore, the scourge of His punishment.
Your Lord surely observes all.
As for man, whenever his Lord tries him with honour and with favours
   He bestows on him, he says, "My Lord has honoured me".
But whenever He tries him by stinting his means, then he says, "My
   Lord has left me humiliated."
No indeed; but you show no kindness to the orphan,

nor do you urge one another to feed the needy.
You devour the orphans' inheritance greedily,
and you love wealth passionately.
No indeed! When the earth is systematically levelled down,
and your Lord comes, with the angels rank on rank,
and Gehanna is, then, brought near,
Then man will remember, but how will that remembrance profit him?
He shall say, "Oh, would that I had prepared for my life!"
On that day none shall chastise as He chastises,
nor shall any bind with chains as He binds.
"Oh soul at peace, return to your Lord, well pleased and well pleasing.
Enter you among My servants!
Enter My Paradise!"

Surah 89   The Dawn (*Al-Fajr*)

The present *surah* follows, in general, the line of this thirtieth part of the Qur'an, inviting the human heart to faith, urging man to awake, meditate and follow the path of piety. It uses different kinds of emphasis, connotation and rhythm. It constitutes, nevertheless, a single harmonious piece of music varying in tones but maintaining the same cadence. Some of its scenes have a touch of quiet beauty and a light, pleasant rhythm. This is particularly evident in its opening, which describes certain charming scenes in the universe and provides at the same time an aura of worship and prayer: *"By the dawn; by the ten nights; by that which is even and that which is odd; by the night as it journeys on!"* Other scenes are tense and dramatic in both what they describe and their music, like this violent, frightening scene: *"When the earth is systematically levelled down; and your Lord comes, with the angels rank on rank; and Gehanna is, then, brought near, then man will remember, but how will that remembrance profit him? He shall say, 'Oh, would that I had prepared for my life!' On that day none shall chastise as He chastises; nor shall any bind with chains as He binds."* Others are pleasing, gentle and reassuring, striking perfect harmony between the subject matter and the rhythm. This is true of the ending of the *surah:* *"Oh soul at peace, return to your Lord, well pleased and well pleasing. Enter you among My servants! Enter My Paradise."* The *surah* also includes some references to the destruction that had befallen some insolent people of the past. The rhythm here is somewhere in between that of easy narration and that of violent destruction: *"Have you not heard how your Lord dealt with Aad who belonged to Iram and were tall as pillars . . . Your Lord surely observes all".* We also have an outline of some human concepts and values which are at variance with faith. This part has its own style and rhythms: *"As for man, whenever his Lord tries him with honour and with favours He bestows on him, he says, 'My Lord has honoured me'. But whenever He tries him by stinting his means then he says, 'My Lord has left me humiliated'."* A refutation of these erroneous concepts and values is provided through an exposition of the human conditions which give rise to them. Here we have two kinds of style and rhythm: *"You show no kindness to the orphan, nor do you urge one another to feed the needy. You devour the orphans' inheritance greedily, and you love wealth passionately."* It is noticeable that the latter style and rhythm serves as a bridge between that of the statement of the erroneous human ways and that of the explanation of their attendant fate. These verses are immediately followed by the scene of

In the Shade of the Qur'an

the earth as it is levelled down.

This brief survey reveals to us the numerous colours of the scenes described and explains the change of metre and rhyme according to the change of scenes. The *surah* is indeed an excellent example of an exceptionally beautiful style which is varied and harmonious at the same time.

"By the dawn, by the ten nights, by that which is even and that which is odd, by the night as it journeys on! Is there not in that an oath for a man of sense?" This opening of the *surah* groups together a few scenes and creatures who have familiar, pleasant, and transparent souls.

"By the dawn" refers to the time when life starts to breathe with ease and happiness, the time which gives a feeling of fresh, friendly companionship. The dormant world gradually wakes up in a prayer-like process.

"By the ten nights". The Qur'an does not specify which are the ten nights referred to here. Several explanations, however, have been advanced. Some say they are the early part of the month of *Thul-Hijja*; some say they are in *Al-Muharram*; and others state that they are the last ten nights of *Ramadan*. As it leaves them undefined, the Arabic reference acquires an added amiable effect. They are merely ten nights known to Allah but the expression connotes that these ten nights have a special character, as if they were living creatures with souls and there was mutual sympathy between them and us, transmitted through the Qur'anic verse.

"By that which is even and that which is odd". This verse adds an atmosphere of worship to that of the dawn and the ten nights. According to At-Tirmithi, the Prophet says: "Some prayers are of even number and some are odd." This is the most appropriate import to be attached to this verse, in the general context of the *surah*. It suggests a mutual response between the souls of the worshippers and those of the selected nights and the brightening dawn.

"By the night as it journeys on." The night here is personified as if it were journeying on in the universe like an insomniac walking on and on in the darkness, or a traveller who prefers to start his long journey at night. What a beautiful expression, describing a pleasant scene with a superb rhythm! The harmony between this verse and the dawn, the ten nights and the even and the odd is perfect. These are not mere words and expressions: they provide a feeling of the breeze of dawn, and the morning dew diffusing the fragrance of flowers.

Surah 89   The Dawn (*Al-Fajr*)

This is the effect of a gentle whisper to the heart and soul, and an inspiring touch upon the conscience. The beauty of this loving address is far superior to any poetic expression because it combines the beauty of originality with the statement of a certain fact. Hence it is concluded with a rhetorical question: *"Is there not in that an oath for a man of sense?"* The oath and the conviction are certainly there for anyone with a meditative mind. Although the positive meaning is intended, the interrogative form is used because it is gentler. Thus, harmony with the preceding gentle address is maintained.

The subject of the oath is omitted, but it is explained by the following discussion of tyranny and corruption. The chastisement inflicted by Allah on the insolent, tyrannical and corrupt peoples is a law of nature asserted by this oath. The assertion takes the form of a hint suitable to the generally light touches of this *surah*: *"Have you not heard how your Lord dealt with Aad who belonged to Iram and were tall as pillars, the like of whom had not been created in the whole land? And with the Thamoud, who used to cut the rocks of the valley? And with Pharoah, of the tent-pegs? They were all tyrannical and transgressors and infested the land with much corruption. Your Lord let loose on them, therefore, the scourge of His punishment. Your Lord surely observes all."*

The interrogative form in such a context is more effective in drawing the attention of the addressee, who is, in the first instance, the Prophet (peace be on him) and then to all those who may ponder over the fates of those nations of the past. The people of the Prophet's generation, who were the first to be addressed by the Qur'an, were aware of what happened to these nations. Their fates were also explained in reports and stories conveyed by one generation to another. The description of these fates as the deeds of Allah is comforting and reassuring to the believers. It was particularly so to those believers in Makka who, at the time when this *surah* was revealed were subjected by the disbelievers to relentless persecution and great hardship.

These short verses refer to the fates of the most powerful and despotic nations in ancient history. They speak of the earlier tribe of Aad of Iram, a branch of the extinct Arabs. They used to dwell at Ahqaf, a sandy piece of land in southern Arabia, midway between Yemen and Hadramout. Aad were nomadic people who used posts and pillars to erect their tents. They are described elsewhere in the Qur'an as extremely powerful and aggressive. Indeed, they were the most powerful and prestigious of all contemporary Arabian tribes:

In the Shade of the Qur'an

"The like of whom had not been created in the whole land." The distinction here is restricted to that particular age. *"And with Thamoud, who used to cut the rocks in the valley?"* The tribe of Thamoud used to live at Al-Hijr, a rocky tract in northern Arabia, on the road from Medina to Syria. Thamoud excelled in using rocks to build their palaces and homes. They also dug shelters and caves in the mountains. *"And with Pharoah, of the tent-pegs."* The term "tent-pegs" denotes the pyramids which are as firm in their construction as pegs well dug in the ground. The Pharoah referred to here is that despot who was Moses's contemporary.

All these people *"were tyrannical and transgressors, and infested the land with much corruption"*. Corruption is an inevitable result of tyranny, and it affects the tyrant and his subjects alike. Indeed, tyranny ruins all human relations. It forces human life out of its healthy, constructive and straight path and diverts it into a line which does not lead to the fulfilment of man's role as Allah's vicegerent on earth. Tyranny makes the tyrant captive of his own desires because he is uncommitted to any principle or standard and unrestrained within any reasonable limits. Thus the tyrant is always the first to be corrupted by his own tyranny. He assumes for himself a role other than that of a servant of Allah, entrusted with a specific mission. This is evident in Pharoah's boastful claim: *"I am your Lord, the most high."*[1]

Here we have an example of the corrupting influence of despotism in Pharoah's aspiration to something greater than the status of an obedient creature, an aspiration which made him very insolent. Tyranny also corrupts the masses, as it humiliates them and compels them to suppress their discontent and the hatred they feel towards the tyrant. It kills all feelings of human dignity and wastes all creative talents, which cannot flourish except in an atmosphere of freedom. A humiliated soul inevitably rots away and becomes a breeding ground for the germs of sickly desires. Hence, digression from the right path becomes the order of the day as clear vision becomes an impossibility. In such conditions no aspiration to a higher human standard can be entertained. The net result of all this is spreading corruption.

Tyranny also destroys all healthy standards and concepts because they constitute a threat to its existence. Hence, values are falsified

---

[1] The Qur'an. 79; 24.

Surah 89   The Dawn (*Al-Fajr*)

and standards are distorted so that the repulsive idea of despotism becomes acceptable as natural. This, in itself, is great corruption.

When the aforementioned people caused so much corruption, the remedy was, inevitably, a complete purge: *"Your Lord let loose on them, therefore, the scourge of His punishment. Your Lord surely observes all."* Allah is certainly aware of their deeds and He records them. So, when corruption increased, He punished the corrupt severely. The text connotes that the chastisement was very painful as it uses the term *"scourge"*, (or "whip" as the Arabic term literally means) and that it was in large supply as is indicated by the use of the phrase *"let loose"*. Thus the corrupted tyrants were made to suffer plentiful and painful retribution.

As the believer faces tyranny in any age or place, he feels great reassurance emanating from far beyond the fates of all those nations. He also feels a particular comfort as he reads the verse: *"Your Lord surely observes all."* Nothing passes unnoticed and nothing is forgotten. So, let the believers be always reassured that Allah will deal, in time, with all corruption and all tyranny.

Thus the *surah* provides some examples of what Allah may do about the cause of faith, which are totally different from the example of the "People of the Pit" outlined in *surah* 85, "The Constellations". All these stories are related for a definite purpose, namely, the education of the believers and their preparation to face whichever course Allah chooses for them. They will be, then, ready for all eventualities and equipped with the Divine reassurance as they submit themselves to Allah and let His will be done.

"Your Lord surely observes all." He sees, records, holds to account and rewards according to a strict and accurate measure which neither errs, nor exceeds the limits of justice. It is never deceived by appearances because it judges the essence of things. Human measures and standards are liable to all sorts of errors. Man sees nothing beyond the appearances unless he adopts the Divine measure.

"As for man, whenever his Lord tries him with honour and with favours He bestows on him, he says 'My Lord has honoured me'. But whenever He tries him by stinting his means, then he says, 'My Lord has left me humiliated'." Such is man's thinking about the various forms of trial Allah may set for him, be it comfort or hardship, wealth or scarcity. Allah may test him with comforts, honour, wealth or position but he does not realise the probationary nature of what he is

given. Rather he considers the gesture as proof that he deserves to be honoured by Allah and as evidence that He has chosen him for a special honour. It is a line of thinking which mistakes trial for reward and test for result. It imagines honour in the sight of Allah to be measured by the amount of worldly comforts given to a certain person. Allah may also try man by stinting his means, and man again mistakes trial for reward and imagines the test to be a retribution. He feels that Allah has made him poor in order to humiliate him.

In both situations the human concept is faulty. Wealth and poverty are two forms of a test Allah sets for His servants. A test with abundance reveals whether a man is humble and thankful to his Lord or arrogant and haughty, while a trial of the opposite kind reveals his patient acceptance or his irritability and fretfulness. A man's reward is given according to what he proves himself to be. What he is given or denied of worldly comforts is not his reward, and a man's standing in the sight of Allah is in no way related to his possessions, for He gives and denies worldly comforts regardless of whether a man is good or bad. A man devoid of faith cannot comprehend the wisdom behind Allah's action of giving worldly comforts or denying them. But when his mind is enlightened with faith and truth becomes apparent to him, he realises the triviality of worldly riches and the value of the reward after the test. So he works for this reward whether he is tried with abundance or scarcity of worldly riches. As he disregards the hollow considerations of wealth and poverty, he feels reassured about his fate and his position in the sight of Allah.

At the time of its revelation, the Qur'an was addressing a kind of people, common to all *Ignorant* societies, who lost all their relations with a world beyond our present life. Such people adopt this mistaken view about Allah's granting or denial of wealth, and apply a set of values which reserve all honour to money and social standing. Hence, their craving for wealth is irresistible. It makes them covetous, greedy and stingy. The Qur'an reveals their true feelings and states that their greed and stinginess are responsible for their inability to understand the true significance of a Divine trial by granting wealth or denying it. *"No, indeed; but you show no kindness to the orphan, nor do you urge one another to feed the needy. You devour the orphans' inheritance greedily, and you love wealth passionately."* The real issue is that when men are given wealth they do not fulfil the duties demanded of the wealthy. They do not look after a young orphan who has lost his father and becomes therefore in need of pro-

Surah 89   The Dawn (*Al-Fajr*)

tection and support. They do not urge one another to contribute to the general welfare. Such a mutual encouragement is indeed an important feature of the Islamic way of life. Since those people do not comprehend the significance of the trial, they do not even try to come out of it successfully by looking after the orphans and urging one another to feed the needy. On the contrary, they devour the orphans' inheritance greedily, and crave unrestrainedly for wealth. It is a craving which kills all nobility in their minds and leaves no room for generous gestures or goodwill towards the poor.

    In Makka, Islam was facing a situation characterised by a common urge to accumulate wealth by every possible means, an urge which makes hearts hard and unsympathetic. The weak positions of the orphans, and orphan girls in particular, tempted many to deprive them of their inheritance in different ways. The ardent love of wealth, the craving to accumulate it through usury and other means, was a distinctive feature of the Makkan society before the advent of Islam. Indeed, it is a distinctive feature of all *Ignorant* societies in all ages and in the present age.

    These few verses do not merely expose the true nature of their attitude. They also condemn this attitude and urge its discontinuation. The condemnation is evident in the repetition in these verses, their rhythm and metre which provide a strong feeling of the urge to accumulate wealth: *"You devour the orphans' inheritance greedily, and you love wealth passionately."*

    Once their erroneous concept of the trial with wealth and poverty is outlined, and their vile attitude has been exposed, there follows a stern warning about the Day of Judgement which comes after the result of the test is known. Here the rhythm is very powerful: *"No, indeed! When the earth is systematically levelled down, and your Lord comes, with the angels rank on rank, and Gehanna is, then, brought near, then man will remember, but how will that remembrance profit him? He shall say, 'Oh would that I had prepared for my life!' On that day none shall chastise as He chastises, nor shall any bind with chains as He binds."* The total destruction of all that is on earth and the systematic levelling down is one of the upheavals which will take place in the universe on the Day of Resurrection. Allah's coming with the angels is unexplained; but the expression overflows with connotations of reverence, awe and fear. The same applies to the bringing closer of Gehanna: we take it to mean that Gehanna will be on that day very close to its prospective dwellers. What actually happens and how it happens is part of the Divine knowledge Allah has chosen to withhold until that day. These verses, with their captivating rhythm and sharp notes, portray nevertheless a scene which strikes fear into the hearts, and makes it apparent in the eyes. The earth is being systematically levelled down: Allah the Almighty sits to judge everyone: the angels stand there rank on rank and Gehanna is brought near and set in readiness. At that moment *"man will remember"*. Man, who lived unaware of the wisdom behind the trial with worldly riches or with deprivation; who devoured the inheritance of orphans greedily; who craved for money and did not care for the orphans or the needy; who tyrannised, spread corruption and turned away from the Divine guidance will then remember the truth and take account of what he beholds. But alas! it is too late: *"but how will that remembrance profit him?"* The time for remembrance is over, so remembrance on the Day of Judgement and Reward will not profit anybody. It serves merely as an act of grief for a chance given but not taken in the first life.

When man is fully aware of the true nature of his situation he says despairingly, *"Oh, would that I had prepared for my life!"* For the true life, the only one that deserves the name is indeed the life hereafter. It is the one which is worth preparing for. *"Oh, would that I had . . ."* It is a sigh of evident regret and grief, but it is the most a man can do for himself in that second life.

The *surah* goes on to portray the fate of that man after his desperate sigh and useless wish: *"On that day none shall chastise as He chastises, nor shall any bind with chains as He binds."* It is Allah, the Supreme Victor, the Almighty Who inflicts His incomparable chastisements, and Who binds as no one can bind. The Divine punishment and binding are explained in detail in other parts of the Qur'an as it outlines various scenes of the Day of Judgement. But the reference to them here is very brief, stressing mainly their incomparability to human chastisement and binding. The reference to the Divine punishment here brings to mind the earlier reference to human tyranny in the given examples of Aad, Thamoud and Pharoah. Those tyrants are stated to have spread much corruption in the land, which includes the infliction of physical torture on people and binding them with chains and ropes. These last verses serve as an address to the Prophet and the believers, reminding them that their Lord will chastise and chain those who used to torture people and chain them. But the two kinds of punishment and chaining are entirely different.

Surah 89   The Dawn (*Al-Fajr*)

Meagre is the torture that any creature can administer, but great is that inflicted by the Creator. Let the tyrants continue with their punishment and persecution; they will have their turn and be the sufferers of a punishment which is beyond all imagination.

Amidst all this unimaginable horror comes an address from on high to the believers: *"Oh soul at peace, return to your Lord, well pleased and well pleasing. Enter you among My servants! Enter My Paradise!"* It is a tender, compassionate and reassuring address: *"Oh soul at peace"*. It speaks of freedom and ease, after the earlier reference to chains and affliction: *"return to your Lord"*. After your alienation on earth and your separation from the one you belong to, return now to your Lord with Whom you have strong ties: *"well-pleased and well-pleasing."* It is a gentle address which spreads an atmosphere of compassion, and satisfaction. *"Enter you among My servants"*, among those servants chosen to enjoy this Divine grace. *"Enter My Paradise"*, to receive Allah's mercy and protection. As it opens, this address generates an aura of heaven: *"Oh soul at peace"*. The believer's is a soul at peace with its Lord, certain of its way, certain of its fate. It is a soul satisfied in all eventualities: happiness or affliction, wealth or poverty. It entertains no doubts; it is free from transgressions. The gentle music adds a feeling of intimacy and peace. The majestic face of Allah, the Compassionate, the Merciful, with all His splendour looks from above.

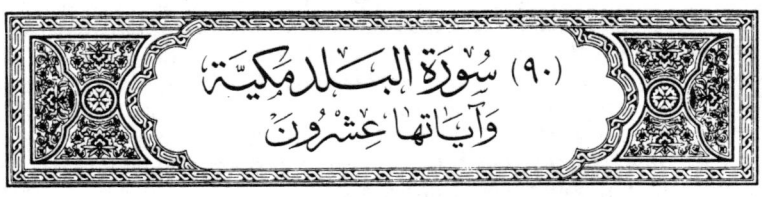

(٩٠) سورة البلد مكية وآياتها عشرون

بِسْمِ ٱللَّهِ ٱلرَّحْمَٰنِ ٱلرَّحِيمِ

لَآ أُقْسِمُ بِهَٰذَا ٱلْبَلَدِ ۝ وَأَنتَ حِلٌّۢ بِهَٰذَا ٱلْبَلَدِ ۝ وَوَالِدٍ وَمَا وَلَدَ ۝ لَقَدْ خَلَقْنَا ٱلْإِنسَٰنَ فِى كَبَدٍ ۝ أَيَحْسَبُ أَن لَّن يَقْدِرَ عَلَيْهِ أَحَدٌ ۝ يَقُولُ أَهْلَكْتُ مَالًا لُّبَدًا ۝ أَيَحْسَبُ أَن لَّمْ يَرَهُۥٓ أَحَدٌ ۝ أَلَمْ نَجْعَل لَّهُۥ عَيْنَيْنِ ۝ وَلِسَانًا وَشَفَتَيْنِ ۝ وَهَدَيْنَٰهُ ٱلنَّجْدَيْنِ ۝ فَلَا ٱقْتَحَمَ ٱلْعَقَبَةَ ۝ وَمَآ أَدْرَىٰكَ مَا ٱلْعَقَبَةُ ۝ فَكُّ رَقَبَةٍ ۝ أَوْ إِطْعَٰمٌ فِى يَوْمٍ ذِى مَسْغَبَةٍ ۝ يَتِيمًا ذَا مَقْرَبَةٍ ۝ أَوْ مِسْكِينًا ذَا مَتْرَبَةٍ ۝ ثُمَّ كَانَ مِنَ ٱلَّذِينَ ءَامَنُوا۟ وَتَوَاصَوْا۟ بِٱلصَّبْرِ وَتَوَاصَوْا۟ بِٱلْمَرْحَمَةِ ۝ أُو۟لَٰٓئِكَ أَصْحَٰبُ ٱلْمَيْمَنَةِ ۝ وَٱلَّذِينَ كَفَرُوا۟ بِـَٔايَٰتِنَا هُمْ أَصْحَٰبُ ٱلْمَشْـَٔمَةِ ۝ عَلَيْهِمْ نَارٌ مُّؤْصَدَةٌۢ ۝

SURAH 90

THE CITY
AL-BALAD

In the name of Allah, the Beneficent, the Merciful.

I swear by this city,
this city in which you yourself are a dweller,
by sire and offspring:
indeed, We have created man in affliction.
Does he think that none has power over him?
"I have wasted vast riches," he says.
Does he think that none observes him?
Have We not given him two eyes,
a tongue, and two lips,
and shown him the two paths.
Yet he has not attempted the Ascent.
Would that you knew what the Ascent is.
It is the freeing of a slave,
or the feeding, in a day of hunger,
of an orphaned near of kin,
or a needy man in misery.
Moreover, it is to be of those who believe and counsel one another
    to be steadfast, and enjoin mercy on one another.
Those who do this shall be on the right hand.
And those who deny Our revelations
shall be on the left hand,
with Hell-fire close above them.

In the Shade of the Qur'an

This short *surah* touches on a large number of facts which are of central importance in human life, in a style characterised by its powerful allusions and revealing touches. Such a number of facts is not easy to combine in any form of concise writing except that of the Qur'an, with its unique method of hitting the right chords of the human heart with such swift and penetrating strokes.

The *surah* opens with a forceful vow asserting an inherent fact of human life: *"I swear by this city, this city in which you yourself are a dweller, by sire and offspring: indeed, We have created man in affliction"*. The city is Makka, the sacred House of Allah which was the first temple ever to be erected on this earth as a place of peace where people put down their weapons and forget their quarrels. They meet inside in peace; each is sacred to all. Even the plants, the birds and all creatures that happen to be in this House enjoy full and complete security. It is the House built by Abraham, the father of Ishmail, who is the grandfather of all the Arabs and the Muslims. Allah then honours His Prophet, Muhammad, by mentioning him and his residence in Makka, a fact which adds to the sanctity of the city, its honour and glory. This is a point of great significance in this context; for the believers were violating the sanctity of the House by harassing the Prophet and the Muslims in it. But the House is sacred and the Prophet's dwelling in its neighbourhood makes it even more so. Allah's oath by this city and by the Prophet's residence in it adds even more to its sacredness and glory, which consequently makes the attitude of the disbelievers grossly impertinent and objectionable on all counts. For they claim to be the custodians of the House, the descendants of Ishmail, and the followers of Abraham.

This last reference supports the inclination to take the phrase, *"by sire and offspring"* to refer to Abraham and Ishmail in particular. This reading includes in the oath the Prophet, the city where he lives, the founder of the House and his offspring. However, it does not preclude that the statement can be a general one, referring to the phenomenon of reproduction which preserves the human race. This reference may be taken as an introduction to the discussion of the nature of man, which is indeed the subject matter of the *surah*.

In his commentary on this *surah* in his *"Juz'u 'Amma"*, the late Sheikh Muhammad Abduh, makes a fine remark which is useful to quote here:

"Allah then swears by parent and children to draw our attention to

Surah 90   The City (*Al-Balad*)

the great importance of the stage of reproduction in life, and to the infinite wisdom and perfection which this stage involves. It also emphasises the great suffering encountered by parent and offspring during the process from its inception up to its conclusion, when the newcomer achieves a certain degree of development.

"Think of plants and the tough opposition met by a seed of a plant in the process of growth, until it adapts to the various factors of climate. Think of its attempts to absorb the food necessary for its survival from its surroundings, till it develops branches and leaves. It then prepares for the production of a similar seed or seeds that will repeat its function and add to the beauty of the world around it. Think of all this then consider the more advanced forms of animal and human life and you will see something much greater and far more wonderful concerning reproduction. You will have a feeling of the hardship and suffering met by all sires and offspring for the sake of preserving the species and the beauty of this world. . . ."

The oath reaffirms an intrinsic fact in human life: *"Indeed, We have created man in affliction"*. Indeed, man's life is a process of continued hardship that never ends, as stated in *surah* 84, ("The Rending"), *"O man, you are striving to your Lord laboriously, and you will duly meet Him"*. No sooner does the first living cell settle in the mother's womb than it starts to encounter affliction and to work hard in order to prepare for itself the right conditions for its survival, with the permission of its Lord. It continues to do so until it is ready for the process of birth, which is a great ordeal for both the mother and the baby. Before the baby finally sees the light it undergoes a great deal of pushing and squeezing to the point of near suffocation in its passage out of the womb.

A stage of harder endurance and greater suffering follows. The newborn baby begins to breathe the air, which is a new experience. It opens its mouth and inflates its lungs for the first time with a cry which tells of the hard start. The digestive system and the blood circulation then start to function in a manner which is totally unfamiliar. Then it starts to empty its bowels, encountering great difficulty in adapting its system to this new function. Indeed, every new step or movement is attended by suffering. If one watches this baby when it begins to crawl and walk, one sees the kind of effort required to execute such minor and elementary movements.

Thus, affliction continues with teething, developing the abilities of standing up, walking firmly, learning and thinking and with every single new experience in the same way as in the case of crawling and walking.

Then the roads diverge and the struggle takes different forms. One person struggles with his muscles, another with his mind and a third with his soul. One toils for a mouthful of food or a rag to dress himself with, another to double or treble his wealth. One person strives to achieve a position of power or influence and another for the sake of Allah. One struggles for the sake of satisfying lusts and desires, and the other for the sake of his faith or ideology. One strives but achieves no more than Hell and another strives for Paradise. Everyone is carrying his own burden and climbing his own hills to arrive finally at the meeting place appointed by Allah, where the wretched shall endure their worst suffering while the blessed enjoy their endless happiness.

Affliction, life's foremost characteristic, takes various forms and shapes but it is always judged by its eventual results. The loser is the one who ends up suffering more affliction in the hereafter, and the prosperous is the one whose striving qualifies him to be released from his affliction and ensures him the ultimate repose under his Lord's shelter. Yet there is some reward for the different kinds of struggle which people endure. The one who labours for a great cause differs from the one who labours for a trivial one, in the amount and the quality of gratification each of them gains from his labour and sacrifice.

Having established this fact concerning human nature and human life, the *surah* goes on to discuss some of the claims that man makes and some of the concepts underlying his behaviour. *"Does he think that none has power over him? 'I have wasted vast riches', he says. Does he think that none observes him?"* This creature, man, whose suffering and struggling never come to an end, forgets his real nature and becomes so conceited with what Allah has given him of power, ability, skill and prosperity that he behaves as if he is not accountable for what he does. He indulges in oppression, tyranny, victimisation and exploitation, trying to acquire enormous wealth. He corrupts himself and others in total disregard of anything of value. Such is the character of a man whose heart is stripped of faith. When he is called upon to spend for good causes, he says, *"I have wasted vast riches"* and given more than enough. *"Does he think that none observes him?"* Has he forgotten that Allah is watching over him? He sees what he has spent and for what purposes. But man still ignores this, thinking that Allah is unaware of what he has done.

In view of man's arrogance, which makes him believe that he is invincible, and in view of his meanness and claim of having spent abundantly, the Qur'an puts before him the bounties Allah has bestowed upon him which are manifested in his make-up abilities, although he has depreciated them. *"Have We not given him two eyes, a tongue and two lips and shown him the two paths."*

Man is conceited because he feels himself powerful, but he is granted his power by Allah. He is mean with his wealth while Allah is the One Who provided him with it. He neither follows the right guidance nor shows his gratitude, although Allah has given him the means to do so. He has given him eyes which are marvellous, precise and powerful. He has also granted him the faculty of speech and the means of expression, *"a tongue and two lips"*. He has equipped him with the ability to distinguish good from evil, and right from wrong, *"and shown him the two paths"*, so that he may choose between them; for in his make-up there exists the ability to take either way. It is Allah's will that man should be given such ability and such freedom of choice, to perfect His scheme of creation which assigns to every creature its role in life and equips it with the means necessary for its fulfilment.

This verse explains the essence of human nature. In fact, the basis of the "Islamic Psychological Theory" is contained in this verse as well as the following verse of *surah* 91, "The Sun": *"By the soul and Him who moulded it and inspired it with knowledge of wickedness and piety. Successful is the one who keeps it pure, and ruined is the one who corrupts it."*

These are the favours bestowed on man in his actual make-up to help him to follow the right guidance: his eyes with which he recognises the evidence of Allah's might and the signs indicated all over this universe which should prompt him to adopt the faith, and his tongue and lips which are his means of speech and expression. One word sometimes does the job of a sword or a shotgun and can be even more effective than either. It may, on the other hand, plunge a man in the fire of Hell. Muaath ibn Jabal said, "I was with the Prophet on a journey. One day I was walking beside him when I said, 'Messenger of Allah! point out to me something I may do to take me to Paradise and keep me away from Hell!' He said, 'You have indeed asked about something great, yet it is quite attainable by those for whom Allah has made it easy. Worship Allah assigning to Him no partner, offer your prayers regularly, pay out what is due to the poor of your money, fast in the month of *Ramadhan* and offer pilgrimage.' The Prophet then said, 'Shall I point out to you the gates of good?' I said, 'Yes, Messenger of Allah, please do.' He said, 'Fasting is a safeguard and a means of protecting yourself; charity erases your errors just as water extinguishes a burning fire; and your praying in the late hours of the night is the sign of piety.' He then recited the verse, *'(those) who forsake their beds as they call on their Lord in fear and in hope; and who give in charity of what We have bestowed on them. No soul knows what bliss and comfort is in store for these as reward for their labours.'* [1] The Prophet then went on: 'Shall I tell you what the heart of the matter is, its backbone and its highest grade?' I said, 'Yes, Messenger of Allah, please do.' He said, 'The heart is *Islam*, i.e. submission to Allah, the backbone is prayers, and the highest grade is *Jihad*, i.e. struggle for the cause of Islam.' He then said, 'Shall I tell you what commands all these?' I said, 'Yes, Messenger of Allah, please do.' He said, 'Control this,' and he pointed to his tongue. I said, 'Are we, Prophet of Allah, really accountable for what we say?' He said 'Watch what you are saying.[2] For what else are people dragged on their faces in Hell apart from what their tongues yield?' (Related by Ahmad, At-Tirmithi, An-Nissaie and Ibn Majah).''

All these bounties have not motivated man to attempt the Ascent that stands between him and Paradise. Allah explains the nature of the Ascent in the following verses, *"Yet he (man) has not attempted the Ascent. Would that you knew what the Ascent is. It is the freeing of a slave, or the feeding, in a day of hunger, an orphaned near of kin, or a needy man in misery. Moreover, it is to be of those who believe and counsel one another to be steadfast and enjoin mercy on one another. Those who do this shall be on the right hand."*

This is the Ascent which man, except those who aid themselves

---

[1] The Qur'an. *32; 16*.
[2] The Arabic expression here would be translated literally: "May your mother lose you". The expression, however, has lost its literal meaning and serves as simple exclamation which may be rendered in several forms as suits the context – Translator's note.

Surah 90   The City (*Al-Balad*)

with faith, refrains from attempting, and which separates him from Paradise. If he crosses it he will arrive! Putting it that way serves as a powerful incentive and a stimulus to the human heart to take up the challenge since the Ascent has been clearly indicated and marked as the obstacle depriving him of such an enormous fortune. The importance of attempting the Ascent in the sight of Allah is then emphasised to encourage man to scale it no matter what effort of struggle he may have to put into this. For struggle he must, in any case. But if he attempts it, his struggle will not be wasted but will bring him favourable results.

Then follows an explanation of this Ascent and its nature by means of, first, enumeration of examples of actions which were totally lacking in these particular surroundings that the call of Islam was facing at the time: the freeing of slaves and the feeding of the poor who were subjected to the cruelty of that ungracious and greedy society. It then adds what is applicable to all ages and societies and needed by all who attempt the Ascent: *"Moreover it is to be of those who believe and counsel one another to be steadfast, and enjoin mercy on one another."*

This *surah* was revealed in Makka when Islam was surrounded by powerful enemies and the state that would implement its laws was non-existent. Slavery was widespread in Arabia and the world at large. The treatment meted out to slaves was brutally severe. When some of the slaves or former slaves, like Ammar ibn Yasser and his family, Bilal ibn Rabah, Suhaib and others, accepted Islam their plight became worse, and their cruel masters subjected them to unbearable torture. It then became clear that the only way to save them was to buy them from their masters. Abu Bakr, the Prophet's companion, was, as usual, the first to rise to the occasion, with all the boldness and gallantry it required.

"Ibn Ishaaq related: 'Bilal, Abu Bakr's servant, was owned by some individual of the clan of Jumah as he was born a slave. He was, however, a genuine Muslim and clean-hearted. Umayyah ibn Khalaf, the Jumah master, used to take Bilal out when it became unbearably hot and order him to be laid down on his back on the hot sand of Makka and cause a massive rock to be placed on his chest. Then, he would say to Bilal that he would stay like that until he died or renounced Muhammad and accepted as deities the idols called Al-Lat and Al-'Uzza, the goddesses of the pagan Arabs.

In the Shade of the Qur'an

Under all that pressure, Bilal would simply say, 'One, One,' meaning that there is only one God.'

"One day, Abu Bakr passed by and saw Bilal in that condition. He said to Umayyah 'Do you not fear Allah as you torture this helpless soul? How long can you go on doing this?' Umayyah replied, 'You spoiled him, so you save him.' Abu Bakr said, 'I will. I have a black boy who follows your religion but he is stronger and more vigorous than Bilal. What do you say to an exchange deal?' Umayyah said, 'I accept.' Abu Bakr said, 'Then he is yours'. When Abu Bakr took Bilal he set him free.

"While in Makka, before emigration to Medina, Abu Bakr freed a total of seven people: Amir ibn Faheerah, who fought in the battle of Badr and was killed in the battle of Bir Ma'oonah, was the only other man freed by Abu Bakr. The other five were all women. The first two were Umm Obais and Zaneerah, who lost her eyesight when she was freed. Some people of Quraysh claimed that the two idols Al-Lat and Al-'Uzza caused her loss of her eyesight. Zaneerah said, 'What rubbish! Al-Lat and Al-'Uzza are absolutely powerless'. Allah then willed that she recover her eyesight. Abu Bakr also freed a woman called An-Nahdiyyah and her daughter, who belonged to a woman of the clan of Abduddar. One day he passed by the two women as their mistress was sending them on an errand to prepare some flour. As she gave them her instructions, she declared: 'By God, I will never set you free'. Abu Bakr said to her 'Release yourself of your oath'. She rejoined: 'It was you who spoilt them. Why don't you set them free?' He said, 'How much do you want for them?' She named her price. He said, 'It is a deal, and they are free.' He turned to the two women and told them to give the woman her flour back. They suggested that they should finish preparing it for her first and he agreed. The fifth woman was a Muslim slave of the clan of Muammal. She was being tortured by Umar ibn Al-Khattab, who was then still a disbeliever. He beat her until he was tired and said to her, 'I apologize to you. I have only stopped beating you because I am bored', to which she replied, 'And so Allah shall thwart you.' Abu Bakr bought her and set her free."

Ibn Ishaaq related: "Abu Quhafa, Abu Bakr's father, said to him 'I see you, son, freeing some weak slaves. Why don't you free some strong men who can defend and protect you?' Abu Bakr replied, 'I am only doing this for the sake of Allah, father.'" Thus Abu Bakr scaled the Ascent by freeing those helpless souls, for the sake of Allah. The attendant circumstances in that particular society make such an action one of the most important steps towards scaling the Ascent.

"Or the feeding, in a day of hunger, of an orphaned near of kin, or a needy man in misery." The time of famine and hunger when food becomes so scarce, is a time when the reality of faith is tested. For the orphans in that greedy, miserly and ungracious society were oppressed and mistreated even by their relatives. The Qur'an is full of verses which urge people to treat orphans well. This in itself is a measure of the cruelty of the orphans' surroundings. Good treatment for the orphans is also urged in the Medinan *surahs* as they outline the rules of inheritance, custody and marriage, especially in *surahs* 2 "The Cow" and 4 "Women". The same can be said of feeding the needy on a day of famine, which is portrayed here as another step for scaling the Ascent. For this is again a test which reveals the characteristics of the believer, such as mercy, sympathy, co-operation and lack of selfishness. It also reveals the extent of one's fear of Allah.

These two steps, freeing slaves and feeding the needy, are mentioned in the *surah* as necessary in the existing situation at the time of revelation; yet their implications are general, which accounts for their being mentioned first. They are followed by the widest and most important step of all, *"Moreover, it is to be of those who believe and counsel one another to be steadfast, and enjoin mercy on one another."* The conjunction in the Arabic text is "then" but it does not signify here any time ordering; it is used simply as introduction to the statement of the most important and most valuable step of all towards scaling the Ascent. For what would be the value of freeing slaves or feeding the hungry without faith? It is faith which gives such actions their value and their weight in the sight of Allah, because it relates them to a profound and consistent system. Thus good deeds are no longer the result of a momentary impulse. Their aim is not any social reputation or self-interest.

Steadfastness is an important element in the general context of faith as well as in the particular context of attempting the Ascent. That people should counsel each other to be steadfast is a higher level than that of being steadfast. It is a practical demonstration of the solidarity of the believers as they co-operate closely to carry out their duties as believers in Allah. The society formed by the believers is an integrated structure whose elements share the same feelings and the same awareness of the need of exerting hard efforts in order to establish the Divine system on earth and to carry out its duties fully. Hence, they counsel each other to persevere as they shoulder their common responsibilities. They rally to support one another in order to achieve their common objective. This is something more than the perseverance by the individual although it builds on it, which indicates the individual's role in the believers' society, namely, that he must be an element of strength and a source of hope and comfort to the whole society.

The same applies to enjoining each other to be merciful, which is a grade higher than simply being merciful. Thus the spirit of mercy spreads among the believers as they consider such mutual counselling an individual and communal duty in the fulfilment of which all co-operate. Hence, the idea of "community" is evident in this injunction, as it is emphasized elsewhere in the Qur'an and in the traditions of the Prophet. This idea is central to the concept of the religion of Islam which is a religion and a way of life of a community. Nevertheless, the responsibility and accountability of the individual are clearly defined and strongly emphasised. Those who scale the Ascent, as defined here in the Qur'an, shall have their dwelling place on the right hand, which indicates that they will enjoy a happy recompense for what they do in this life.

"And those who deny Our revelations shall be on the left hand, with Hell-fire close above them." There is no need here to identify this group with more than *"those who deny Our revelations"*, as this is enough to settle the issue. Nothing can be good if coupled with disbelief, and all evil is contained and encompassed by the denial of Allah. There is no point in saying that this group do not free slaves or give food to the needy, and, moreover, they deny Our revelations. For such a denial renders worthless any action they may do. They dwell on the left hand, which indicates their degradation and disgrace. These people cannot scale the Ascent.

"With Hell-fire close above them," that is, they are encircled by it either in the sense that they are locked within it, or in the sense that it is their eternal abode. Its being close above them gives them no chance of breaking away from it. The two meanings are quite interrelated.

Surah 90   The City (*Al-Balad*)

These are then the fundamental facts concerning human life laid down from the point of view of faith, in a limited space but with great power and clarity. This remains the distinctive characteristic of the Qur'anic style which is unique.

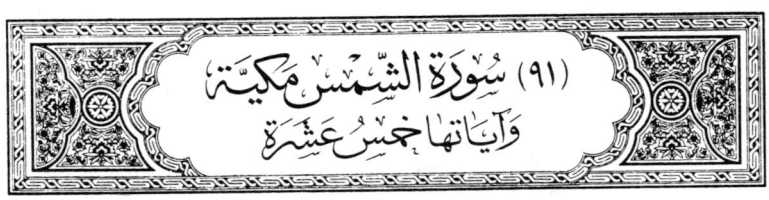

بِسْمِ اللَّهِ الرَّحْمَنِ الرَّحِيمِ

وَالشَّمْسِ وَضُحَاهَا ۝ وَالْقَمَرِ إِذَا تَلَاهَا ۝ وَالنَّهَارِ إِذَا جَلَّاهَا ۝ وَاللَّيْلِ إِذَا يَغْشَاهَا ۝ وَالسَّمَاءِ وَمَا بَنَاهَا ۝ وَالْأَرْضِ وَمَا طَحَاهَا ۝ وَنَفْسٍ وَمَا سَوَّاهَا ۝ فَأَلْهَمَهَا فُجُورَهَا وَتَقْوَاهَا ۝ قَدْ أَفْلَحَ مَنْ زَكَّاهَا ۝ وَقَدْ خَابَ مَنْ دَسَّاهَا ۝ كَذَّبَتْ ثَمُودُ بِطَغْوَاهَا ۝ إِذِ انْبَعَثَ أَشْقَاهَا ۝ فَقَالَ لَهُمْ رَسُولُ اللَّهِ نَاقَةَ اللَّهِ وَسُقْيَاهَا ۝ فَكَذَّبُوهُ فَعَقَرُوهَا فَدَمْدَمَ عَلَيْهِمْ رَبُّهُمْ بِذَنْبِهِمْ فَسَوَّاهَا ۝ وَلَا يَخَافُ عُقْبَاهَا ۝

SURAH 91

THE SUN
ASH-SHAMS

In the name of Allah, the Beneficent, the Merciful.

By the sun and his morning brightness,
by the moon as she follows him,
by the day which reveals its splendour,
by the night when it enshrouds him,
by the heaven and its construction,
by the earth and its spreading,
by the soul and its moulding
and inspiration with knowledge of wickedness and piety.
Successful is the one who keeps it pure,
and ruined is the one who corrupts it.
In their insolence the people of Thamoud denied the truth,
when their most-wretched broke forth.
The Messenger of Allah said to them:
"The she-camel of Allah, let her have her drink".
But they cried lies to him, and hamstrung her.
For that sin their Lord let loose His scourge upon them,
and razed their city to the ground.
He fears not what may follow.

In the Shade of the Qur'an

This *surah*, which maintains a single rhyme and keeps the same musical beat throughout, starts with several aesthetic touches which seem to spring out from the surrounding universe and its phenomena. These phenomena form the framework which encompasses the great truth which is the subject matter of the *surah*, namely, the nature of man, his inherent abilities, his choice of his line of action, and his responsibility in determining his own fate.

This *surah* also refers to the story of the tribe of Thamoud and their negative attitude to the warnings of Allah's messenger to them, and their killing of the she-camel; and finally the collapse of Thamoud and their complete annihilation. This comes as an example of the unpromising prospects which await those who corrupt their souls instead of keeping them pure and do not confine themselves within the limits of piety. *"Successful is the one who keeps it pure, and ruined is the one who corrupts it."*

"By the sun and his morning brightness, by the moon as she follows him, by the day which reveals its splendour, by the night when it enshrouds him, by the heaven and its construction, by the earth and its spreading, by the soul and its moulding and inspiration with knowledge of wickedness and piety. Successful is the one who keeps it pure, and ruined is the one who corrupts it."

Allah swears by these objects and universal phenomena as He swears by the human soul, how it is fashioned and how it is inspired. The oath gives these creatures an added significance and draws man's attention to them. Man ought to contemplate these phenomena and try to appreciate their value and the purpose of their creation.

There exists in fact, some kind of a special language through which the human heart communicates with the universe and its marvellous scenes and phenomena. This language is part of human nature. It is a language which does not use sounds and articulation. It is a communication to the hearts and an inspiration to the souls which come alive whenever man looks up to the universe for an inspiring touch or a cheerful sight. Hence, the Qur'an frequently urges man to reflect upon the surrounding universe. It does this in various ways, sometimes directly and sometimes with hints and incidental touches and stimuli, as in this case where some phenomena of the universe are made the subject of Allah's oath, in order to serve as a framework for what follows in the *surah*. These explicit directives and indirect hints

Surah 91   The Sun (*Ash-Shams*)

are very frequent in this thirtieth part of the Qur'an. There is hardly one *surah* in it which does not encourage man, in one way or another, to communicate with the universe, in their secret language, so that he may appreciate its signs and understand its address.

Here we have an inspiring oath by morning. The oath also specifies the time when the sun rises above the horizon, when it is indeed at its most beautiful. Indeed, mid-morning is, in winter, a time for refreshing warmth. In summer, it is the time when the atmosphere is just mild and fresh before the blazing heat of midday sets in, and the sun is at its clearest.

The oath is also by the moon as she follows the sun and spreads her beautiful and clear light. Between the moon and the human heart there is an age-long fascination that is well established in men's inmost souls. It is a fascination that is born anew everytime the two meet. The moon issues her own special whispers and inspirations to the human heart, and she sings her songs of praise to the Creator, which a poet can almost hear through the tenderness of moonlight. On a clear moonlit night, one can almost feel oneself sailing through the moonlight, clearing off one's worries and enjoying a perfect bliss as one feels the hand of the Maker beyond this perfect creation.

Allah also swears by the day as it exposes the sun. The Arabic wording of this verse makes the pronoun preceding 'splendour' ambiguous. Initially, one tends to take it as if it refers to the sun. The general context, however, suggests that it refers to the earth as it is lit by the sun. This method of changing referents is widely employed in the Qur'an when the change is easily noticeable when the subject matter is familiar. Here we have a discreet allusion to the fact that sunlight does reveal the earth and has a great effect on human life, as is well known. Our familiarity with the sun and his light makes us tend to overlook his beauty and function. This Qur'anic hint reawakens us to this magnificent daily spectacle.

The same applies to the following verse, *"by the night when it enshrouds him"*, that is, the opposite of what happens in the day. Night time is like a screen that covers and hides everything. It also has its own impressions on everyone, and its impact on human life is not less important than that of daytime.

Allah then swears *"by the heaven and its construction."* When heaven is mentioned, our immediate thoughts go to the huge dome-like sky above us in which we see the stars and the planets moving each in its orbit. But we are in fact uncertain of the exact nature of heaven. However, what we see above us does bear the idea of building and construction because it looks to us a firm and solid whole. As to how it is built and what keeps it together as it floats in the infinite space, we have no answer. All that has been advanced in this field is only theory that is liable to be invalidated or modified. We are certain, however, that the hand of Allah is the one which holds this structure together, as emphasised elsewhere in the Qur'an: *"Allah holds the heavens and the earth that they do not collapse. Should they collapse none could hold them back but He."*[1] This is the only definite and absolute truth about the matter.

The oath then includes the earth and its spreading as preparatory to the emergence of life. Indeed, human and animal life would not have been possible had the earth not been spread. It is indeed the special characteristics and the natural laws which Allah has incorporated in the making of this earth that make life on it possible, according to His will and plan. It appears that if any of these laws were to be violated or upset, life on earth would have been impossible or would have changed its course. The most important of these is perhaps the spreading of the earth which is also mentioned in *surah* 79 ("The Pluckers"): *"After that He spread out the earth. He brought out water from it, and brought forth its pastures."*[2]

The *surah* moves on to state the basic truth about man, and relates this truth to the various phenomena of the universe, for man is one of the most remarkable wonders in this harmonious creation: *"by the soul and its moulding and inspiration with knowledge of wickedness and piety. Successful is the one who keeps it pure, and ruined is the one who corrupts it."*

These four verses in conjunction with a verse in the preceding *surah*, "The City": *"And (We have) shown him the two paths"*, and a verse in *surah* 76, "Man", which says: *"We (Allah) have shown him the right path, be he grateful or ungrateful,"*[3] constitute the basis of the "Psychological Theory of Islam". They supplement the verses which point out the duality in man's make-up in *surah* 38, "Sad", which says: *"Your Lord said to the angels, 'I am creating man from clay. When I have fashioned him, and breathed of My spirit into him, kneel down and prostrate yourselves before him.'"*[4] These verses also sup-

---

[1] The Qur'an. 35; 41.
[2] Ibid. 79; 30.
[3] Ibid. 76; 3.
[4] Ibid. 38; 72–3.

Surah 91   The Sun (*Ash-Shams*)

plement and are related to the verses which define man's responsibility and accountability for his actions, as the one in *surah* 74, "The Cloaked One", which reads in translation: *"Every soul is the hostage of its own deeds,"*[1] and the verse in *surah* 13, "Thunder", which states that Allah's attitude to man is directly related to man's own behaviour: *"Allah does not change a people's lot until they change what is in their hearts."*[2] These and similar verses define the Islamic view of man with perfect clarity.

    Allah has created man with a duality of nature and ability. What we mean by duality is that the two ingredients in his make-up, i.e., earth's clay and Allah's spirit, form within him two equal tendencies to good and evil, to follow Divine guidance and to go astray. Man is just as capable of recognising the good as he is of recognising the evil in everything he encounters, and he is equally capable of directing himself one way or the other. This dual ability is deeply ingrained within him. All external factors like Divine messages only serve to awaken his potential and help it take its chosen way. In other words, these factors do not create this potential, which is innate; they only help it develop.

    In addition to his innate ability man is equipped with a conscious faculty which determines his line of action and is, therefore, responsible for his actions and decisions. He who uses this faculty to strengthen his inclinations to what is good and to purify himself and to weaken the evil drive within him will be prosperous and successful; while he who uses this faculty to suppress the good tendency in him will ruin himself: *"Successful is the one who keeps it pure and ruined is the one who corrupts it."*

    There must be, then, an element of responsibility attached to man's conscious faculty and freedom of choice. For if he is free to choose between his tendencies, his freedom must be coupled with responsibility. He is assigned a definite task related to the power given to him. But Allah, the Compassionate, does not leave man with no guidance other than his natural impulses or his conscious, decision-making faculty. Allah helps him by sending him messages which lay down accurate and permanent criteria, and point out to him the signs which should help him choose the right path and which exist within him and in the world around him, and clear his way of any obstructions so that he may see the truth. Thus, he recognises his

---

[1] The Qur'an *74; 38*.   [2] *Ibid. 13; 11*.

way easily and clearly and his conscious decision-making faculty functions with full knowledge of the nature of the direction it chooses, and the implications of that choice.

This is what Allah has willed for man and whatever takes place within this framework is a direct fulfilment of His will.

From this very general outline of the Islamic concept of man emerge a number of vital and valuable facts: firstly, that this concept elevates man to the high position of being responsible for his actions and allows him freedom of choice, (within the confines of Allah's will that granted him this freedom). Responsibility and freedom of choice, therefore, make man the honoured creature of this world, a position worthy of the creature in whom Allah has blown something of His own spirit and whom He has made with His own hand and raised above most of His creation.

Secondly, it puts man's fate in his own hands (according to Allah's will as explained earlier) and makes him responsible for it. This stimulates in him an attitude of caution as well as the positive sense of the fear of God. For he knows then that the will of Allah is fulfilled through his own actions and decisions: *"Allah does not change a people's lot until they change what is in their hearts."* This is in itself a great responsibility which demands that one should be always alert.

Thirdly, it reminds man of his permanent need to refer to the criteria fixed by Allah in order to ensure that his desires do not get the better of him, lead him astray and destroy him. Thus man keeps near to Allah, follows His guidance and illuminates his way by the Divine light. Indeed, the standard of purity man can achieve is limitless.

The *surah* then gives an example of the failure which befalls those who corrupt themselves, and erect a barrier between themselves and Divine guidance: *"In their insolence the people of Thamoud denied the truth, when their most-wretched broke forth. The Messenger of Allah said to them, 'The she-camel of Allah, let her have her drink': But they cried lies to him, and hamstrung her. For that sin their Lord let loose His scourge upon them and razed their city to the ground. He fears not what may follow."*

The story of Thamoud and their Messenger, Salih, is mentioned several times in the Qur'an. A discussion of it is given every time it occurs. The reader may refer to it for further details in the commentary on *surah* 89, "The Dawn", in this volume. The present *surah*,

Surah 91   The Sun (*Ash-Shams*)

however, states that the people of Thamoud rejected their Prophet and accused him of lying simply because they were arrogant and insolent. Their transgression is represented here by their most-wretched breaking forth to hamstring the she-camel. He is the most-wretched as a result of his crime. Their Messenger had warned them in advance, saying, "Beware! never harm Allah's she-camel and never touch her drink." This was his condition when they asked him for a sign. The sign was that she-camel who had the water for herself one day and left it for the rest of the cattle one day. The she-camel must have had something else peculiar to her, but we shall not go into its details because Allah has not told us about it. Thamoud, however, did not heed their Messenger's warnings but hamstrung the she-camel. The person who perpetrated the crime, the arch-sinner, is the most-wretched, but they all were held responsible because they did not take him to task. On the contrary, they applauded what he did. A basic principle of Islam is that the society bears a collective responsibility in this life. This does not conflict with the principle of individual responsibility in the hereafter when everyone is answerable for his own deeds. It is a sin, however, not to counsel and urge one another to adhere to the good and not to punish evil and transgression.

As a result of Thamoud's insolence and their outrageous crime, a calamity befell them: *"For that sin their Lord let loose His scourge upon them and razed their city to the ground."* The Arabic verse uses the verb *'damdama'* for *'let loose His scourge'*, which creates, by its repetitiveness, an added feeling of horror, as we learn that the city was completely razed to the ground.

"He fears not what may follow". All praises and glorification be to Him. Whom, what and why should He fear? The meaning aimed at here is what the statement entails: he who does not fear the consequences punishes most severely. This is true of Allah's punishment.

In conclusion, we say the *surah* provides a link between the human soul, the basic facts of the universe, its constant and repetitive scenes, and Allah's unfailing law of punishing the tyrant transgressors. This He does according to His own wise planning which sets a time for everything and a purpose for every action. He is the Lord of man, the universe and fate.

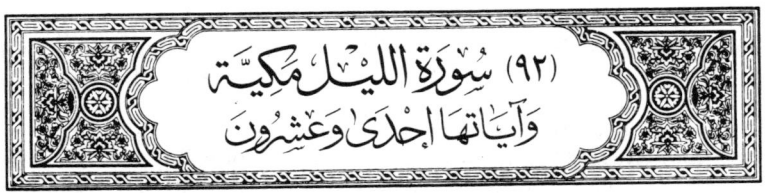

بِسْمِ اللهِ الرَّحْمَنِ الرَّحِيمِ

وَاللَّيْلِ إِذَا يَغْشَى ۝ وَالنَّهَارِ إِذَا تَجَلَّى ۝ وَمَا خَلَقَ الذَّكَرَ وَالْأُنْثَى ۝ إِنَّ سَعْيَكُمْ لَشَتَّى ۝ فَأَمَّا مَنْ أَعْطَى وَاتَّقَى ۝ وَصَدَّقَ بِالْحُسْنَى ۝ فَسَنُيَسِّرُهُ لِلْيُسْرَى ۝ وَأَمَّا مَنْ بَخِلَ وَاسْتَغْنَى ۝ وَكَذَّبَ بِالْحُسْنَى ۝ فَسَنُيَسِّرُهُ لِلْعُسْرَى ۝ وَمَا يُغْنِي عَنْهُ مَالُهُ إِذَا تَرَدَّى ۝ إِنَّ عَلَيْنَا لَلْهُدَى ۝ وَإِنَّ لَنَا لَلْآخِرَةَ وَالْأُولَى ۝ فَأَنْذَرْتُكُمْ نَارًا تَلَظَّى ۝ لَا يَصْلَاهَا إِلَّا الْأَشْقَى ۝ الَّذِي كَذَّبَ وَتَوَلَّى ۝ وَسَيُجَنَّبُهَا الْأَتْقَى ۝ الَّذِي يُؤْتِي مَالَهُ يَتَزَكَّى ۝ وَمَا لِأَحَدٍ عِنْدَهُ مِنْ نِعْمَةٍ تُجْزَى ۝ إِلَّا ابْتِغَاءَ وَجْهِ رَبِّهِ الْأَعْلَى ۝ وَلَسَوْفَ يَرْضَى ۝

SURAH 92

THE NIGHT
AL-LAIL

In the name of Allah, the Beneficent, the Merciful.

By the night when she lets fall her darkness,
by the day in full splendour,
by Him who created the male and the female:
surely your striving is diverse.
For him who gives and is godfearing
and believes in that which is the Best
We shall smooth the way to perfect ease.
But as for him who is a miser and deems himself self-sufficient,
and calls the Best a lie
We shall smooth his way to affliction.
His wealth will not avail him when he falls headlong.
It is for Us to give guidance,
and to Us belong the End and the Beginning.
I warn you, therefore, of the fiercely blazing fire,
in which none shall burn but the most wretched,
who denies the truth and turns away.
Preserved from it will be the righteous
who gives away his money to purify himself,
not in recompense of any favour done him by anyone.
He simply seeks the pleasure of His Lord, the Most High.
He shall indeed be well content.

In the Shade of the Qur'an

Within a framework of scenes taken from the universe and the realm of human nature, this *surah* states emphatically the basic facts of action and reward. This issue had diverse aspects: *"Surely your striving is diverse. For him who gives and is godfearing, and believes in that which is the Best, We shall smooth the way to perfect ease. But as for him who is a miser and deems himself self-sufficient, and calls the Best a lie, We shall smooth his way to affliction."* The end in the hereafter is also varied, according to the type of action and the direction taken in this life: *"I warn you, therefore, of the fiercely blazing fire in which none shall burn but the most wretched, who denies the truth and turns away. Preserved from it will be the righteous who gives away his money to purify himself."*

The subject matter of the *surah*, i.e., action and reward, is by nature double directional, so the framework chosen for it at the beginning of the *surah* is of dual colouring. It is based on contrasting aspects in the creation of man and the universe: *"By the night when she lets fall her darkness, by the day in full splendour, by Him who created the male and the female."* This is one form of artistic harmony extensively used in the Qur'an.[1]

"By the night when she lets fall her darkness; by the day in full splendour, by Him who created the male and the female." Allah swears by these two of His signs, namely, the night and the day, and describes them by the scene each produces on the horizon: the night as she enshrouds everything with her veil of darkness, and the day as it attains its full splendour. The night covers and conceals the land and all there is on it, and the day brightens up and makes every object apparent and visible. The two times are contrasting in the astrological cycle and in their respective scenes, qualities and effects. Allah also swears by His creation of all species in two contrasting sexes: *"by Him who created the male and the female."* This completes the contrast in the general atmosphere of the *surah* as well as in the facts it emphasises. The night and the day are two general phenomena which carry a certain message with which they inspire the human heart. The human soul is automatically affected by the cycle of the

---

[1] For a fuller treatment of this reference may be made to the chapter entitled "Artistic Harmony" in the author's book *"The Qur'anic Art of Picture Drawing"* (Arabic).

Surah 92   The Night (*Al-Lail*)

night and its curtain and the day and its splendid brightening. This continuous succession of night and day specks the universe, its mysterious secrets and phenomena over which man has no control. It suggests that there is a power which controls time in the universe as if it was a simple wheel. It also tells of the never-ending change in the universe.

As one contemplates and meditates upon these phenomena one is bound to conclude that there is an able hand which controls the universe and alternates the night and the day in that perfect, unfailing accuracy. One is also bound to conclude that the hand of Allah also controls the lives of men. He has not created them in vain, and He does not abandon them to lead a life without purpose.

However the disbelievers try to drown this reality and divert attention away from it, the human heart remains responsive to this universe. It receives its intimations and ponders over its changes and phenomena. Contemplation and meditation endorse its innate feeling that there is a Controller whose presence is bound to be felt and recognised in spite of all nonsense and conceited denials.

The same applies to the creation of male and female. In man and the mammals it all starts with a living germ settling in a womb, a sperm which unites with a cell. What is the reason then for this difference in outcome? What is it that says to one germ, "Be a male", and to another, "Be a female"? Discovery of the operative factors does not make the matter any different. How do the male factors exist in one case and the female ones in the other? What makes the end product, i.e., division of the species into two sexes, so fitting with the course of life as a whole and a guarantee of its continuity through procreation?

Is it all a coincidence? Even coincidence has a rule which deems it impossible for all those elements to come together accidentally. The only explanation is that there is a Controller in charge Who creates the male and the female according to a carefully worked-out plan which has a definite objective. There is no room for chance in the order of this universe.

Moreover, the male and female division is not limited to mammalia alone: it is applicable to all animate species, including plants. Singularity and oneness belong only to the Creator Who has no parallel whatever.

In the Shade of the Qur'an

Allah swears by these contrasting aspects of the universe and of man's creation and constitution that the striving of human beings is diverse, the roads they follow lead to different ends. Hence, their reward is also diverse. Good is not the same as evil, following the right guidance is unlike wrong-doing, and righteousness is different from corruption. Generosity and godfearing are unlike hoarding and conceit. The faithful are unlike those devoid of faith. Variance of ways necessitates variance of destinations. The reward is also appropriately different: *"Surely your striving is diverse. For him who gives and is godfearing, and believes in that which is the Best, We shall smooth the way to perfect ease. But as for him who is a miser and deems himself self-sufficient, and calls the Best a lie, We shall smooth his way to affliction. His wealth will not avail him when he falls headlong."*

"Your striving is diverse." It varies in essence, motives, directions and results. Men have diverse temperaments, environments, concepts and concerns, so much so that every man seems to be a distinct world by himself living in his own, special planet.

This is a fact, but along with it there is another general fact which applies to all beings and their different worlds. It groups them in two distinct classes and two contrasting positions. It assigns to each its distinctive label: *"who gives and is godfearing and believes in that which is the Best;"* and, *"who is a miser and deems himself self-sufficient and calls the Best a lie."*

These are the two positions at which the disparate souls line up where all the diverse striving and the divergent ways of life end. Each group has its way in this life smoothed, all obstructions removed: *"For him who gives and is godfearing, and believes in that which is Best, We shall smooth the way to perfect ease."* He who is charitable and godfearing and believes in the ideology which has the Best as its title has indeed done his best to purify himself seeking right guidance. Hence, he deserves the help and grace which Allah has, by His own will, committed Himself to provide. For without this grace man finds himself absolutely helpless. He whose path to perfect ease and comfort is made smooth by Allah achieves something certainly great, and achieves it with ease and in this life. He lives in ease. Ease flows from him to all around him. Ease becomes characteristic of his movement, action and handling of all things and situations. Success coupled with quiet contentedness becomes the distinctive mark of his life, all its details and its general aspects. He attains the highest grade of all, in the sense that he joins the Prophet as recipients of Allah's promise

Surah 92   The Night (*Al-Lail*)

to His messenger: *"We will indeed facilitate for you the way to perfect ease."*[1]

"But for him who is a miser and deems himself self-sufficient, and calls the Best a lie We shall smooth his way to affliction. His wealth will not avail him when he falls headlong."

He who sacrifices nothing of himself or his wealth, professes that he is in no need of His Lord or His guidance and disbelieves in His message and religion, makes himself most vulnerable to evil. He deserves for so doing that everything should be made hard for him. Hence, Allah makes easy his path to affliction, and withholds from him all kinds of help. Allah makes every stride he takes really hard, drives him away from the path of the right guidance, and leaves him to traverse the valleys of misery, although he may imagine himself to be taking the road to success. How greatly mistaken he is! He loses balance so he tries to avoid falling only to go down heavily, and finds himself further away from the path set by Allah, deprived of His pleasure. When he falls headlong eventually he can make no use of the wealth he has hoarded and which has caused him to imagine himself in no need of Allah or His guidance. *"His wealth will not avail him when he falls headlong."* Facilitating evil and sin is the same as facilitating the way to affliction, even though the sinful person may be successful and prosperous in this life. For is there any affliction worse than Hell? Indeed, Hell is affliction itself.

Thus the first part of the *surah* ends having made clear that there are only two ways for all mankind in all times and places. All humanity is in two parties under two headings however numerous are their colours and forms.

The second part states the fate of each group. It emphasises firstly that the end and reward of each group is fair and inevitable, for guidance has been provided and warnings have been issued: *"It is for Us to provide guidance, and to Us belong the End and the Beginning. I warn you, therefore, of the fiercely blazing fire, in which none shall burn but the most wretched who denies the truth and turns away. Preserved from it will be the righteous, who gives away his money to purify himself, not in recompense of any favour done him by anyone. He simply seeks the pleasure of His Lord, the Most High. He shall indeed be well content."*

One aspect of Allah's grace and mercy to His servants is that He

---

[1] The Qur'an. 87; 8. Reference may be made to the commentary on this verse in this volume.

In the Shade of the Qur'an

has taken upon Himself to provide clear guidance readily acceptable to human nature, and to explain it as well through His messages and messengers, and by means of the signs He has provided. Thus, no one will have a valid argument for his deviation, and no one will suffer injustice: *"It is for Us to give guidance."*

Then follows a straightforward statement of the essence of the power which has control over man and all around him, from which he can have no shelter: *"and to Us belong the End and the Beginning."*

By way of elaboration on the two facts just mentioned, namely, Allah's provision of guidance and that to Him belongs this life and the hereafter, i.e., the realms of actions and reward, there is a reminder to us that He has cautioned and warned: *"I warn you, therefore, of the fiercely blazing fire."* It is only the most wretched of mankind who are thrown in this fire. Indeed there is no wretchedness worse than suffering in Hell: *"in which none shall burn but the most wretched."* Then follows a description of the most wretched. It is he *"who denies the truth and turns away."* He denies this message and turns away from Divine guidance. He does not answer his Lord's beckoning to him so that He may guide him as He has promised any one who comes towards Him with open mind.

"Preserved from it will be the righteous," who will be the happiest in contrast with the most wretched. The righteous, the *surah* explains, is the one *"who gives away his money to purify himself"*, not for any vanity or to satisfy any snobbish feeling. He spends it voluntarily not out of any indebtedness to anybody, seeking no gratitude from anyone. His only objective is the pleasure of his Lord, the Most Exalted: *"not in recompense of any favour done him by anyone. He simply seeks the pleasure of his Lord, the Most High."*

What can the righteous person expect in return for spending his money in self-purification, for the pleasure of his Exalted Lord? The reward which the Qur'an states is indeed astonishing: *"He shall indeed be well content."* It is the satisfaction which fills the believer's heart and soul, animates everything in his life, and radiates through him. What a reward, and what grace! *"He shall indeed be well content."* He will be satisfied with his religion, his Lord and his destiny. He will be content with whatever befalls him of comfort or discomfort, and whether he is poor or wealthy. He will be free of anxiety and hard feelings. He does not worry about his burden being too heavy or his objective too far. This satisfaction is in itself a reward, great beyond description. Only the person who sacrifices himself and his wealth for it and who seeks to purify himself and to win the pleasure of Allah deserves this reward. It is Allah alone Who can pour such a reward into the hearts which submit to Him with all sincerity and pure devotion. Having paid the price, the believer *"shall indeed be well content."* At this point, the reward comes as a surprise, but it is a surprise awaited by the one who attains the standard of the righteous, whose main qualifications are spending for self purification and seeking the pleasure of Allah. Such a person will be well pleased and well satisfied.

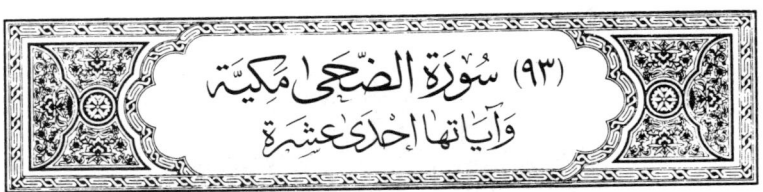

بِسْمِ اللهِ الرَّحْمَنِ الرَّحِيمِ

وَالضُّحَى ۝ وَاللَّيْلِ إِذَا سَجَى ۝ مَا وَدَّعَكَ رَبُّكَ وَمَا قَلَى ۝ وَلَلْآخِرَةُ خَيْرٌ لَكَ مِنَ الْأُولَى ۝ وَلَسَوْفَ يُعْطِيكَ رَبُّكَ فَتَرْضَى ۝ أَلَمْ يَجِدْكَ يَتِيمًا فَآوَى ۝ وَوَجَدَكَ ضَالًّا فَهَدَى ۝ وَوَجَدَكَ عَائِلًا فَأَغْنَى ۝ فَأَمَّا الْيَتِيمَ فَلَا تَقْهَرْ ۝ وَأَمَّا السَّائِلَ فَلَا تَنْهَرْ ۝ وَأَمَّا بِنِعْمَةِ رَبِّكَ فَحَدِّثْ ۝

SURAH 93

THE FORENOON
AD-DHUHA

In the name of Allah, the Beneficent, the Merciful.

By the white forenoon
and the brooding night
your Lord has neither forsaken you, nor does He hate you.
Surely the life to come will be better for you than this present life.
And certainly your Lord will be bounteous to you and you will be
    satisfied.
Did He not find you an orphan and give you a shelter?
Did He not find you in error and guide you?
Did He not find you poor and enrich you?
Therefore do not wrong the orphan,
nor chide away the beggar,
but proclaim the goodness of your Lord.

In the Shade of the Qur'an

This *surah*, with its subject matter, mode of expression, scenes, connotations and rhythm is a touch of tenderness and mercy. It is a message of affection; it is a benevolent hand which soothes pains and troubles and generates an air of contentment and confident hope. The *surah* is dedicated in its entirety to the Prophet (peace be on him). It is a message from his Lord which touches his heart with pleasure, joy, tranquillity and contentment. Altogether it is a flow of mercy and compassion to his restless soul, and suffering heart.

Several accounts mention that the revelation of the Qur'an to the Prophet came, at one stage, to a halt and that Jibril stopped coming to him for a while. The unbelievers therefore said, "Muhammad's Lord has bidden him farewell!" Allah therefore revealed this *surah*.

Revelation, Jibril's visits and the link with Allah were the Prophet's whole equipment along his precarious path. They were his only solace in the face of hard rejection and his sole comfort against outright repudiation. They were the source from which he derived his strength to stand steadfast against the unbelievers who were intent on rebuff and refusal, and bent on directing a wicked, vile attack against the Prophet's call, faith and guidance.

So when the Revelation was withheld, the source of strength for the Prophet was cut off. His lifespring was sapped and he longed for his heart's friend. Alone he was left in the wilderness, without sustenance, without water, without the accustomed companionship of the beloved friend. It was a situation which taxes human endurance heavily.

Then this *surah* was revealed and it came as a rich flow of compassion, mercy, hope, comfort and reassurance. *"Your Lord has neither forsaken you, nor does He hate you. Surely the life to come will be better for you than this present life. And certainly your Lord will be bounteous to you, and you will be satisfied."* Your Lord has never before left you or rejected you, or even denied you His mercy or protection. *"Did He not find you an orphan and give you a shelter? Did He not find you in error and guide you? Did He not find you poor and enrich you?"*

Do you not see the proof of all this in your own life? Do you not feel it in your heart? Do you not observe it in your world? *"Your Lord has neither forsaken you, nor does He hate you."* Never had His mercy been taken away from you and it never will be. *"Surely the life to come will be better for you than this present life."* And there will be much more: *"And certainly your Lord will be bounteous to you and you will be satisfied."*

Surah 93   The Forenoon *(Ad-Dhuha)*

This statement of the fact of the matter, made in excellent style and fine rhythm, is given in the framework of a universal phenomenon: *"By the white forenoon and the brooding night."* The expression spreads an air of affection, kindliness and complete satisfaction. *"Your Lord has not forsaken you, nor does He hate you. Surely the life to come will be better for you than this present life. And certainly your Lord will be bounteous to you and you will be satisfied. Did He not find you an orphan and give you shelter? Did He not find you in error and guide you? Did He not find you poor and enrich you?"* That tenderness, that mercy, that satisfaction, that solace are all felt in the sweet expressions and the soothing words and phrases which softly thread along the *surah* with gentle echoes and lively rhythm as they are contained within the frame of the morning hours and the still night which are the times of the day and night most conducive to clarity. During these periods one's reflections flow like a stream, and the soul is best able to communicate with the universe and its Creator, and feels the universe worshipping its Lord and turning towards Him in praise with joy and happiness. In addition, the night is described as "brooding". It is not the dark gloomy night as such but the "brooding" night that is clear, silent and tranquil, covered with a light cloud of sweet longing and kind reflection. It is a picture similar to that of the orphan's life. More still, the night is cleared away by the crossing morning and thus the colours of the picture beautifully match with those of the framework, and harmony is achieved.

The scene drawn here is one of perfect beauty. Such perfection is Divine, unparalleled and inimitable.

"By the white forenoon, and the brooding night: your Lord has neither forsaken you, nor does He hate you. Surely the life to come shall be better for you than this present life. And certainly your Lord will be bounteous to you and you will be satisfied."

Allah vows by these two calm and inspiring periods of time and establishes a relationship between natural phenomena and human feelings. Thus, mutual response is encouraged between human hearts and the universe, which is beautiful, alive and sympathetic to all living beings. Hence, hearts live in peace with the world, relaxed and happy.

This mode of expression is particularly appropriate in this *surah* as the feeling of fellowship is stressed here as if to tell the Prophet right from the beginning of the *surah* that his Lord had already blessed him with the fellowship of the world around him and that he was by no means forsaken or left alone.

Then follows a straightforward assertion. *"Your Lord has neither forsaken you, nor does He hate you."* He has not left you, nor has He been harsh to you as is alleged by those who want to afflict your heart and soul or trouble your feelings. For He is your Lord and you belong to Him. He is your sustainer and protector. Allah's favours on you have neither run out nor have they been stopped. You, Muhammad, are to get much more and better favours in the hereafter than you are getting in this life. *"Surely the life to come will be better for you than this present life."*

Allah is saving for you, Muhammad, what will satisfy you in your mission and ease your hard path and bring about the victory of your call and the vindication of the truth you advocate. These thoughts were in fact preoccupying the Prophet's mind as he was encountering his people's outright rejection, ill-treatment, and malice. *"Your Lord will be bounteous to you and you will be satisfied."*

The *surah* then goes on to remind the Prophet of his Lord's attitude towards him from the very beginning of his mission so that he may reflect on how favourably Allah has been treating him. This is to make him recall the happy memories of the Divine kindness which is a joy revived by the words, *"Did He not find you an orphan and give you a shelter? Did He not find you in error and guide you? Did He not find you poor and enrich you?"* Reflect on your present life and on your past. Has He ever forsaken you or hated you even before He charged you with the assignment of prophethood.

You were born an orphan but Allah protected you. He made so many people kind to you, especially your uncle Abu Talib, though he followed a religion different from yours. You were poor and He made your heart rich with contentment, and made you rich through your business gains and the wealth of your wife, Khadeejah, so that you would not suffer from poverty or yearn for the riches that abound all around you.

You were also brought up in an *Ignorant* society, full of confusion of beliefs and concepts, where erring ways and practices abounded. You did not like those beliefs, concepts and practices but you could not find a clear and suitable way out. You could find your way neither in the *Ignorant* world nor with the followers of Moses and Jesus, who adulterated their beliefs, distorted their original form and

Surah 93   The Forenoon (*Ad-Dhuha*)

went astray. But Allah has guided you through His revelations and the way of life He has set which establishes a firm bond between Him and you.

This "guidance" in the wilderness of disbelief and confusion is the greatest favour of them all. The happiness and reassurance it brings about cannot be matched. The Prophet had been greatly perturbed and afflicted because of the cessation of revelation, and the malicious attitude of the polytheists during the period of its cessation. Hence comes this reminder to put his heart at ease and reassure him of his Lord's promise never to abandon him.

Allah takes the opportunity of mentioning the Prophet's earlier orphanhood, error and poverty in order to instruct the Prophet and all Muslims to protect every orphan, to be charitable to every beggar, and to speak of the great favours they enjoy from Allah, the first of which is guidance to the religion of Islam. *"Therefore, do not wrong the orphan, nor chide away the beggar, but proclaim the goodness of your Lord."*

As we have already mentioned repeatedly, these instructions reflect the needs of the day, in that greedy and materialistic society in which the weak, who could not defend their own rights, were not catered for. Islam came to reform that society with Allah's laws which establish equity, justice and good-will.

Speaking of Allah's bounties, especially those of guidance and faith, is a form of expressing gratitude to Him, the Giver. It is a practical manifestation of thanks on the part of the recipient.

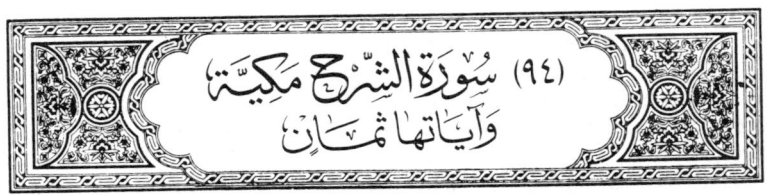

بِسْمِ اللَّهِ الرَّحْمَٰنِ الرَّحِيمِ

أَلَمْ نَشْرَحْ لَكَ صَدْرَكَ ۝ وَوَضَعْنَا عَنكَ وِزْرَكَ ۝ الَّذِي أَنقَضَ ظَهْرَكَ ۝ وَرَفَعْنَا لَكَ ذِكْرَكَ ۝ فَإِنَّ مَعَ الْعُسْرِ يُسْرًا ۝ إِنَّ مَعَ الْعُسْرِ يُسْرًا ۝ فَإِذَا فَرَغْتَ فَانصَبْ ۝ وَإِلَىٰ رَبِّكَ فَارْغَب ۝

SURAH 94

SOLACE
ASH-SHARH

In the name of Allah, the Beneficent, the Merciful.

Have We not lifted up your heart,
and relieved you of your burden,
which weighed down your back?
And have We not given you high renown?
With hardship comes ease.
Indeed, with hardship comes ease.
When you have completed your task resume your toil
and seek your Lord with all fervour.

In the Shade of the Qur'an

This *surah* was revealed soon after the revelation of *surah* 93, 'The Forenoon', as if it was a continuation of it. Here, also, abound the feelings of sympathy and the atmosphere of delightful, friendly discourse. It portrays the Divine care for the Prophet and explains the measures taken out of concern for him. The *surah* also carries glad tidings of the forthcoming relief, points out to the Prophet the secret of ease, and emphasises the strong tie with Allah.

"*Have We not lifted up your heart, and relieved you of your burden which weighed down your back? And have We not given you high renown?*" This suggests that the Prophet was troubled in his soul for some reason concerning the message he was entrusted with, and the obstacles in its way and the plots against it. These verses also suggest that the difficulties facing his mission weighed heavily on his heart and made him feel that he urgently needed help and backing. Hence came this comforting address and delightful discourse.

"*Have We not lifted up your heart*", so that it may warm to this message? Have We not facilitated it for you, endeared it to you defined its path and illuminated it for you to see its happy end? Look into your heart! Do you not see it to be full of light, happiness and solace? Reflect on the effects brought about by all the favours bestowed on you! Do you not feel comfort with every difficulty, and find contentment with every kind of deprivation you suffer?

"*And relieved you of your burden which weighed down your back?*" We have relieved you of your burden which was so heavy that it almost broke your back. The relief took the form of lifting up your heart so that you might feel your mission easier and your burden not difficult to shoulder. Another aspect of the relief was the guidance you received on how to discharge your mission and how to appeal to men's hearts. Furthermore, there is relief for you in the revelation of the Qur'an which explains the truth and helps you to drive it home to people easily and gently. Do you not feel all that when you think of the burden which weighed down your back? Do you not feel it to be lighter after We have lifted up your heart?

"*And have We not given you high renown?*" We exalted you among those on high, on earth and in the whole universe. We raised your fame high indeed as we associated your name with that of Allah whenever it is pronounced. "No Deity but Allah, Muhammad is the Messenger of Allah." Indeed, this is the highest degree of exaltation. It is the position granted only to Muhammad and to no other human being. For Allah has willed that one century should turn after

Surah 94   Solace (*Ash-Sharh*)

another and generations succeed generations with millions and millions of people in all corners of the world honouring the blessed name of Muhammad with prayers for peace and blessings to be granted to him, and with his profound love entrenched in their hearts. Your fame spread far and wide when your name became associated with this Divine way of life.

Certainly the mere fact that you were chosen for this task is an exaltation to which no one else in this universe can ever aspire. How can there remain any feeling of affliction or hardship after this favour which heals up all hardships and difficulties?

Allah, nevertheless, addresses His beloved messenger kindly. He comforts and reassures him and explains to him how He has given him unceasing ease. *"With hardship comes ease. Indeed, with hardship comes ease."* Hardship never comes absolute, without some ease accompanying it. When your burden became too heavy We lifted up your heart and relieved the sting of hardship for you.

This is strongly emphasised by a literal repetition of the statement: *"With hardship comes ease. Indeed, with hardship comes ease."* The repetition suggests that the Prophet had endured serious hardship and suffered much affliction. This reminder recalls the various aspects of care and concern shown to the Prophet and then reassures him emphatically. A matter which afflicts Muhammad's soul so much must be very serious indeed.

Then follows a statement pointing out the aspects of comfort and the factors contributing to the lifting up of hearts and spirits, which is of great help to Muslims as they travel along their hard and long way: *"When you have completed your task resume your toil and seek your Lord with all fervour."*

With hardship goes ease, so seek relief and solace. When you have finished whatever you may have to do, be it a matter relating to the conveyance of your message or an affair of this life then turn with all your heart to what deserves your toil and striving, namely devotion and dedication in worship. *"And seek your Lord with all fervour."* Seek Him alone and let nothing whatsoever distract you. Do not even think of the people you call to believe in Him. A traveller must have his food with him and this is the real food for your journey; and a fighter for a cause needs to have his equipment and this is the equipment necessary for you. This will provide you with a feeling of ease in every difficulty you may encounter, and with comfort against every kind of affliction you may suffer.

The *surah* ends on the same note as the preceding *surah*, "The Forenoon". It leaves us with two intertwined feelings. The first is a realisation of the great affection shown to the Prophet, which overwhelmed him because it was the love of his Lord, the Compassionate, the Merciful. The other feeling is one of sympathy to his noble self. We can almost feel what was going on in his blessed heart at that time which required this reminder of the delightful affection.

It is this mission of Islam: a grave trust and a burden which weighs down his back. It is nevertheless the rising of the Divine light, the link between mortality and eternity, existence and non-existence.

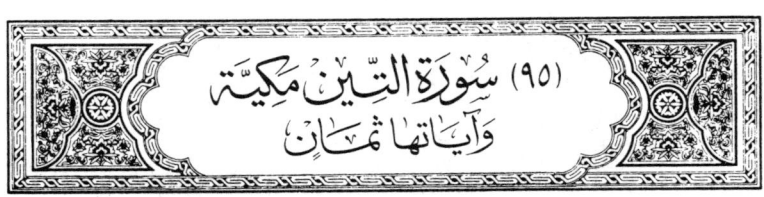

بِسْمِ اللهِ الرَّحْمَنِ الرَّحِيمِ

وَالتِّينِ وَالزَّيْتُونِ ۝ وَطُورِ سِينِينَ ۝ وَهَذَا الْبَلَدِ الْأَمِينِ ۝ لَقَدْ خَلَقْنَا الْإِنسَانَ فِي أَحْسَنِ تَقْوِيمٍ ۝ ثُمَّ رَدَدْنَاهُ أَسْفَلَ سَافِلِينَ ۝ إِلَّا الَّذِينَ آمَنُوا وَعَمِلُوا الصَّالِحَاتِ فَلَهُمْ أَجْرٌ غَيْرُ مَمْنُونٍ ۝ فَمَا يُكَذِّبُكَ بَعْدُ بِالدِّينِ ۝ أَلَيْسَ اللهُ بِأَحْكَمِ الْحَاكِمِينَ ۝

SURAH 95

THE FIG
AT-TEEN

In the name of Allah, the Beneficent, the Merciful.

By the fig and the olive,
and the Mount of Sinai,
and this secure city,
We indeed have created man in the fairest form.
Then We brought him down to the lowest of the low,
except for those who believe and do righteous deeds,
for theirs shall be an unfailing recompense.
Who, then, can give you the lie as to the Last Judgement?
Is not Allah the most Just of judges?

In the Shade of the Qur'an

The basic fact outlined in this *surah* is that of the upright nature which Allah has given man. This upright nature is essentially in perfect harmony with the nature of faith. With faith it attains its ultimate perfection. But when man deviates from this upright nature and from the straight path of faith he sinks into the lowest of ranks.

Allah swears to the validity of this by the fig *"teen"*, the olive *"zaitoon"*, the Mount of Sinai *"Toor Sineen"* and the secure city of Makka *"al-balad al-ameen"*. As we have already seen in many *surahs* of this thirtieth part of the Qur'an, this oath is the framework which perfectly fits the essential fact presented within it.

The Toor of Sinai is the Mount on which Moses received the Divine summons. The secure city is Makka, Allah's Holy House. The relationship between the two on the one hand and religion and faith on the other is obvious. But a similar relationship is not readily clear with regard to the figs and olives. Suggestions as to the significance of the figs and olives are numerous. It is said that the fig refers to the fig tree in heaven with the leaves of which Adam and his wife, Eve, tried to cover their private parts. Another suggestion is that the reference here is to the place where the fig tree appeared on the mountain where Noah's ship embarked.

As for the olive, it is suggested that it is a reference to the Mount of Toor Zaita in Jerusalem. It is also said that it refers to Jerusalem itself. Another suggestion is that it refers to the olive branch brought back by the pigeon which Noah released from the ship to examine the state of the floods. When the pigeon brought back the olive branch, he knew that the land had reappeared and that vegetation was growing.

A different opinion posits that the fig and olive mentioned in the *surah* are simply those two kinds of food with which we are familiar. Alternatively, it is claimed, they are symbols of growth out of land.

There is another reference in the Qur'an to the olive tree in association with the Mount. The verse there reads as follows: *"And a tree issuing from Mount Sinai which bears oil and seasoning for all to eat"*.[1] The olive tree is mentioned here for the only time in the Qur'an.

Hence, we cannot say anything definite on this matter. However, on the basis of parallel frameworks in other *surahs* of the Qur'an, the most likely explanation of the fig and olive mentioned here is that they refer to certain places or events which have some relevance to re-

---

[1] The Qur'an. *23; 20.*

ligion and faith or to man as the creature fairest in shape and form. (This may have been established in Heaven where man's life began.) The harmony between this detail and the main fact outlined in the *surah* is yet another example of the unique method of the Qur'an whereby the framework and the fact within it fits perfectly.

The essential fact of the *surah* is embodied in the verses: *"We indeed have created man in the fairest form. Then We brought him down to the lowest of the low, except for those who believe and do righteous deeds, for theirs shall be an unfailing recompense."*

Allah has perfected all His creation; and the special emphasis laid here and elsewhere in the Qur'an on man's being endowed with perfect form shows clearly that this creature, man, has enjoyed extra care. Moreover, Allah's care for this creature despite his distortion of his upright nature and the corruption he indulges in suggests that Allah has given him a special rank and a special weight in the universe. Allah's care is most clearly apparent in the moulding of his highly complicated physical structure and his unique spiritual and mental make up.

The emphasis here is on man's spiritual qualities since these are the ones which drag man down to the most ignoble state when he deviates from the upright nature and turns away from belief in Allah which is perfectly harmonious with this nature. It is needless to say that man's physical structure does not sink down into such a low level. Moreover, the superiority of man's creation is most clearly apparent in the spiritual qualities. He is made in a way which enables him to attain a sublime standard, superior to that of the highest-ranking angels. This is illustrated in the story of the Prophet's ascension to Heaven. Then, Jibril stopped at a certain level and Muhammad, the human being, was elevated much higher.

At the same time, man is given the dubious ability to sink down to levels unreached by any other creature: *"Then We brought him down to the lowest of the low."* In this latter case, the animals become superior to him and more upright since they do not violate their nature. They praise the Lord and fulfil their function on earth as they are guided to do. But man who has been given the fairest form and abilities denies his Lord and sinks right down.

"We have created man in the fairest shape and form". This is a reference to his nature and abilities. *"Then We brought him down to the lowest of the low."* That is, when he forces this nature away from the line Allah has defined for him. Having laid down the way, Allah left

man to choose whether to follow it or not.

"Except for those who believe and do righteous deeds." For these are men who stick to the upright nature, consolidate it with faith and righteous deeds, elevate it towards its destined level of perfection until they finally attain a life of perfection in the world of perfection: *"for theirs shall be an unfailing recompense."* But those who cause their nature to sink to the lowest of the low go down with it along their slippery road until they reach the lowest level, that is, in Hell where their humanity is shed and they are completely debased. Both ends are natural results of two widely different starts and lines of action.

Thus, the importance of faith in human life becomes clear. Faith is the elevating path through which upright human nature ascends to its ultimate perfection. It is the rope stretched between man and his Maker. It is the light showing him where to put his feet along the elevating path. When the rope is cut and the light put out, the inevitable result is the fall down the steep path into the lowest of the low. The clay element in man's make-up separates from the spiritual element and man, along with stones, becomes fuel for the hell-fire.

In the light of this fact, the Prophet is addressed in this manner *"Who, then, can give you the lie as to the Last Judgement? Is not Allah the most Just of judges?"* What makes you, man, belie this religion after you have known this fact, after having realised the importance of faith in the life of humanity, and after becoming aware of the destiny awaiting those who disbelieve, turn away from this light and refuse to follow the straight path laid down by Allah?

"Is not Allah the most Just of judges?" Is not He the most Just when He gives this ruling concerning the destiny of creation? Is not Allah's wisdom clearest and most reassuring as He rules between the believers and the disbelievers? Justice is certainly clear and wisdom is manifest. Hence, we are taught in the tradition *(Hadith)* related by Abu Hurairah that when one reads this *surah* one should answer the rhetorical question *"Is not Allah the most Just of judges?"* by saying: "Indeed, and I am a witness to that."

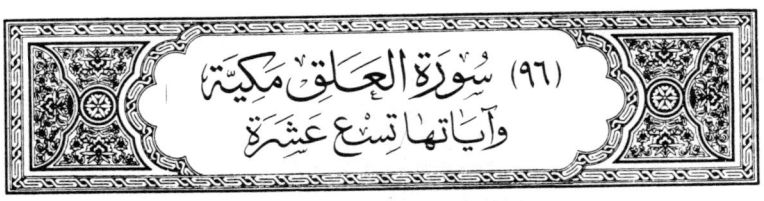

بِسْمِ اللَّهِ الرَّحْمَنِ الرَّحِيمِ

اقْرَأْ بِاسْمِ رَبِّكَ الَّذِي خَلَقَ ۝ خَلَقَ الْإِنسَانَ مِنْ عَلَقٍ ۝ اقْرَأْ وَرَبُّكَ الْأَكْرَمُ ۝ الَّذِي عَلَّمَ بِالْقَلَمِ ۝ عَلَّمَ الْإِنسَانَ مَا لَمْ يَعْلَمْ ۝ كَلَّا إِنَّ الْإِنسَانَ لَيَطْغَىٰ ۝ أَن رَّآهُ اسْتَغْنَىٰ ۝ إِنَّ إِلَىٰ رَبِّكَ الرُّجْعَىٰ ۝ أَرَأَيْتَ الَّذِي يَنْهَىٰ ۝ عَبْدًا إِذَا صَلَّىٰ ۝ أَرَأَيْتَ إِن كَانَ عَلَى الْهُدَىٰ ۝ أَوْ أَمَرَ بِالتَّقْوَىٰ ۝ أَرَأَيْتَ إِن كَذَّبَ وَتَوَلَّىٰ ۝ أَلَمْ يَعْلَم بِأَنَّ اللَّهَ يَرَىٰ ۝ كَلَّا لَئِن لَّمْ يَنتَهِ لَنَسْفَعًا بِالنَّاصِيَةِ ۝ نَاصِيَةٍ كَاذِبَةٍ خَاطِئَةٍ ۝ فَلْيَدْعُ نَادِيَهُ ۝ سَنَدْعُ الزَّبَانِيَةَ ۝ كَلَّا لَا تُطِعْهُ وَاسْجُدْ وَاقْتَرِب ۩

SURAH 96

THE BLOOD CLOTS
AL-ALAQ

In the name of Allah, the Beneficent, the Merciful.

Read in the name of your Lord who created,
created man from clots of blood.
Read! your Lord is the most Bounteous,
Who has taught the use of the pen,
has taught man what he did not know.
Indeed, man tyrannises, once he thinks himself self-sufficient.
Surely to your Lord all things return.
Observe the man who rebukes a servant of Allah when he prays!
Think: does he not follow the right guidance and enjoin true piety?
Think: if he denies the truth and turns his back,
does he not realise that Allah sees all?
Let him desist, or We will drag him by the forelock,
his lying, sinful forelock.
Then let him call his henchmen.
We will call the guards of Hell.
No, never obey him, but prostrate yourself and draw closer to Allah.

In the Shade of the Qur'an

It is universally agreed that the opening of this *surah* was the first Qur'anic revelation. The accounts stating that other verses were revealed first are not authentic. Imam Ahmad transmits the following *hadith* attributing it to Aisha, the Prophet's wife:

> The first aspect of revelation to Allah's Messenger was that his dreams came true. Whatever vision he might have in his sleep would occur exactly as he had seen. Then, he began to enjoy seclusion. He used to retreat alone into the cave of Hira where he would spend several days in devotion before going back to his family. He used to take some food with him, and when he came back he would take a fresh supply for another period. He continued to do so until he received the truth while in the cave of Hira. The angel came to him and said, "Read." He replied, "I am not a reader." The Prophet says, "He held me and pressed hard until I was exhausted, then he released me and said, "Read." and I replied, "I am not a reader". So, he held me and pressed me hard a second time until I was exhausted, then he released me and said, "Read." I replied, "I am not a reader." He then held me and pressed me hard for the third time. Then he said, *"Read, in the name of your Lord Who created, created man from clots of blood. Read! your Lord is the most bounteous, Who has taught the use of the pen, has taught man what he did not know."* The Prophet returned home to Khadeeja trembling and said, "Wrap me! Wrap me!" They wrapped him and his fear subsided. He turned to Khadeeja and exclaimed, "What has happened to me?" and related to her what had happened and said, "I fear for myself." And Khadeeja replied, "Fear not, be calm and relax. Allah will not let you suffer any humiliation, because you are kind to your relatives, you speak the truth, you assist anyone in need, you are hospitable to your guests and you help in every just cause." Then she took him to Waraqa ibn Nawfal, her paternal cousin who was a Christian convert and a scholar with good knowledge of Arabic, Hebrew and the Bible. He had lost his eyesight as he had grown very old. Khadeeja said to Waraqa, "Cousin, would you like to hear what your nephew has to say?" Waraqa said, "Well, nephew,[1] what have you seen?" The

---

[1] Waraqa was not the Prophet's uncle. Khadeeja's reference to Muhammad as his nephew was in accordance with the standards of politeness prevalent in Arabia at the time. – Translator's note.

Surah 96   The Blood Clots (*Al-Alaq*)

Prophet related to him what he had seen. When he finished, Waraqa said, "It is the same revelation as was sent down to Moses. I wish I was a young man so that I might be alive when your people turn you away from this city." The Prophet exclaimed, "Would they turn me away?" Waraqa answered "Yes! No man has ever preached a message like yours but was met with enmity. If I live till that day, I will certainly give you all my support." But Waraqa died soon after that . . .

This *hadith* is transmitted in both of the most authentic books of the Prophet's traditions and was related by Al-Zuhri.

Al-Tabari also transmitted the following tradition, related by Abdullah ibn Az-Zubair:

"The Prophet said, 'While I was asleep he came to me carrying a case of a very rich material in which there was a book. He said, 'Read.' I replied, 'I am not a reader.' He pressed me so hard that I felt I was about to die. Then he released me and said, 'Read.' I asked, 'What shall I read?' (and I said this only out of fear that he might repeat what he had done to me before.) He said, *'Read: In the name of your Lord who created . . . taught man what he did not know.'* I read it. He stopped, then left me and went away. I woke up feeling that it was actually written in my heart'." The Prophet went on to say, "No man was ever more loathsome to me than poets or deranged persons. I could not bear even looking at either. I thought, 'The man (meaning himself) is undoubtedly a poet or deranged. This shall not be said about me amongst the Quraish. Let me climb high up in the mountain and throw myself and get rid of it all.' I went to carry out this intention. When I was half way up in the mountain I heard a voice coming from the heavens saying, 'Muhammad, you are the Messenger of Allah and I am Jibril.' I raised my head up to the sky and I saw Jibril in the image of a man with his feet one next to the other, up on the horizon. He said again, 'Muhammad, you are the Messenger of Allah and I am Jibril.' I stood in my place looking up at him; this distracted me from my intention. I was standing there unable to move. I tried to turn my face away from him and to look up at the sky, but wherever I looked, I saw him in front of me. I stood still, moving neither forward nor backward. Kahdeeja sent her messengers looking for me and I remained standing in my place all the while until they went back to her. He then left me and I went back to my family...'"

This tradition is also related in more details by Ibn Ishaq, on the authority of Wahb ibn Kayssan.

I reflected for a while upon this event. We all have read it many times in books; either those of the Prophet's biography or those explaining the meaning of the Qur'an. But we either read it casually or gave it little thought and went on with our reading.

Yet this is an event which has immense significance. It is an event which has important bearing on the life of humanity; but much as we try today to perceive its great value, many of its aspects will remain beyond our perception. It is no exaggeration to describe this event as the greatest in the long history of human existence.

The true nature of this event is that Allah, the Great, the Compeller, the Almighty, the Supreme, the Sovereign of the whole universe, out of His benevolence, has turned to that creation of His which is called "man", and which takes its abode in a hardly visible corner of the universe, the name of which is the "Earth". He has honoured this species of His creation by choosing one of its numbers to be the recipient of His Divine light and the guardian of His wisdom.

This is something infinitely great. Some aspects of its greatness become apparent when man tries, as best as he can, to perceive the essential qualities of Allah: absolute power, freedom from all limitations and everlastingness; and when he reflects, in comparison, on the basic qualities of Allah's servants who are subject to certain limitations of power and life duration. One may then perceive the significance of this Divine care for man. He may realise the sweetness of this feeling and manifest his appreciation with thanksgiving, prayers and devotion. He feels that the whole universe shares in the general happiness spread by the revelation of Divine words to man in his obscure corner of the universe.

What is the significance of this event? With reference to Allah, it signifies that He is the source of all the great bounties and unfailing compassion. He is the Benevolent, the Loving, Who bestows His mercy and benefactions for no reason except that benevolence is one of His Divine attributes. As for man, this event signifies that Allah has bestowed on him an honour the greatness of which he can hardly ever appreciate and for which he can never show enough gratitude,

Surah 96   The Blood Clots (*Al-Alaq*)

not even if he spends all his life in devotion and prostration. This honour is that Allah has taken notice and care of him, established contact with him and chosen one of the human race as His messenger to reveal to him His words; that the earth, man's abode has become the recipient of these Divine words, which the whole universe echoes with submission and devotion.

This great event began to bear on the life of humanity as a whole right from the first moment. It marked a change in the course of history, following the change it brought about in the course followed by human conscience. It specified the source man should look up to in order to derive his ideals, values and criteria. The source is heaven and the Divine revelations, not this world and man's own desires. When this great event took place the people who recognised its true nature and adapted their lives accordingly enjoyed Allah's protection and manifest care. They looked up to Him directly for guidance in all their affairs, big and small. They lived and moved under His supervision. They expected that He would guide them along the road, step by step, stopping them from error and leading them to the right. Every night they expected to receive some Divine revelations concerning what they had on their minds, providing solutions for their problems and saying to them, "Do this and leave that."

The period which followed the event was certainly remarkable: twenty-three years of direct contact between the human race and the Highest Society. The true nature of this period cannot be recognised except by those who lived in that period and went through its experience, witnessed its start and its end, relished the sweet flavour of that contact and felt the Divine hand guiding them along the road. The distance which separates us from that reality is too great to be defined by any measure of length this world has known. It is a distance in the world of conscience incomparable to any distance in the material world, not even when we think of the gaps separating the stars or galaxies. It is a gap that separates the earth and the Heaven; a gap between human desires and Divine revelation as sources from which concepts and values are derived; a gap between *Ignorance* and Islam, the human and the Divine.

The people who lived in that period were fully aware of its uniqueness, recognised its special place in history and felt the great loss when the Prophet passed away to be in the company of the Supreme Companion. This marked the end of this remarkable period which our minds can hardly imagine but for its actual occurrence.

In the Shade of the Qur'an

Anas related that Abu Bakr said to 'Umar after the death of the Prophet "Let us go to visit Umm Ayman[1] as the Prophet used to do." When they went to her she burst into tears. They said, "What are you crying for? Don't you realise that Allah's company is far better for the Prophet?" She replied, "That is true, I am sure. I am only crying because revelation has ceased with his death." This made tears spring to their eyes and the three of them cried together. (Transmitted by Muslim).

The impact of that period has been in evidence in the life of humanity ever since its beginning up to this moment, and it will remain in evidence until the day when Allah inherits the earth and all that walks on it. Man was reborn when he started to derive his values from Heaven rather than earth and his laws from the Divine revelation instead of his own desires. The course of history underwent a change the like of which has never been experienced before or since. That event, the commencement of revelation, was the point at which the roads crossed. Clear and permanent guidelines were established which cannot be changed by the passage of time or effaced by events. Human conscience developed a concept of existence, human life and its values unsurpassed in comprehensiveness, clarity and purity of all worldly considerations as well as its realism and practicability in human society. The foundations of this Divine code have been firmly established in the world and its various aspects and essential standards have been made clear, *"so that he who perishes may perish after having received a clear sign and he who lives may live after having received a clear sign."*[2]

The beginning of revelation was a unique event at a unique moment marking the end of one era and the start of another. It is the demarcation line in the history of mankind, not merely in the history of a certain nation or a particular generation. It has been recorded by the universe and echoed in all its corners. It has also been recorded in the conscience of man which today needs to be guided by what Allah has revealed and never to lose sight of it. It needs to remember that this event was a rebirth of humanity which can take place only once in history.

---

[1] Umm Ayman was the nurse who took care of the Prophet in his childhood. He remained grateful to her throughout his life. – Translator's note.
[2] The Qur'an. *8; 42.*

Surah 96   The Blood Clots (*Al-Alaq*)

It is self evident that the rest of the *surah* was not revealed at the same time as its opening but at a later date. For it refers to a certain situation and to events in the life of the Prophet which took place later, after he was instructed to convey his message and commanded to offer his worship in public, and after he was met with opposition by the polytheists. This is indicated in the part of the *surah* which begins: *"Observe the man who rebukes a servant of Allah when he prays . . ."* Yet there is perfect harmony between all parts of the *surah*. The facts it relates after the opening part are also arranged in a perfect order. These two factors make the *surah* one perfectly harmonious unit.

"Read in the name of your Lord Who created, created man from clots of blood. Read! your Lord is the most Bounteous, Who has taught the use of the pen, has taught man what he did not know."

This is the first *surah* of the Qur'an so it starts with the name of Allah. It instructs the Messenger of Allah right at the very first moment of his blessed contact with the Highest Society and before taking his very first step along the way of the message he was chosen to deliver, to read in the name of Allah, *"Read in the name of your Lord."* The first attribute of Allah it mentions is that of creation and initiation: *". . . your Lord Who created."* Then it speaks in particular of the creation of man and his origin: *"created man from clots of blood."* He is created from a dried drop of blood which sticks to the womb: a cheap and unsophisticated substance. This reflects the grace and mercy of the Creator as much as it reflects His power. It is out of His grace that He has elevated this clot of blood to the rank of man who can be taught and who can learn: *"Read! your Lord is the most Bounteous, Who has taught the use of the pen, has taught man what he did not know."* The gulf between the origin and the outcome is very wide indeed. But Allah is Able and He is Bounteous, hence this change which makes us dizzy with wonder.

Here also emerges the fact of the teaching of man by the Creator. The pen has always been the most widespread means of learning and it has always had the most far-reaching bearing on man's life. This fact was not as clear at the time of revelation as it is now. But Allah knows the value of the pen; hence, this reference to the pen at the beginning of this His final message to humanity, in the first *surah* of the Qur'an. Yet the Messenger charged with the conveyance of this message could not write. Had the Qur'an been his own composition, he would not have stressed this fact at the first moment. But the Qur'an is Allah's revelation and a message from the Divine.

The *surah* then states the source of learning, which is Allah. From Him man receives all his knowledge, past, present and future. From Him man learns any secret revealed to him about this universe, life and himself.

This single paragraph revealed at the very first moment of the Messenger's contact with the Highest Society states the comprehensive basis of faith and its concepts. Everything starts, works and moves in His name. He is the One Who creates, originates and teaches. Whatever man learns and whatever experience and knowledge he acquires come originally from Allah. He has taught man what he did not know. The Prophet recognised this basic Qur'anic fact. It governed his feelings, teachings and actions for the rest of his life because it is the principal fact of faith.

Imam Ibn Qayyim al-Jawziyyah summarises in his book *"Zad al-Ma'ad"* the Messenger's teaching respecting the remembrance of Allah:

> The Prophet was the most perfect man with regard to his remembrance of Allah, the Exalted. Indeed whatever he spoke was in the line of such remembrance. His commands, prohibitions, legislations, his teaching concerning the Lord and His attributes, judgements, actions, promises and threats were all part of this remembrance. So were his praise and glorification of the Lord, his prayers to Him, his feelings of fear and hope of Him and even his silence. He was conscious of Allah at all times and in every state. His praise of Allah was part of his very nature as if he praised Him with every breath. Indeed he praised Him as he stood up, sat or reclined and when walking, riding, moving, at home or travelling.
>
> When he woke up he used to say, "Praise be to Allah Who has given us life after He had caused us to die. To Him we shall be resurrected." Aisha said that the Prophet used to say when he woke up at night, "Allah is the greatest," and would repeat it ten times. Then he would repeat ten times the statement, "There is no deity but Allah," and pray, "My Lord, I seek refuge with You against constraint in this life and on the Day of Resurrection," ten times. Then he would start his formal prayers. Aisha also said that when the Prophet woke up at night for his devotion he would say, "There is no God but You, my Lord. Praise be to You. I beseech You to forgive my sins and appeal to You for mercy. My Lord,

Surah 96   The Blood Clots (*Al-Alaq*)

enrich my knowledge and cause not my heart to go astray after You have granted me Your guidance. Grant me Your mercy, for You are the most Bounteous." (Transmitted by Abu Dawood) The Messenger has also taught us that whoever gets up at night and says, "There is no God but Allah alone; He has no partner; to Him belongs the Sovereignty and praise; He is able to do everything; all grace is His; Glorified be He; there is no deity but Allah; Allah is the greatest; no power can operate without His permission; He is the Great, the Supreme," and after this says, "My Lord, forgive me," or any other prayer, his prayers will be answered. Should he make ablution and offer prayers, these will be accepted.

The Messenger once stayed for a night at Ibn Abbas's home. The latter related that when he, the Messenger, woke up he raised his hand to the sky and read the last ten verses of *surah "Aal-'Imran."* Then he went on to pray, "My Lord, to You belongs all praise; You are the light of heaven and earth and all therein; Praise be to You, the true Lord; Your promise is true; whatever You say is true; the Meeting with You is true; Heaven is true; Hell is true; the Prophets are true; and the Hour is true. I submit myself to You; I believe in You and depend on You. To You I return. Any dispute I may enter into is for You. To You I turn for judgement. Forgive me all my sins, past and future, public and secret. You are my Lord and there is no God but You. No power can operate without the permission of Allah, the Great, the Supreme."

Aisha related that when the Prophet woke up at night to worship he used to say, "My God, the Lord of Jibril, Mikaeel and Israfeel, the Creator of heaven and earth, Who knows what is concealed and what is made public. You judge amongst Your servants in their disputes. Guide me, with Your own will, to the truth over which people argue and dispute, for You guide whom You will to the straight path." She might have also said that he used to say this at the start of his prayers.

After offering the *"witr"* prayer, the Messenger used to repeat three times, "Glorified be Allah, the Holy One." When he went out of his house he would say, "In the name of Allah. I depend on Allah. My Lord, I appeal to You to guard me against going astray or causing anyone to go astray, and against any slip, and being unjust to anyone or being victim to any injustice by others, and against acting ignorantly, or being ignorantly done by."

The Messenger said, "Whoever says as he leaves his home, 'In the name of Allah. I depend on Allah. No power is operative without the permission of Allah,' he will receive the answer. 'You are rightly guarded and well protected,' and the devil will be made to turn away from him."

Referring to the night when he was host to the Messenger, Ibn Abbas said that when the Messenger left for the mosque for the dawn prayers he said, "My Lord, give me light in my heart, tongue, ears and eyes: give me light in front of me, over me and below me and make the light You give me great."

Abu Said al-Khudri related that the Prophet said, "When a man goes out to the mosque for prayers and says, 'My Lord, I appeal to You by the right of those who pray to You, and the right of my journey to You. I have not come out with any feeling of self-sufficiency, nor in hypocrisy or conceit, nor to seek reputation. I have come out with the hope of avoiding Your anger, seeking Your pleasure. I pray you, save me from Hell and forgive me my sins; You are the Only One Who forgives sins;' seventy thousand angels will be charged with praying for his forgiveness and Allah will receive and welcome him until he finishes his prayers."

Abu Dawood transmitted that the Prophet used to say when he entered the mosque, "I seek refuge with Allah, the Great, and His Holy face, and His old power against Satan, the Outcast." When a man says this the Devil says, "He is now protected against me for the rest of the day."

The Prophet said, "Whenever any of you comes to the mosque, let him pray and ask peace for the Prophet and say, 'My Lord, open to me the doors of your mercy.' When he leaves the mosque, let him say, 'My Lord, I pray You to give me out of Your grace.'" It is also related that when the Prophet entered the mosque, he would ask peace for Muhammad (himself) and his household, then he would say, "My Lord, forgive me my sins and open the doors of Your mercy to me." When he left, he would again ask peace for Muhammad and his household, and say, "My Lord, forgive me my sins and lay open to me the doors of Your grace." After offering the dawn prayers, Allah's Messenger used to stay in his praying place until sunrise, utilising his time in the remembrance of Allah, the Exalted. In the morning, he would say, "Our Lord, we have lived till this morning by Your will, and we also live till evening by Your will. We live and die by Your will. To You we will return." He also used to say, "Morning has appeared. This morning all sovereignty belongs to Allah, praised be He. There is no God but Allah alone. He has no partner, to Him belongs all the universe and to Him is all praise. He is the Almighty, able to do what He wills. My Lord, I pray to You to give me of the best of this day and the best of the days to follow. I seek refuge with You against the evil of this day and the days to follow. My Lord, I seek Your refuge against laziness and the evils of old age, against suffering in Hell and suffering in the grave." In the evening he would repeat the same prayer substituting evening for morning (Transmitted by Muslim).

Once Abu Bakr, the Prophet's most distinguished companion, said to him, "Teach me some prayers to say in the morning and in the evening." Allah's Messenger taught him the following prayer, "My Lord, the Creator of heaven and earth. Who knows the visible and the unseen, the perceptible and the imperceptible, the Lord and Possessor of all, I declare that there is no God but You. I appeal to You to protect me against my own evil and the evil of Satan; I seek Your refuge against doing myself any harm or causing harm to any Muslim." The Messenger told Abu Bakr to say this prayer in the morning, evening and before going to bed. (*Zad al-Ma'ad* contains numerous traditions on the same subject.)

... When Allah's Messenger had a new garment, he would mention it by name (e.g. a shirt, a gown or a turban) and say, "My Lord, praise be to You. You have given me this. I pray You to give me its goodness and the goodness for which it was made. I pray to You to rid me of its evil and the evil for which it was made."

The Messenger is reported to have been in the habit of saying the following prayer when he returned home, "Praise be to Allah who has given me this shelter and what is sufficient for me; and praise be to Allah Who has given me food and drink, and praise be to Allah Who has given me much (of His generosity). I pray You to extend Your protection to me against Hell."

It is confirmed in the two authentic books of the Messenger's traditions that, when he entered the toilet, he used to say,

"My Lord, I pray You to rid me of evil things." When he left, he used to say, "Praise be to Allah Who has ridden me of harm and given me good health." (Transmitted by Ibn Majjah).

It is also confirmed that he once put his hand in a water container and said to his companions, "Make ablutions in the name of Allah." When he saw the new moon, he used to say, "My Lord, let it come to us with security, faith, safety and submission to You. New moon, Allah is my Lord and Your Lord." (Transmitted by At-Tirmithi).

When he started eating, he used to say, "In the name of Allah." He also said, "When any of you eats, let him mention the name of Allah. If he forgets to do so, let him say (when he remembers), in the name of Allah at the beginning and at the end."

Thus was the life of the Messenger of Allah. It was conditioned, down to every single detail, by the Divine instruction which he received at the very first moment of his message. This instruction helped his faith to be established on a genuine basis.

It is Allah, then, Who creates, teaches and bestows His abundant bounties on man. This implies that man should acknowledge Allah's benevolence and be grateful for it. But what actually happens is something different.

The second part of the *surah* deals with man's transgression. *"Indeed man tyrannises once he thinks himself self-sufficient. Surely to your Lord all things return."* It is Allah Who gives to man in abundance and makes him independent. He also creates and teaches him and extends to him His generous treatment. But men in general (excluding those guarded by faith) are not thankful for their independence which is made possible by what they are given. They do not recognise the source of this grace, which is the same as the source of their creation, knowledge and livelihood. They tyrannise and transgress all limits and show their conceit instead of being dutiful and thankful.

The portrait of the transgressor, conceited because he has forgotten his origin, is followed by a comment charged with an implicit warning, *"Surely to your Lord all things return."* Where can this proud tyrant then turn? At the same time one of the fundamental rules of the Islamic ideological concept is emphasised. That is, all must refer to Allah in every matter, thought or action. He is the only resort and refuge. The good and the bad, the obedient and the sinner, the righteous and the wrong-doer, the rich and the poor, will all return to Him. Even the man who tyrannises when he thinks himself

Surah 96   The Blood Clots *(Al-Alaq)*

independent will come to Him eventually.

Thus, the first two parts of the *surah* state together the ideological concept of Islam: creation and teaching belong to Allah alone and to Him all return: *"Surely to your Lord all things return."*

The third part tackles a particularly appalling form of tyranny. Its description in the inimitable Qur'anic style fills one with wonder and dismay that it should take place at all. *"Observe the man who rebukes a servant of Allah when he prays. Think: does he not follow the right guidance and enjoin true piety? Think: if he denies the truth and turns his back, does he not realise that Allah sees all?"*

The feelings of wonder and dismay are aroused by the manner of expression which takes the form of address and conversation using short sentences that follow in rapid succession. The effect can hardly ever be produced by ordinary written language. *"Observe"* this ghastly business actually taking place! *"Observe the man who rebukes a servant of Allah when he prays."* Have you seen this repulsive sight? Have you realised how repugnance is doubled by the fact that the person being dissuaded from his prayers is in fact following Divine guidance. He merely enjoins righteousness and piety, yet he is discouraged and told to desist!

Yet the transgressor outdoes himself by taking a still more abhorrent stand, *"Think: if he denies the truth and turns his back."* The closing note is one of implicit warning, similar to that of the previous paragraph, *"Does he not realise that Allah sees all?"* He sees everything: the denial of truth, the turning away from it, as well as the forbidding of the believers from offering their prayers. Since Allah sees all there is something which follows His seeing. This is the implicit warning.

Thus, we have a scene of tyranny trying to suppress the call of faith and obedience to Allah which is followed immediately by a stern warning stated explicitly this time, *"Let him desist, or We will drag him by the forelock."* The Arabic term used for "drag" has a marked tone of violent action. The dragging is by the forelock as it is the part of the head raised high by every conceited tyrant. It undoubtedly deserves to be hit violently: *"His lying, sinful forelock!"* The tyrant may think of calling his clan and supporters to come to his aid: *"Then let him call his henchmen."* On the other side, *"We will call the guards of Hell,"* and they are powerful and ruthless. The outcome of the battle is never in doubt.

In the light of this frightening destiny of the disbelievers, the *surah* concludes with an instruction to the obedient servants of Allah to persevere and follow the path of faith: *"No, never obey him, but prostrate yourself and draw closer to Allah."* Do not obey this tyrant who tries to stop you from offering your devotion and conveying your message. Prostrate yourself to your Lord and bring yourself closer to Him through worship and obedience. As for the tyrant, leave him to the guards of Hell who are sure to mete out to him what he deserves.

Some authentic reports say that the *surah,* with the exception of the first part, refers to Abu Jahl who once passed by the Prophet while he was praying at the Ka'aba. He turned to him and said, "Muhammad, have I not ordered you to stop these practices?" He also added some warnings to the Prophet who gave him a stern reply. This was possibly the time when the Prophet seized Abu Jahl by the collar and warned him of his impending doom. Abu Jahl said, "Muhammad, what do you threaten me with? I am sure I have the largest following in this valley." Hence, the revelation, *"Let him call his henchmen."* Ibn Abbas, the Prophet's companion, said in comment "Had he called them, the angels charged with meting out punishment would have taken him away there and then."

The *surah,* however, is general in its significance. It refers to every obedient believer calling men to follow the path of Allah and to every tyrant who forbids prayer, threatens to punish the believers and act conceitedly. The concluding Divine instruction is therefore, *"No, never obey him, but prostrate yourself and draw closer to Allah."*

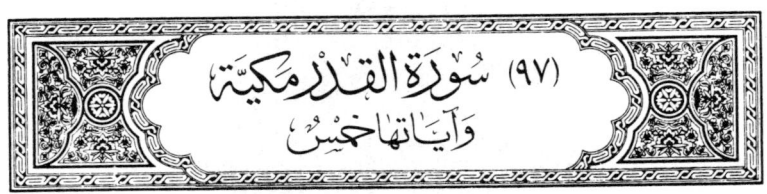

بِسْمِ اللهِ الرَّحْمَنِ الرَّحِيمِ

إِنَّا أَنزَلْنَهُ فِى لَيْلَةِ ٱلْقَدْرِ ۝ وَمَا أَدْرَىٰكَ مَا لَيْلَةُ ٱلْقَدْرِ ۝ لَيْلَةُ ٱلْقَدْرِ خَيْرٌ مِّنْ أَلْفِ شَهْرٍ ۝ تَنَزَّلُ ٱلْمَلَٰٓئِكَةُ وَٱلرُّوحُ فِيهَا بِإِذْنِ رَبِّهِم مِّن كُلِّ أَمْرٍ ۝ سَلَٰمٌ هِىَ حَتَّىٰ مَطْلَعِ ٱلْفَجْرِ ۝

SURAH 97

POWER
AL-QADR

In the name of Allah, the Beneficent, the Merciful.

We revealed it (the Qur'an) on the Night of Power.
Would that you knew what the Night of Power is like.
Better is the Night of Power than a thousand months.
On that night the angels and the Spirit descend by their Lord's
    permission, with all His decrees.
That night is peace, till the break of dawn.

In the Shade of the Qur'an

This *surah* speaks about the promised great night which the whole universe marked with joy and prayers. It is the night of perfect communion between this world and the Highest Society. It is the night which marked the beginning of the revelation of the Qur'an to Muhammad (peace be on him), an event unparalleled in the history of mankind for its splendour and the significance it has for the life of mankind as a whole. Its greatness is far beyond human realisation. *"We revealed it on the Night of Power. Would that you knew what the Night of Power is like. Better is the Night of Power than a thousand months."*

The Qur'anic statements which relate this great event radiate with Allah's clear and shining light: *"We revealed it on the Night of Power."* There is also the light of the angels and the Spirit moving between the earth and the Highest Society. *"On that night the angels and the Spirit descend by their Lord's permission with all His decrees."* In addition, there is also the light of dawn which the *surah* represents as perfectly harmonious with the light of the Qur'an and the angels as well as with the spirit of peace: *"That night is peace, till the break of dawn."*

The night in question here is the same night referred to in *surah* 44, ("Smoke"): "We revealed it (the Qur'an) on a blessed night, for We would warn (mankind), on a night when every precept was made plain as a commandment from Us. We have ever sent forth messengers as a blessing from your Lord, who hears all and knows all." It is established that it is a night in the month of *Ramadhan*, as stated in *surah* 2, ("The Cow"): *"In the month of Ramadhan the Qur'an was revealed, a book of guidance distinguishing right from wrong."* This means that the Night of Power marked the beginning of the revelation of the Qur'an to the Prophet and his charge of conveying it to mankind.

Ibn Ishaq related that the first revelation, consisting of the opening of *surah* 96, ("The Blood Clots"), took place in the month of *Ramadhan*, when the Messenger of Allah was at his devotion in the cave of Hira.

A number of traditions specifying this night have come down to us: some stress that it is the twenty-seventh of *Ramadhan*, others the twenty-first; a few others say it is one of the last ten days and some others do not go beyond saying that it is in *Ramadhan*.

Its title "The Night of Power" may be taken to mean assignment, designation and organisation, or it may mean value, position and

Surah 97   Power (*Al-Qadr*)

rank. Both meanings are relevant to that great universal event of the revelation of the Qur'an and the assigning of the message to the Prophet. For it is the greatest and most precious of all events which the universe has witnessed. It is also the event which explains more clearly than any other the place of assignment, designation and organisation in the life of mankind. This night is better than a thousand months. The figure here and elsewhere in the Qur'an does not signify its precise number. It simply denotes a very high number. Many thousand months and many thousand years have passed without leaving behind a fraction of the changes and results brought about in that blessed and happy night.

This night is of an essence too sublime to be understood by human intellect: *"Would that you knew what the Night of Power is like."* There is no reason to attach any value to the legends circulating among the masses concerning this night. It is great because Allah has chosen it for the revelation of the Qur'an, so that its light may spread throughout the universe, and Divine peace may spread in human life and conscience. That night is great because of what the Qur'an includes: an ideology, a basis for values and standards and a comprehensive code of moral and social behaviour, all of which promote peace within the human soul and in the world at large. It is great because of the descent of the angels, and Jibril in particular, by their Lord's permission carrying the Qur'an which was first sent down on that night. They fill all the space between heaven and earth in such a splendid, universal celebration, vividly portrayed in this *surah*.

When we look today in retrospect, after the lapse of numerous generations, at that glorious and happy night, and imagine the fascinating celebration the world witnessed on that night, and ponder over the essence of revelation and its far-reaching effects on human life and its values, we appreciate the greatness of this event. We can then understand, to some extent, why the Qur'anic reference to that night is made in such an equivocal way: *"Would that you knew what the Night of Power is like"*.

On that night every matter of significance was made plain and distinct; new values and standards were established; the fortunes of nations were determined; and values and standards were sifted.

Humanity, out of ignorance and to its misfortune, may overlook the value and importance of the Night of Power. When humanity ignores all that, it loses the happiest and most beautiful sign of grace which Allah bestowed on it. It loses the real happiness and peace gifted to it by Islam, namely, the peace of conscience, family and society. What it has otherwise gained of material civilisation cannot be adequate compensation for its loss. Humanity is miserable in spite of higher production levels and better means of existence. The splendid light which once illuminated its soul has been put off; the brilliant touch of happiness which carried it high up to the Highest Society has been smothered; the peace which overflowed on the hearts and minds has disappeared. Nothing can compensate for the happiness of the soul, the heavenly light and the elevation to the loftiest ranks.

We, the believers in Islam, are commanded not to forget or neglect this event. The Prophet has taught us an easy and enjoyable way to commemorate that night, so that our souls may always be in close communion with it and with the universal event which took place in it. He has urged us to spend this night of each year in devotion. He said, "Seek the Night of Power in the last ten nights of *Ramadhan.*" "He who spends the Night of Power in worship, with a pure motive of faith and devotion, will have all his past sins forgiven." Islam is not mere formalities. Hence, the Prophet specified that the consecration of that night must be motivated by faith and devotion. This would make its consecration by an individual an indication of his full awareness of the far-reaching effects of what took place in that night.

The Islamic method of character building links worship with faith and the truth it establishes in the heart and conscience of the individual. In this method, worship is considered a means for maintaining full awareness of this truth, its clarification and firm establishment in one's mind, heart and soul. This method has been proved to be the best for the revival of this truth so that it may have a constant influence on men's consciences and behaviour. The theoretical understanding of this truth cannot, on its own and without worship, establish it or give it the necessary impetus for its operation in the life of the individual or the life of the society. This link between the anniversary of the Night of Power and its consecration in faith and devotion is a part of the successful and upright method of Islam.

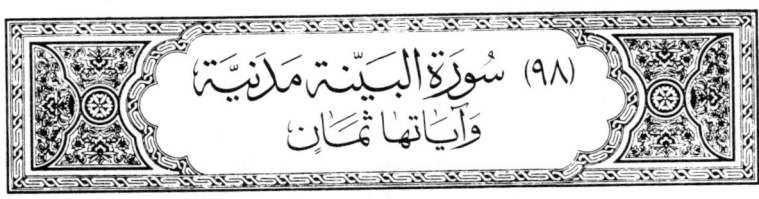

(٩٨) سورة البينة مدنية
وآياتها ثمان

بِسْمِ اللهِ الرَّحْمَنِ الرَّحِيمِ

لَمْ يَكُنِ ٱلَّذِينَ كَفَرُوا۟ مِنْ أَهْلِ ٱلْكِتَٰبِ وَٱلْمُشْرِكِينَ مُنفَكِّينَ حَتَّىٰ تَأْتِيَهُمُ ٱلْبَيِّنَةُ ۝ رَسُولٌ مِّنَ ٱللَّهِ يَتْلُوا۟ صُحُفًا مُّطَهَّرَةً ۝ فِيهَا كُتُبٌ قَيِّمَةٌ ۝ وَمَا تَفَرَّقَ ٱلَّذِينَ أُوتُوا۟ ٱلْكِتَٰبَ إِلَّا مِنۢ بَعْدِ مَا جَآءَتْهُمُ ٱلْبَيِّنَةُ ۝ وَمَآ أُمِرُوٓا۟ إِلَّا لِيَعْبُدُوا۟ ٱللَّهَ مُخْلِصِينَ لَهُ ٱلدِّينَ حُنَفَآءَ وَيُقِيمُوا۟ ٱلصَّلَوٰةَ وَيُؤْتُوا۟ ٱلزَّكَوٰةَ ۚ وَذَٰلِكَ دِينُ ٱلْقَيِّمَةِ ۝ إِنَّ ٱلَّذِينَ كَفَرُوا۟ مِنْ أَهْلِ ٱلْكِتَٰبِ وَٱلْمُشْرِكِينَ فِى نَارِ جَهَنَّمَ خَٰلِدِينَ فِيهَآ ۚ أُو۟لَٰٓئِكَ هُمْ شَرُّ ٱلْبَرِيَّةِ ۝ إِنَّ ٱلَّذِينَ ءَامَنُوا۟ وَعَمِلُوا۟ ٱلصَّٰلِحَٰتِ أُو۟لَٰٓئِكَ هُمْ خَيْرُ ٱلْبَرِيَّةِ ۝ جَزَآؤُهُمْ عِندَ رَبِّهِمْ جَنَّٰتُ عَدْنٍ تَجْرِى مِن تَحْتِهَا ٱلْأَنْهَٰرُ خَٰلِدِينَ فِيهَآ أَبَدًا ۖ رَّضِىَ ٱللَّهُ عَنْهُمْ وَرَضُوا۟ عَنْهُ ۚ ذَٰلِكَ لِمَنْ خَشِىَ رَبَّهُۥ ۝

SURAH 98

THE CLEAR PROOF
AL BAYYINAH

In the name of Allah, the Beneficent, the Merciful.

Those who disbelieve among the people of the earlier revelations and the polytheists could have never departed (from their erring ways) until there had come to them the Clear Proof:
a Messenger from Allah reciting purified pages, containing books of high value and importance.
Nor were the people of the earlier revelations divided until the Clear Proof had been given to them.
Yet they are ordered to do nothing more than to serve Allah, to worship Him alone with sincerity, and with purity of faith, to attend to their prayers and to pay the purifying alms (zakat). That is surely the faith of the upright nation.
Those who disbelieve among the people of the earlier revelations and the polytheists shall burn forever in the fire of Hell. They are the worst of all creatures.
But those who believe and do righteous deeds are the best of all creatures.
Their Lord will reward them with the gardens of Eden underneath which rivers flow, where they shall dwell forever. Allah is well pleased with them and they with Him. This is the reward of the god-fearing.

In the Shade of the Qur'an

As stated in our copies of the Qur'an and according to the greater number of reports, this *surah* is a Medinan revelation. There are, however, some reports which classify it as Makkan. Although its classification as Medinan carries more weight in view of these reports and its mode of expression and style, yet the possibility of its being Makkan cannot be ruled out. The fact that it mentions *"the purifying alms" (zakat)* and "the people of earlier revelations" is not clear cut argument against the Makkan possibility. Some *surahs* which are indisputably Makkan mention the people of earlier revelations. Also, there were some of these people in Makka; some of them adopted Islam and some did not. Moreover, the Christians from Najran came to the Prophet when he was still in Makka, and they accepted the Islamic faith, as it is known. Moreover, *"zakat"* or *"the purifying alms"* is mentioned in some Makka *surahs*.

This *surah* deals in a positive manner with a number of facts relating to history and faith. The first fact is that the sending of the Messenger, Muhammad (peace be on him), was essential to the transformation of those of the people of the earlier revelations and the polytheists who had ended up in disbelief. They could not have departed from their erring ways without the help of this prophetic mission: *"Those who disbelieve among the people of the earlier revelations and the polytheists could have never departed (from their erring ways) until there had come to them the Clear Proof: a Messenger from Allah reciting purified pages containing books of high value and importance"*.

The second fact is that religious discord and conflict among the people of the earlier revelations did not arise out of their ignorance of, or from any obscurity or ambiguity in, their religion. On the contrary, they ran into discord after they had received true knowledge and the clear proof: *"Nor were the people of the earlier revelations divided until the Clear Proof had been given to them."*

The third fact is that, in regard to its origin, religion is one. Its fundamentals are simple and clear and do not, by themselves and by their plain and easy nature, make for divisions or conflicts: *"Yet they are ordered to do nothing more than to serve Allah, to worship Him alone with sincerity and with purity of faith, to attend to their prayers and to pay the stated alms. That is surely the faith of the upright nation."*

The fourth fact is that those who disbelieved after receiving the clear proof are the worst creatures of all, while those who believe and

Surah 98   The Clear Proof *(Al-Bayyinah)*

do good deeds are the best creatures. Hence the rewards of the two types are totally different: *"Those who disbelieve among the people of the earlier revelations and the polytheists shall burn forever in the fire of Hell. They are the worst of all creatures. But those who believe and do righteous deeds are the best of all creatures. Their Lord will reward them with the gardens of Eden underneath which rivers flow, where they shall dwell for ever. Allah is well pleased with them and they with Him. This is the reward of the godfearing.*

All these four facts are greatly valuable for the full understanding of the role of the Islamic ideology which is the final Divine message, as well as for the formulation of one's concepts of faith.

"Those who disbelieve among the people of the earlier revelations and the polytheists could have never departed (from their erring ways) until there had come to them the Clear Proof: a Messenger from Allah reciting purified pages, containing books of high value and importance."

The world was terribly in need of a new message. Corruption had spread around the whole world to the extent that there was no hope of reform except by means of a new message, a new method of orientation and a new movement. Disbelief crept into and became the characteristic of all creeds and doctrines whether those of the people of earlier revelations (i.e. the Jews and the Christians) who previously knew the Divine religions and distorted them or those of the polytheists in the Arabian Peninsula and beyond, all alike. They were not to turn away from this disbelief into which they had sunk except by means of this new message and at the hands of a messenger who would himself be a clear proof, distinctive and specific. *"A Messenger from Allah reciting purified pages"*, that is, purified of all idolatory and disbelief, *"containing books of high value and importance."* The term "book" is used for reference to the subject discussed, for example, book of purity, book of prayers, book of destiny and book of resurrection. These pure pages are indeed the Qur'an which contains valuable and important books.

Hence this message and the messenger came at a perfectly suitable time. These scriptures also came with all that they contain of books and facts to bring about a far reaching reform of this world. As to how badly the world needed this message and messenger we shall be content to indicate by quoting some inspiring remarks from the valuable book written by the Muslim author Sayyid Abul-

In the Shade of the Qur'an

Hassan Ali Nadwi and entitled *"Islam and the World"*. This book is the clearest as well as the briefest that we have read on this subject. The author writes in chapter one:

> The sixth Century of the Christian era, it is generally agreed, represented the darkest phase in the history of our race. Humanity had reached the edge of the precipice, towards which it had been tragically proceeding for centuries, and there appeared to be no agency or power in the whole world which could come to its rescue and save it from crashing into the abyss of destruction.
>
> In his melancholy progress from God forgetfulness to self-forgetting, man had lost his moorings. He had grown indifferent to his destiny. The teachings of the prophets had been forgotten: the lamps that they had kindled either had been put out by the storms of moral anarchy or the light they shed had become so feeble that it could illumine the hearts of but a few men, most of whom had sought refuge in passivity and resignation. Having been vanquished in the battle between spiritualism and materialism, they had shut themselves up in monasteries or gone into wilderness. Such of them as were still left in the whirlpool of life had aligned themselves with the ruling classes of their lands. They helped them in the satisfaction of their sensual desires and in the maintenance of unjust political and economic systems and co-operated with them in reaping unlawful benefits out of the wealth of the people. . . .
>
> Great religions became playthings in the hands of debased ecclesiastics who corrupted and twisted them beyond recognition, so much so that if it were possible for their founders to return to the physical life, they could not have recognised them. In consequence of the moral debasement of the great centres of civilisation and general disorder and unrest, people everywhere got entangled in their internal problems. They had no message to offer to the world. The world had become hollow from within; its life-springs had dried up. It possessed neither the light of religious guidance for their personal conduct nor any abiding and rational principles for running a state.

This outlines briefly the condition of mankind and religions just before the advent of Prophet Muhammad (peace be on him). The Qur'an refers in various parts to the aspects of this disbelief which spread amongst the people of the earlier revelations as well as the polytheists. Among these references to the Jews and Christians are: *"The Jews say, 'Ezra is the son of Allah', and the Christians say, 'the Messiah is the son of Allah'"*[1] and *"The Jews say, 'the Christians follow nothing true', and the Christians say, 'the Jews follow nothing true'."*[2] The Qur'an also refers to the Jews: *"The Jews have said, 'Allah's hand is fettered'. Fettered are their hands, and cursed they are for what they say. His hands are outspread: He bestows as He wills"*.[3] It says about the Christians: *"They are surely disbelievers who say, 'Allah is the Messiah, son of Mary'"*[4] and, *"They are surely disbelievers who say, 'Allah is one of a trinity'"*[5] The Qur'an also speaks about the polytheists: *"Say: "Disbelievers! I do not worship what you worship. Nor do you worship what I worship. I shall never worship what you worship, neither will you worship what I worship. You have your own religion and I have mine'."*[6] There are many other statements in the Qur'an which support this view.

In addition to this disbelief, there were backwardness, divisions, ruin as well as other evils spread all over the world.

"In short there was no nation on earth with an upright thinking. There was neither a society built on a foundation of morality and virtue, nor a government based on justice and mercy, nor a leadership founded on knowledge and wisdom, nor a true religion that came through the prophets".[7]

Hence, the Divine grace extended to mankind required that a Messenger be sent from Him reciting purified scriptures containing valuable and important books. There was no way of putting an end to the widespread corruption except by the sending of this Messenger, the deliverer, the guide and himself the Clear Proof.

Having made this fact clear at the outset, the *surah* goes on to state that the people of the earlier revelations in particular did not experience religious conflicts and divisions as a result of ignorance on their part or confusion or complication on the part of their religion. Their divisions occurred after the true knowledge and the clear signs of their religion were delivered to them through the Messengers sent to them: *"Nor were the people of the earlier revelations divided until the Clear Proof had been given to them."*

---

[1] The Qur'an. *9; 30.*
[2] *Ibid. 2; 113.*
[3] *Ibid. 5; 64.*
[4] *Ibid. 5; 72.*
[5] *Ibid. 5; 73.*
[6] *Ibid. 109; 1–6.*
[7] Abul Hassan Ali Nadwi. *Islam and the World.*

In the Shade of the Qur'an

The first division was among the Jews who split into sects and groups before the prophethood of Jesus. Although their prophet was Moses and the Torah was their book, they split up into five main sects, namely, the Sadducees, the Pharisees, the Asians, the Extremists and the Samaritans. Each had their own characteristics and their own ways. Later on the division between the Jews and the Christians took place in spite of the fact that Jesus is the last prophet sent to the Children of Israel. He came to endorse the Torah and confirm it. Nevertheless, the quarrel between the Jews and the Christians reached the level of violent enmity and wicked hatred. History tells us about the horrifying massacres that took place between the two parties.

"The mutual jealousy and hatred between the Christians and the Jews, which did not permit them to forego any opportunity of settling an old score was brought to its climax towards the close of the sixth century. In 610 A.D. the Jews of Antioch rebelled against the Christians, and the Emperor Phocas sent his famous general Bonosus to put down the uprising, who set about his business with such enthusiasm that the whole of the Jewish population was wiped out. Thousands of Jews perished by the sword, while hundreds of them were drowned or burnt alive or thrown to the wild beasts."[1]

"This was repeated again and again between the Jews and the Christians. Al-Maqrizi says in his Book of Plans (*Al Khitat*), "During the reign of the Byzantine Emperor Phocas, Chosroes, the Shah of Persia, dispatched his armies to Syria and Egypt. They destroyed the churches of Jerusalem, Palestine and the rest of the Syrian land. They wiped out all the Christians and pursued them to Egypt, where they slaughtered them in large numbers and enslaved an unimaginable number. The Jews helped them in fighting the Christians and destroying their churches. They poured from all directions to help the Persians and came from Tiberia, the Mount of Galilee, Nazareth village and the City of Tyre and all around Jerusalem. They committed all sorts of atrocities against the Christians, organised ghastly massacres, destroyed two Christian churches in Jerusalem, burnt their places, stole a piece of the pillar of the Cross and captured the Patriarch of Jerusalem and a great

---

[1] Abul Hassan Ali Nadwi, *Islam and the World*, English Edition pp. 17–18.

Surah 98   The Clear Proof (*Al-Bayyinah*)

many of his friends and companions. . . ." Al-Maqrizi goes on to relate the Persian conquest of Egypt; then he writes: "At that time, the Jews in the City of Tyre rebelled and sent messengers from among themselves to other cities and towns and all agreed to lay a trap for the Christians and kill them. A war broke out between the Jews and Christians in which the number of the Jews was around 20,000. They destroyed the Christian churches around Tyre. But the Christians surrounded them and raised much greater numbers, so the Jews suffered a ghastly defeat and a great number of them were killed. At the time Heraclius ascended to power in Constantinople. He defeated the Persians by setting a trap for the Shah, who left him eventually and went away. Then he marched from Constantinople to re-establish his authority over Syria and Egypt and to renew what the Persians had destroyed. The Jews from Tiberia and other places went out to meet him. They presented him with precious gifts and begged him to guarantee their security and to take an oath to this effect. He granted their request. He went on to Jerusalem where he was received by the Christian population holding up their Bibles, crosses, and incense, and burning candles. He was very much displeased at seeing the city and its churches destroyed. He expressed his sorrow to the local Christians who told him about the uprising by the Jews and their siding with the Persians, the massacre of the Christians and the destruction of their churches. They told Heraclius to level a blow to the Jews but he protested that he had already guaranteed their security and had taken an oath to that effect. Their monks, cardinals and priests gave their judgement that the killing of the Jews was justifiable on the grounds that they had played a trick in order to win that assurance from him before he knew what they had done. The clergy also pledged to atone for Heraclius' oath by committing themselves and all Christians to fast a certain Friday every year for the rest of time. Thus he leaned to their argument and wreaked such a savage vengeance upon the Jews that in the Byzantine provinces of Syria and Egypt those alone could save themselves who could take to flight or go into hiding."

These reports give us an idea about the degree of savagery the two parties, the Christians and the Jews, had reached, their watching for a chance to strike against the enemy and their heeding no rules in all that.[1]

---
[1] Abul Hassan Ali Nadwi, *Islam and the World,* first Arabic edition pp. 9–11.

In the Shade of the Qur'an

Then divisions and differences broke out amongst the Christians themselves in spite of the fact that their book is one and their messenger is one. They were divided first in matters of faith; then they split up into hostile and warring sects. The differences were concerned with the nature of Jesus and whether he had a Divine or a human nature, and with the nature of Mary, his mother, and also with the nature of the Trinity which constitutes God, as they claim. The Qur'an relates two or three of their sayings on these issues: *"They are surely disbelievers who say: 'Allah is the Messiah, son of Mary'"*,[1] *"They are surely disbelievers who say: 'Allah is one of a trinity'"*,[2] and, *"Allah said: 'Jesus, son of Mary! Did you ever say to people: "Worship me and my mother as gods beside Allah"?'"*[3]

The most violent of doctrinal divisions was that which erupted between the Byzantine State and the Christians of Syria and the Christians of Egypt, or, in a more accurate definition, the Melkites and the Monophysites. The main dispute was over the alleged combination of the Divine and the human natures in Jesus. The Melkite Christians of Syria held that he was both Divine and human, while the Monophysites of Egypt insisted upon his being truly Divine, the human part of his nature having lost itself in the Divine as a drop of vinegar loses its identity in the ocean. The dispute between the two parties became much stronger in the sixth and seventh centuries so that it looked as if it was a ceaseless war between two rival religions, or a dispute between Jews and Christians. Every group kept saying to the other that its stand was without foundation.

Emperor Heraclius (610–641) tried after his victory over the Persians in 638 to reconcile the contending creeds in his state and to unite them by compromise. This compromise took the shape of a general ban on indulging in any argument on the nature of Jesus Christ, the Messiah, and whether he had a single or dual nature. But everyone had to accept the doctrine of a single energy in Christ.[4] Agreement on this was established at the beginning of

---

[1] The Qur'an. *5; 72.*

[2] *Ibid. 5; 73.*

[3] *Ibid. 5; 116.*

[4] The doctrine of a single energy in "Christ" was that the allegedly Divine and human natures in Jesus had one active force.

Surah 98   The Clear Proof *(Al-Bayyinah)*

631, and thus the Menothelian creed was declared the official creed of the state and all those of its populations who belonged to the Christian church. Heraclius was determined to give the new creed overall supremacy, and he utilised all means for this end. But the Copts disputed his authority and declared their total rejection of this innovation and deviation. They took the opposing stand and sacrificed their all for their old faith. The Emperor tried once again to unite all the creeds and settle the differences. He was content that people should accept that there is a single will for Christ.[1] As for the other issue, namely, the realisation of that will by action, he deferred taking a stand on it altogether. He also banned all people from indulging in arguments and debates on these issues. He included all that in an official message which he delivered to all parts of the Eastern world. But the message failed to end the storm. Instead, brutal persecution was administered by the Emperor in Egypt for ten years which witnessed what would send a shiver of terror into any mortal being. Men were tortured savagely before being put to death by drowning. Big torches were lit and directed to the miserable prisoners until the fat ran from both sides of their bodies to the floor. Prisoners were put in sacks which were then filled with sand and thrown into the sea. These and other ghastly brutalities were committed.[2]

All these disputes among the people of earlier revelations took place after *"the Clear Proof had been given to them"*. They were not lacking in knowledge and proof, but they were blindly driven by their desires into deviation.

Yet religion is clear in its original form and the faith is simple in its essence: *"Yet they are ordered nothing more than to serve Allah, to worship Him alone with sincerity, and with purity of faith, to attend to their prayers and to pay the purifying alms (zakat). That is surely the faith of the upright nation."* This is the basis of the Divine religion throughout the ages and in all its forms. It is simply the worship of Allah alone, sincere and pure submission to Him, detachment from polytheism and the polytheists, the establishment of regular worship and payment of the prescribed alms: *"That is surely the faith of the upright nation."* It is a pure and sincere faith in the heart, worship of the

---

[1] The doctrine of the single energy was repudiated, and the doctrine of a single will (the Monothelete formula) was propounded in 638.
[2] Abul Hassan Ali Nadwi, *Islam and the World*, Arabic edition pp. 3–5.

Divine Being which is a translation of this faith, and spending money for the cause of Allah as He has stated. He who fulfils these injunctions has met the requirements of faith, as the people of the earlier revelations were commanded to do, and as these requirements are outlined in all the forms of the Divine religion. It is one religion, the same faith in all the successive messages and as preached by the successive messengers of Allah. It is a religion free from all ambiguity and complication; a faith which gives no reason for division and dispute. It is very clear and very simple. How completely different this religion is from those complicated and confusing concepts and from those lengthy polemics.

Since clear proof has been given to them formerly in their own religions through their own prophets, and since clear proof had been given to them again, full of life, in the form of a Messenger from Allah reciting purified pages, and offering them a clear and simple faith, then the true path becomes very clear. So does the destiny of the disbelievers, and that of the believers: *"Those who disbelieve among the people of the earlier revelations and the polytheists shall burn forever in the fire of Hell; they are the worst of all creatures. But those who believe and do righteous deeds are the best of all creatures. Their Lord will reward them with the gardens of Eden underneath which rivers flow where they shall dwell forever. Allah is well pleased with them and they with Him. This is the reward of the godfearing."*

Muhammad (peace be on him) was the last messenger, and Islam, which he preached, the final message. Messengers from Allah came successively every time corruption spread in the world. Their objective was to make mankind return to righteousness. Those who deviated from the right path had one chance after another to correct their behaviour. But now that Allah has willed to close His messages to earth by this final, comprehensive, perfect and accomplished message, then the last chance has been given. It is either the adoption of faith and salvation, or the denial of faith and destruction. For disbelief now is an established evidence of unlimited evil, while accepting the faith is proof of goodness which goes to its absolute end.

"Those who disbelieve among the people of the earlier revelations and the polytheists shall burn forever in the fire of Hell. They are the worst of all creatures." It is a clear and absolute verdict which gives no room for argument of dispute. It is applicable even if some of their actions, values or systems were good, since these are not based on be-

Surah 98   The Clear Proof (*Al-Bayyinah*)

lieving in this final message and final messenger. No appearance of goodness will make us entertain even the slightest doubt in this judgement, since this apparent goodness is detached from the upright method of living laid down by Allah.

"Those who believe and do righteous deeds are the best of all creatures." This is also an absolute verdict that makes for no dispute or argument. Its condition is also clear, free from any ambiguity or deception. The condition is faith, not merely being born in a land which claims to be Islamic, or in a family which claims to belong to Islam. Neither is it a few words which one repeats again and again. It is the acceptance of faith which establishes its effects on the actual life, *"and do righteous deeds."* It is entirely different from the words that go no further than the lips. As for the *"righteous deeds"*, these are everything Allah has commanded to be done in matters of worship, behaviour, action and day-to-day dealings. The first and most important of these *"righteous deeds"* is the establishment of Allah's law on this planet, and the government of people according to what Allah has legislated. Those who act accordingly are the best creatures of all.

"Their Lord will reward them with the gardens of Eden underneath which rivers flow, where they shall dwell forever." These gardens are a specially prepared, permanent and happy dwelling. The happiness is symbolised here by security against death and by the prevalent feeling of contentment as against the feelings of anxiety which mar and disrupt all earthly comforts. It is also symbolised by the rivers flowing underneath these gardens; a picture which adds a sense of ease, life and beauty.

The *surah* then adds some refined touches to the picture it portrays of their perpetual happiness: *"Allah is well pleased with them and they with him."* This pleasure of Allah with them is much more exalted and far more enjoyable than any happiness. Moreover, in their inmost souls they feel their pleasure with their Lord. They are well pleased with the destiny He has set for them, delighted with the grace He has granted them, enchanted with this relationship with their Lord. It is a pleasure which fills the heart and soul with security and contentment as well as delight and happiness, deep and pure. It is an expression which suggests unique connotations: *"Allah is well pleased with them and they with him."*

"This is the reward of the godfearing." This is the final assertion. It stresses that all that has been said is dependent on the nature of the

relationship between man's heart and Allah. It also depends on man's having a feeling of Allah which urges him to all sorts of good deeds and militates against all sorts of deviation. It is a feeling which removes the barriers, lifts the curtains and makes man's heart stand bare before Allah, the One, the All Powerful. It is a feeling which helps make worship and submission to Allah pure and purges human actions from all elements of hypocrisy and polytheism, in all forms. So he who truly fears his Lord cannot allow his heart to entertain the slightest shred of influence by any being other than Allah, the Creator of all beings. Such a man knows that Allah rejects any deed by which the doer seeks any being beside Allah. For Allah is in no need of partners. Every action must be pure for Him or else He rejects it.

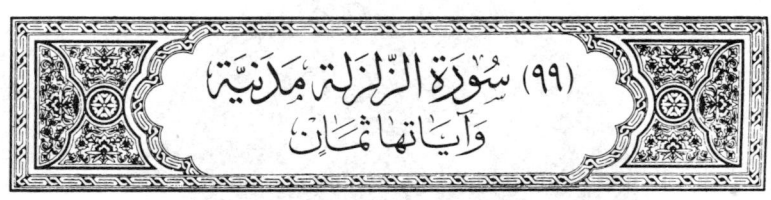

بِسْمِ اللهِ الرَّحْمَٰنِ الرَّحِيمِ

إِذَا زُلْزِلَتِ الْأَرْضُ زِلْزَالَهَا ۝ وَأَخْرَجَتِ الْأَرْضُ أَثْقَالَهَا ۝ وَقَالَ الْإِنْسَانُ مَا لَهَا ۝ يَوْمَئِذٍ تُحَدِّثُ أَخْبَارَهَا ۝ بِأَنَّ رَبَّكَ أَوْحَىٰ لَهَا ۝ يَوْمَئِذٍ يَصْدُرُ النَّاسُ أَشْتَاتًا لِيُرَوْا أَعْمَالَهُمْ ۝ فَمَنْ يَعْمَلْ مِثْقَالَ ذَرَّةٍ خَيْرًا يَرَهُ ۝ وَمَنْ يَعْمَلْ مِثْقَالَ ذَرَّةٍ شَرًّا يَرَهُ ۝

SURAH 99

THE EARTHQUAKE
AZ-ZALZALAH

In the name of Allah, the Beneficent, the Merciful.

When the Earth is rocked with her (final) earthquake,
when the Earth shakes off her burdens,
and man cries: "What is the matter with her?"
on that day she will tell her news,
that your Lord has inspired her (with His command).
On that day men will issue forth in small groups to be shown their labours.
Whoever has done an atom's weight of good will see it then,
and whoever has done an atom's weight of evil will see it then also.

Surah 99   The Earthquake (*Az-Zalzalah*)

According to some reports, this *surah* is a Medinan revelation but other reports say it was revealed in Makka. The latter report seems to us to be more valid, because the *surah's* mode of expression and its subject matter are more in line with the style and subjects of Makkan *surahs*.

The *surah* gives a violent shake to drowsy hearts; the subject matter, the scene drawn and the rhythm all contribute to the effect of a violent jolt. It is a powerful blast that makes the earth and all that is on it quake and tremble. Men hardly recover their senses when they find themselves confronted with the reckoning, weighing and evaluating of actions and deeds, and with recompense. All this is expressed in a few short phrases, which is characteristic of this thirtieth part of the Qur'an as a whole and is forcefully portrayed in this *surah*.

"When the Earth is rocked with her (final) earthquake, when the Earth shakes off her burdens, and man cries, 'What is the matter with her?' on that day she will tell her news, that your Lord has inspired her (with His command)".

It is the Day of Judgement when the firm earth trembles and quakes violently, yields up her long-carried loads of bodies and metals and other matters which have weighed heavily on her.

It is a scene that makes every firm and solid object under the feet of the listeners shake and totter. They think themselves to be staggering and toddling and the earth beneath them shuddering and quaking. It is a scene which cuts the heart from everything on earth it clings to, thinking it to be firm and everlasting. This is the first impression created by these scenes which the Qur'an portrays. The Qur'an imparts to them a kind of movement which is transmitted almost to the very sinews of the listener as soon as he hears these unique expressions. This impact is all the more forceful because man is portrayed as confronting the scene described and revealing his reaction and reflexes while beholding it: *"And man cries: 'What is the matter with her?''*.

It is the question advanced by the bewildered, astonished, surprised and puzzled who sees something unfamiliar to him, encounters what is imperceptible to his senses and beholds what makes him impatient and agitated. So he bursts out, "What is the matter with her? What is quaking and shaking her so violently?" He cries as he reels and staggers, trying to hold on to anything which may support him or keep him upright. But all around him waver and totter violently.

Man has experienced earthquakes and volcanoes which have filled him with awe and terror and have brought to him ruin and destruction. But when man witnesses the quake of the Day of Resurrection he sees no similarity between it and the earthquakes and volcanoes of this world. He neither knows its secrets, nor does he remember anything similar to it. It is something august and dreadful, taking place for the first time ever.

"On that day", when this quake occurs, leaving man entirely shaken, *"she (the Earth) will tell her news, that your Lord has inspired her"*. This earth will then tell her news, describe her condition and what has happened to her. It all will have been brought about simply because *"your Lord has inspired her"*, ordered her to shake and quake so fiercely and to shake off her burdens. She obeys only the Lord's orders *"in true submission"* to Him.[1] She will relate her news because what will be taking place is a simple and clear account of what lies behind it of Allah's orders and inspiration to the earth.

At this point when man is astonished and puzzled, and as the rhythm gasps with dread and terror, with surprise and wonder, tottering and shuddering – at this point when man can hardly keep his breath, crying "What is the matter with her? What has happened to her?" – at this point he encounters the scene of resurrection, reckoning, weighing and recompense. *"On that Day men will issue forth in small groups to be shown their labours. Whoever has done an atom's weight of good will see it then, and whoever has done an atom's weight of evil will see it then also."*

In the twinkling of an eye we behold the scene of people coming out of their graves; *"On that Day mankind will issue forth in small groups"*. We behold them issuing forth from all over the globe: *"as if they were swarming locusts"*.[2] This is also a scene unknown to man; it is something unprecedented, unique in nature, with all human generations issuing forth here and there, all over the globe. *"On that Day, the Earth will split asunder and they will come out in haste"*.[3] Wherever you look you behold a ghost coming up; then he hurries away, caring for nothing and never looking back nor turning his face either left or

---

[1] The Qur'an. *84; 2.*
[2] *Ibid. 54; 7.*
[3] *Ibid. 50; 44.*

Surah 99   The Earthquake (*Az-Zalzalah*)

right. They all are *"rushing to the Summoner"*[1], with their heads down and their eyes staring forward, *"for each one of them will on that day have enough preoccupations of his own"*.[2]

It is a scene indescribable in human language. It is ghastly and it is also astonishing. All these adjectives and all their synonymous and analogous terms in the dictionary cannot describe this scene, while it would be better conceived with a stretch of imagination and contemplation within the limits and capacity of the human mind.

"On that Day men will issue forth in small groups to be shown their labours". This is far more terrible and dreadful. They go to where they will be shown their deeds. They have to face their deeds and their rewards or punishments. Encountering one's deeds may be, sometimes, far more severe than any punishment. Man sometimes does things which he avoids even thinking about when he is alone.

In a spell of repentance and remorse, man would even turn his face from some of his deeds because they are ghastly. Then, in what condition will he be on that day when he faces his deeds in front of all mankind and in the presence of Allah, the Great, the Almighty, the All-Powerful? It is a terrible and frightful punishment, although it is only that they are shown their deeds and have to confront their labours. But following this confrontation (between men and their deeds) comes the accurate reckoning which does not leave an atom's weight of good or evil unassessed or without reward. *"Whoever has done an atom's weight of good will see it then, and whoever has done an atom's weight of evil will see it then also"*.

"An atom's weight": the early commentators on the Qur'an explain this phrase as "a mosquito" or "a particle of dust" which could be seen only when exposed to the light of the sun. These were the smallest things they could think of, and which may be referred to as an "atom". But now we know that the word "atom" refers to a definite thing which is much smaller than that "particle of dust" seen in the sunlight. For the particle of dust can be seen by the human eye, while it is impossible to see the atom, even with the help of the most powerful microscopes in laboratories. It is only "conceived" by the scientists. None of them has seen it either with his eyes or with his microscope. All that they have seen is its effects. This atom, or what is similar to it in weight, whether good or bad, will be brought forth and shown to its doer, who will then receive its reward. At that time

---

[1] The Qur'an. *54; 8.*   [2] *Ibid. 80; 37.*

Surah 99   The Earthquake (*Az Zalzalah*)

man does not undervalue any of his actions and deeds, whether good or bad. He does not say, "Oh, this is a trivial thing which has no weight or consideration". On the contrary, his conscience will be as sensitive to everything he has done as an accurate scale registering even the weight of an atom favourably or unfavourably. There is nothing parallel or similar to this measure in this world, except the believing heart. For the believing heart is sensitive to even an atom's weight of either good or evil. But there are some hearts in this world which are unmoved even by mountains of sins and crimes. They remain unaffected while suppressing fountains of good which are far firmer than the mountains. These hearts are conceited in this earth, but on the Day of Judgement they are crushed under their own burdens.

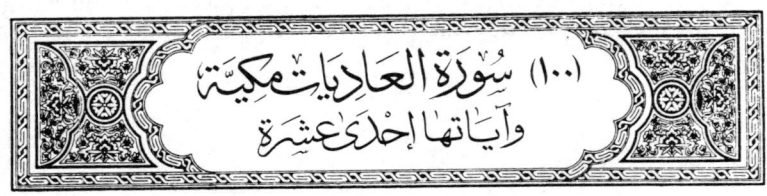

بِسْمِ اللهِ الرَّحْمٰنِ الرَّحِيمِ

وَالْعَادِيَاتِ ضَبْحًا ۝ فَالْمُورِيَاتِ قَدْحًا ۝ فَالْمُغِيرَاتِ صُبْحًا ۝ فَأَثَرْنَ بِهِ نَقْعًا ۝ فَوَسَطْنَ بِهِ جَمْعًا ۝ إِنَّ الْإِنْسَانَ لِرَبِّهِ لَكَنُودٌ ۝ وَإِنَّهُ عَلَىٰ ذَٰلِكَ لَشَهِيدٌ ۝ وَإِنَّهُ لِحُبِّ الْخَيْرِ لَشَدِيدٌ ۝ ۞ أَفَلَا يَعْلَمُ إِذَا بُعْثِرَ مَا فِي الْقُبُورِ ۝ وَحُصِّلَ مَا فِي الصُّدُورِ ۝ إِنَّ رَبَّهُمْ بِهِمْ يَوْمَئِذٍ لَخَبِيرٌ ۝

SURAH 100

THE COURSERS
AL-'ADIYAT

In the name of Allah, the Beneficent, the Merciful.

By the snorting coursers,
striking sparks of fire,
by those which scour to the raid at dawn,
blazing a trail of dust,
cleaving into the centre of the enemy;
man is surely ungrateful to his Lord,
and of this he himself is a witness;
and truly, he is passionate in his love for worldly riches.
But is he unaware that when the contents of the graves are
    scattered about,
and what is in the breasts is brought out,
surely their Lord will on that day know all about them.

In the Shade of the Qur'an

This *surah* is presented in rapid and violent touches. The text moves swiftly from one scene to another. As we come to the last verse, everything – the verbal expressions, the connotations, the subject matter and the rhythm – settle down in a manner similar to that of a courser reaching the finishing point.

The *surah* starts with the scene of war steeds running, snorting, striking sparks of fire with their hoofs, launching a raid at dawn and blazing a trail of dust, cleaving suddenly into the centre of the enemies, taking them by surprise and striking terror and fear in their hearts.

Then follows a picture of the human self: a scene of ingratitude, ignobleness, greed and extreme miserliness. Immediately after that there is a description of graves laid open and their contents scattered, and the secrets of hearts poured out. Finally the trail of dust, ingratitude and miserliness, the contents of the graves and the dragged out secrets all come to the same terminus. They come to Allah and settle down: *"surely their Lord will on that day know all about them"*.

The rhythm of the *surah* is robust and thunderous and thus fits well with the dusty and clamorous atmosphere generated by the upturned graves and the secrets violently pulled out of the breasts. These characteristics of the rhythm are also appropriate to the picture of ingratitude, thanklessness and extreme miserliness. A framework for this picture is provided by a dusty and tumultuous atmosphere of horses racing and thundering. Thus the frame and the picture are in perfect harmony with each other.

"By the snorting coursers, striking sparks of fire, by those which scour to the raid at dawn, blazing a trail of dust, cleaving into the centre of the enemy; man is surely ungrateful to his Lord. And of this he himself is a witness; and truly, he is passionate in his love for worldly riches".

Allah swears by the war horses and describes their movements one after the other – running, snorting and neighing. They strike their hoofs against rocks, producing sparks of fire. They wage their attack early at dawn in order to take the enemy by surprise, producing a trail of dust during the unexpected battle. They pierce swiftly the enemy ranks creating disorder and confusion amongst them. These successive stages were well known to those who were first addressed by the Holy Qur'an. The fact that Allah swears by the horses pro-

Surah 100   The Coursers (*Al-'Adiyat*)

vides an emphatic suggestion that the movement portrayed is a lovable one and men should respond to it actively. This they do only after realising how precious it is in the measure of Allah, which is reflected in His paying attention to it. Added to all this is the harmony between this scene and the scenes which are the subject of the Divine oath, namely the state of the human soul when it is devoid of faith and its impetus. The Qur'an draws man's attention to this state in order that he may gather all his willpower to combat it. For Allah is perfectly aware of how deeply it is ingrained in man and what great pressure it exercises on him.

"*Man is surely ungrateful to his Lord and of this he himself is a witness; And truly, he is passionate in his love for worldly riches*". It is a fact that man reacts with ingratitude to all the bounties of his Lord. He denies the favours which Allah confers on him. His thanklessness and ingratitude is reflected in a host of actions and verbal statements which will serve as witness against him. Or perhaps, on the Day of Judgement, he may testify against himself, admitting his ingratitude: "*and of this he himself is a witness*". For on the Day of Judgement he will speak the plain truth even against himself, without any contentions or excuses. "*And truly, he is passionate in his love for worldly riches*". Man is a passionate self-lover. But he loves only what he imagines to be good for him: wealth, power and the pleasures of this world. This is his nature unless he has faith which changes his concepts, values and even his concerns. Faith changes his ingratitude to humble thankfulness. It changes his greed and miserliness to benevolence and compassion. It makes him aware of the proper values which are worthy of being the object of ambition and hard competition. Indeed these are much more exalted than money, power and mundane pleasures.

Man without faith is an ignoble creature having only trivial ambitions and petty concerns. However big his desires, however strong his ambitions and high his objectives may seem, he remains sunk in the cesspool of this earth, confined within the limits of this life, imprisoned in self. He cannot be freed or elevated except by an attachment to a world superior to this earth, extending beyond this life; a world which originates from Allah who is the First Being[1] and returning to

---

[1] The Arabic term "*Azali*" which refers to Allah as the "First Being", has an important implication that He is independent of time. – Translator's note.

Allah the Eternal; a world into which this life and the life hereafter converge and which has no end.

Hence, the final touch in the *surah* provides the cure for ingratitude, greed and miserliness. It portrays the scene of resurrection in a way which makes man shudder, and puts his love for wealth and indulgence in worldly riches out of his mind, unshackling his soul and setting it free from earthly attachments: *"But is he unaware that when the contents of the graves are scattered about, and what is in the breasts is brought out, surely their Lord will on that day know all about them"*. It is a violent and frightening scene in which we witness the "scattering about" of the contents of the graves and the bringing out of the secrets of the hearts which were closely guarded, kept away from everyone. The Arabic terms used here for scattering and pulling are very forceful, suggesting an atmosphere of violence and force.

Does he not know when this will take place? The mere awareness of all this is enough to inspire man to seek an answer and explore every avenue in search of it, while at the same time discerning all that may result from these wild movements. These nimble and agile movements finally come to where every matter and destiny is settled: *"surely their Lord will on that day know all about them"*. So to their Lord is their end. He *"on that day"* knows them and all their affairs and secrets. Allah certainly knows everything at all times and in all conditions but the knowledge of *"that day"* has some effects to which their attentions are drawn here. It is a knowledge which necessitates the reckoning and reward. This implicit meaning is the one underlined here.

The *surah* is a swift, vehement and breathless piece, with a sudden terminus of meaning, expression and rhythm. It reflects a unique Qur'anic method of expression.

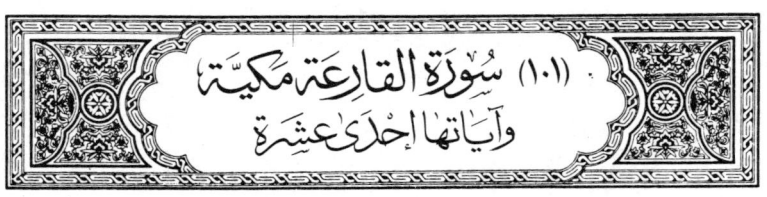

بِسْمِ اللَّهِ الرَّحْمَنِ الرَّحِيمِ

الْقَارِعَةُ ۝ مَا الْقَارِعَةُ ۝ وَمَا أَدْرَاكَ مَا الْقَارِعَةُ ۝ يَوْمَ يَكُونُ النَّاسُ كَالْفَرَاشِ الْمَبْثُوثِ ۝ وَتَكُونُ الْجِبَالُ كَالْعِهْنِ الْمَنفُوشِ ۝ فَأَمَّا مَن ثَقُلَتْ مَوَازِينُهُ ۝ فَهُوَ فِي عِيشَةٍ رَاضِيَةٍ ۝ وَأَمَّا مَنْ خَفَّتْ مَوَازِينُهُ ۝ فَأُمُّهُ هَاوِيَةٌ ۝ وَمَا أَدْرَاكَ مَا هِيَهْ ۝ نَارٌ حَامِيَةٌ ۝

SURAH 101

THE STRIKER
AL-QARI'AH

In the name of Allah, the Beneficent, the Merciful.

The Striker!
What is the Striker?
Would that you knew what the Striker is!
The day when men shall be like scattered moths,
and the mountains like carded wool.
Then he whose scales are heavy,
shall enjoy a life of satisfaction.
But he whose scales are light,
shall have the abyss for his home.
Would that you knew what this is like!
It is a raging fire.

In the Shade of the Qur'an

"Al-Qaari'a" or the Striker is the resurrection named in other places in the Qur'an as the Overwhelming One, the Deafening Shout, the Stunning Blast and the Enveloper. The term *al-Qaari'a* also connotes hitting and knocking hard. It hits the hearts with its engulfing horrors.

The *surah* as a whole deals with the Striker, its essence, what takes place in it and what it leads to in the end. Thus the *surah* portrays one of the scenes of the resurrection.

The scene portrayed here is one of horror directly affecting man and mountains. In this scene men look dwarfish in spite of their great number. For they are *"like scattered moths";* they fly here and there, having no power or weight, experiencing the dilemma and perplexity of moths which rush to destruction, having no aim or purpose. Besides, mountains which used to be firm and solidly based seem to be like carded wool carried away by winds, and even by a light breeze. Thus, it is in harmony with this image that the Day of Resurrection is described as the one that strikes or knocks out. The connotations of the expressions used and the rhythm are in consonance with the effects of the Striker on both men and mountains. The *surah* spreads an air of awe and expectation of the outcome of the reckoning.

"The Striker! What is the Striker! Would that you knew what the Striker is!" This *surah* starts with the single word *"Al-Qaari'a"* which stands for "the Striker". It is thrown alone like a shot without any further information or any predicate or adjective. As such it creates through its sound and connotations a feeling of resounding awe. The word is immediately followed by a question suggesting something alarming: *"What is the Striker?"* It is that dreadful and formidable thing which arouses curiosity and questioning. Then comes the answer in the form of a cryptic exclamation, giving no clear indication: *"Would that you knew what the Striker is!"* It is too great to be comprehended or imagined. Then follows the answer which states what takes place in it but refrains from stating its exact nature: *"The day when men shall be like scattered moths and the mountains like carded wool"*.

This is the first scene of the Striker, a scene that leaves the hearts in panic and makes the limbs tremble with fear. The listener feels that everything he clings to in this world is flying all around him like

Surah 101 — The Striker (*Al-Qari'ah*)

dust. Then comes the end of all mankind. *"Then he whose scales are heavy shall enjoy a life of satisfaction. But he whose scales are light shall have the abyss for his home. Would that you knew what this is like! It is a raging fire".* It is useful for us to consider the *"scales"* and their being heavy or light. This means that there are standards which Allah credits with being valuable and others that are valueless. This is the general meaning of the statement which Allah wants to convey. He, however, knows best the exact nature of these *"scales"*. To indulge in a sophisticated, logical and linguistic dispute about the meaning of this term is in itself a departure from the Qur'anic spirit and indicates that the reader is not interested in the Qur'an and in Islam.

"He whose scales are heavy" according to Allah's measures and His evaluation, *"shall enjoy a life of satisfaction"*. Allah makes this statement general without any detailed information. Thus, the statement imparts to man's feelings the connotations of content and satisfaction or, indeed, pure happiness.

"But he whose scales are light", according to the same measures of Allah and His evaluation, *"shall have the abyss for his home"*. The Arabic text uses the term "mother" for what is rendered here as "home". It is to his mother that a child turns for help and protection as he seeks shelter and security at home. But such people with light scales can turn and resort only to the abyss! The expression is a fine one, beautifully ordered. It has also a shade of obscurity preparing the way for subsequent clarification which adds to the depth of the intended effect: *"Would that you knew what this is like!"* It is again the cryptic exclamation used often in the Qur'an which emphasises that it is beyond comprehension and vision. Then comes the answer in the closing note: *"It is a raging fire"*. So this is the mother of the one whose scales are light. This is his mother to whom he turns for help and protection and for security and comfort. But what does he find with such a mother? – The abyss and the raging fire.

It is a sudden shock rendered by the expression to represent the hard reality.

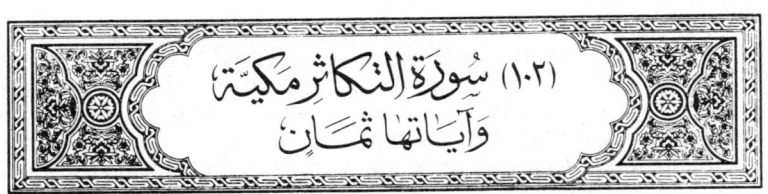

بِسْمِ اللهِ الرَّحْمَنِ الرَّحِيمِ

أَلْهَىٰكُمُ التَّكَاثُرُ ۝ حَتَّىٰ زُرْتُمُ ٱلْمَقَابِرَ ۝ كَلَّا سَوْفَ تَعْلَمُونَ ۝ ثُمَّ كَلَّا سَوْفَ تَعْلَمُونَ ۝ كَلَّا لَوْ تَعْلَمُونَ عِلْمَ ٱلْيَقِينِ ۝ لَتَرَوُنَّ ٱلْجَحِيمَ ۝ ثُمَّ لَتَرَوُنَّهَا عَيْنَ ٱلْيَقِينِ ۝ ثُمَّ لَتُسْـَٔلُنَّ يَوْمَئِذٍ عَنِ ٱلنَّعِيمِ ۝

SURAH 102

RIVALRY FOR WORLDLY GAIN
AT-TAKATHUR

In the name of Allah, the Beneficent, the Merciful

Rivalry for worldly gain distracts you,
until you visit your graves.
Indeed you shall know!
Again, you shall certainly come to know.
Indeed, were you to have certain knowledge . . .
You shall certainly see the fire of Hell.
Yes, you will see it with your very eyes.
Then, on that day, you shall be questioned about your joys and comforts.

In the Shade of the Qur'an

This *surah* has a rhythm that is majestic and awe-inspiring — as if it were the voice of a warner standing on a high place and projecting his voice which rings out in weighty emphasis. He calls out to people who are drowsy, drunken, confused. They approach a precipice with their eyes closed and their feelings numbed. So the warner increases the volume of his voice to the limit: *"Rivalry for worldly gain distracts you until you visit your graves"*.

You drunken and confused lot! You who take delight and indulge in rivalry for wealth, children and the pleasures of this life — from which you are sure to depart! You who are absorbed with what you have, unaware of what comes afterwards! You who will leave the object of this rivalry, and what you seek pride in and go to a narrow hole wherein there is no rivalry or pride! Wake up and look around, all of you! For indeed, *"rivalry for worldly gain distracts you until you visit your graves"*.

With a deep and grave rhythm the Qur'an then strikes their hearts with the terror awaiting them after coming to the graves: *"Indeed, you shall know"*. Then it repeats the same note with the same words and with the same firm and terrifying rhythm: *"Again, you shall certainly come to know"*. Then it adds to the depth and awe of this assurance, and hints at the grave future that lies beyond, the terrifying essence of which they do not recognise in the flush of intoxication and rivalry for worldly riches: *"Indeed, were you to have certain knowledge . . ."* The conditional sentence is not completed in the text. This is acceptable as a refined form of Arabic. It adds to the feeling of awe generated by the *surah*. The inference here is that had they known what they should know for certain, they would have not indulged in such rivalry for petty gains. The *surah* then discloses the fearful fact which has been withheld: *"You shall certainly see the fire of Hell"*.

Then it emphasises this fact and deepens its striking impact on people's hearts: *"Yes, you will see it with your very eyes"*. Finally, it puts the last statement which makes the drunken sober, the lethargic conscious, the confused attentive and the self-indulgent tremble and feel apprehension at his indulgence in comforts and pleasures: *"Then on that day you shall be questioned about your joys and comforts"*.

You will be questioned concerning all that: How did you get it? How did you dispense with it? Was it obtained from a lawful source and dispensed with in a lawful way? Or from a forbidden source and in a sinful manner? Was it legal or illegal? Have you praised and

Surah 102   Rivalry for Worldly Gain (*At-Takathur*)

thanked Allah for it? Have you given the poor their due? Have you given some of it to others? Or have you monopolised it all for yourselves? *"You shall be questioned"* about your rivalry in gathering and amassing wealth and about what you take pride in. It is a burden which you, in your preoccupation and enjoyment, think little of. But beyond it lie heavy responsibilities.

This is a self-expressing *surah*. It leaves its impact on man's feelings by its meaning and rhythm. It leaves the heart occupied, burdened with the problem of the Hereafter, inattentive to the trivialities of this worldly life and its petty concerns which please hollow-minded people.

This *surah* portrays the life of this world as a fleeting wink in the long span of existence: *"Rivalry for worldly gain distracts you until you visit your graves"*. The wink of this life is over and its small leaf is turned. Thereafter time stretches on and so do the burdens. The style of the *surah* produces this inference, achieving harmony between the actual reality and the manner of expressing it.

Whenever a human being reads this awe-inspiring and majestic *surah*, he feels its rhythm which travels upwards in space at the beginning and travels downwards to the deep, deep level at the end. He feels the burden of this wink of a life on his shoulders as he walks heavily along the road. Then he starts questioning himself about the smallest and even the most trivial of his deeds.

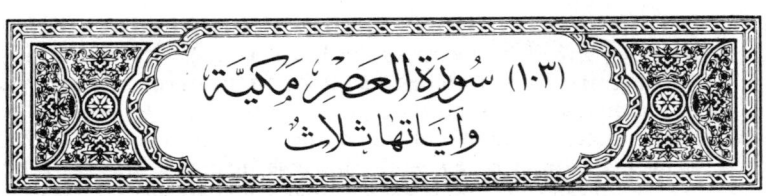

بِسْمِ اللَّهِ الرَّحْمَنِ الرَّحِيمِ

وَالْعَصْرِ ۝ إِنَّ الْإِنسَانَ لَفِي خُسْرٍ ۝ إِلَّا الَّذِينَ آمَنُوا وَعَمِلُوا الصَّالِحَاتِ وَتَوَاصَوْا بِالْحَقِّ وَتَوَاصَوْا بِالصَّبْرِ ۝

SURAH 103

THE DECLINING DAY
AL-'ASR

In the name of Allah, the Beneficent, the Merciful.

I swear by the declining day,
that man is a certain loser,
save those who have faith and do righteous deeds and counsel one another to follow the truth and counsel one another to be steadfast.

This short *surah* of three verses outlines a complete system for human life based on the Islamic viewpoint. It defines, in the clearest and most concise form, the basic concept of faith in the context of its comprehensive reality. In a few words the whole Islamic constitution is covered and in fact, the nation of Islam is described in its essential qualities and its message in one verse only: the third. This is the eloquence of which Allah alone is capable.

The great fact which this *surah* affirms is simply that throughout the history of man there has been one worthwhile and trustworthy path – that which the *surah* indicates and describes. All other paths lead only to loss and ruin. As it says in outline, that path is first the adoption of faith, followed up with good deeds and exhortation to follow the truth and to steadfastness.

What does the adoption of faith then signify? We shall not give here its juristic definition. Instead, we shall describe its nature and its importance in human life.

Faith is the characteristic by which the minute, transient human being attains closeness to the Absolute and Everlasting Originator of the universe and all that exists in it. He thus establishes a link with the whole world, which springs from that One Origin, with the laws governing it and with the powers and potentialities created in it. As a result, he breaks away from the narrow boundaries of his trivial self to the broadness of the universe, from his inadequate power to the immensity of the unknown universal energies, and from the limits of his short life to the "Eternity" that Allah alone comprehends.

This proximity grants the human being a certain power, limitless scope and freedom. It endows him with great enjoyment of life, its beauty and its constituents with whose "souls" he lives in mutual friendship. Thus life becomes a pleasant journey for mankind everywhere and at all times. From this everlasting happiness, delightful joy and true intimate understanding of life and all creation are derived. This is the invaluable gain, to lack which is an immeasurable loss.

The qualities of faith are also precisely those of sublime and dignified humanity, such as the worship of one God which elevates man above servitude to others and establishes within him the truth of the equality of all men so that he neither yields nor bows down his head to any but the One, the Absolute. The result is that man will enjoy true liberty, which radiates from within his conscience following his reali-

Surah 103   The Declining Day (*Al-'Asr*)

sation of the fact that there is only one power and one Lord in this world. This liberation is spontaneously developed from such an awareness, for it is the only logical sequence.

Godliness is the second quality of dignified humanity. This quality determines for man the source from which he derives his concepts, values, criteria, considerations, doctrines, laws and whatever brings him into relation with Allah, the world at large and with human beings. Thus, equity and justice replace personal desires and self-interest. This strengthens the believer's realisation of the value of his way of life and keeps him above ignorant concepts, values and interests and above all strictly mundane values. This is so even when the believer is the only one of his kind. For he counters these features with those which he derives directly from Allah and which therefore rank highest in value and are the most sound and the most deserving of devotion and esteem.[1]

A third quality of faith and dignified humanity is the clarity of the relationship between the Creator and the created, the restricted creature is connected with the Everlasting Truth without any mediator. It supplies man's heart with light, his soul with contentment and gives him confidence and purpose. It eliminates from his mind perplexity, fear, anxiety and agitation as well as unlawful haughtiness on earth and unjustifiable tyranny over people.

Steadfastness along the path ordained by Allah is the next quality of such humanity. This must be maintained so that good does not occur casually, incidentally or without deliberation but springs from definite motives and heads towards certain aims. People united for Allah's cause collaborate. Thus, with a single definite purpose and a single distinguished banner, the Muslim community is raised. This is true for all generations that are similarly welded together.

Another quality is belief in the dignity of man in the sight of Allah. This heightens man's regard for himself and restrains him from aspiring for a position higher than that which the Creator has defined for him. For man to feel that he is dignified in Allah's sight is the loftiest conception he may attain of himself. Any ideology or concept which abases this valuation and ascribes a dishonourable origin to man, separating him from the Highest Society of Allah is, in effect, inviting him to abjection and derogation, though it may not say so

---

[1] For more detailed discussion of this point, see the commentary on *surah* 80 "The Frowning" in this volume.

openly. Hence, the effects of Darwinism, Freudianism and Marxism are among the most horrid disasters human nature has encountered. For they teach mankind that all abasement and downright animalism are natural phenomena with which we should be familiar and of which we need not be ashamed.

Purity of motivation is yet another quality of the dignified humanity established by faith. This directly follows the realisation of man's dignity in Allah's sight, His supervision over men's conscience and His knowledge of their innermost undertakings. The normal human being whom the theories of Freud, Karl Marx and their type have not deformed is bashful that another human being may come to know what incidental unhealthy feelings he may have. The believer feels the awesome presence of Allah in his innermost consciousness and his awareness makes him tremble. He therefore attends to self-purification and spiritual cleansing. A refined moral sense is the natural fruit of faith in a just, kind, compassionate, generous and forbearing God who abhors evil and loves goodness and who knows the furtive look and the secret thought. From this follows the responsibility of the believer which results from his free will and the comprehensiveness of Allah's supervision over him. It stimulates within him healthy awareness, sensitivity, serenity and foresight. It is a communal responsibility rather than an individual one and it is a responsibility towards all humanity in relation to goodness, pure and simple. The believer feels all these in every action. He achieves a higher degree of self-respect and calculates the results before taking any steps. He is of value in the world and the whole realm of existence and has a role in its smooth running.

The final quality is man's elevation above greed for worldly gains and the choice of Allah's richer, everlasting reward for which all men should strive, as the Qur'an directs them to do and which results in elevation, purification and cleansing of their souls. Of immense help in this regard is the fact that the believer has a broad scope to move in: between this life and the next and between the heavens and the earth. The elevation of man lessens his anxiety about the results and fruits of his deed. He does good only because it is good and because Allah requires it. It is never his concern whether it leads to further goodness in his own short lifetime. Allah, for whom he performs the good, never dies nor does He forget nor ignore any of men's deeds. The reward is not to be received here, for this life is not the last. Thus, the believer acquires the power to continue to perform good deeds

Surah 103   The Declining Day (*Al-'Asr*)

sustained by this overwhelming belief. This it is that guarantees that doing good becomes a deliberate way of life and not a casual incident or motiveless event. It is this belief that supplies the believer with the power and the fortitude to face evil, whether manifested in the despotism of a tyrant or in the pressures of *Ignorance* or in the frailty of his will-power to control his passions which arise primarily from his feeling of the shortness of his life to achieve aims and enjoyments and from his inability to comprehend the deeper results of the good, and witness the victory of right over evil. Faith tackles these feelings radically and perfectly.

Faith is the great root of life from which goodness springs in its various forms and to which all its fruits are bound. What does not spring from faith is a branch cut from a tree: it is bound to fade and perish, it is indeed a devilish production, limited and impermanent! Faith is the axis to which all the fine fabric of life's network is connected. Without it life is a loose event, wasted through the pursuit of yearnings and fantasies. It is the ideology which collects diversified deeds under a consonant system, following the same route and geared to the same mechanism, possessing a definite motive and a predetermined goal.

Hence, all deeds not stemming from this origin and not related to that path are completely disregarded by the Qur'an. Islam is invariably candid over this. In *surah* 14, "Abraham", we read what may be translated as: *"The likeness of those who disbelieve in their Lord: their works are like ashes which the wind blows furiously on a tempestuous day. They have no power over anything they have earned"*. In surah 24, "Light", we have: *"As for those who disbelieve, their deeds are like a mirage in a desert. The thirsty traveller thinks it is water but when he comes near he finds that it is nothing"*. Now these are clear statements discrediting every deed not related to faith, which, in turn, gives it a motive that is connected with the origin of its existence and an aim that is compatible with the purpose of the world in all creation. This is a logical view of an ideology that attributes all events to Allah. Whoever dissociates himself from Him, vanishes and loses the reality of his existence.[1]

---

[1] The eminent scholar, Imam Muhammad Abduh in his commentary on the Qur'anic verse: *"Whoever has done an atoms weight of good shall see it then, and whoever has done an atoms weight of evil shall see it then"*, says: "... and what some scholars relate, that the consensus of opinion is that good deeds

In the Shade of the Qur'an

Faith is a sign of health in a person's nature and soundness in his disposition. It also indicates man's harmony with the nature of the whole universe, and a sign of mutual effect between man and the world around him. His life, as long as his behaviour is straightforward, must bring about an orientation which ends up in his adoption of faith because of what this universe itself possesses of signs and testimonies about the absolute power that so created it. Were the contrary the case, something must then be wrong or lacking in the state of the recipient – i.e. the human being – which would be a sign of corruption that only leads to loss and nullifies any deed which might somehow give an appearance of righteousness.

So extensive and comprehensive, so sublime and beautiful, so happy is the believer's world that the world of the disbelievers around appears to him minute, trivial, low, feeble, ugly and miserable – that is, in a state of ruin and complete loss.

Doing what is righteous is the natural fruit of faith and a spontaneous activity generated at the same time as the reality of faith settles inside the human heart and mind. For faith is a positive and active concept which, once it has pervaded the human conscience, hastens to activate it to the outside world in good deeds. This is the Islamic view of faith. It must be dynamic. If it is not, then it is either phoney or non-existent, just as a flower cannot withhold its fragrance which, if present, naturally spreads, or else it is not in the flower at all.

From all this we recognise the values of faith: dynamism, activity, creativeness and productiveness devoted to Allah's pleasure and not narrowness, negativity or isolation into self. It is not just sincere and innocent intentions, that never develop into actions. This is the distinguishing characteristic of Islam that makes it a creative power in practical life.

All this is logical only as long as faith remains the link with the Divinely ordained path. This path is characterised by perpetual dynamism in the world among people. It is founded according to a specific plan and orientated towards a definite goal. Moreover, faith

---

do not benefit a disbeliever on the Day of Judgement or lessen the penalty due for him for any of his evil deed, is unfounded." But here we can see that this view is not based on "consensus of opinion" but on Qur'anic injunctions that are themselves the source of judgement.

Surah 103   The Declining Day (*Al-'Asr*)

propels humanity towards implementing that which is good, pure, constructive and utilitarian.

Counselling one another to follow the truth and to steadfastness reveals a picture of Islamic society which has its own very special entity, a unique inter-relationship between its individual members and a single destination and which fully understands its entity as well as its duties. It realises the essence of its faith and what it has to do of good deeds which include, among other tasks, the leadership of humanity along its own path. To execute this tremendous duty, counselling and exhortation becomes a necessity.

From the meaning and nature of the very word "counsel" appears the loftiest and most magnificent picture of that integrated, coordinated, righteous and enlightened nation or society which caters for right, justice and goodness on this earth. This exactly is how Islam wants the Islamic nation to be.

Mutual counsel aimed at that which is right is a necessity because it is hard always to maintain what is right, bearing in mind that the obstacles in its way are innumerable: egoistic passions and predilictions, the false concepts in the environment, and the tyranny, inequity and despotism of some. Hence the mutual exhortation urged here means reminding, encouraging and expressing the unity in aim and destination and equality in responsibility and charge. It also collects the individual efforts into a unified whole and thus increases the feelings of brotherhood in every guardian of truth, that there are others with him to exhort, encourage, support and love him. This is precisely the case with Islam, the righteous way of life whose establishment requires the care of a co-ordinated, interdependent, self-sufficient and self-supporting community.

Counsel and exhortation to be steadfast are also a necessity because the sustenance of faith and good deeds and catering for right and equity are the hardest tasks ever to carry out. This makes endurance utterly indispensible. Endurance is also necessary when adapting oneself to the Islamic way of life, when confronting others, when afflicted with maltreatment and hardship. Steadfastness is necessary when evil and falsehood triumph. It is necessary for traversing the length of the route, putting up with the slowness of the process of reform, the obscurity of road-posts and the lengthy road leading to the destination.

Exhortation to endurance and steadfastness widens the capacities by inspiring unity of aim and direction and the feeling of togetherness in everyone, equipping them with love, fortitude and determination. It generates vitality in the community where the truth of Islam can survive and through which it is implemented.

Judging by the doctrine which the Qur'an outlines for the life of the successful group which attains salvation, we are gravely shocked to see the loss and the ruin in which humanity finds itself everywhere on this earth today. We are shocked by the frustrations humanity suffers in this present world and by witnessing how humanity turns away, in vain, from the goodness Allah has bestowed upon it. We are the more distressed by the absence of a righteous and faithful authority to stand up for the Truth. Moreover, the Muslims, or rather people claiming to be Muslims, are the farthest of all from what is good and the most averse to the ideology Allah ordained for their nation and the one route He prescribed for their deliverance from loss and ruin. People, in the very realm where this righteousness took its roots, have deserted the banner Allah raised for them, that of faith, to raise instead banners of race which have never done them any good all through their history or given them any reputation either on earth or in the heavens. Islam it was that raised for them the banner totally conforming to Allah's will, flying in His name only and identified with Him alone. Under this banner the Arabs triumphed, were predominant and gave humanity a righteous, strong, enlightened and successful leadership for the first time in their history and the long history of humanity.

Professor Abul Hassan Ali Nadwi outlines the characteristics of this unique leadership in Chapter 3 of his valuable book *"Islam and the World"*:

Once the Muslims were aroused, they quickly burst the bounds of Arabia and threw themselves zealously into the task of the fuller working out of human destiny. Their leadership held the guarantee of light and happiness for the world; it gave the promise of turning humanity into a single divinely-guided society. Some of the characteristics of Muslim leadership were:

The Muslims had the unique advantage of being in possession of the Divine Book (the Qur'an) and the Sacred Law (the *Shari'at*). They did not have to fall back on their own judgement on the vital questions of life, and were thus saved from

Surah 103   *The Declining Day (Al-'Asr)*

the manifold difficulties and perils that are attendant upon such a course. The Divine Word had illumined all the avenues of life for them and had enabled them to progress towards a destination which they clearly envisaged. With them it was not to be a case of trial and error. Says the Holy Qur'an:

"Can he who is dead, to whom We give life and a Light whereby he can walk amongst men, be like him who is in the depths of darkness from which he can never come out?" (Al-Qur'an. 6; 122).

They were to judge among men on the basis of the Revealed Word; they were not to diverge from the dictates of justice and equity; their view was not to be blurred by enmity, hatred or desire for revenge.

"O you who believe, stand out firmly for God as witnesses to fair dealing, and let not the hatred of others to you make you swerve to wrong and depart from justice. Be just; that is nearer to piety; and fear God, for God is well acquainted with all that ye do." (Al-Qur'an. 5; 8).

They had not by themselves leapt into power all of a sudden from the abysmal depth of degradation. The Qur'an had already beaten them into shape. They had been brought to a high level of nobility and purity by the Prophet through long years of unremitting care. The Prophet had conditioned them to a life of austerity and righteousness; he had instilled into their hearts the virtues of humility and courageous self-denial; he had purged them clean of greed and of striving after power, renown or wealth. It was laid down by him as a fundamental principle of Islamic polity that "We shall not assign an office under the government to anyone who makes a request for it, or shows his longing for it in any other way."[1]

The Muslims were as far removed from falsehood, haughtiness and mischief as white is from black. The following words of the Qur'an had not in vain been grounded into them night and day:

"That Home of the Hereafter We shall give to those who intend

---

[1] Al-Bukhari and Muslim.

not high-handedness or mischief on earth; and the End is (best) for the righteous." (Al-Qur'an. 28; 33).

Instead of aspiring for positions of authority and trust, they accepted them with great reluctance and when they did accept an official position they accepted it as a trust from God, to Whom they would have to render full account of their sins of omission and commission on the Day of Judgement. Says the Holy Qur'an:

"God commands you to render back your trusts to those to whom they are due; and when you judge between man and man, that you judge with justice." (Al-Qur'an. 4; 58).

"It is He Who has made you (His) vicegerents on the earth. He has raised you in ranks, some above others, that He might try you in the gifts you receive; for your Lord is quick in punishment; yet He is indeed Oft-Forgiving, Most Merciful." (Al-Qur'an. 6; 165).

Further, the Muslims were not the agents of any particular race or country; nor were they out to establish Arab imperialism. Their mission was a universal mission of faith and freedom. They were happily free from all the sickly obsessions of colour and territorial nationality. All men were equal before them. The Qur'an had pointedly said:

"O mankind, We created you from (a single pair of) a male and a female; and made you into nations and tribes, that you may know each other (not that you may despise each other). Verily the most honoured of you in the sight of God is (he who is) the most righteous of you. And God has full knowledge and is Well-Acquainted (with all things)." (Al-Qur'an. 49; 13).

Once the son of 'Amr ibn al-'As, the Governor of Egypt, struck an Egyptian commoner with a whip. The matter was brought to the notice of Caliph 'Umar. The Caliph did not show the least regard for the high status of the offender's father, and ordered the Egyptian straightaway to avenge himself for harm done to him. To the offender's father he administered this telling rebuke, "Why have you made them slaves when they were born free?"[1]

---

[1] Ibn Jauzi. *Tarikh-Umar bin Khattab*.

Surah 103 The Declining Day (*Al-'Asr*)

The Arabs were not stingy in making the benefits of Faith, culture and learning available to the non-Arabs. They did not care for the nationality or the family connections of the recipients when it came to the conferment of high honours and positions in the State. They were, as it were, a cloud of bliss that rained ungrudgingly over the entire world, and from which all peoples, everywhere freely profited according to their own capacity.[1]

The Arabs allowed a free and equal partnership to all nations in the establishment of a new socio-political structure and in the advancement of mankind towards a fuller and richer moral ideal. There were no national divisions, no colour bars, no vested interests, no priesthood and no hereditary nobility in the Islamic Commonwealth. No special benefits were reserved for anyone. There was nothing to prevent the non-Arabs from surpassing the Arabs in the various fields of life. Even as Doctors of *Fiqh*[2] and *Hadith*[3] a number of non-Arabs attained to distinction for which the Muslims in general and the Arabs in particular feel proud. Ibn Khaldun writes: "It is an amazing fact of history that though their religion is of Arabian origin and the Law that the Prophet had brought had an Arab complexion, with a few exceptions, all eminent men of learning in the Muslim *Millat*, in the field of theological as well as secular sciences, are non-Arabs. Even those who are Arabs by birth are non-Arabs by education, language and scholarship."[4] During the later centuries, too, the non-Arab Muslims continued to produce leaders, statesmen, saints and savants of

---

[1] It is related by Abu Musa Ash'ari that the Holy Prophet once said, "The message with which God has sent me into the world can be compared to a heavy shower of rain that fell over a vast stretch of land. Part of this land was soft and smooth and it absorbed the rain and was turned into a meadow; part of it was uneven and hard and it retained the water which proved to be of great benefit to mankind; people drank it themselves and gave it to others to drink; part of it was altogether flat and barren, which could neither retain the water nor grow anything. The first two instances apply to those who drank in the Divine message to their own advantage and to the advantage of their fellow-beings, while the last one refers to those who paid no heed to what God had revealed to me." Al-Bukhari, *Kitab-ul-Ilm*.
[2] Islamic Jurisprudence.
[3] The Traditions of the Prophet.
[4] Ibn Khaldun. *Muqaddima, p. 499*.

exceptional merit. This would obviously not have been possible, had the Arabs been mean or prejudiced in sharing their opportunities with the people of other nationalities in the Islamic world. Humanity has many sides – physical, emotional, social, moral, mental and spiritual. We cannot neglect any one of them for the benefit of another. Humanity cannot progress to its highest level unless every human instinct is brought into proper play. It would be futile to hope for the establishment of a healthy human society till an intellectual, material, moral and spiritual environment is created in which a man is enabled to develop his latent potentialities in harmony with God's plan of creation. We learn from experience that this goal must remain a dream so long as the reins of civilization are not held by those who attach due importance to both the material and the spiritual yearnings of life, and can, together with having a high moral and spiritual sense, fitly appreciate the claims of flesh and blood upon man and the interrelationship between the individual and the society."

He then speaks of the reign of the first four Caliphs who ruled after the Prophet:

We, consequently, find that no period in the recorded history of the human race has been more auspicious for it in the true sense of the term than what is known among the Muslims as *Khilafat-i-Rashida* (i.e. the reign of the first four Caliphs). During this epoch, all the material, moral and spiritual resources of man were brought into use to make him an ideal citizen of an ideal State. The Government was judged by the yard-stick of morality, and the morals were judged by their utility to lift humanity in permanent values and establishing justice in human society. Though the Islamic Commonwealth was the richest and the most powerful State of its time, the popular heroes and ideal personalities in it used to be drawn from among those who possessed, not earthly glory, but purity and nobleness of character. There was no disparity between power and morality. Material advancement was not allowed to out-run moral progress. That is why in the Islamic world the incidence of crime was very low in spite of the abundance of wealth and the great heterogeneity of its population. To put it in a nut-

Surah 103 The Declining Day (*Al-'Asr*)

shell, this epoch was the most beautiful springtime mankind has to this day experienced.[1]

We know some features of that glorious period of human history whose generation lived under the Islamic Constitution, the pillars of which this particular *surah* erects and under the banner carried by the group of believers who performed righteous deeds and encouraged each other to follow the truth and to be steadfast. Now what, in the light of all this, is the "loss" humanity is suffering everywhere and how great is its failure in the battle between good and evil because of a blind eye it turns to that great message the Arabs conveyed to it when they raised the banner of Islam and thus assumed the leadership of mankind? Having abandoned Islam, the Arab nation is in the forefront of the caravan which is heading towards loss and ruin. Since then, the banners of mankind have been for Satan, falsehood, error, darkness and loss. No banner has been raised for Allah, truth, guidance, light or success. The banner of Allah, however, is still there awaiting the arms that will raise it and the nation which under this banner will advance towards righteousness, guidance and success.

All that has been said so far concerned gain and loss in this life which, though of great importance, is very trivial in comparison with the hereafter. There is an everlasting life and a world of reality – the real gain and the real loss, the attainment or deprivation of Paradise and the pleasure of Allah. There man either accomplishes the highest of perfection allowed for him or completely collapses so that his humanity is crushed and ends up as worthless as pebbles or even worse in condition *"on a day when a man will look on what his hands have forwarded and the disbeliever will cry: 'Would that I were dust' "*.[2]

This *surah* is unequivocal in indicating the path leading humanity away from loss, *"save those who have faith and do righteous deeds, and counsel one another to follow the truth and counsel one another to be steadfast"*. There is one right path and one only – that of faith, good deeds and the existence of a Muslim community whose members counsel each other to follow the truth and to show endurance and steadfastness.

---

[1] A.H.A. Nadwi: *Islam and the World*. English edition, Lucknow, India, 1967, pp 75 to 80
[2] The Quran. 78; 40.

Consequently, whenever two companions of the Messenger of Allah were about to depart from each other, they would read this *surah*, after which they would shake hands. This was indicative of a pledge to accept this doctrine fully, to preserve this faith, piety and a willingness to counsel each other to follow the truth and remain steadfast. It was a mutual compact to remain good elements in an Islamic society established according to that doctrine and to preserve the foundation of this society.

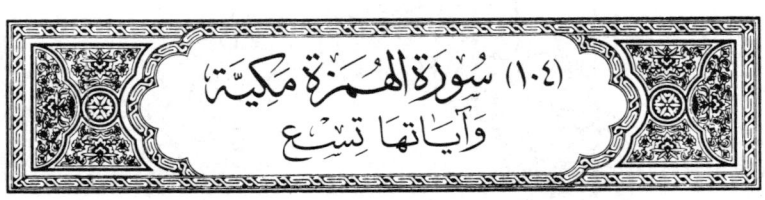

بِسْمِ اللهِ الرَّحْمَنِ الرَّحِيمِ

وَيْلٌ لِّكُلِّ هُمَزَةٍ لُّمَزَةٍ ۞ الَّذِي جَمَعَ مَالًا وَعَدَّدَهُ ۞ يَحْسَبُ أَنَّ مَالَهُ أَخْلَدَهُ ۞ كَلَّا لَيُنبَذَنَّ فِي الْحُطَمَةِ ۞ وَمَا أَدْرَاكَ مَا الْحُطَمَةُ ۞ نَارُ اللهِ الْمُوقَدَةُ ۞ الَّتِي تَطَّلِعُ عَلَى الْأَفْئِدَةِ ۞ إِنَّهَا عَلَيْهِم مُّؤْصَدَةٌ ۞ فِي عَمَدٍ مُّمَدَّدَةٍ ۞

SURAH 104

THE SLANDERER
AL-HUMAZAH

In the name of Allah, the Beneficent, the Merciful.

Woe to every taunting slanderer and backbiter,
who piles up wealth and keeps counting it again and again,
thinking that his wealth will make him immortal.
By no means! He will indeed be flung into the crushing one.
Would that you knew what the crushing one is!
It is Allah's own kindled fire,
which rages over men's hearts.
It is closed on them from every side,
in towering columns.

In the Shade of the Qur'an

This *surah* portrays one of the actual scenes in the early days of the Islamic call. Yet this scene is a pattern which is repeated in every environment and society. It is the scene of the vile, mean one who is given wealth and uses it to tyrannise over others – until even he cannot bear himself. He thinks that wealth is the supreme value in life, the value before which all values and all standards come toppling down. He feels that since he possesses wealth, he controls other people's destiny without being accountable for anything he does. He imagines that his money and his wealth is a god, capable of everything without exception – even of resisting death, making him immortal and stopping the judgement of Allah and His retribution.

Deluded as he is by the power of his wealth, he counts it and takes pleasure in counting it again and again. A wicked vanity is let loose in his being which drives him on to mock other people's positions and dignity, to taunt and slander them. He criticises others with his tongue, mocks them with his movements, either by imitating their movements and voices or by ridiculing their looks and features – by words and mimicry, by taunts and slander.

It is a vile and debased picture, one of the pictures of human beings devoid of the ideals of manhood and generosity and stripped of faith. Islam despises this abject sort of people because of its own high standards of morality. Islam emphatically forbids mockery and ridicule and fault-finding in others. But in this case the Qur'an describes these actions as sordid and ugly and adds warnings and threats to anyone who indulges in them. This suggests that it is referring to an actual case of some polytheists who have subjected the Prophet and the believers to their taunts and slander. The reply to these actions comes in the form of strong prohibition and fearful warning. There are some reports which name certain people as being the traducers meant here, but they are not authentic, so I will not discuss them, but shall be content with what I have just stated.

The warning comes in the form of a scene of the hereafter portraying the mental and physical sufferings and giving an image of Hell which is both palpable and telling. It takes care to relate the crime to the punishment inflicted and to its effect on the culprit. On the one side there is the image of the taunting slanderer and backbiter who is given to mocking other people and ridiculing them while he gathers wealth thinking that he is guaranteed immortality in this way. This image of the cynical calumniator who seeks power through wealth is

Surah 104   The Slanderer (*Al-Humazah*)

contrasted with the image of the slighted, neglected one flung into a crushing instrument which destroys all that comes in its way and thus crushes his structure and his pride.

The crushing instrument is *"Allah's own kindled fire"*. Its identification as the fire of Allah suggests that it is an exceptional, unfamiliar sort of fire and makes it sound full of terrors. This fire *"rages"* over his heart and mind from which spring mockery and ridicule and in which lie his vanity and conceit. To complete the image of the slighted, neglected and crushed, this fire closes in on him from all directions and locks him in. None can save him and none asks about him. Inside he is tied to a column, as animals are tied, without respect.

The tone of the vocabulary used in this *surah* is very strong: *"Keeps counting it again and again; by no means! he will indeed be flung; rages; towering."* In the meaning of the expressions, forcefulness is conveyed by various forms of emphasis: *"He will indeed be flung into the crushing one. Would that you knew what the crushing one is! It is Allah's own kindled fire"*. The generalisation and cryptic expression first, then the exclamation suggesting great horrors, and then the clear answer – all these are forms of forceful expression. The style also conveys warnings: *"Woe; he will be flung into; the crushing one; Allah's kindled fire; which rages over men's hearts; it is closed on them; in towering columns."*

In all this there is a kind of harmony between imagery and feelings and the actions of the *"taunting slanderer and backbiter"*.

At the time of its revelation, the Qur'an was following up the incidents faced by the Islamic call and leading it simultaneously along its road. The Qur'an is the infallible weapon which destroys the cunning of the conspirators, shakes the hearts of enemies, and fills the believers with courage and steadfastness. Indeed we recognise two significant facts in Allah's care here as He denounces this sordid example: firstly, we are shown the ugliness of moral decline and how people are rendered so abject. Secondly, we realise that He defends the believers, preserves their souls against their enemies' insults, shows them that Allah knows and hates what is inflicted on them, and that He will punish the wrong-doers. This is enough to elevate their souls and to make them feel their position high above any wicked designs.

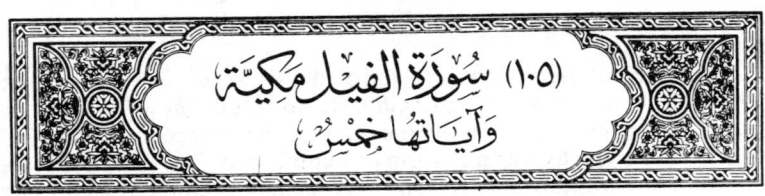

بِسْمِ اللهِ الرَّحْمَنِ الرَّحِيمِ

أَلَمْ تَرَ كَيْفَ فَعَلَ رَبُّكَ بِأَصْحَابِ ٱلْفِيلِ ۝ أَلَمْ يَجْعَلْ كَيْدَهُمْ فِي تَضْلِيلٍ ۝ وَأَرْسَلَ عَلَيْهِمْ طَيْرًا أَبَابِيلَ ۝ تَرْمِيهِم بِحِجَارَةٍ مِّن سِجِّيلٍ ۝ فَجَعَلَهُمْ كَعَصْفٍ مَّأْكُولٍ ۝

SURAH 105

THE ELEPHANT
AL-FEEL

In the name of Allah, the Beneficent, the Merciful.

Have you not seen how your Lord dealt with the people of the Elephant?
Did He not cause their treacherous plan to be futile,
and send against them flights of birds,
which pelted them with stones of sand and clay?
Thus He made them like devoured dry leaves.

In the Shade of the Qur'an

This *surah* refers to a widely famous incident in the Arabian Peninsula which took place before the commencement of the Islamic message. The incident shows very clearly how Allah protected the Holy land, which He willed to be the focal point of the last enlightenment, the cradle of the new ideology, from where it was to begin its blessed and holy march to exterminate *Ignorance* from all corners of the world and to establish in its place Allah's infallible guidance.

The various reports on this incident relate that after the Abyssinians had expelled the Persians from Yemen and established their rule there, the Abyssinian governor of Yemen, Abrahah, built a superbly luxurious church in his area giving it the name of the Abyssinian emperor at the time. He did this after he had witnessed the love and enthusiasm of Yemeni Arabs – which were the same as those felt all over the Arab land – to the Ka'ba, the Holy Mosque at Makka, with the aim of making them forsake their attachment to the Mosque of Makka and turn instead to his new luxurious church.

But the Arabs did not turn away from their Holy House. They believed themselves to be the descendants of Abraham and Ishmael who built the House. For them, this fact was a source of pride in line with their tradition of taking pride in their forefathers. Besides, vain and hollow as they were, their beliefs were, in their eyes, better and more profound than those of the people of earlier revelations (Jews and Christians). They knew how the latter beliefs were conflicting and futile.

As a result, Abrahah made up his mind to pull down the Ka'ba in order to achieve his objective of turning the Arabs away from it. He therefore marched at the head of a great army equipped with elephants. In the front was a very big elephant which enjoyed special fame among Abrahah's men. The news of Abrahah's march and his objective travelled in the Arab land and there spread among the Arabs very strong feelings against the destruction of their Holy House. A nobleman of the royal family of Yemen, called Thu Nafar, tried to stop the Abyssinian governor, calling on his people and other Arabs to fight Abrahah and defend the Holy House. Some Arab tribes joined him in a battle against Abrahah which Thu Nafar lost before he was taken prisoner. Later, while Abrahah was on his way, he was attacked by Nafeel ibn Habab Al Khath'ami, who had mobilised two Arab tribes as well as troops from other supporting tribes, but Abrahah won the battle again and captured Nafeel. Nafeel then agreed to act as a guide for Abrahah to show him the way in the Arab

Surah 105   The Elephant (*Al-Feel*)

land. When the Abyssinian governor approached Ta'if,[1] a number of its leaders went to him to say that the House he wanted to pull down was in Makka and not at Ta'if. They did this in order that he would not destroy the house they had built for their idol "Al-Lat". They also provided him with a guide to show him the way to the Ka'ba.

    Then on arrival at Al-Mughammas (a valley mid-way between Ta'if and Makka), Abrahah despatched one of his commanders to Makka where he looted some belongings of the Quaraish and other Arabs, including two hundred camels which belonged to Abdulmuttalib ibn Hashim, the chief of Makka and the Prophet's grandfather. Quraish, Kinana, Huthail and neighbouring Arab tribes gathered to fight Abrahah but then they realised that they stood no chance of winning, so they did not proceed. Then Abrahah sent a messenger to Makka to meet its chief and convey to him that the governor of Yemen did not come to fight the Makkans but to pull down the House; if they left him to accomplish what he had come for, he would be pleased not to cause any bloodshed. Abrahah also ordered his messenger to bring with him the Makkan chief if the latter did not propose to fight. When the messenger communicated his master's message to Abdulmuttalib, the latter said: "By God, we do not want to fight him and we have no power to resist him. This is God's sacred House, built by His chosen friend, Abraham. If He protects it against him, it is because the House is His, and if He leaves it to him to destroy, we cannot defend it". Abdulmuttalib then went with the messenger to Abrahah.

    Ibn Ishaq said that Abdulmuttalib was a most handsome, charming and attractive person. When Abrahah saw him he felt much respect for him. He felt that Abdulmuttalib was too noble to sit beneath his royal bed but at the same time he did not wish to be seen by the Abyssinians sitting with him on his royal bed, so he came down and sat with Abdulmuttalib on the carpet. Then Abrahah ordered his interpreter to ask his guest what he wanted. Abdulmuttalib said he wanted to request the king to give him back his two hundred camels which were looted by his commander. Abrahah ordered his interpreter to tell Abdulmuttalib on his behalf: "I admired you when I first saw you but when I spoke to you I was disappointed. Do you come to talk to me about two hundred looted camels and forget about the House which is an embodiment of your and your fore-

---

[1] A town fifty miles from Makka.

fathers' religion and which I have come to destroy? You did not even say a word to persuade me to spare it". Abdulmuttalib said: "I am only the master of my camels, but the House has its own Lord who is sure to protect it". Abrahah snapped, "It cannot be defended against me". The Makkan chief said: "You take your chance!" Abrahah returned his camels to him.

Abdulmuttalib went back to the Quraish and told them of his encounter with the Abyssinian commander and ordered them to leave Makka and seek shelter in the mountains surrounding it. Then he went with a few personalities of the Quraish to the Ka'ba where he held the ring on its door in his hand. They all prayed hard to Allah for his help and protection of the House. Abdulmuttalib is reported to have recited the following lines of poetry in his prayer:

> Our Lord, a creature protects his property, so protect Yours.
> Let not their cross and their might ever overcome Your might.
> If You are leaving them to destroy our House of worship, then
>   You surely have something in mind.

Abrahah, on the other hand, ordered his army to march with the elephants to complete their mission, but just outside Makka the renowned big elephant sat down and refused to go any further. The soldiers exerted all efforts to persuade the elephant to enter the city but their efforts were in vain. This incident is a fact acknowledged by the Prophet. When his she-camel, Al-Qaswa', sat down some distance away from Makka, on the day when the Hudaibiyah peace agreement was concluded, the Prophet said to those of his companions who claimed she had become mulish, that she had not and that mulishness was not part of her nature. "But", the Prophet added, "she has been prevented by the same will which debarred the Elephant from entering Makka".[1] On the day of the conquest of Makka, the Prophet said: "Allah protected Makka against the Elephant but He allowed His messenger and the Believers to conquer it. Its sanctity today is the same as yesterday. Let those who hear this convey it to those absent".[2]

Then Allah's will to destroy the Abyssinian army and its commander was fulfilled. He sent groups of birds to stone the attackers with stones of sand and clay, leaving them like dry and torn leaves, as

---
[1] Transmitted by Al-Bukhari.
[2] Transmitted by Al-Bukhari and Muslim.

Surah 105   The Elephant (*Al-Feel*)

the Holy Qur'an tells. Abrahah suffered physical injuries. The remainder of the army carried him on their way back to Yemen but his limbs began to separate from the rest of the body and he started losing one finger after another, until they arrived at Sana'a. Abrahah died after his chest was broken apart, according to various reports.

Versions relating to this event vary with regard to the description of those groups of birds, their size and the nature of stones and the manner of their effect. Some of these versions add that smallpox and measles broke out in Makka in that year. Those who are inclined to limit the scale of miracles and imperceptible phenomena and who seek to explain all events as resulting from the operation of familiar natural phenomena, prefer to explain this event as an actual outbreak of smallpox and measles among the army. They further explain that "the birds" could have been flies or mosquitoes carrying germs. The word "bird" in Arabic refers to all that flies.

Imam Muhammad 'Abduh, explaining this *surah* in his commentary on the thirtieth part of the Qur'an, says:

> On the second day the epidemic of smallpox and measles broke out among the soldiers. Ikrimah said: "It was the first time smallpox had appeared in the Arab land". Yakoub ibn Utbah said: "That was the year when measles and smallpox appeared in Arabia. The diseases had an almost unparalleled effect on their bodies: their flesh began falling apart. The soldiers and their commander were horror-stricken and ran away. Abrahah was also hit; his flesh continued falling off his body, finger by finger, until eventually his chest broke and he died at Sana'a". This is what different reports have mentioned and what is logically acceptable. This holy *surah* shows us that the smallpox and measles were produced by solid stones carried and thrown on the soldiers by colossal groups of birds which are usually carried by winds.

It is in line to believe that those birds referred to in the *surah* were a kind of fly or mosquito which carries the germs of some diseases, and that the stones were of dried and poisonous clay which the wind carried and which might have stuck to the legs of those birds. When this clay touched any organism, it penetrated deep into it and then caused complications of wounds and injuries which upset the whole body, leading to the dropping off of the flesh. Many kinds of these powerless birds are, as a matter of fact, the most efficient troops of Allah, which He uses for the destruction of whomsoever He wills. That little organism called nowadays "germ" is within this classification. It gathers in big groups, the number of which is unknown except to the Creator. It is not essential for the manifestation of Allah's might that the birds should be as big as mountain tops, or of a certain shape or colour; and it is not essential for this manifestation that we should know the size of those stones and the way they work. For Allah has troops of all kinds: "In everything He has a sign attesting to His Unity", as the saying goes.

There is no force in the universe but is subject to His power. To that tyrant (Abrahah) who wanted to destroy the House, Allah sent birds carrying smallpox and measles. Both he and his people were destroyed before entering Makka. That was a grace and a blessing from Allah bestowed on the neighbours of His sanctuary, in spite of their polytheism. Allah wished to protect His House until He sent the one who would protect it with the force of faith and ideology, that is, the Prophet. At the same time, it was a punishment from Allah inflicted on His enemies, the people of the Elephant, who wanted to destroy the House without any reason to justify their action.

This can be taken as a basis for understanding this *surah*. Nothing else can be accepted without logical explanation, even if it is authentically reported. The Divine power would be exhibited more strikingly when those who manifested their might by recruiting elephants (the biggest four-legged animals) should be destroyed and crushed by a tiny animal invisible to human eyes. For the wise, this is certainly greater, more fascinating and miraculous.

Neither this assumption (of smallpox or measles resulting from clay infected with germs of these diseases) advanced by the well-versed Imam, nor the opposite one described in some narratives, that the stones (thrown by the birds) split the heads and bodies of the Abyssinians and went through in them to tear their bodies apart leaving them like remnants of dry leaves – neither of the two explanations outweighs the other in manifesting Allah's might and neither needs be taken as a better explanation of the event. To me, both are the same with regard to their possibility and the exhibition of Allah's power. Whether the natural phenomena known and familiar to man operated to destroy the people Allah willed to be destroyed, or His purpose was accomplished through some Divine rules and phenomena of which man has no knowledge, are in my view exactly the same.

The Divine rules of nature are not circumscribed by the boundaries of man's knowledge or what is familiar to him. For man knows of the Divine rules of nature only a fraction which Allah has put before him and which is proportionate to his capacity of understanding and thought nourished by his experience through the ages. Hence, the so-called miracles are part of the rules of nature laid down by Allah, but they are miracles only when measured by human knowledge and experience.

Hence, there is no need for unease or doubt when faced with a supernatural event. Nor is there any need to seek an explanation for it, if the reports mentioning it are authentic, or if there are enough reasons, based on what is in the texts, to suggest that it was supernatural and did not comply with known natural laws. That a certain event should run according to familiar natural laws is not, in my opinion, less significant or less effective than its following supernatural laws. The natural rules familiar to men are in fact miraculous when weighed in the measures of man's powers and abilities. Sunrise is a miracle, though it occurs every day, and the birth of every child is superhuman in spite of its happening every minute. If anyone wants to challenge this, let him try to devise a birth! The employment of birds of any kind to carry ground stones infected with germs of smallpox and measles, then to throw them at that particular place and time, to afflict the raiding army with these epidemics at the moment when the army was about to overwhelm the city and destroy the House, is indeed a great miracle. That Allah's will should have been realized in that way would comprise several miracles with each as a clear manifestation of Allah's might and will. Had that course been followed, it would not have been less significant or less striking than sending a certain kind of bird, carrying unfamiliar kinds of stones, to afflict human bodies with a peculiar sort of affliction at that particular time. The two courses are the same; both are supernatural and superhuman.

As for the event in question, the opinion advocating an unfamiliar, superhuman course carries more weight. This opinion visualises that Allah sent groups of unfamiliar birds, carrying strange stones which caused extraordinary affliction to human bodies. To accept this opinion does not necessitate the acceptance of those narratives which describe the birds in a most striking and fascinating way, similar to descriptions of other incidents which betray exaggeration.

In the Shade of the Qur'an

The general tone of this *surah* and the circumstances of the event tend to support this opinion. Allah had a scheme for the House: He wanted to preserve it as a refuge for mankind where everyone finds peace, and to make it a gathering point for the followers of the new faith to march out in security in a free land, not subject to any external force or to any tyrannical government which might try to smother the new message in its cradle. Allah also wanted to make this event a permanent lesson, clear to everyone in all ages, so much so that in this *surah* He reminds the Quraish even after the Prophethood[1] of Muhammad (peace be on him) of this grace He bestowed on them, and gives it as an example of how He protects His sanctuaries and preserves them. There is no need for any attempt to impart a familiar image to this event that is exceptional and singular in essence and circumstances. This is all the more so especially when we take into consideration the fact that what we know of smallpox and measles and their effects on man does not fit in with what was reported of the effects of the incident on the bodies of the soldiers and their commander. Neither of the two diseases causes the falling off of man's limbs, finger by finger and organ by organ, and neither of them causes the breaking up of one's chest. The Qur'an's narrative suggests very clearly that this is what happened: *"Thus He made them like devoured dry leaves"*.

Moreover, the reports of Ikrimah and Yakoub ibn 'Utbah do not state that smallpox hit the army. Neither report says anything more than that smallpox broke out that year for the first time in the Arabian peninsula. Neither of the two men suggested that Abrahah and his army particularly fell victims to this epidemic. Besides, if the army only was hit with the disease while the Arabs around remained safe – that is, if the birds were meant to hit only the army – then this is again preternatural. Since the event is in any case supernatural, why trouble ourselves in limiting it to a certain explanation only because this explanation is based on what is familiar to human senses?

The motives of the rational school of which Imam Muhammad 'Abduh was the leading thinker, to limit the field of the supernatural and the imperceptible to our senses when explaining the Holy Qur'an, are commendable and understandable. This school tried to explain such events within the bounds of the known and familiar natural laws. It was confronted with the superstitious trend which

---

[1] Forty years after the incident took place.

Surah 105   The Elephant (*Al-Feel*)

tightened its grip on the minds of the masses at that time. Moreover, it was facing a flood of legends and Thalmudic narratives with which books explaining the Qur'an were overburdened, while the fascination with modern technology and science and doubt in the principles of religion was reaching its zenith. The rational school tried, therefore, to preserve the place of religion taking the standpoint that whatever it says is compatible with reason. Hence, this school strived to keep religion pure from any association with any kind of legend and superstition. It also tried to establish a religious mentality which understood the natural laws and recognised that they were constant and infallible, and which attributed all human and universal functions and operations to these natural laws. This mentality is in essence the Qur'anic mentality. For the Qur'an refers men to the natural laws as they constitute the permanent and infallible rule which organizes individual operations and diverse phenomena.

But resisting the pressures of superstition on the one side and fascination with technology on the other left their stamps on that school. It became extra cautious, tending to make the familiar natural laws the only basis of the Divine Laws of nature. Hence the Qur'anic explanations of Sheikh Muhammad 'Abduh and his two disciples Sheikh Rasheed Rida and Sheikh Abdul Qadir Al-Mughrabi show clearly a strong desire to reduce the greater number of miracles to only the more familiar of Allah's natural laws rather than the supernatural. They explain some of these miracles in a way that would be in line with what is called "rational", and they are excessively cautious in accepting what is imperceptible to human senses.

But with this understanding and appreciation of the environmental factors behind this trend of the rational school, it may be noted that it has gone too far in overlooking the other side of the comprehensive concept which the Qur'an aims to implant in the minds of the Muslims. This is that Allah's will and power are absolute, limitless and go far beyond the universal rules and laws He ordained, whether familiar to man or not. This absoluteness does not accept the human mind as a final arbiter. Neither does it accept the limits of the human mind as binding in such a way as to classify as probable only what may be acceptable to human reason, and to demand "rational" explanations for all which may be unacceptable to it. This demand is frequently stated by the advocates of this school.

Moreover, the Divine laws of the universe are not only those familiar to man. Indeed, what is familiar to man is only a fraction of these laws. Both these and the unfamiliar laws are the same in manifesting the greatness of the Divine power and the exactness and precision of Allah's designs.

Nevertheless, we must be well guarded against superstition and at the same time reject any unfounded legend with conscious moderation, so that we do not succumb to the influence of particular environments nor be motivated by the need to resist a common tradition of a certain age.

There is a safe rule for approaching the Qur'anic texts which may be appropriately stated here, viz, we cannot approach what the Qur'an states with prejudiced minds and preconceived ideas, whether generally or in relation to the subject matter of the statements under study. The opposite is the right way: WE MUST APPROACH THE QUR'ANIC STATEMENTS IN ORDER TO DERIVE OUR CONCEPTS AND FORMULATE OUR IDEAS FROM THEM. What the Qur'an states is final as it is. For what we call "reason" and its adjudication on what the Qur'an relates of events in the universe or in the history, in the world of man or of the imperceptibles, is no more than the net result of our finite human existence and experiences. Although this reason is, in essence an absolute force, not subject to, or limited by individual experiences or events, yet, it is, after all, confined to our human existence. This existence does not reflect "The Absolute" as this belongs to Allah. The Qur'an comes from Allah, the Absolute. Hence, it is binding on us in the sense that whatever it states is the basis of our very "rational" concepts. Then, no one can say about a certain statement of the Qur'an: "It is unacceptable to reason, so a logical explanation must be sought for it," as the advocates of the rational school frequently say. This does not mean that we should accept superstitions; it only stresses that human reason is not the arbiter of what the Qur'an states. When the expressions of a Qur'anic text are clear and straightforward, they determine how our reasons should approach it in order to formulate our views concerning its subject matter as well as regarding other universal facts.

Now we proceed to discuss the *surah* itself and try to understand the significance of the story.

"Have you not seen how your Lord dealt with the people of the Elephant?" It is a question which draws attention to the wonders involved in the incident itself and stresses its great significance. The

Surah 105   The Elephant (*Al-Feel*)

incident was so well known to the Arabs that they used to consider it a sort of beginning of history. They used to say, "This incident happened in the Elephant year", and, "That event took place two years before the Elephant year", or, "This dates to ten years after the Elephant year". It is well known that the Prophet was born in the Elephant year itself. This is perhaps one of the fascinatingly perfect arrangements of the Divine will.

The *surah* then is not relating to the Arabs something they did not know. It is a reminder of an event well known to them, aiming at achieving something beyond the actual remembrance of it.

After this opening note, Allah goes on to tell the rest of the story in the form of a rhetorical question: *"Did He not cause their treacherous plan to be futile?"*, which means that the designs of the people of the Elephant were useless, incapable of achieving anything at all. They were like someone who lost his way and thus could not get to his own destination. Perhaps this is a reminder to the Quraish of the grace Allah bestowed on them when He protected and preserved the House at the time when they felt too weak to face the mighty aggressors, the people of the Elephant. Such remembrance may make them feel their disgrace when they persist in denying Allah after He has helped them out of their weakness. It may also curb their conceit and heavy-handedness in their treatment of Muhammad and the few believers who supported him. Allah destroyed the powerful aggressors who wanted to pull down His House and sanctuary. Allah then may destroy these aggressors who try to persecute His messenger and suppress His message.

The Qur'an superbly portrays how the defeat of the aggressors' designs were brought about: *"And send against them flights of birds, which pelted them with stones of sand and clay. Thus He made them like devoured dry leaves"*. The birds were flying in groups. The Qur'an uses a Persian term, *"sijjeel"*, which denotes "stone and clay" to describe the substance with which the birds struck the aggressors. The dry leaves were described as *"devoured"* to denote that insects or other animals had eaten them. It is a vivid image of the physical shattering of the Abyssinian soldiers when they were stricken with these muddy stones. There is no need to go into such explanations as that it was an allegorical description of their destruction with smallpox or measles.

In the Shade of the Qur'an

The significance of this event is far reaching and the lessons deduced from mentioning it in the Qur'an are numerous. It first suggests that Allah did not want the polytheists to take the responsibility of protecting His House, in spite of the fact that they held it in deep respect and sought security in being its neighbours. When He willed to preserve the House and made it clear that He Himself was its protector who looked after it, He left the polytheists to be defeated by the Abyssinians. The Divine Will then directly intervened to repel the aggression and preserve the sacred House of Allah. Thus the polytheists did not have the chance to hold the protection of the House as a 'favour they did to Allah' or as "an act of honour". If they did, they would have been prompted by the fanatic impulses of *Ignorance*. This point gives considerable weight to the argument that the Divine Will of destroying the aggressors was accomplished through preternatural rules.

This direct intervention by Allah to protect the Holy House should have prompted the Quraish and the rest of the Arabian tribes to embrace Islam, the Divine religion, when it was conveyed to them by the Prophet. Surely, their respect and guardianship of the House, and the paganism they spread around it, should not have been their reason for rejecting Islam! Allah's reminder to them of this event is a part of His campaign against them and His drawing attention to their amazingly stubborn attitude.

The event also suggests that Allah did not allow the people of earlier revelations, represented in this case by Abrahah and his army, to destroy the sacred House or to impose their authority over the Holy land, even when it was surrounded by the impurity of polytheism and the polytheists were its custodians. Thus the House remained free from any human authority, safe against all plottings and designs. Allah preserved the freedom of the land in order that the new faith would grow up there completely free, not subjected to the authority of any despot. Allah revealed this religion as the force which keeps under its fold all other religions and all mankind and takes over the leadership of humanity. This was Allah's will concerning His House and religion. It was accomplished long before any human being knew that the Prophet, who was to convey the new message, was born in the same year. We feel contented and reassured when we realize this aspect of the significance of the event. We know the wicked ambitions of international crusading forces and world Zionism concerning the Holy lands. We realize that these forces spare no effort to

Surah 105   The Elephant (*Al-Feel*)

achieve their wicked ambitions. But we are not worried. For Allah who protected His House against the aggression of the people of earlier revelations when its custodians were polytheists will protect it again, if He wills, and will protect Medina the city of His Messenger, against the plottings and designs of the evil doers.

The third aspect the event refers to concerns the reality of the Arabian situation at the time. The Arabs did not have any role to play on the face of the earth; they did not even have an identity of their own before Islam. In the Yemen they were subjugated by either the Persians or the Abyssinians. If they had any government of their own it was under the protection of the Persians. In the north, Syria was subject to the Byzantine rule which was either direct or in the shape of an Arab government under the protection of the Byzantines. Only the heartland of the Arabian Peninsula escaped foreign rule. But this also was in a state of tribalism and division which deprived it of any weight in world power politics. Tribal war could drag on for forty years or more, but neither individually nor as a group did these tribes count as a power in the eyes of the neighbouring mighty empires. What happened with regard to the "Elephant" aggression was a correct assessment of the real force of these tribes when faced with a foreign aggressor.

Under Islam the Arabs had, for the first time in history, an international role to play. They also had a powerful state to be taken into consideration by the world powers. They possessed a sweeping force that destroys thrones, conquers empires, and brings down the false, deviating and ignorant leaderships in order to take over the leadership of mankind. But what facilitated these achievements for the Arabs for the first time in their history was that they forgot their Arabism. They forgot the racial urges and fanaticism. They remembered that they were Muslims, and Muslims only. They carried the message of a forceful and all-comprehensive faith, which they delivered to humanity with mercy and compassion. They did not uphold any sort of nationalism or factionalism. They were the exponents of a Divine idea which gives mankind a Divine, not earthly, doctrine to be applied as a way of life. They left their homes to struggle for the cause of Allah alone. They were not after the establishment of an Arab empire under which they may live in luxury and conceit. Their aim was not to subjugate other nations to their own rule after freeing them from the rule of the Byzantins or the Perisans. It was an aim clearly defined by Rabaie ibn Amir, the Muslims' messenger to the Persian commander, when he said in the latter's headquarters: "Allah ordered us to set out in order to save humanity from the worship of creatures and bring it to the worship of Allah alone, to save it from the narrowness of this life so that it may look forward to the broadness of the life hereafter, and from the oppression of other religions so that it may enjoy the justice of Islam".

Then, and only then, did the Arabs have an identity, a power and a leadership. But all of these were devoted to Allah alone. They possessed their power and leadership as long as they followed the right path. But when they deviated and followed their narrow nationalistic ideas, and when they substituted for the banner of Islam that of factional bonds, they came under subjugation by other nations. For Allah deserted them whenever they deserted Him; He neglected them as they neglected Him.

What are the Arabs without Islam? What is the ideology that they gave, or they can give to humanity if they abandon Islam? What value can a nation have without an ideology which it may present to mankind? Every nation which assumed the leadership of humanity in any period of history advanced an ideology. Nations which did not, such as the Tartars who swept over the east, or the Berbers who crushed the Roman Empire in the west, could not survive for long. They were assimilated by the nations they conquered. The only ideology the Arabs advanced for mankind was the Islamic faith which raised them to the position of human leadership. If they forsake it they will no longer have any function or role to play in human history. The Arabs should remember this well if they want to live and to be powerful and to assume the leadership of mankind. It is Allah who provides guidance for us lest we go astray.

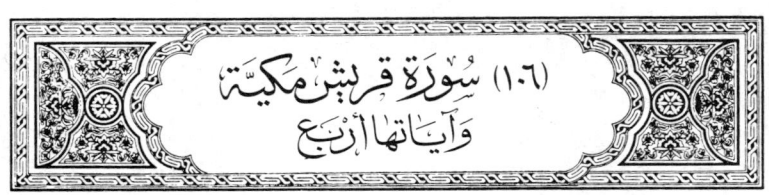

بِسْمِ اللَّهِ الرَّحْمَٰنِ الرَّحِيمِ

لِإِيلَٰفِ قُرَيْشٍ ۝ إِۦلَٰفِهِمْ رِحْلَةَ الشِّتَاءِ وَالصَّيْفِ ۝ فَلْيَعْبُدُوا رَبَّ هَٰذَا الْبَيْتِ ۝ الَّذِي أَطْعَمَهُم مِّن جُوعٍ وَءَامَنَهُم مِّنْ خَوْفٍ ۝

SURAH 106

QURAISH

In the name of Allah, the Beneficent, the Merciful

For the tradition of Quraish:
their tradition of travelling in winter and summer. Let them worship the Lord of this House,
Who provides them with food lest they should go hungry, and with security lest they should live in fear.

In the Shade of the Qur'an

When Abraham, the friend *(khalil)* of Allah, completed the building of the house of worship (the Ka'ba) and had purified it he turned to Allah with the following prayer: *"Lord, make this a city of peace and sustain its inhabitants with the fruits (of the earth)."*[1] So Allah made that House one of peace; He made it free from all human authority and free from all tyranny. He granted security and peace to anyone seeking shelter in that House, while fear was all around it. Even when the people transgressed, ascribed Divinity to beings other than Allah and worshipped idols, there was peace and security; for Allah had designed a purpose for this sacred House.

When the people of the Elephant marched to destroy the House, there happened to them what is described in the preceding *surah*, "The Elephant". Allah preserved for the House its peace, security and sacredness. Of those who lived around it, Allah says: *"Do they not then see that We have made a secure Sanctuary, and that men are being snatched away from all around them?"*[2]

The Elephant incident had an added effect in greatly enhancing the sanctity of the House amongst the Arabs all over the Arabian peninsula. It also strengthened the position of the Quraish, the custodians of the House, in all Arabia. They were thus able to travel far and wide in peace and security. Wherever they went they met with generosity and high esteem. This encouraged them to establish two great routes for their commercial caravans, to the Yemen in the south and to Syria in the north. They organised two enormous trading expeditions; one to the Yemen in the winter and the other to Syria in the summer.

In spite of very poor conditions of security in all parts of the Arabian peninsula at the time, and in spite of all the looting and plundering raids that were very common in that land, the sanctity of the House in the eyes of all Arabs guaranteed security and peace in their flourishing business to those who lived near it and were its custodians. It created for the Quraish a distinct and exclusive position and opened up to them extensive and guaranteed means of sustenance in peace, security and contentment. The Quraish became accustomed to these two profitable and peaceful trips, which were soon established among their traditional habits.

This is the specific grace of which Allah reminds the Quraish, as

---

[1] The Qur'an. *2; 126.*
[2] *Ibid. 29; 67.*

Surah 106   *Quraish*

He had reminded them of the Elephant incident in the previous *surah*. It is the grace of their being accustomed to the trips of winter and summer, and the abundance with which He endowed them in these two fruitful journeys. It is by the grace of Allah that while their land is desolate and dry, they still live a comfortable life. Out of His grace He secured them from fear whether in their hearths and homes, next to Allah's house, or in their trips and journeys. Their security is the result of their being the custodians of the House, the sanctity of which is ordained and preserved by Allah against any violation.

Allah reminds them of these graces in order that they may be ashamed of their submission to other beings, while He is the Lord of the House. Allah says to them in effect: for this tradition of Quraish, namely their trips of winter and summer, let them submit to the Lord of this House Who guaranteed their security and so encouraged them to take such beneficial trips. *"Let them worship the Lord of this House, Who provides them with food lest they should go hungry."* As their land is infertile, they would have starved had it not been for the sustenance supplied to them by Allah. *"And with security lest they should live in fear."* Poor as they are, and living in an insecure surroundings, their life would have been one of fear and apprehension. But Allah granted them security and allayed their fear.

And this is a reminder which generates and leaves a deep shame in the hearts of the Quraish, who were not unaware of the great value of the House and the effect of its sanctity on their lives. At the moment of danger and difficulty, the Quraish used to appeal only to the Lord of that House and seek only His help. This was the case with Abdulmuttalib[1] who did not confront Abrahah[2] with any army or physical strength. Instead Abdulmuttalib addressed himself only to the Lord of the House, because He was the only one who could protect His House. Abdulmuttalib did not appeal to any of the idols or graven images for any help. He did not even say to Abrahah that these "gods" will protect their House. He only said to him, "I am only the master of the camels, but the House has its own Lord who is sure to protect it." But *Ignorance* does not listen to any logic, or acknowledge what is right, or accept any reasonable argument.

---

[1] The grandfather of Prophet Muhammad and the chief of the Quraish at the time of Abyssinian attack aimed at the destruction of Ka'ba. – Translator's note.
[2] The commander of the Abyssinian aggressors. – Translator's note.

In the Shade of the Qur'an

This *surah* seems to be an extension of the preceding one, "The Elephant," with regard to its subject matter and general tone. Nevertheless, it is an independent *surah* with the usual beginning of the Qur'anic *surahs*, namely, *"In the name of Allah, the Beneficent, the Merciful"* Authorities state that nine *surahs* were revealed between the revelation of *surah* "The Elephant" and *surah* "Quraish", but these two were put next to each other in the Qur'an because of their close similarity of subject.

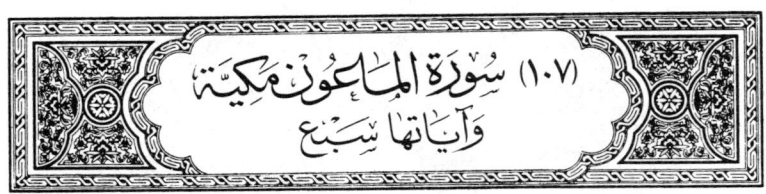

بِسْمِ اللَّهِ الرَّحْمَٰنِ الرَّحِيمِ

أَرَأَيْتَ الَّذِي يُكَذِّبُ بِالدِّينِ ۝ فَذَٰلِكَ الَّذِي يَدُعُّ الْيَتِيمَ ۝ وَلَا يَحُضُّ عَلَىٰ طَعَامِ الْمِسْكِينِ ۝ فَوَيْلٌ لِلْمُصَلِّينَ ۝ الَّذِينَ هُمْ عَن صَلَاتِهِمْ سَاهُونَ ۝ الَّذِينَ هُمْ يُرَاءُونَ ۝ وَيَمْنَعُونَ الْمَاعُونَ ۝

SURAH 107

SMALL KINDNESS
AL-MA'OUN

In the name of Allah, the Beneficent, the Merciful.

Have you seen him who denies Our religion?
It is he who harshly repels the orphan
and does not urge others to feed the needy.
Woe to those who pray
but are heedless of their prayers;
who put on a show of piety
but refuse to give even the smallest help to others.

In the Shade of the Qur'an

This *surah* is a Makkan revelation according to some authorities and a Makkan-Medinan one according to others (the first three verses are said to have been revealed in Makka and the rest in Medina). The latter opinion is perhaps more accurate. Yet the *surah* is one interwoven entity, aiming at the establishment of one of the most fundamental aspects of Faith. For this reason we are more inclined to take it as being an entirely Medinan revelation. Its subject matter is more in line with the topics of the part of the Qur'an revealed in Medina. It is related to the phenomena of hypocrisy and false appearances which were unheard of among the Muslim community in Makka. But there is no need to reject the assertion that the *surah* is a Makkan-Medinan revelation, because it is possible that the last four verses were sent down in Medina and integrated with the first three on grounds of similarity of subject. Having said that, let us now consider the *surah* and its theme.

This *surah* of seven short verses tackles an important and vital issue which could very well change the common meanings normally assigned the terms "faith" or *"Iman"* and "disbelief" or *"Kufr"*. Moreover, it brings forth the fundamental truth intrinsic in the nature of the Islamic faith, the enormous benefit it offers to all humanity and the abundant blessings with which Allah favoured mankind when He sent them His last Message.

Islam is not a way of life built on ostentation and superficiality. The apparent aspects of the different acts of worship are, according to Islam, meaningless unless they are motivated by sincerity and devotion to Allah. Worship sincerely motivated produces effects within the individual's heart which then cause him to act righteously and which are reflected in a social behaviour which elevates man's life on this earth.

No less true is the fact that Islam is not a loose, fragmentary, disjointed system from which one can pick and choose at leisure. On the contrary, it is a complete way of life with acts of worship and rites as well as individual and collective obligations that are mutually complementary. Together they lead to a goal of which mankind is the sole beneficiary, a goal which ensures that hearts are purified, life is ennobled, and men co-operate for the common good and progress, a goal wherein abounds the blessings of Allah.

A man can profess to be a Muslim, that is, he accepts this religion and all its principles, offers prayers regularly and observes other acts

Surah 107   Small Kindness (*Al-Ma'oun*)

of worship, and yet be lacking in the essence of faith and sincerity of belief. In fact, he may be very far from these. For there are signs which indicate the firm establishment of these qualities in men's hearts.

As explained in the commentary on *surah* 103, "The Declining Day", the essence of faith once firmly rooted in the hearts and minds, will begin immediately to operate and manifest itself in men's behaviour. The *surah* stresses unequivocally that, if this is not the case, there is no faith.

"Have you seen him who denies Our religion? It is he who harshly repels the orphan and does not urge others to feed the needy." The *surah* starts with a question addressed to all who can "see", generating suspense and holding their attention in order to make them discover the target and subject of the *surah*. Ah! Who is this creature identified by the Qur'an as the one who denies the religion of Islam? Hence, the answer: *"It is he who harshly repels the orphan and does not urge others to feed the needy."*

This definition of the disbelievers may sound surprising when compared with the traditional definition of faith, but this is the core of the whole matter. Indeed the one who denies the faith is he who wickedly repels the orphan, humiliating him and hurting his feelings, and who does not care for the needy or their welfare. For if the truth of Islam has in any degree touched his heart, he would commit no such acts. True belief in Islam is not a spoken word but an overall change of the individual's heart, motivating him to benevolence and goodwill for all his fellow beings that are in need of his care and protection. Allah does not want mere words from His servants but demands deeds to support the spoken words which, otherwise, are as weightless and valueless as blown ash. Nothing can be more forceful than these three verses in affirming this fact which represents most aptly the nature of Faith.

We do not intend here to indulge in a juristic discussion on the boundaries of faith and Islam. These are required in legal affairs, whereas this *surah* states the facts from Allah's point of view and judgement, which is quite different from the legal aspect.

Next, Allah offers a practical illustration of what is meant above: *"Woe to those who pray, but are heedless of their prayers."* These verses contain Allah's invocation against, or a threat of destruction to those who offer prayers but are careless about them. Who exactly are such? They are those *"who put on a show of piety but refuse to give even the smallest help to others,"* those who perform prayers but do not aptly meet their requirements. They execute the mechanical aspects and pronounce the verbal formulae of prayers but their hearts are never alive to them, nor are they nourished by praying. The essence and purpose of prayer and its component parts (recitation, supplication and exaltation of Allah) are never present in their souls. They offer prayers only to deceive others and not out of devotion to Allah. Hence, they are inattentive when they pray. They only outwardly perform their prayers. Muslims are required to offer their prayers regularly, having in mind that their prayers are a manifestation of their servitude to Allah alone. Thus, prayer leaves no result in those who are neglectful and inattentive to it. Consequently, they refuse to be kind or helpful to their fellow beings and deny the slightest charity to any of the servants of Allah.

Once again, we find ourselves presented with the fundamental truth and the nature of this religion; a Qur'anic verse threatens with destruction certain people who offer prayers precisely because they carry out meaningless movements devoid of any spirit or sense of purpose, intended for deceit and pretence, and not devoted to Allah. Since their prayers have not affected their hearts and behaviour, they are not merely useless but rather a sin for which they are liable to severe punishment.

From all these, we gather the purpose behind what Allah demands of His servants when He instructs them to believe in, and worship Him. He seeks no benefit thereof for Himself, as He is All-Affluent, but all He cares for is their own welfare and prosperity, purification of their hearts and happiness in their lives. Allah wishes human life to be elevated, happy, based on pure motives and characterised by mutual compassion, brotherhood and purity of hearts and behaviour.

To where then is humanity driving itself? Away from this abundance of mercy? Away from this wonderful and sublime path? How can mankind debase itself to living in the wilderness of a wretched and gloomy *Ignorance* when it beholds the sparkling light of faith before its very eyes at the cross-roads where it now stands?

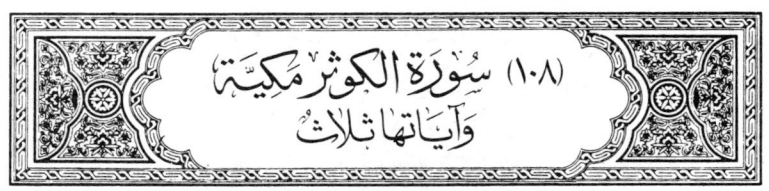

(١٠٨) سُورَةُ الكوثرِ مكيةٌ وآياتُها ثلاثٌ

بِسْمِ اللَّهِ الرَّحْمَنِ الرَّحِيمِ

إِنَّا أَعْطَيْنَاكَ الْكَوْثَرَ ۝ فَصَلِّ لِرَبِّكَ وَانْحَرْ ۝ إِنَّ شَانِئَكَ هُوَ الْأَبْتَرُ ۝

SURAH 108

ABUNDANCE
AL-KAWTHAR

In the name of Allah, the Beneficent, the Merciful.

Indeed We have given you abundance.
So pray to your Lord and sacrifice to Him.
Surely, he who hates you is the one cut off

In the Shade of the Qur'an

Similar to *surahs* 93 and 94, "The Forenoon" and "Solace", this *surah* exclusively concerns the Prophet, cheering him up and assuring him of happier prospects in his struggle. In it Allah threatens the enemies of the Prophet with destruction while directing the Prophet to the path of thanksgiving.

The *surah* represents a glimpse of the life of the Prophet and the course of his mission in the early period at Makka. It deals with the plots and insults directed against the Prophet and the Divine message he conveys. The *surah* is an instance of Allah's actual protection of His servant and the few who followed the Prophet and believed in Allah. It is an instance of Allah's direct support to the believers in their struggle, supplying them with fortitude, restraint and promise, while threatening a terrible fate to their antagonists.

In this way, the *surah* symbolises the reality of guidance, goodness and faith on the one hand and that of error, evil and disbelief on the other; the former category is one of abundance, profusion and expansive goodness, the latter one of scantiness, shrinking resources and annihilation.

Among the people of the Quraish (the Arab tribe which was dominant in Makka) there were some impudent folk who viewed the Prophet and his mission with no small degree of antagonism. They would resort to machinations and taunts against him to deter the people from listening to the Truth, which he conveyed to them in the form of a Divine message. Among them were people like Al-Aas ibn Wa'il, 'Uqba ibn Abi Mu'yat, Abu Lahab, Abu Jahl and others. They used to say about the Prophet that he was a man with no posterity, referring to the early death of his sons. One of them once remarked, "Do not be bothered with him; he will die without descendants and that will be the end of his mission."

Such a trivial and cunning taunt had a wide impact in the Arab society of the time, which set great store by sons. This sharp taunt delighted the enemies of the Prophet and undoubtedly this was a source of depression and irritation to his noble heart. This *surah* was therefore revealed, comforting the Prophet and assuring him of the abiding and profuse goodness which Allah had chosen for him and of the deprivation and loss awaiting his persecutors.

"Indeed We have given you abundance." The word used in the *surah* and rendered here as "abundance" is *"kawthar"*, derived from the

Surah 108   Abundance (*Al-Kawthar*)

stem word *"kathrah"* which signifies "abundance" or "a multitude". This *"kawthar"* is unrestricted and unlimited. It indicates the opposite meaning to the one the impudent folk of Quraish tried to attach to the Prophet. *"We have given you"* that which is plentiful, overflowing and rich, unstinting and unending.

If anyone wishes to pursue and observe this abundance which Allah has given to His Prophet, he would find it wherever he looks and reflects. He would find it in Muhammad's prophethood itself, this link with the great Reality and the great Being, Who has no parallel and no partner. What indeed can the one who has found Allah be said to have lost?

He would find it in this Qur'an which was revealed to Muhammad, every chapter of which is a fountain of richness which flows incessantly.

He would also find this *kawthar* or abundance manifest in the of the Prophet's *Sunnah* (way of life) throughout the centuries, in the far-flung corners of the earth, in the millions upon millions who follow in his footsteps, in the millions upon millions who pronounce his name with respectful affection and the millions upon millions of hearts that cherish, and would cherish his example and memory even to the Day of Resurrection.

He would also find this *Kawthar* or abundance manifest in the goodness and prosperity which have accrued to the human race as a result of his message, and which reach those who know and believe in him and those who do not. He would also discern this abundance in various and manifold phenomena, attempting to enumerate which would at best give only a passing feeling of a great reality.

This indeed is abundance in its absolute unlimited sense. The *surah* therefore does not give it a specific definition.

Several accounts relate that *"Al-Kawthar"* is a river in Paradise granted to the Prophet but Ibn Abbas, a learned companion of the Prophet, contends that the river is but one part of the abundance which Allah has furnished for His Prophet. Keeping the circumstances and the whole context in mind, Ibn Abbas's view is the more valid.

"So pray to your Lord and sacrifice to Him." Having assured the Prophet of this munificent gift, which disproves what the calumniators and conspirators say, Allah directs the Prophet to be completely and sincerely thankful to Him for His bounty;

to devote himself to Him alone in worship and ritual slaughter, taking no heed whatsoever of all forms of polytheism and refusing to participate in the worship of the polytheists, especially when they pronounce any name other than that of Allah in their offerings.

Islam frequently lays emphasis on the pronouncing of Allah's name when slaughtering animals. It prohibits anything that is consecrated to any other being, which indicates the importance Islam attaches to the purification of human life from all forms of polytheism and all that leads to it. Islam does not aim merely at purifying the imagination and conscience, for it is the religion based on the unity of Allah in every sense. It pursues polytheism in all its manifestations, striving to eliminate its marks in the conscience of man, in his worship and rituals, and in his behaviour generally. Life, Islam says, is one indivisible entity and must be treated as such. It must be cleansed inside out and completely oriented towards Allah, in all its aspects and spheres – worship, tradition and social behaviour.

"Surely he who hates you is the one cut off". In the first verse, Allah specified that Muhammad was not the one who had no posterity but, on the contrary, was the one endowed with abundance. In this verse, Allah throws back the taunt on those who hated and reviled the Prophet. Indeed, the promise of Allah has come true. For, the influence and the legacy of Muhammad's enemies was short-lived, while his impact on human history and human life has grown and deepened. Today we are witnessing the truth of this Divine pronouncement as clearly as no one among those addressed by the Qur'an for the first time ever did or imagined.

Faith and goodness cannot be barren: they leave deep-rooted influence; but falsehood, error and evil – no matter how fast they grow and spread – do ultimately come to nothing.

Allah's criteria are different from the criteria laid down by man. Men are often deceived when they vainly believe their sense of judgement to be the criterion. Before us is the eloquent and enduring example of the Prophet. Of what value or interest to humanity have those slanderers and foes of Muhammad been to anyone?

On the other hand, calling others to the religion of Allah, to truth and goodness, can never be called futile. Neither can the righteous and the true be called deprived or cut off. How can it be, when this message itself comes from and is supported by Allah, the Immortal, the Eternal? But deprived and sterile indeed are disbelief, error and evil as are their votaries, however strong and widespread they may appear to be at a particular moment.

Allah affirms the truth; the wily opponents are but liars!

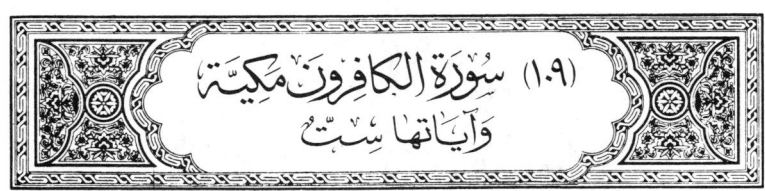

بِسْمِ اللهِ الرَّحْمَنِ الرَّحِيمِ

قُلْ يَٰأَيُّهَا ٱلْكَٰفِرُونَ ۝ لَآ أَعْبُدُ مَا تَعْبُدُونَ ۝ وَلَآ أَنتُمْ عَٰبِدُونَ مَآ أَعْبُدُ ۝ وَلَآ أَنَا۠ عَابِدٌ مَّا عَبَدتُّمْ ۝ وَلَآ أَنتُمْ عَٰبِدُونَ مَآ أَعْبُدُ ۝ لَكُمْ دِينُكُمْ وَلِيَ دِينِ ۝

SURAH 109

THE DISBELIEVERS
AL-KAFIROON

In the name of Allah, the Beneficent, the Merciful.

Say: "Disbelievers!
I do not worship what you worship
nor do you worship what I worship.
I shall never worship what you worship
neither will you worship what I worship.
You have your own religion and I have mine."

In the Shade of the Qur'an

Although the Arabs before Islam were not disavowing Allah, they did not know Him by the true identity He accorded Himself as the One and the Eternal. They did not only depreciate Him and inaptly worship Him but they also ascribed to Him, as partners, idols that were supposed to represent their great and pious ancestors or, in some cases, the angels whom they claimed to be the daughters of Allah. Moreover, they alleged a kinship between Him and the jinn. They often ignored all these qualifications, however, and worshipped those idols themselves. But in all cases, as the Qur'an quotes them as saying, they only *"worship them (the various gods) so that they may bring us near to Allah."* [1]

The Qur'an also states: *"If you ask them who it is that has created the heavens and the earth, and subjected the sun and the moon (to fixed laws) they will say: 'Allah' "*.[2] And again: *"If you ask them who it is that sends down water from the sky, and thereby revives the earth after it has died, they will say: 'Allah' "*.[3] Moreover, Allah superseded their gods in their oaths and supplications.

But in spite of their belief in Allah, the polytheism they entertained fouled their conceptions as well as their traditions and rites to the extent that they assigned to their alleged gods a portion of their earnings and possessions, and even their offspring; in fact, they had often been obliged to sacrifice their children. Concerning this, the Qur'an has the following to say:

They set aside for Allah a share of what He has produced in abundance of crops and cattle, saying: "This is for Allah" – so they pretend – "and this for the partner-gods we associate with Him" But nothing of the share of their partner-gods may ever go to Allah while the share of Allah may go to their partner-gods. How ill they judge! Thus those partner-gods of theirs have induced many polytheists to kill their children so that they may ruin them and confuse them in their faith. Had Allah willed, they would not have done so; so leave them to their false inventions. They say: "Such cattle and crops are forbidden; no one may eat of them save those whom we permit" – so they assert. Further, there are cattle which they prohibit men from riding, and others over which they do not pronounce the name of Allah. All these are lies they assert against Allah. He will surely pun-

---

[1] The Qur'an. *39; 3.*
[2] *Ibid. 29; 61.*
[3] *Ibid. 29; 63.*

Surah 109 The Disbelievers (*Al-Kafiroon*)

ish them for their invented lies. They also say: "What is in the wombs of these animals is reserved to our males, forbidden to our females." But if it is still born, then they all partake of it. Allah will surely punish them for what they impute to Him. He is surely wise and He knows all. "Lost are they who, in their ignorance, wantonly slay their children, and make unlawful what Allah has provided for them, inventing lies against Allah. They have indeed gone astray and heeded no guidance."[1]

The Arabs were also convinced that they were the followers of the religion of Abraham and that they were better guided than the People of the Scriptures (i.e. Jews and Christians) inhabiting the Arabian peninsula at the time: the Jews and the Christians preached respectively that Ezra and Jesus were the sons of Allah whereas they, the Arabs, worshipped angels and jinn – the true offspring of Allah according to them. Their belief, they maintained, was more logical and more conceivable than that of the Christians and the Jews. Nonetheless, all was polytheism.

When Muhammad (peace be on him) declared his religion to be that of Abraham, they argued that there was no reason for them to forsake their beliefs and follow Muhammad's instead, since they too were of the same religion. In the meantime, they sought a sort of compromise with him proposing that he should prostrate himself before their gods in return for their prostration to his God, and that he should cease denouncing their gods and their manner of worship in reciprocation for whatever he demanded of them!

This confusion in their concepts, vividly illustrated by their worship of various gods while acknowledging Allah, was perhaps what led them to believe that the gulf between them and Muhammad was not unbridgeable. They thought an agreement was somehow possible by allowing the two camps to co-exist in the region and by granting him some personal concessions!

To clear up this muddle, to cut all arguments short and firmly distinguish between one form of worship and the other, between one doctrine and concept and the other this *surah* was revealed in such a decisive, assertive tone. It was revealed in this manner to demarcate monotheism (*tawheed*) from polytheism (*shirk*), and to establish a true criterion, allowing no further wrangling or vain arguments.

Using all the mentioned means, the *surah* goes on to emphasise a

---

[1] The Qur'an. 6; 137–41.

negation in one sentence and an affirmation in another. *"Say"* – this denotes a clear-cut Divine order which conveys the fact that the whole affair of the religion belongs exclusively to Allah, nothing of it belongs to Muhammad himself, and that Allah is the only One to order and decide. Address them, Muhammad, by their actual and true identity: *"Say: 'Disbelievers!'"* They follow no prescribed religion, nor do they believe in you. No meeting-point exists between you and them anywhere. Thus the beginning of the *surah* brings to mind the reality of a difference which cannot be ignored or settled.

"I do not worship what you worship" is a statement affirmed by *"I shall never worship what you worship"*. *"Nor do you worship what I worship"* is also repeated for more emphasis and in order to eliminate all chances of doubt or misinterpretation.

Finally, the whole argument is summed up in the last verse, *"You have your own religion, and I have mine"*, meaning that you (disbelievers) and I (Muhammad) are very far apart, without any bridge to connect us – a complete distinction and a precise, intelligible demarcation.

Such an attitude was essential then in order to expose the fundamental discrepancies in the essence of the two beliefs and doctrines, in the source of the two concepts and in the nature of the two paths of monotheism and polytheism, faith and disbelief. Faith on the one hand, is the way of life which directs man and the whole world towards Allah alone and determines for him the source of his religious concept, laws, values, criteria, ethics and morals. That source is Allah and nobody else. Thus life proceeds for him accordingly, devoid of any form of polytheism which, on the other hand, represents another way of life entirely dissimilar to that of faith. The two never meet.

On the whole, the distinction we are dealing with here is indispensable both for those who invite people to Islam and the people themselves, because *Ignorant* concepts are likely to be mixed with those of Islam especially in those societies which previously followed the Islamic method, but have later deviated from it. They are, to be sure, the most rigid and the most hostile to the idea of regaining faith in its healthy, clear and straightforward form – certainly more so than those who have not known Islam originally. They take it for granted that they are righteous while they grow more and more complicatedly perverse!

Surah 109   The Disbelievers (*Al-Kafiroon*)

The existence of noble and base beliefs and thoughts in those societies may tempt the advocate of the Islamic system to hope for their quick return, thinking he may be able to strengthen the good aspects of their life and rightly correct undesirable features! This temptation is dangerously misleading. For *Ignorance* is nothing but *Ignorance* and Islam is altogether different from it. The only way to bridge the gulf between the two is for *Ignorance* to liquidate itself completely and substitute for all its laws, values, standards and concepts their Islamic counterparts.

The first step that should be taken in this field by the person calling on people to embrace Islam is to segregate himself from *Ignorance*. He must be separated to the extent that any agreement or intercourse between him and *Ignorance* is absolutely impossible unless and until the people of *Ignorance* embrace Islam completely: no intermingling, no half measures or conciliation is permissible, however clever *Ignorance* may be in usurping the role of Islam or reflecting it. The chief basis of the personality of the person inviting others to Islam is the clear manifestation of this fact within himself and his solemn conviction of being radically different from them. They have their own religion, and he has his. His task is to orientate them so that they may follow his path without any fraud or pretence. Failing this, he must withdraw completely, detach himself from their life and openly declare to them: *"You have your own religion, and I have mine."*

This is a *sine qua non* for the contemporary advocates of Islam. They badly need to realise that they are calling for Islam today in entirely *Ignorant* surroundings amongst ex-Muslim peoples whose hearts have grown harder and whose beliefs have now deteriorated considerably. They need to understand that there is no room for short-term or half solutions, compromises, or partial redemption or adjustment, and that their call is for uniquely distinguished Islam, in contrast to what these people conceive of as Islam. They must face these people bravely and explicitly put it to them: *"You have your own religion, and I have mine."* Our religion is based on absolute monotheism whose concepts, values, beliefs and laws cover all aspects of human life and are all received from Allah and none else.

Without this basic separation confusion, double-dealing, doubt and distortion will certainly persist. And let it be clear in our minds here that the movement advocating Islam can never be constructed on any ambiguous or feeble foundations, but has to be built upon firmness, explicitness, frankness and fortitude as embodied in

Allah's instruction to us to declare: *"You have your own religion, and I have mine."* Such was the way adopted by the Islamic call in its early days.

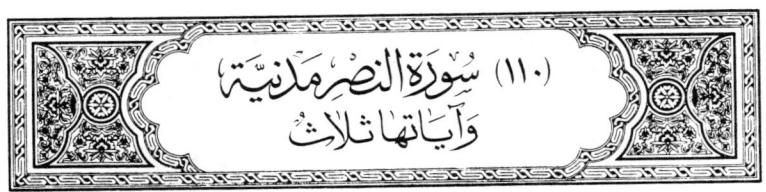

(١١٠) سورة النصر مدنية وآياتها ثلاث

بِسْمِ اللَّهِ الرَّحْمَنِ الرَّحِيمِ

إِذَا جَاءَ نَصْرُ اللَّهِ وَالْفَتْحُ ۝ وَرَأَيْتَ النَّاسَ يَدْخُلُونَ فِي دِينِ اللَّهِ أَفْوَاجًا ۝ فَسَبِّحْ بِحَمْدِ رَبِّكَ وَاسْتَغْفِرْهُ إِنَّهُ كَانَ تَوَّابًا ۝

SURAH 110

VICTORY
AN-NASR

In the name of Allah, the Beneficent, the Merciful.

When the victory granted by Allah and the Conquest come,
and you see people embracing the religion of Allah in large numbers,
then celebrate the praises of your Lord, and seek His forgiveness.
   He is ever disposed to mercy.

In the Shade of the Qur'an

This short *surah* brings the good news to Allah's Messenger concerning the advent of victory, the Conquest and peoples' collective acceptance of Allah's religion. It instructs him to turn towards his Lord in a devoted adoration and a humble request for His forgiveness. The *surah* also presents the nature and the righteousness of this Faith and its ideology – how high humanity ascends to an ideal and brilliant summit unattainable otherwise than by responding to the call of Islam.

Of the several traditions regarding the revelation of this *surah*, we quote that of Imam Ahmad which goes as follows: "Aisha said that the Messenger of Allah used to repeat very frequently, towards the end of his life, 'Exaltations and praises be to Allah, whose forgiveness I ask; I repent of my sins.' He also said, 'My Lord told me I would see a sign in my nation. He ordered me to praise Him, the Forgiving, and ask His pardon when I see this sign. Indeed, I have. *'When the victory granted by Allah and the Conquest come . . .'*"[1]

Ibn Katheer said in his commentary on the Qur'an: "'The Conquest'; it is unanimously agreed, is a reference to the conquest of Makka. The Arab tribes were awaiting the settlement of the conflict between Quraish and the Muslims, before accepting Islam, saying: 'If he, Muhammad, prevails over his people, he would indeed be a prophet.' Consequently, when that was accomplished they accepted Islam in large numbers. Not two years were to pass after the conquest of Makka when the whole Arabian Peninsula was dominated by Islam, and, all thanks to Allah, every Arab tribe had declared its belief in Islam."

Al-Bukhari in his *Sahih* related "Amr ibn Salamah said that when Makka was conquered, every tribe hastened to declare acceptance of Islam to Allah's Messenger. They were waiting for it to take place saying, Leave them to themselves. He would indeed be a prophet if he prevailed over them." This version is the one which agrees chronologically with the beginning of the *surah* in the sense that its revelation was a sign of something to follow with some instructions to the Prophet, on what he should do when this event took place.

There is, nevertheless, another fairly similar version in agreement with the one we have chosen and it is that by Ibn 'Abbas which says: "''Umar used to let me join the company of elders who were present

---

[1] Transmitted by Muslim.

Surah 110   Victory *(An-Nasr)*

at Badr, some of whom felt uneasy and asked why I should be allowed with them when I was young. But 'Umar said to them, 'You know that he is of high standing.' One day 'Umar invited them all and invited me as well. I felt that he wanted to show them who I was, so he asked them, 'What do you make of Allah's saying, *'When the victory granted by Allah and the Conquest come?''* Some of them replied, 'He ordered us to praise Him and seek His forgiveness when He helps us to triumph and bestows His favours on us.' The others remained silent. Then 'Umar asked me, 'Do you agree with this view, Ibn Abbas?' I answered in the negative. 'Umar asked me again. 'What then do you say?' I replied, 'It was a sign from Allah to His Messenger indicating the approach of the end of his life, meaning, when the victory from Allah and the Conquest come, your end is near, so extol the praises of your Lord and seek His forgiveness.' 'Umar commented, 'I have known no more than what you have said.'"[1]

So it is possible that the Messenger, having witnessed his Lord's sign, realized that he had fulfilled his mission on this earth and that it was time for him to leave, which was what Ibn 'Abbas actually meant.

However, there is another account narrated by Al-Hafiz al-Baihaqi also attributed to Ibn 'Abbas who according to it said, "When this *surah* was first revealed, the Messenger of Allah called Fatimah and said, 'My death has been announced to me.' She was seen to start crying, then she smiled. She explained later, 'I cried when he told me of his approaching death. But he said to me, "Be restrained, because you will be the first of my family to join me", so I smiled.'"

According to the last tradition quoted the time of the revelation of the *surah* is actually fixed as coming later than the sign, that is, the Conquest and the people's collective movement into Islam. When events took place in this fashion the Messenger of Allah knew that his life would soon come to a close. But again the first account is more authentic and fits in more suitably with the outline of the beginning of the *surah*, especially as the Fatimah incident is related in a different form which gives more weight to what we have suggested. This other form goes as follows: Umm Salamah, the Prophet's wife said, "The Messenger of Allah called Fatimah to him sometime during the

---

[1] Transmitted by Al-Bukhari.

year of the Conquest and he said something to her. She cried. Then he spoke to her again and she was smiling. After he had died, I asked her about the incident and she explained 'The Messenger of Allah told me he was soon to die, so I cried. Then he told me that I would be the next most celebrated woman in Paradise after Mariam (Mary), the daughter of Imran, so I smiled.' This narration agrees with the general meaning of the Qur'anic text and with what Imam Ahmad related which appears in the *Sahih* of Muslim — that is, there was a sign (in the *surah*) between Allah and His Messenger and when the Conquest was accomplished the latter knew that he was soon to meet his Lord, so he spoke to Fatimah in the manner described by Umm Salamah.

Let us now consider the actual text of the *surah* and the injunction it gives for all time:

"When the victory granted by Allah and the Conquest come, and you see people embracing the religion of Allah in large numbers. Then, celebrate the praises of your Lord and seek His forgiveness. He is ever disposed to mercy."

The beginning of the first verse implicitly presents a concept of what goes on in this universe: the events that take place in this life, and the actual role of the Messenger of Allah and his followers in the progress of Islam, and to what extent it depends on their efforts. *"When the victory granted by Allah"* denotes that it is Allah's victory and Allah is the One who brings it about in His own good time, in the form He decides and for the purpose He determines. The Prophet and his companions have nothing to do with it at all, and they obtain no personal gain from it. It suffices them that He does it through them, appoints them as its guards and entrusts it to them. This is all they acquire from the victory of Allah, the Conquest and the people's acceptance *en masse* of His religion.

According to this concept, the duty of the Messenger and his companions whom Allah chose and gave the privilege of being the instruments of His victory, was to turn to Him at the climax of victory in praise, expressing gratitude and seeking forgiveness. Gratitude and praise are for His being so generous as to have chosen them to be the standard bearers of His religion; for the mercy and favour He did to all humanity by making His religion victorious; and for the Conquest of Makka and the people's collective acceptance of Islam.

His forgiveness is sought for the various unrevealed, defective feel-

Surah 110   Victory (*An-Nasr*)

ings, such as vanity, which sometimes creep into one's heart at the overwhelming moment of victory attained after a long struggle. Human beings can hardly prevent this happening and therefore Allah's forgiveness is to be sought for it. Forgiveness also has to be sought for what might have been insinuated into one's heart during the long and cruel struggle and for petulance resulting from the belatedness of victory or the effects of convulsive despair, as the Qur'an brings out elsewhere: *"Or think you that you will enter Paradise while yet there has not come to you the like of that which came to those who passed away before you? Affliction and adversity befell them; they were shaken as with earthquake, till the Messenger (of Allah) and those who believed along with him said: 'When will Allah's help come?' Now surely Allah's help is near."* [1]

It is also necessary to seek Allah's forgiveness for one's shortcomings in praising Allah and thanking Him for His favours which are perpetual and infinite. *"And if you were to count the favours of Allah, never will you be able to number them."* [2] However much one's efforts in this respect, they are never adequate. Another touching thought is that seeking forgiveness at the moment of triumph arouses in one's mind the feeling of impotence and imperfection at a time when an attitude of self-esteem and conceit seems natural. All these factors guarantee that no tyranny will afflict the conquered. The victorious is made to realize that it is Allah who has appointed him – a man who has no power of his own and is devoid of any strength – for a predetermined purpose; consequently the triumph and the conquest as well as the religion are all His, to Whom all things ultimately return.

This is the lofty, dignified ideal the Qur'an exhorts people to toil towards and attain, an ideal in which man's exaltation is in neglecting his own pride and where his soul's freedom is in his subservience to Allah. The goal set is the total release of human souls from their egoistic shackles, their only ambition being to attain Allah's pleasure. Along with this release there must be exerted a striving which helps man to flourish in the world, promote human civilisation and provide a rightly-guided, unblemished, constructive, just leadership devoted to Allah.

In contrast, man's efforts to liberate himself while in the grip of egoism, shackled by his zest for worldly things, or overpowered by

---

[1] The Qur'an. *2; 214*.   [2] *Ibid. 16; 18*.

his cravings, turn out to be absolutely in vain unless he sets himself free from self and lets his loyalty to Allah override everything else, particularly at the moment of triumph and the collecting of booty. Such a standard of behaviour, which Allah wants humanity to aspire towards and to attain, was the characteristic feature of the Prophets at all times.

So it was the case with Prophet Yussuf (Joseph), when all he wanted was achieved and his dream came true: *"and he placed his parents high on the throne of dignity and they fell down prostrate before him. He said: 'Father! This is the fulfilment of my dream of old. My Lord has made it come true. He has been gracious to me. He has released me from prison and has brought you from the desert after Satan had stirred-up strife between me and my brothers. My Lord is gracious with all that He plans to do. He is full of knowledge and wisdom.'"*[1] Then, at that moment of climax, Yussuf took himself away from the jubilations and from the embracing arms to turn towards his Lord, praising him with a pure feeling of gratitude: *"my Lord! You have given me something of sovereignty and power and have taught me something of the interpretation of visions. Creator of the heavens and the earth! You are my Protector in this world and the hereafter. Let me die in submission and join the righteous."*[2]

Thus vanished the feeling of predominance and reputation and the happiness brought by his reunion with his family, and the picture we are left with is of that individual, Yussuf, praying to Allah to help him remain submissive to Him until he dies and to let him, out of His mercy and grace, join His righteous servants.

So, it was also with Prophet Sulaiman (Solomon), when he saw the Queen of Sheba's throne brought into his very reach in a flash: *"And when he (Sulaiman) saw it set in his presence he said: 'This is of the bounty of my Lord, that He may try me whether I give thanks or remain ungrateful. He who gives thanks does so for his own good, and he who is ungrateful . . . . my Lord is all sufficient and bountiful.'"*[1]

And so indeed it was with Muhammad all through his life. In the moment of triumph, as the Conquest of Makka was accomplished, he entered it on the back of his camel with his head bowed down. He forgot the joy of victory and thankfully bowed his head seeking his Lord's forgiveness, though he had just conquered Makka, the city

---

[1] The Qur'an. *12; 100.*   [2] *Ibid. 12; 101.*

Surah 110   Victory (*An-Nasr*)

whose people had openly and unashamedly persecuted and expelled him. This also was the practice of his companions after him.

Thus, upon belief in Allah, was that great generation of humanity raised very high, reaching an unparalleled standard of greatness, power and freedom.

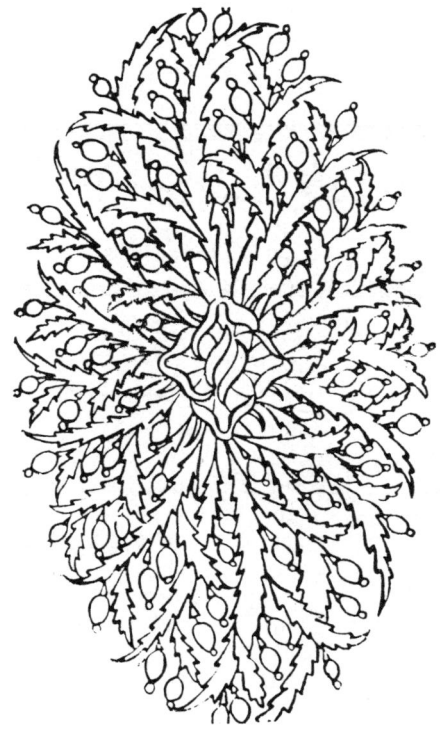

---

[1] The Qur'an. 27; 40.

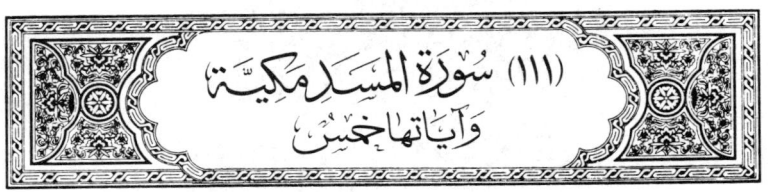

بِسْمِ اللَّهِ الرَّحْمَٰنِ الرَّحِيمِ

تَبَّتْ يَدَا أَبِي لَهَبٍ وَتَبَّ ۝ مَا أَغْنَىٰ عَنْهُ مَالُهُ وَمَا كَسَبَ ۝ سَيَصْلَىٰ نَارًا ذَاتَ لَهَبٍ ۝ وَامْرَأَتُهُ حَمَّالَةَ الْحَطَبِ ۝ فِي جِيدِهَا حَبْلٌ مِّن مَّسَدٍ ۝

SURAH 111

FIRE FLAMES
AL-MASAD

In the name of Allah, the Beneficent, the Merciful.

May the hands of Abu Lahab perish; doomed he is.
His wealth and his gains shall not avail him.
He shall be plunged in a flaming fire,
and his wife, the carrier of firewood
shall have a rope of palm fibre round her neck.

In the Shade of the Qur'an

Abu Lahab, whose real name was Abduluzza ibn Abdulmuttalib, was an uncle of the Prophet. He was so nicknamed because of the radiant look he had on his face. With his wife Abu Lahab was one of the most unbending foes of the Messenger and the ideas he was propagating.

Ibn Ishaq related the report made by Rabiah ibn 'Abbad Ad-Daili who said, "When I was a youngster I once watched with my father Allah's Messenger preaching Islam to the Arab tribes saying 'O sons of... (calling their respective names), I am Allah's Messenger sent to order you to submit to and worship Him and nothing else beside Him, and to believe in me and protect me until I carry out what Allah has entrusted me with.' A cross-eyed, bright-faced man was behind him, who used to say, after he had finished, 'O sons of... this man wants you to forsake Al-Lat and Al-Uzza (two prominent idols worshipped by the pagan Arabs) and your allies of the *jinn*, the children of Malik ibn Aqmas and to substitute for them these innovations and nonsense he has brought. Do not harken to him, nor follow what he preaches.' I asked my father who that man was and he told me that it was Abu Lahab, the Prophet's uncle." (Imam Ahmad and Tabarani also had the same version.)

This is but one incident of Abu Lahab's intimidation and ill-will towards the Messenger and his call. His wife Arwa, the daughter of Harb Ibn Ummya, a sister of Abu Sufyan, gave him unfailing support in his virulent, relentless campaign.

Such was the attitude of Abu Lahab towards the Prophet from the very start of his Divine mission. Al-Bukhari related, on the authority of Ibn Abbas, that the Prophet went out to Batha' (a large square in Makka) one day, mounted a hill and summoned the people of Quraish. When they came to him he addressed them and said, "Were I to tell you that an enemy is drawing near and will attack you tomorrow morning or evening, would you believe me?" "Yes," they replied. "So listen to me," he went on, "I am warning you of gruesome torment (from Allah)." Abu Lahab was there and snapped at him, "Damn you![1] For this you have called us?" (Another version goes: "Abu Lahab stood up shaking the dust off his hands and saying, 'Damn you all day long...'") Then this *surah* was revealed.

Another instance was when the Hashimi clan (the Prophet's own clan) decided on grounds of tribal loyalties, under the leadership of

---

[1] Literally, "Perish you!"

Surah 111   Fire Flames (*Al-Masad*)

Abu Talib to protect the Prophet despite their rejection of the religion he was preaching. Abu Lahab was the only one to take a different stand. He joined with the Quraish instead, and was with them in signing the document to boycott the Hashimi clan completely and starve them till they gave up the Prophet to them.

Abu Lahab also ordered his two sons to renounce the daughters of Muhammad, to whom they had been engaged before Muhammad's prophetic assignment, so as to burden him with the expenses of their maintenance and welfare.

Thus, Abu Lahab and his wife, Arwa, who was also called Umm Jamil, continued to launch their persistent onslaught against the Prophet and his message. The fact that they were close neighbours of the Prophet made the situation worse still. We are told that Umm Jamil used to carry thorns and sharp wood and place them in the Prophet's path (though it is thought that the phrase "the carrier of firewood" in the *surah* is used only metaphorically to indicate her lies and malice about him).

This *surah* was revealed as a counter-attack against their hostile campaigns; Allah had taken over the command of the battle. *"May the hands of Abu Lahab perish, doomed he is."* The Arabic term rendered here as *"perish"* also signifies failure and cutting off. The term is used twice in two different senses. It is used first as an appeal, while in the second occurence it implies the granting of the appeal and its fulfilment. So, in one short verse, an action is realised which draws the curtains upon a scene of a completed battle. What later follows is merely a description of what took place with the remark that *"his wealth and his gains shall not avail him."* He can have no escape. He is defeated, vanquished and damned.

That was his fate in this world, but in the Hereafter *"he shall be plunged in a flaming fire."* And his wife, the wood-carrier, will reside there with him having around her neck a rope of palm-fibre with which, as it were, she is being dragged into Hell; or which she used for fastening wood bundles together, according to whether a literal or metaphorical interpretation of the text is adopted.

The language of this *surah* achieves a remarkable degree of beautiful harmony between the subject matter and the atmosphere built around it. Abu Lahab will be plunged into a fire with *"Lahab"*, which is the Arabic word for flames of fire; and his wife who carries the wood, a fuel, will be met with the same fire with a palm-fibre rope around her neck. *"Jahannam"* or Jehanna with fiercely burning *"Lahab"* will be inhabited by Abu Lahab. And his wife, who wraps up thorns and sharp woods, materials which, significantly, can increase the blaze of a fire, and puts them in the Prophet's way, will be subsequently dragged to Hell with a rope tied to her neck, bundled like firewood. How perfect is the matching between the words and the pictures; the punishment is presented as of the same nature as the deed – wood, ropes, fire and *Lahab!*

Phonetically, the words are arranged in a way which provides a wonderful harmony between the sounds made by the pulling of the wood and the neck by ropes. Read in Arabic, the verse, *"Tabbat yada abi Lahabin watab,"* makes one feel a kind of hard sharp pull, analogous to that of bundles of wood or of dragging an unwilling person by the neck into a wild fire; all is in phase with the fury and the violent, bellicose tone that goes with the theme of the *surah*. Thus, in five short verses of one of the shortest *surahs* of the Qur'an, the vocal melodies click neatly with the actual movements of the scene portrayed.

This extremely rich and brilliant style led Umm Jamil to claim that the Prophet was in fact "satirizing" her and her husband. The arrogant and vain Arab woman could not get over being referred to with such a humiliating phrase as *"the carrier of firewood,"* who *"shall have a rope of palm-fibre round her neck."* Her rage grew wilder when the *surah* became popular among the Arab tribes who esteemed such a literary style!

Ibn Ishaq related: "Umm Jamil, I was told, having heard what the Qur'an said about her and her husband, came to the Prophet who was with Abu Bakr at the Ka'aba. She was carrying a handful of stones. Allah took her sight away from the Prophet and she saw only Abu Bakr to whom she said, 'Where is your comrade? I have heard that he has been satirizing me. Were I to find him, I would throw these stones right into his face. I, too, am gifted in poetry.' Then she said before leaving:

'The contemptible we obey not!
Nor what he says shall we accept!'

"Abu Bakr turned around to the Prophet and said, 'Do you think

Surah 111   Fire Flames (*Al-Masad*)

that she saw you?' 'No,' replied the Prophet, 'Allah made her unable to see me.'"

Al-Hafiz Abu Bakr Al-Bazar also related, on the authority of Ibn Abbas, that when this *surah* was revealed Abu Lahab's wife sought the Prophet. While he was with Abu Bakr she appeared and Abu Bakr suggested, "She will not harm you if you hide yourself away!" "Don't worry," said the Prophet in a soothing manner. "She will not see me." She came to Abu Bakr and said, "Your friend has lampooned us!" "By the Lord of this Ka'aba, he has not," Abu Bakr assured her. "He is no poet and what he says is not poetry," he added. She said, "I believe you," and then left. Abu Bakr then enquired from the Prophet whether she had seen him and he said, "No, an angel was shielding me all the time she was here." So much was her fury and her indignation at what she thought was poetry and which Abu Bakr rightly refuted.

Thus, the humiliating picture of Abu Lahab and his wife has been recorded to last forever in this eternal book, the Qur'an, to show Allah's anger with them for their animosity to His Messenger and the ideas he was advocating. All those who choose to take a similar attitude towards Islam, therefore, shall meet with the same disgrace, calamity and frustration, both in this life and in the Hereafter, as fitting punishment and reward!

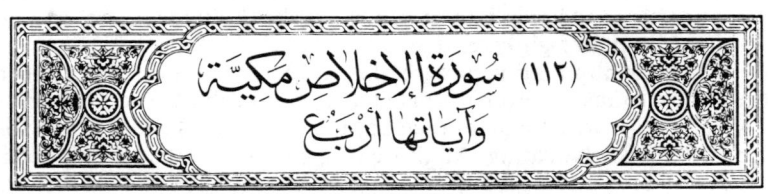

(١١٢) سورة الإخلاص مكية
وآياتها أربع

بِسْمِ اللَّهِ الرَّحْمَنِ الرَّحِيمِ

قُلْ هُوَ اللَّهُ أَحَدٌ ۞ اللَّهُ الصَّمَدُ ۞ لَمْ يَلِدْ وَلَمْ يُولَدْ ۞ وَلَمْ يَكُنْ لَهُ كُفُوًا أَحَدٌ ۞

SURAH 112

PURITY OF FAITH
AL-IKHLAS

In the name of Allah, the Beneficent, the Merciful.

Say: He is Allah, the one and only God,
the Eternal, the Absolute.
He begot none, nor was He begotten,
and there is none comparable to Him.

In the Shade of the Qur'an

This short *surah* is "equivalent to one third of the Qur'an". Al-Bukhari, the leading traditionist, was told about someone who had heard a man reciting, *"Say: He is Allah..."* repeatedly and had gone to the Prophet the following morning and told him disapprovingly about what he had heard. The Prophet commented, "I swear by Him in Whose hand is my soul that it (the *surah*) is equivalent to one third of the Qur'an."

And, indeed, there is nothing surprising in that. For the unity of Allah which the Messenger was ordered to declare to the whole world is a belief to be ingrained in our beings, an explanation of human existence and a way of life in itself. From this standpoint, the *surah* can be said to have embraced in the clearest terms the principal and most fundamental ideas of the great truth of Islam.

The Arabic term *"Ahad"* used here to refer to the unity of Allah is much more precise than the much more frequently used term *"Wahid"* which means "one". *"Ahad"* has the added connotations of absolute and continuous unity and the absence of equals.

The unity of Allah is such that there is no reality and no true and permanent existence except His. Moreover, every other being acquires whatever power it possessed from the effective power of Allah which rules over this world. Nothing else whatsoever plans anything for the world nor decides, for that matter, anything in it.

This is the belief that should be entrenched in us. It is a full explanation of human existence. Once this belief has become clear and that explanation has established itself in the human mind, the heart is purified of all falsities and impurities and it is released from all ties except those of the one and unique Being who alone possesses the reality of being and who is the only effective power in this world. The human heart is then released from bondage to anything in this world, if not from attributing existence to anything else altogether. Indeed, why should men's hearts aspire to something that has no permanent reality nor has any independent power to function in this world, since the real being is that of the Divine Being and the truly effective power is the Divine Will?

When the human heart releases itself from believing in anything but the one Truth, the Truth of Allah, and upholds this everlasting Truth, it liberates itself from all shackles, false ideas, evil desires, fear of earthly powers and from the confusions that mislead in this life. For when the human heart finds Allah, it benefits and loses nothing. So why should it desire anything but the pleasure of Allah? And why

Surah 112   Purity of Faith (*Al-Ikhlas*)

should it fear anything, since there is no absolutely effective power but that of Allah?

When a conception that sees nothing in the world but the reality of Allah establishes itself in the human mind and heart, it is accompanied by the vision of this genuine, permanent reality in every other being that has sprung from it. This is the stage at which the heart feels the hand of Allah in everything and beyond which it feels nothing but Allah in the whole universe. There would be no other reality to be felt.

It is also accompanied by the attribution of every event and every movement in this life and in this universe to the first and only cause, that is, Allah, that brings other causes about and influences their effectiveness. The Qur'an takes great care to establish this truth in the Muslims' concept of faith. It has always put aside apparent causes and associated events directly with the will of Allah. It says, *"When you threw (a handful of dust) it was not your act, but Allah's."* [1] *There is no triumph except that given by Allah,"* [2] *"You have no will except as llah wills."* [3]

By disregarding all apparent causes and connecting matters directly with the will of Allah, a feeling of relief gently penetrates the human heart so that it knows the only Saviour from whom it can ask whatever it wishes and by whom it is rescued from all it fears. It becomes unimpressed by the apparent influences, reasons and causes that bear no reality or true existence in themselves.

These are the steps of the way some mystics tried to climb, but they deviated too far from it. For Islam wants people to follow this route struggling with the realities of life with all its varied conditions and qualities, and to lead a human life in which they exercise their role of vicegerency of Allah on earth with all their resources and the obligations laid upon them.

From this concept of the unity of Allah, stems a perfect path of life based on the explanation of human existence and whatever outlooks, feelings, and traits it stimulates. Such a path is based on the worship of Allah alone, who is the only real and permanent being, and whose will is the only effective power in the world. It is the path that makes its followers turn towards Allah alone and seek refuge in Him in times of need and fear, happiness and discomfort, luxury and

---

[1] The Qur'an. *8; 17.*   [3] *Ibid. 76; 30.*
[2] *Ibid. 8; 10* and *3; 126.*

hardship. For what is the use of turning towards a non-existent or a powerless being? This path has as its benefactor Allah alone. From Him we receive our beliefs, outlook, values, criteria, legislations, institutions, systems, ethics and traditions. Such qualities must be obtained from the One and Permanent Being and the One Truth.

It is a path for performing activities, doing work and making sacrifices absolutely and only for Allah, and for wishing to be nearer the truth. This path also strengthens the links of love, brotherhood, mutual sympathy and responsiveness between all beings and individual hearts. For when we speak of the liberation from complete submission to these feelings we by no means suggest that people should despise or hate them or escape from practising them. They all arise from the creative hand of Allah and they all owe their existence to Him. They are a gift to us from the Beloved and, therefore, they deserve our love.

It is a sublime and lofty path by whose standards this earth is so small, life is so short, its enjoyments and luxuries are worthless; and the breaking away from the various hindrances and falsifications is a supreme wish and a great aim for humanity. But in Islam, however, this release does not mean seclusion and neglect, nor does it mean contempt for or escape from life, but it simply means a continuous and sincere endeavour and an everlasting struggle to lead humanity to the submission of everything in human life to Allah alone. Consequently, as was stated earlier, it is the fulfilment of man's role as Allah's vicegerent on earth with all its obligations.

The liberation of the human soul by priesthood and extreme spiritualism is available and easy to achieve but Islam does not approve of it, because, according to it, man's vicegerency on earth and the leadership of mankind are a part of its Divine path of liberation. This is a harder way that guarantees and secures the humanity of man and achieves the victory of the Divine will within his being. This is the real liberation, the flight of the human soul unto its Divine source and the achievement of its sublime truthfulness within the scope its wise Creator has chosen for it.

For the sake of all this, the first call to Islam was devoted to the establishment of the reality of the unity of Allah in the hearts and minds of men. For in this form it is a belief by the human soul, heart and mind, a full explanation of human existence, a way of life and not merely a spoken word or an inert belief. It is life in its entirety and re-

Surah 112   Purity of Faith (*Al-Ikhlas*)

ligion in its totality and whatever results follow after it are no more than the natural fruits of its establishment in the hearts and minds of mankind.

All the deviations that afflicted the followers of earlier Divine religions, and which corrupted their beliefs, ideas and life arose, in the first place, from the deterioration of the concept of the absolute unity of God in their minds. But what distinguishes this concept in the Islamic faith, is its deep-rootedness in the entire human life and the construction of the latter on its basis and its being considered as a foundation for the realistic and practical system of human life with its effects clearly appearing in legislation as well as in belief.

"He is Allah, the one and only God," means that He is *"the Eternal and the Absolute,"* and that, *"He begot none nor was He begotten,"* and that *"there is none comparable to Him."* But the Qur'an states it all in detail for more emphasis and clarification.

"The Eternal, the Absolute" means the supplicated Lord without whose permission nothing is decided. Allah is the One Lord. He is One in His Divinity and all the other beings are but His servants. To Him and Him alone are addressed all supplications. He and only He decides everything independently. No one decides with Him. And since He is the one and only God this quality is already His.

"He begot none, nor was He begotten," means that the reality of Allah is deep-rooted, permanent and everlasting. No changeable circumstances ever affect it. Its quality is absolute perfection at all times. Birth is descent and multiplication and implies a developed being after incompleteness or nothingness. It requires espousal which is based on similarity of being and structure. All this is utterly impossible in the case of Allah. So the quality of "One" includes the renouncement of a father and a son.

"There is none comparable to Him" means that no one resembles Him in anything or is equivalent to Him in any respect, either in the reality of being, or in the fact that He is the only effective power, or in any of His qualities or attributes. This is implied in the statement of his being "One" made in the first verse, but it is repeated thus to confirm and elaborate on that fact. It is a renunciation of the two-god belief which implies that Allah is the God of Good while Evil has its god who – as the belief goes – is in opposition to Allah, spoils His good deeds and propagates evil on earth. The most well-known two-god belief was that of the Persians, who believed in a god of light and

a god of darkness. This belief was known to the people in the south of the Arabian Peninsula, where the Persians once had a state and exercised sovereignty.

This *surah* is a firm establishment and a confirmation of the Islamic belief in the unity of Allah as was *surah* 109, "The Disbelievers", a denunciation of any similarity or meeting point between the unity of Allah and anthropomorphic belief. Each *surah* deals with the unity of Allah from a different angle. The Prophet used to start off his day reciting these two *surahs* in his morning prayer (*fajr*). This, surely, was significant.

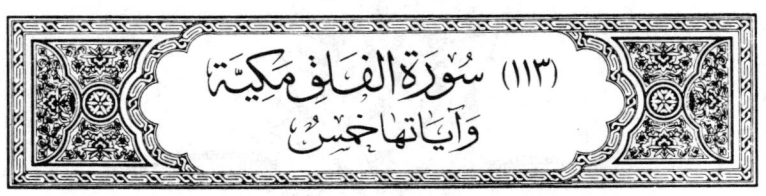

بِسْمِ اللَّهِ الرَّحْمَنِ الرَّحِيمِ

قُلْ أَعُوذُ بِرَبِّ ٱلْفَلَقِ ۝ مِن شَرِّ مَا خَلَقَ ۝ وَمِن شَرِّ غَاسِقٍ إِذَا وَقَبَ ۝ وَمِن شَرِّ ٱلنَّفَّٰثَٰتِ فِى ٱلْعُقَدِ ۝ وَمِن شَرِّ حَاسِدٍ إِذَا حَسَدَ ۝

SURAH 113

THE DAYBREAK
AL-FALAQ

In the name of Allah, the Beneficent, the Merciful.

Say: I seek refuge in the Lord of the Daybreak,
from the evil of what He has created;
from the evil of darkness when it gathers;
from the evil of conjuring witches;
from the evil of the envier when he envies.

In the Shade of the Qur'an

This *surah*, along with the following one, "Men", contains a directive from Allah primarily to His Prophet and secondly to the believers at large, to take refuge in Him and seek His protection in the face of any source of fear, hidden or visible, known or unknown. It is as if Allah, the Exalted, is unfolding His world of care, and embracing the believers in His guard, and is kindly and affectionately calling on them to resort to His care wherein they will feel safe and peaceful: "I know that you are helpless and surrounded by foes and fears, . . . Come on here for safety, contentment and peace . . ." Thus the two *surahs* start off with, *"Say: I seek refuge in the Lord of the Daybreak,"* and *"Say: I seek refuge in the Lord of men."*

Several accounts have been handed down concerning the revelation and popularity of this *surah* and they all fit in neatly with the above interpretation, that is, of Merciful Allah unfolding His care and offering shelter to His faithful servants. The Messenger of Allah himself loved this *surah* deeply, as is clearly apparent in his traditions.

According to Uqba ibn 'Amir, the Prophet's companion, the Messenger of Allah once said "Have you not heard the unique verses that were revealed last night, *'Say: I seek refuge in the Lord of the Daybreak'* and *'Say: I seek refuge in the Lord of men.'*" (Transmitted on the authority of Malik, Muslim, At-Tirmithi, Abu Dawood and An-Nissai).

Jabir, the Prophet's companion, said "The Messenger of Allah said to me once, 'Jabir, recite!' and I asked, 'What shall I recite?' He replied, 'Recite *"Say: I seek refuge in the Lord of the Daybreak,"* and *"Say: I seek refuge in Lord of men."'* So I recited them and he commented, 'Recite them (as often as you can) for you shall never recite anything equivalent to them.'" (Transmitted by An-Nissai)

Tharr ibn Hubaish said that he had enquired from Ubay ibn Ka'ab, the Prophet's companion, about *Al-Mu'awwathatain* (as the two *surahs* are called) saying, "Abu Al-Munthir,[1] your brother, Ibn Masoud says so and so. (For some time Ibn Masoud was under the false impression that these two *surahs* were not part of the Qur'an, but he later admitted his mistake). What do you think of that?" He replied, "I asked Allah's Messenger about this and he told me that he had been instructed to say the context of the *surahs* and he had car-

---

[1] Local habits in Arabia consider that addressing a man as father (*Abu*) of his eldest son a gesture of respect. – Translator's note.

ried out the instruction. We surely say the same as Allah's Messenger has said." (Transmitted by Al-Bukhari). All these reports throw powerful light on that underlying factor of Allah's kindness and love to which the two *surahs* draw attention.

Allah, the Exalted, refers to Himself in this *surah* by His attribute, *"The Lord of the Daybreak."* The Arabic term *"falaq"* simply means "daybreak" and yet it could be taken to mean "the whole phenomenon of creation" with reference to everything breaking out into life. This interpretation is supported by Allah's saying in *surah* 6, "The Cattle": *"Allah it is who splits (faliq) the seed and the fruit-stone (for sprouting). He brings forth the living from the dead . . . He is the cleaver (faliq) of the daybreak, and He has ordained the night for rest, and the sun and the moon for reckoning."*[1] If the meaning "daybreak" is adopted, refuge is being sought from the unseen and the mysterious with the Lord of the daybreak, Who bestows safety as He kindles the light of day. If, however, *"faliq"* is taken to mean "creation", then refuge from the evil of some creature is being sought with the Lord of all creation. In both cases, harmony with the theme of the *surah* is maintained.

"From the evil of what He has created." The phrase contains no exceptions or specifications. Mutual contact between various creatures, though no doubt advantageous, brings about some evil. Refuge from it is sought with Allah by the believer in order to encourage the goodness such a contact produces. For He who created those creatures is surely able to provide the right circumstances that lead them on a course where only the bright side of their contacts prevails.

"From the evil of darkness (ghasiq) when it gathers (waqab)." From the linguistic point of view, *"ghasiq"* means "substantially pouring out" and *"waqb"* is the name given to a little hole in a moutain through which water issues forth; *"waqab"* is the verb denoting such an action. What is probably meant here is the night, with all that accompanies it when it rapidly engulfs the world. That is horrifying in itself; in addition it fills hearts with the possibility of an unknown, unexpected discomfort caused by a savage beast, an unscrupulous villain, a striking enemy or a hissing poisonous creature, as well as anxieties and worries (which entail depression and uneasiness) and

---

[1] The Qur'an. 6; 96–97.

evil thoughts and passions that are liable to revive in the dark during one's state of solitude at night. This is the evil against which the believer needs the protection of Allah.

"From the evil of conjuring witches" refers to the various types of magic, whether by deceiving physical human senses or by influencing people's will power and projecting ideas onto their emotions and minds. (The verse specially refers to a form of witchcraft carried out by women in Arabia at the time who tied knots in cords and blew upon them with an imprecation.)

Magic is the production of illusions, subject to a magician's designs, and it does not offer any kind of new facts or alter the nature of things. This is how the Qur'an describes magic when relating the story of Moses in *surah 20,* "Ta Ha": *"They (the magicians of Pharaoh) said, 'Moses, Will you throw down your gear first or shall we be the first to throw?' He said: 'Throw down yours.' And by the power of their magic, their cords and staffs appeared to him as though they were running. Moses conceived a secret fear within him. But We said: "Fear not! You shall have the upper hand. Throw that which is in your right hand! It will swallow up that which they have made. That which they have made is but the deceitful show of witchcraft. Come where he may, a magician shall never be successful.'"* [1] Thus, their cords and staffs did not actually turn into snakes but it seemed so to the onlookers, Moses included, to the point where he felt uneasy inside. He was restrained by the transformation of his stick into a real snake, by Allah's own doing, to destroy the phoney ones.

This is the nature of magic as we ought to conceive it; that through it one is capable of influencing other people's minds, causing them to think and act according to one's suggestions. We refrain from going any further with this. It is indeed an evil from which Allah's protection needs to be sought.

A few unsupported narratives, some of which have been quoted by authentic sources, allege that Labid ibn 'Assam, a Jew, hypnotised the Prophet for several days or months in Medina so that, as some relate, he felt he was having a marital relationship with his wives when he was not; or, according to others, thought of having done something when he did not do so. This surah and the next one "Men", according to these narrations, were revealed to release him from that state by reciting them.

---

[1] The Qur'an. *20;* 65–9.

Surah 113   The Daybreak (*Al-Falaq*)

But surely these stories contradict the idea of the infallibility of the Prophet in word and deed and do not agree with the belief that all his actions are exponent of the Islamic way of life for all Muslims. Above all, they conflict with the Qur'anic emphatic denial of his being influenced by any kind of magic whatsoever, as claimed by some opponents of Islam. Hence, we dismiss such stories, on the grounds that the Qur'an is the ultimate arbiter, and that singularly narrated traditions are left out in matters concerning the faith. These stories have not had proper backing and such backing is an essential qualification for a tradition to be rated as authentic. What weakens the stories most, however, is that the two *surahs* were revealed in Makka while these stories relate the incident as having taken place in Medina!

"*And from the evil of the envier when he envies.*" Envy is the evil, begrudging reaction one feels towards another who has received some favours from Allah. It is also accompanied by a very strong desire for the annihilation of such favours. Some harm to the envied may result from such a baseless grudge. Now, this may either be the outcome of some direct physical action of the envier or may result from the suppressed feelings alone.

We should try not to feel uneasy on learning that there is a countless number of inexplicable mysteries in life. There are several phenomena for which no account has been offered up till now. Telepathy and hypnosis are examples of such phenomena.

Very little is known about the mysteries of envy and the little that is known has often been uncovered by chance and coincidence. In any case, there is in envy an evil from which the refuge and protection of Allah must be sought. For He, the Most Generous, Most Merciful and the One who knows all has directed His Messenger and his followers to seek His refuge from this evil. It is unanimously agreed by the Islamic schools of thought that Allah will always protect His servants from such evils, should they seek His protection as He has directed them to do.

Al-Bukhari related that Aisha said that the Prophet would blow into both hands when getting into bed to sleep, and recite: "*Say: He is Allah, the One . . .,*" and, "*Say: I seek refuge in the Lord of the Daybreak . . .*" and, "*Say: I seek refuge in the Lord of men*", and starting with his head, face and front part of his body, he would then run his palms all over the rest of his body. He did that three times. (Also transmitted by the other major traditionists).

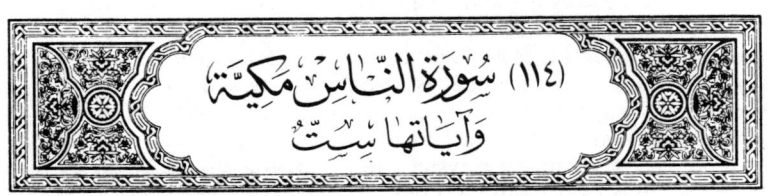

بِسْمِ اللهِ الرَّحْمَنِ الرَّحِيمِ

قُلْ أَعُوذُ بِرَبِّ النَّاسِ ۝ مَلِكِ النَّاسِ ۝ إِلَهِ النَّاسِ ۝ مِن شَرِّ الْوَسْوَاسِ الْخَنَّاسِ ۝ الَّذِي يُوَسْوِسُ فِي صُدُورِ النَّاسِ ۝ مِنَ الْجِنَّةِ وَالنَّاسِ ۝

SURAH 114

MEN
AN-NAS

In the name of Allah, the Beneficent, the Merciful

Say: I seek refuge in the Lord of men,
the King of men,
the God of men,
from the mischief of the slinking prompter,
who whispers in the hearts of men,
from among jinn and men.

In this *surah,* as can be seen, refuge is sought in the Lord, Sovereign and God of mankind from the insidious whisperer, *jinn* or human, who prompts evil ideas into people's minds. The *surah* presents the relevant attributes of Allah to keep away this invisible evil which the mind on its own cannot shut out. For the Lord is He who preserves, directs, cherishes and protects mankind; the Sovereign is He who owns, governs and independently runs the world; and the Deity is He who supercedes all other beings and absolutely supervises over all their affairs. The particular mention of mankind here brings man closer to Allah's protection and care.

Allah, the Merciful, instructs His Messenger and his nation or followers to recognise these attributes of His and seek His protection against this sneaking evil which locates itself within their hearts. For they cannot rid themselves of such an evil which creeps into their hearts surreptitiously and imperceptibly without the aid of Allah, the Lord, the Sovereign, the Deity.

The nature of this evil-importing medium is identified in the text first as *"the slinking prompter."* Its function is outlined as to *"whisper in the hearts of men"*. Then its origin is specified as *"from among jinn and men."*

The style adopted here is quite significant because it draws one's attention fully to the identity of this sneaking whisperer after describing its nature in order to show the process by which that evil is insinuated, so that one is alerted to watch and confront it. For when one is given the full picture one knows that this sneaking whisperer operates secretly. One also realises that it is *jinn* as well as human, for human beings are not exceptions in spreading evil while unseen.

We do not know how the *jinn* perform this whispering, but we certainly find its repercussions in the behaviour of individuals as well as in human life generally. We know for sure that the battle between Adam (man) and Iblis (Satan) is a very old one. War between the two was declared by Satan out of the evil inherent in him, his conceit and his envy and resentment of man. He was given Divine permission to carry out this battle for some purpose which Allah alone comprehends. But, significantly, man has not been left alone, dispossessed of the necessary means of protection. He has been provided with power of faith or *"Iman"*, (that is, conscious belief in and knowledge of Allah and His attributes through conviction and sincere devotion). Meditation and seeking refuge in Allah are among the most effective weapons. When man neglects these means of security and defence, he indeed has only himself to blame.

Ibn Abbas related that the Messenger of Allah had said, "Satan besieges the individual's heart; he subsides whenever one conscientiously remembers Allah, but insinuates his evil whenever one is unthoughtful of Him."

As for humans we know a great deal of their curious ways of whispering and prompting and some types like the following are more devilish than the Devil:

> a bad companion who injects evil into his comrade's heart and mind while he is unaware, as he is thought to be trustworthy;
> a ruler's counsellor or advisor who "whispers" to him and turns him into a destructive tyrant;
> an unscrupulous slanderer who fabricates and decorates tales and makes them sound factual and convincing;
> a hustler of immoral business and dealings who tries to get through to people by exploiting their sensual, unhealthy desires;
> a hundred other "whisperers" who lay various traps inconspicuously utilising people's different weak points which they detect and look for.

They are more devilish than even the *jinn* themselves. Faced with evil in this guise, man is not capable of ensuring his own safety. Allah therefore points out to him in this *surah* the means he can employ in this fierce battle.

And there is a very direct significance in identifying the "prompter" as "slinking". For while this description indicates the secretiveness of this whisperer on the one hand, it is, on the other hand, an illusion to its intrinsic feebleness whenever it is discovered or resisted. It subsides and meekly withdraws when met in the open; or, as the Messenger said in his accurate illustrations, "He (Satan) subsides whenever one conscientiously remembers Allah, but insinuates his evil whenever one is unthoughtful of Him!" This presentation fortifies the believer's heart in face of this timid, subsiding whisperer.

Nevertheless, the battle is everlasting since this "prompter" is always watchful for the right moment (when one neglects the remembrance of Allah) to implant its evils. For the believer to be conscious of Allah once in a while is not sufficient, as the war is continuous till the end of time; this the Qur'an vividly states in a lucid picture:

> "And when We (Allah) said to the angels, 'Fall down prostrate before Adam', they fell prostrate except Iblis (Satan) who said, 'Shall I bow down before him whom You have created of clay? Do you see this creature whom You have honoured above me? If You give me grace until the Day of Resurrection, I will certainly destroy his offspring, save but a few'. 'Begone!' said He. 'But you and whoever of them follows you will have Hell for reward. An ample reward it shall be. Rouse with your voice whomever you are able. Muster against them your horsemen and your footmen. Be their partner in their wealth and in their offspring. Make them promises. Whatever Satan promises them is only for deceit. But over My true servants you shall have no power.' Your Lord is their all-sufficient Guardian.''[1]

This concept of the battle and the source of evil in it, whether provoked by Satan himself or by his human agent, fully inspires man to feel that he is not helpless in it; since his Lord, Sovereign and Deity controls all creations and events. Though He has permitted Satan to attack, He has supreme power over him and He has also provided guidance for man. Allah leaves to Satan only those who neglect Him, their Lord, Sovereign and Deity, but those who live in consciousness of Him are safe and protected against his intimidations and incitements. Thus, righteousness is supported by the only true power of the Lord, Sovereign and Deity, whereas evil is backed by a slinking prompter, a sneaky whisperer, cowardly in the open field, quick to retreat in war, and easily defeated by one's seeking refuge with Allah.

This is the most perfect conception of the battle between good and evil. It is a conception which protects the being against defeat and provides him with strength confidence and contentment.

Praise be to Allah at the beginning and at the end. From Him we derive confidence and success. To Him we turn for unfailing support.

---

[1] The Qur'an. *17; 61–5.*